CTA

Awareness Paper

FA 2009

PRACTICE & REVISION KIT

FOR THE EXAMS IN MAY AND NOVEMBER 2010

TQT
Tax Qualification Training

Second edition February 2010

ISBN 9780 7517 7636 2

British Library Cataloguing-in-Publication Data
A catalogue record for this book is available from the British Library

www.bpp.com/learningmedia

Printed in the United Kingdom

All our rights reserved. No part of this publication may be reproduced, stored in a retrieval system or transmitted, in any form or by any means, electronic, mechanical, photocopying, recording or otherwise, without the prior written permission of BPP Learning Media Ltd.

While every care has been taken in the preparation of this kit to ensure its accuracy, no responsibility for loss occasioned by any person acting or refraining from acting as a result of any statement made herein can be accepted by BPP Learning Media or Kaplan Financial.

We are grateful to the Chartered Institute of Taxation for permission to reproduce past examination questions.

Your learning materials, are printed on paper sourced from sustainable, managed forests.

A note about copyright

Dear Customer

What does the little © mean and why does it matter?

Your market-leading TQT books, course materials and e-learning materials do not write and update themselves. People write them: on their own behalf or as employees of an organisation that invests in this activity. Copyright law protects their livelihoods. It does so by creating rights over the use of the content.

Breach of copyright is a form of theft – as well as being a criminal offence in some jurisdictions, it is potentially a serious breach of professional ethics.

With current technology, things might seem a bit hazy but, basically, without the express permission of BPP Learning Media:

- Photocopying TQT materials is a breach of copyright.

- Scanning, ripcasting or conversion of TQT digital materials into different file formats, uploading them to Facebook or e-mailing them to your friends is a breach of copyright.

You can, of course, sell your books, in the form in which you have bought them – once you have finished with them. (Is this fair to your fellow students? We update for a reason.)

©
BPP Learning Media Ltd
2010

Contents

Page

Finding questions

Question index iv
Using your TQT Practice and Revision Kit vi

Passing exams

Revising and taking CTA exams ix
How to revise x
How NOT to revise xi
How to PASS your exams xii
How to FAIL your exams xiii
Using your TQT products xiv

Passing the CTA Awareness paper

Revising the CTA Awareness Paper xvii
Tackling questions xviii
Exam information xix
VAT Supplement xix
TQT talks to the Examiners xx

Questions and answers

Questions 1
Answers 87

Exam practice

Mock exam 1
- Questions 221
- Answers 241

Mock exam 2
- Questions 267
- Answers 285

Mock exam 3
- Questions 305
- Answers 321

Tax Tables 341

Review form

Question index

The headings in this checklist/index indicate the main topics of questions.

	Marks	Time allocation Mins	Page number Question	Answer
Part A: VAT including stamp taxes				
VAT basics and treatment of supplies	95	95	3	89
Input tax	95	95	6	93
Land and buildings	45	45	8	97
Overseas and miscellaneous issues	65	65	10	99
VAT administration	85	85	11	101
Stamp taxes	40	40	13	105
Part B: Inheritance tax, trusts and estates				
IHT basics	115	115	17	109
APR, BPR and post mortem sales	60	60	21	115
Overseas aspects and anti-avoidance	85	85	23	118
IHT and trusts	60	60	26	123
Trust income tax and CGT	35	35	28	127
General CGT	35	35	30	129
Estates in administration	30	30	31	131
Part C: Corporation tax				
The corporation tax computation	90	90	35	137
Loan relationships, intangibles and R & D	60	60	38	142
Capital gains and companies with investment business	60	60	39	145
Single company losses	55	55	41	149
Groups of companies	90	90	44	154
Personal service companies and overseas aspects	70	70	49	159
Part D: Taxation of individuals				
The income tax computation and property income	80	80	55	165
Employment income & NIC	110	110	57	168
Investments and pensions	30	30	60	174
CGT basics	75	75	61	176
CGT reliefs	20	20	64	180
Overseas aspects of IT and CGT	40	40	64	181
Administration of IT and CGT	75	75	66	183
Part E: Taxation of unincorporated businesses				
Trading income	165	165	71	189
Trading losses	45	45	78	201
CGT basics	50	50	79	204
Partnerships	45	45	80	207
CGT reliefs	75	75	82	211
NIC and administrative aspects of IT and CGT	45	45	85	217

	Marks	Time allocation Mins	Page number Question	Page number Answer
Mock exam 1 (Pilot Paper)				
Module A	60	60	225	243
Module B	60	60	228	247
Module C	60	60	230	252
Module D	60	60	233	256
Module E	60	60	236	261
Mock exam 2 (May 2009)				
Module A	60	60	271	287
Module B	60	60	273	290
Module C	60	60	276	293
Module D	60	60	278	296
Module E	60	60	281	301
Mock exam 3 (November 2009)				
Module A	60	60	309	323
Module B	60	60	310	326
Module C	60	60	312	329
Module D	60	60	315	332
Module E	60	60	317	336

Using your TQT Practice and Revision Kit

Tackling revision and the exam

You can significantly improve your chances of passing by tackling revision and the exam in the right ways. Our advice is based on recent feedback from CTA examiners.

- We look at the dos and don'ts of revising for, and taking, CTA exams
- We focus on the CTA Awareness Paper; we discuss, what to do (and what not to do) in the exam, how to approach different types of question and ways of obtaining easy marks

Selecting questions

Even within the real exam, the questions will vary in terms of difficulty. Recognising the easier questions and performing well on these is key to passing the exam. Remember, your approach to a less challenging requirement is likely to be different from your approach to a challenging question.

Attempting mock exams

There are three mock exams that provide practice at coping with the pressures of the exam day. We strongly recommend that you attempt them under exam conditions.

Notes page

Notes page

CTA AWARENESS PAPER (02/10)

REVIEW FORM

Name: _____   Address: _____

_____

How have you used this Kit?
(Tick one box only)

☐ Home study (book only)
☐ On a course _____
☐ Other _____

Why did you decide to purchase this Kit?
(Tick one box only)

☐ Have used TQT Kits in the past
☐ Recommendation by friend/colleague
☐ Recommendation by a lecturer
☐ Saw advertising
☐ Other _____

During the past six months do you recall seeing/receiving either of the following?
(Tick as many boxes as are relevant)

☐ Our advertisement in *Tax Adviser*
☐ Our Publishing Catalogue

Which (if any) aspects of our advertising do you think are useful?
(Tick as many boxes as are relevant)

☐ Prices and publication dates of new editions
☐ Information on Kit content
☐ Facility to order books off-the-page
☐ None of the above

Your ratings, comments and suggestions would be appreciated on the following areas of this Kit.

	Very useful	Useful	Not useful
Question bank	☐	☐	☐
Answer bank	☐	☐	☐
Quality of explanations	☐	☐	☐
Legislative references	☐	☐	☐
Mock exams	☐	☐	☐

	Excellent	Good	Adequate	Poor
Overall opinion of this Kit	☐	☐	☐	☐

Do you intend to continue using TQT Products?   ☐ Yes   ☐ No

Please note any further comments and suggestions/errors on the reverse of this page. The TQT author of this edition can be e-mailed at: suedexter@bpp.com

Please return to: Sue Dexter, Tax Publishing Director, BPP Learning Media Ltd, FREEPOST, London, W12 8BR. BPP Learning Media Ltd is a member of the TQT joint venture.

CTA AWARENESS PAPER (02/10)

REVIEW FORM (continued)

TELL US WHAT YOU THINK

Please note any further comments and suggestions/errors below.

Passing CTA exams

Revising and taking CTA exams

To maximise your chances of passing your CTA exams, you must make best use of your time, both before the exam during your revision, and when you are actually doing the exam.

- Making the most of your revision time can make a big, big difference to how well-prepared you are for the exam
- Time management is a core skill in the exam hall; all the work you have done can be wasted if you do not make the most of the three hours you have to attempt the exam

In this section we simply show you what to do and what not to do during your revision, and how to increase and decrease your prospects of passing your exams when you take them. Our advice is grounded in feedback we have had from CTA examiners. You may be surprised to know that much examiner advice is the same whatever the exam, and the reasons why many students fail do not vary much between subjects and exam levels. So if you follow the advice we give you over the next few pages, you will **significantly** enhance your chances of passing **all** your CTA exams.

How to revise

☑ Plan your revision

At the start of your revision period, you should draw up a **timetable** to plan how long you will spend on each subject and how you will revise each area. You need to consider the total time you have available and also the time that will be required to revise for other exams you are taking.

☑ Practise Practise Practise

The **more exam-standard questions** you do, the **more likely you are to pass** the exam. Practising an entire module will mean that you will get used to the time pressure of the exam. When the time is up, you should note where you have got to and then complete the module, giving yourself practice at everything the module tests.

☑ Revise enough

Make sure that your revision covers the breadth of the syllabus as any topic can be examined and all questions are compulsory. However it is true that some topics are **key** – they appear regularly or are a particular interest of the examiner – and you need to spend sufficient time revising these. Make sure you also know the **basics** – the fundamental calculations, proformas and layouts.

☑ Deal with your difficulties

Difficult areas are topics you find dull and pointless, or subjects that you found problematic when you were studying them. You must not become negative about these topics; instead you should build up your knowledge by reading the **Passcards** and using the **Quick quiz** questions in the Study Text to test yourself. When practising questions in the Kit, go back to the Text if you are struggling.

☑ Learn from your mistakes

Having completed a question you must look at your answer critically. Look for easy marks to see how you could have quickly gained credit on the questions that you have done. As you go through the Kit, it is worth noting any traps you have fallen into, and referring to these notes in the days before the exam. Aim to learn at least one new point from each question you attempt, a technical point perhaps or a point on style or approach.

☑ Complete all three mock exams

You should attempt the **Mock exams** at the end of the Kit under **strict exam conditions**, to gain experience of selecting questions, managing your time and producing answers.

How NOT to revise

☒ Revise selectively

Examiners are well aware that some students try to forecast the contents of exams, and only revise those areas that they think will be examined. Examiners try to prevent this by doing the unexpected, for example setting the same topic in successive sittings or setting topics that have previously never been examined.

☒ Spend all the revision period reading

You cannot pass the exam just by learning the contents of Passcards, Course Notes or Study Texts. You have to develop your **application skills** by practising questions.

☒ Audit the answers

This means reading the answers and guidance without having attempted the questions. Auditing the answers gives you **false reassurance** that you would have tackled the questions in the best way and made the points that our answers do. The feedback we give in our answers will mean more to you if you have attempted the questions and thought through the issues.

☒ Practise some types of question, but not others

The CTA awareness paper contains compulsory short form questions. You need to make sure you can get some marks on the harder questions, and more marks on the easier questions.

☒ Get bogged down

Do not spend a lot of time worrying about all the minute detail of certain topic areas, and leave yourself insufficient time to cover the rest of the syllabus. Remember that a key skill in the exam is the ability to **concentrate on what is important** and this applies to your revision as well.

☒ Overdo studying

Studying for too long without interruption will mean your studying becomes less effective. A five minute break each hour will help. You should also make sure that you are leading a **healthy lifestyle** (proper meals, good sleep and some times when you are not studying).

How to PASS your exams

☑ Prepare for the day

Make sure you set at least one alarm (or an alarm call), and allow plenty of time to arrive at the exam hall. You should have your route planned in advance and should listen on the radio for potential travel problems. You should check the night before to see that you have pens, pencils, erasers, watch, calculator with spare batteries, also exam documentation and evidence of identity.

☑ Plan your three hours

You need to make sure that you spend the right length of time on each question. Each mark carries with it a **time allocation** of **1 minute**, so each short form question should take you 5 minutes, and you should complete each module in 1 hour.

☑ Read the questions carefully

To score well, you must follow the requirements of the question, understanding what aspects of the subject area are being covered, and the tasks you will have to carry out. The requirements will also determine what information and examples you should provide. Remember to answer all parts of the question, in the format required.

☑ Show evidence of application of knowledge

Remember that examiners are predominantly looking for a display of knowledge; but even in this paper you will need to show you can **apply** the knowledge you have. Evidence of application will include writing answers that only contain **relevant** material, using the facts to **support** what you say and stating any **assumptions** you make.

☑ Stay until the end of the exam

Use any spare time to **check and recheck** your script. This includes checking you have filled out the candidate details correctly, you have labelled question parts and workings clearly, you have used headers and underlining effectively and spelling, grammar and arithmetic are correct.

How to FAIL your exams

☒ Don't finish

If you do not attempt all of the questions on the paper, you are making it harder for yourself to pass the questions that you do attempt. Historically, paper 1 (the equivalent paper under the old syllabus) was a very time pressured exam, and students often found they ran out of time at the end of the exam. Generally, those students who had no time to attempt the last three or four short form questions, failed the exam. Remember, failing to attempt all of the paper is symptomatic of poor time management.

☒ Include irrelevant material

Markers are given detailed mark guides and will not give credit for irrelevant content. The markers will only give credit for what is **relevant**.

☒ Don't do what the question asks

Failing to provide all the examiner asks for will limit the marks you score.

☒ Present your work poorly

Markers will only be able to give you credit if they can read your writing. There are also plenty of other things that will make it more difficult for markers to reward you. Examples include:

- Not using black or blue ink
- Not showing clearly which question you are attempting
- Contradicting yourself
- Not showing clearly workings or the results of your calculations
- Crossing out your workings; never do this they may be right!

☒ Get lost in the legislation

The legislation is a valuable tool in the exam, but you need to be familiar with it before you enter the exam hall. Using the indexes, contents pages and footnotes are useful skills, but you do not have time in the exam to develop them. Often it is better to accept that you do not know the answer and move onto a question you can attempt, rather than waste 20 minutes to obtain only a few marks.

Using your TQT products

This Kit gives you the question practice and guidance you need in the exam. Our other products can also help you pass:

- **Passcards** provide you with clear topic summaries and exam tips

Passing the Awareness paper

Revising the Awareness Paper

The Awareness Paper contains compulsory questions which are each 5 marks.

Based on the pilot paper and the May and November 2009 papers, you can expect a mix of questions, some covering core areas and some covering more complex areas, or peripheral areas.

In order to pass this paper, you will need to combine time management skills with the ability to compensate for harder questions, by spotting and performing well on the easier questions.

Question spotting is never a good idea where all the questions are compulsory, and at this early stage of the syllabus it is particularly inadvisable. This means you need to ensure your revision covers the breadth of the syllabus to maximise your chances of passing the exam.

Topics to revise

That said, you must have sound knowledge in the following fundamental areas if you are to stand a chance of passing the exam. You should therefore revise the following areas particularly well.

Module A: VAT

- Registration and deregistration
- Input tax recovery – blocked input tax
- Partial exemption
- Capital goods scheme
- Land and buildings
- VAT penalties and administration

Module B: Inheritance tax, trusts and estates

- Lifetime gifts
- Transfers of value
- Death estate
- BPR and APR
- Inheritance tax for relevant property trusts
- Income tax for trusts
- Basic capital gains tax computations

Module C: Corporation tax

- The corporation tax computation, including capital allowances in detail
- Chargeable gains: replacement of business asset relief
- Loan relationships and IFAs – how they are treated and how relief is given for losses
- Loss relief
- Group relief, and chargeable gains groups

Module D: Taxation of individuals

- The income tax computation, including personal allowances
- Employment income
- Calculation of capital gains and the capital gains tax liability
- Capital gains tax reliefs
- Overseas aspects of income tax and capital gains tax
- Income tax and capital gains tax administration
- National insurance contributions

Module E: Taxation of unincorporated businesses

- Income tax and national insurance liabilities from trading income
- The calculation of trading income including the basis period rules
- Capital allowances
- Calculating capital gains tax liabilities arising from the sale of business assets
- Applying capital gains tax reliefs on the disposal of business assets

Question practice

Question practice under timed conditions is essential, so that you can get used to the pressures of answering exam questions in **limited time** and practise not only the key techniques but allocating your time between different requirements in each question.

Tackling questions

You will improve your chances by following a step-by-step approach along the following lines.

Step 1   Read the requirement

Identify the knowledge areas being tested and see precisely what the examiner wants you to do. This will help you focus on what is important in the question.

Step 2   Read the question actively

You will already know which knowledge area(s) are being tested from having read the requirement so whilst you read through the question think about how you will use the information in your answer or calculations.

Step 3   Write your answer

Keep to your time allocation. Write as quickly as you can while still being legible. Bullet point answers are appropriate in the Awareness paper. Computations should be clear, but as brief as possible. Take care not to overrun.

Exam information

Format of the exam

Time allowed: 3 hours

Tax rates and allowances will be provided in the examination paper.

The CTA Awareness paper is split into the following five modules.

- Module A: VAT
- Module B: Inheritance tax, trusts and estates
- Module C: Corporation tax
- Module D: Taxation of individuals
- Module E: Taxation of unincorporated businesses

Candidates must attempt three modules.

Candidates cannot take the same options at both awareness and advisory level.

Each module contains 12 five mark short form questions. All questions in the chosen modules should be attempted.

The marks for all three modules are aggregated and the total marks are scaled down by $^{100}/_{80}$ to determine the result of the paper. The pass mark is 50%.

VAT Supplement

Until 30 November 2008, the standard rate of VAT had been 17.5% for many years. The standard rate of VAT was reduced from 17.5% to 15% on 1 December 2008. It remained at 15% until 31 December 2009. From 1 January 2010 it reverted to 17.5%.

In your CTA exams, you should use the correct VAT rate according to each date in the question.

TQT talks to the Examiners

1. **Prospective legislation**

    Question: When is prospective / new legislation examinable?

    Examiner Response: Legislation enacted at least 5 months prior to the exam is examinable in any given exam even if it has yet to come into force ie the legislation may still be prospective at the date of the exam. In relation to FA09 changes, the following items will therefore be examinable in 2010:

    New administration and compliance rules

    Harmonised interest rules

    Changes to personal allowances where income exceeds £100,000 and higher rate of income tax

    VAT cross border changes

    Disclosure of tax avoidance schemes in relation to SDLT

    World-wide debt cap

2. **Marking guides**

    Question: Would the CIOT consider publishing its marking guides for all papers again?

    Examiner Response: There are no plans to make these guides available...all marking guides are flexible and credit will always be given to candidates who make relevant comments not within the marking guide/model answer.

3. **Interest rates for unpaid / late tax**

    Question: Will rates be given in the exam? And where the rate is 0% (eg IHT and repayment supplement) presume no point in examining?

    Examiner Response: Rates of interest on unpaid and overpaid tax due vary from time to time and in some cases the calculation will span a change of rate date so it would not be appropriate to assume there is no point in examining merely because the current rate is nil. Where relevant the rates will usually be supplied in the question.

4. **New compliance rules**

    Question: Many of the new compliance rules will not come into effect until April 2010 – are they going to be examined now?

    Examiner Response: Questions may be set on prospective legislation passed more than five months prior to the examination date even if coming into force in the future. It would be examined on the basis of that legislation rather than on any subsequent changes.

    TQT Comments: Following the CIOT's response, the material for the 2010 examinations was prepared (in August 2009) on the basis that the administration changes in FA 2009 apply even where their implementation date was unknown at the time.

5. **New harmonised interest regime**

    Question: As the new harmonised regime for interest on overdue/overpaid tax introduced by FA 2009 does not apply until Royal Assent at the earliest can we assume that it will not be examined in the 2010 exams?

    Examiner Response: The rules will be examinable in 2010.

6   **Historic compliance rules**

    Question   Can we assume that any compliance rules which ceased to apply from April 2009 are no longer examinable? Eg penalties for incorrect returns for IT, CT and VAT (misdeclaration penalty)?

    Examiner Response: We will not examine the historic rules in 2010.

7   **Share pooling**

    Question   Given the recent changes to the share pooling rules in FA 2008 is it reasonable to assume that the detailed share pooling rules for companies will not be examined?

    Examiner Response: Not examinable.

8   **Intra-spouse transfers & indexation**

    Question   Where an intra-spouse transfer has been made would candidates be given the indexed cost to the spouse or be expected to calculate the relevant amounts from the tables?

    Examiner Response: Candidates need to calculate the indexation.

9   **Rollover relief**

    Question   Rollover relief is not examinable in the Corporation Tax module of the Awareness paper, but groups and transactions within groups are. Can we assume that questions about groups would not include rollover relief? Would this include the potential for rollover of a de-grouping charge?

    Examiner Response: Correct.

10 **Gift relief**

    Question   Gift of business assets is only examinable in the Taxation of Unincorporated Businesses module – would this exclude gifts of shares in view of the fact that disposals of shares in general is only examinable in the Taxation of Individuals Awareness module?

    Examiner Response: The syllabus includes all forms of business asset.

11 **March 1982/April 1965 assets**

    Question   Are assets held at 31 March 1982 / 6 April 1965 examinable in the Awareness paper?

    Examiner Response: 31 March 1982 - yes
                             6 April 1965 - no

12 **CGT administration**

    Question   To what extent is CGT administration examinable in the Awareness papers?

    Examiner Response: We would not expect candidates to have a detailed knowledge of the administration of CGT. The thrust of the Awareness papers is to enable candidates to spot issues rather than to be able to deal with the detailed administration of the tax.

13 **NIC**

    Question   NIC is included in the syllabus for the Taxation of Individuals Awareness module. What is the position with regard to Class 1A and Class 1B NIC as these are not paid by the individual. Would these be excluded from this paper?

    Examiner Response: This includes Class 1A and Class 1B. Please also note that the operation of the PAYE system is included in this paper.

14 PAYE

Question: The operation and application of the PAYE system is examinable in Taxation of Individuals Awareness module. Can we assume this is from the individual's perspective and so things like due dates for the employer submitting forms, details re PSAs would not be examinable?

Examiner Response: No, this also covers employer aspects.

15 Unincorporated businesses

Question: Are we correct to assume that just basic income tax computations involving trading income would be examinable in this paper?

Examiner Response: Yes

16 Pension forestalling rules

Question: Are the pension forestalling rules examinable?

Examiner Response: Yes.

17 World-wide debt cap

Question: Is the new world-wide debt cap examinable at Awareness level?

Examiner Response: Not examinable at Awareness level, but will be examinable for both the Taxation of Owner-Managed Businesses paper (at a basic level) and Advanced Corporation Tax (in depth) Advisory papers.

18 Foreign dividends

Question: To what extent are the old rules examinable for receipt of foreign dividends prior to 1 July 2009?

Examiner Response: For Awareness level, foreign dividends received prior to 1 July 2009 are not examinable. At Awareness level it is acceptable to assume that all foreign dividends received are exempt from tax in the UK and that the exclusions from exemption are not examinable.

19 Cars transitional rules – leases and capital allowances

Question: To what extent are the transitional rules for cars in relation to capital allowances and leases examinable?

Examiner Response: Transitional rules are examinable. Existing expenditure on pre April 2009 cars is therefore examinable as are leases entered into before April 2009.

20 Capital allowances changes

Question: To what extent are the old rules examinable?

Examiner Response: Pre April 2008 first year allowances, the old long life asset pool, and pre April 2008 rates are no longer examinable.

21 Industrial buildings allowance

Question: Can you confirm that IBA/ABA/Hotels are outside the syllabus.
Examiner Response: Yes

Module A
VAT

Questions

Module A: VAT

VAT basics and treatment of supplies

1   You are the tax adviser for a number of businesses:

    (1) Vogi Ltd manufactures and sells car seat covers. The company's associate Igov Ltd, in which it owns a 30% interest, manufactures plastic zips used for the seat covers, which are also sold to third parties.

    In recent years, it has purchased the following assets:

		VAT paid £
15 August 2006	New computer	732
15 June 2008	New printer	386

    It also rents large tools from a local supplier, incurring VAT of £80 per month on average.

    (2) Michael owns a furniture shop and a carpet cleaning business.

    (a) **Assuming that all businesses make taxable supplies which exceed the registration threshold, explain briefly how many VAT registrations are required.**

    (b) **Assuming any VAT registration is effective from May 2010, what effect will it have in respect of the VAT that has already been paid by Vogi Ltd?**

2   The bookkeeper of Travelbiz Ltd is raising two invoices as follows:

    (a) An invoice to a customer for £3,560, being the cost of an international air ticket, which includes a sum for in-flight meals.

    (b) An invoice to a customer for £4,200, being the cost of a Mediterranean cruise, which also includes a sum for on-board meals at any of the high quality restaurants on board.

    He is unsure of whether to charge one or two rates of tax.

    Explain briefly the VAT status of these supplies.

3   Blythe has the following transactions:

    (a) Blythe produced the following invoice on 1 April 2010 for the sale of goods to one of her customers:

	£
50 barbecues @ £80 each	4,000
Less: quantity discount 20%	(800)
	3,200

    The invoice also states that a further 5% discount is available if payment is received within 14 days of the invoice date. Payment was received 30 days after the invoice date.

    (b) Blythe gave gas barbeque sets costing £80 each to 12 of her biggest customers in the year ended 31 March 2010. She has also given samples of a new line in wine coolers, costing £5 each, to many other customers.

    Explain the VAT implications of the above transactions.

4   Carla is a trader selling children's clothes. Her turnover is £50,000 per annum. She incurs annual expenditure of £18,000 (VAT exclusive) including £10,000 of standard rated goods. She is not registered for VAT.

    Darla runs a coffee shop. Her turnover is also £50,000 per annum. She incurs annual expenditure of £21,000 (VAT exclusive) including £8,000 of standard rated goods. She is also not registered for VAT.

    Advise Carla and Darla if it is possible to register for VAT, state any advantages and any recommendation you would give. Assume you are writing in May 2010.

5   On 1 April 2009, Gaby began trading as an author and editor of popular fiction. She makes taxable supplies of £8,000 per month throughout her first year.

   On 15 August 2009 she signed a contract to write a book. The terms will result in additional income as follows:

		£
15 August 2009	Advance fee paid on signing contract	13,000
30 November 2009	Further payment on delivery of manuscript	6,000
31 December 2009	Final payment on publication	12,000

   When should Gaby inform HMRC of her need to register for VAT and from what date will she need to charge VAT on her supplies?

6   **State the advantages and disadvantages of VAT group registration.**

7   In certain circumstances, companies are able to form a VAT group.

   (a)   **What are the consequences of forming a VAT group**
   (b)   **What are the conditions that must be satisfied for companies to form a VAT group?**

8   **State the VAT liability of the following items:**

   (a)   **A child's car seat**
   (b)   **Medical care provided by a registered doctor**
   (c)   **A train ticket**
   (d)   **A newspaper**
   (e)   **An educational CD-ROM.**

9   There have been numerous cases appealed to the Tribunal, in respect of whether there is a single supply with a single VAT liability, or multiple supplies, with potentially multiple VAT liabilities.

   List the features that may be considered when determining if a supply is a mixed supply or a composite supply

10   The question as to whether an undertaking constitutes business activity has often been considered by VAT Tribunals.

   List the tests that might commonly be applied to decide if an activity is performed in the course or furtherance of business.

11   You notice that in your local fast food outlet, the price list shows that VAT is not charged on certain items if you buy the food to eat away from the premises.

   You are required to explain why this is, and also why it is that for some items VAT is charged regardless of where the items are eaten.

12   (a)   Aris Ltd ceased to make taxable supplies on 1 September 2009 although it continued to trade making only exempt supplies.

      Explain how this will affect the company's VAT registration.

   (b)   Beta Ltd is considering voluntary deregistration.

      Advise the company in which circumstances this is possible and from when it would be effective.

13   Many charities operate shops, selling a mixture of goods which are donated to the charity, and goods which are bought in for resale.

   You are required to explain the VAT liability and accounting rules which apply to such sales.

14 On 14 May 2010, Very Fry Ltd signs a contract with a large retailer to supply them with 10,000 frying pans to be delivered on 3 June 2010, with payment due on delivery. The contract is worth £80,000. Very Fry Ltd is a new company and is not yet VAT registered.

Steamy Limited commenced to trade on 1 February 2010. The company makes a mixture of zero rated and standard rated supplies, to the value of £8,000 per month.

State the date by which the two companies above must notify their liability to register for VAT, and the date from which their registrations will take effect.

15 India Ltd commenced trading as a wholesaler on 1 November 2009.

The company had the following turnover:

	£
November 2009	6,000
December 2009	7,500
January 2010	12,500
February 2010	14,700
March 2010	28,550
April 2010	33,700
May 2010	54,600
June 2010	70,400

State the date that India Ltd will be required to register for VAT, and the date of the VAT registration will be effective.

State the circumstances in which India Ltd will be allowed to recover input tax incurred on goods purchased and services incurred prior to the date of VAT registration.

16 H Ltd owns 70% of A Ltd and 100% of B Ltd. H Ltd makes standard rated supplies, A Ltd makes zero rated supplies and B Ltd makes exempt supplies, the latter suffering input VAT of £7,000 pa, which is much less than either A Ltd or H Ltd.

H Ltd frequently sells goods and supplies services to A Ltd and B Ltd.

Explain which companies, if any, should join in a group registration

17 Tuition Ltd is a VAT registered business. It provides a 1 day course at all an inclusive cost of £500. The course comprises a set of notes and teaching by an expert tutor.

The cost to Tuition Ltd of writing and printing the notes is £100. The tutor has a daily charge out rate of £200.

All amounts are stated exclusive of VAT.

Explain the status of this supply and advise how much VAT Tuition Ltd should charge for a course in March 2010.

18 **You are required to list five types of services which are treated as made where physically carried out, regardless of where the customer belongs.**

19 When there is a supply of goods for no consideration, in most cases output VAT is still due. It is therefore necessary to determine the consideration upon which the output VAT is calculated.

You are required to list the alternative methods that may be used to determine the consideration for the supply.

Input tax

20 In the VAT quarter to 31 March 2010, Sean makes standard rated supplies of £215,500 (excluding VAT) and exempt supplies of £59,780.

His input tax for the same quarter was:

	£
Wholly attributable to taxable supplies	34,000
Wholly attributable to exempt supplies	5,600
Attributable partly to taxable and partly to exempt supplies	9,500

In addition to the above, Sean also incurs input VAT of £2,200 on the purchase of a new car, which is to be used partly for business and partly privately, and £120 on entertaining clients. Sean uses the VAT recovery percentage for the current quarter to calculate his recoverable input tax.

Calculate the input tax reclaimable for the quarter.

21 Martin, who has been in business as a market gardener for several years, has just bought a car that will be used partly for business and partly privately.

Explain briefly the extent to which VAT paid on the cost of buying and running the car will be recoverable.

22 Pauline, a VAT registered trader, makes the following supplies in the quarter ended 31 December 2009:

	£
Taxable supplies (excluding VAT)	36,400
Exempt supplies	7,800

Her input tax for the period is analysed as follows:

Wholly attributable to:

	£
Taxable supplies	1,725
Exempt supplies	1,035
Non-attributable (overheads)	1,380

Pauline uses the recovery percentage of the actual return period to calculate the input VAT recoverable.

Calculate the amount of input tax that Pauline may recover and describe the calculation of the annual adjustment.

23 **State the items which should be included on a 'less detailed tax invoice' issued by a retailer. What is the maximum value for which a less detailed invoice can be issued?**

24 Kindly Ltd intends to purchase a van for deliveries of its goods for business purposes. However, as a perk, Kindly Ltd has stated in advance of this new purchase that all employees will be able to borrow the van at weekends and evenings if they need it to move personal belongings, so long as they replace the fuel used. It is anticipated that this offer will be popular.

Briefly explain what the input tax implications are and advise how the Lennartz mechanism could be used in this situation.

25 Kwik Kall Ltd is a partly exempt business which is registered for VAT. The company operates the standard partial exemption method. During the VAT quarter ending 31 March 2010, which is also the VAT year end, it made the following sales:

	£
Taxable supplies	100,000
Exempt supplies	20,000
Input VAT directly attributable to taxable supplies	30,000
Input VAT directly attributable to exempt supplies	350
Input VAT attributable to head office costs	7,500

Kwik Kall uses the recovery percentage of the current return period to calculate the reclaimable input VAT for a period.

(a) Calculate the amount of VAT that the company may recover on the March 2010 VAT return.
(b) State when the annual adjustment calculation needs to be made.

26 Liela, a VAT registered trader, has incurred the following expenditure in the quarter to 31 March 2010:

	£
Car lease payments (20% private use)	1,200
Entertaining employees	320
Telephone calls (30% private use)	180
Purchase of the business of a competitor	320,000
New BMW	28,000
Delivery charges for new BMW	150

All figures are exclusive of VAT.

Calculate, with explanations, the amount of VAT recoverable.

27 A partially exempt business purchased building A in October 2008 and building B in December 2008. The costs of the buildings were £200,000 (plus VAT) and £400,000 (plus VAT) respectively. Both buildings have exempt and taxable use. The business' partial exemption recovery rates are as follows:

	%
Y/e 31 December 2008	50
Y/e 31 December 2009	40

Calculate the amount of input tax that can be reclaimed in the year of purchase and any adjustment required in the following year. Assume a standard rate of VAT of 17.5% throughout.

28 **Give five examples of expenditure on which recovery of VAT is blocked (ie VAT is non-deductible), for VAT registered businesses.**

29 **State the conditions for the recovery of input tax.**

30 When performing a partial exemption calculation under the standard method, supplies of certain goods and/or services are excluded from supplies when calculating the partial exemption percentage.

Give five examples of goods and/or services which are excluded when calculating the partial exemption percentage.

31 Banana Ltd buys a new computer on 2 January 2010, incurring £9,000 of input VAT.

Taxable use of the computer is as follows:

	%
Year ended 31 March 2010	60
Year ended 31 March 2011	80

The computer was sold on 1 December 2011 for £6,000 plus VAT. You may assume that the taxable use of the computer continued at 80% from 1 April 2011 to sale.

Calculate the adjustments that are required under the capital goods scheme for all relevant years.

32 State:

(a) Which assets are subject to the capital goods scheme.
(b) The adjustment periods for each.
(c) When the adjustments should be made.

33 Bones Funeral Services is an 80% exempt trader. The company's premises are to be extended by 15% (by floor area) in 2010. The company is considering either using contractors to do the work or to offer 6 month employment contracts to a variety of contractors. The value of the work has been estimated at £200,000 plus VAT.

Outline the VAT implications of each of these options.

34 What alternative methods are available to the standard method of allocating unattributable input tax for a partially exempt trader? In what situation can HMRC impose a special method rather than the standard method?

35 On 1 January 2010 Rafi, a VAT registered trader buys a new car (CO_2 emissions = 235g/km) costing £15,000 excluding VAT which he will use 90% for business purposes. A month later he has a CD player costing £100 excluding VAT fitted into the car. In the quarter ended 31 March 2010 Rafi spent £500 (inclusive of VAT) on fuel. Rafi has opted to apply the fuel scale charge in respect of the private fuel used.

State the VAT implications of these transactions.

36 Tim has set up a new business manufacturing and selling clothes and has registered voluntarily for VAT.

His supplies in the past year were:

	£
Sales of adult clothes (standard rated supplies)	82,000
Sales of children's clothes (zero rated supplies)	71,000

In addition, he received fees of £15,000 in relation to setting and marking exams for Townville University art and design degree courses.

Explain how the exam fees received could affect the recoverability of his input tax.

37 Your client is a firm of solicitors who are a partnership. The senior partner has a history of involvement in motor racing. He has purchased a single seater racing car to race in a new competition series in the UK. His stated objective in entering these races is to secure promotion for the firm by way of articles and features in the local press and in specialist magazines. The firm's accounts department are not sure whether they should recover the VAT on the purchase of the racing car, and have asked you for advice.

You are required to draft a short note for the accounts department, advising them on whether or not they should recover the VAT and giving an explanation for your conclusion.

38 On 1 April 2007, HM Revenue & Customs introduced new conditions on businesses which want to implement a special partial exemption method. Such businesses now have to provide an additional declaration, to support the special partial exemption methodology being proposed.

You are required to explain:

(a) What the declaration is.
(b) How it should be made.
(c) When it should be made.
(d) The statutory reference which gives HM Revenue & Customs the right to require such a declaration.

Land and buildings

39 Frump Ltd is planning to renovate and sell an office block. Two prospective purchasers have been identified:

(a) A bank
(b) A clothes retailer.

Frump Ltd will pay a large amount of VAT on the renovation and is therefore planning to elect to opt to tax the office block.

Outline the implications of opting to tax this property.

40 What is the VAT treatment of the:

(a) Grant of a 60 year lease in a newly built factory.
(b) Sale of a freehold house by the builder who constructed it.
(c) Sale of the freehold of a 12 month old office block.
(d) Sale of a plot of land acquired for investment purposes.
(e) Sale of a new freehold building to a charity, who will use the building entirely for charitable purposes.

41 **(a)** State whether the following supplies are standard rated, zero rated or exempt:

      (i) Sale of a house by the present owner/occupier.
      (ii) Hire of a hotel conference room for a meeting.
      (iii) Sale of a two year old commercial building.
      (iv) The grant of an eight year lease in a commercial building.

(b) Briefly explain if an option to tax could affect the liability of any of these supplies.

42 Alpha Ltd is considering entering into a property development agreement, whereby it would construct a new building and lease it to a tenant, Beta Ltd, who has already agreed to accept a 25 year lease on the property. Alpha's lawyers have recommended that they should exercise their option to tax.

You are required to draft a short note to Alpha Ltd explaining how they should go about opting to tax. You are NOT required to explain the effect of the option to tax, or any benefits and/or disadvantages which might result.

43 Your local Society for the Preservation of Historic Oldtown has asked you to give a presentation on the application of VAT on the costs of maintaining a Listed Building.

You are required to prepare brief notes for the presentation you will give.

44 **List five uses a building may be put to which would qualify as a relevant residential purpose for the purposes of the zero rating provisions.**

45 Penguin Ltd, a construction company, has incurred the following subcontractor costs in the construction of some of its current properties:

- Subcontractor fees on the construction of a block of flats (labour and building materials).

- Architects fees on the construction of a block of flats (invoiced directly to Penguin Ltd).

- Subcontractor fees on the construction of a building for Oxfam (the building will be used entirely for a charitable purpose and Penguin Ltd holds the appropriate certificate for zero rating).

Penguin Ltd sold a freehold interest in the above properties in March 2010.

You are required to determine the VAT treatment of the subcontractor and architects fees above, and comment upon how Penguin Limited will recover the VAT (if any) so charged.

46 Your client incurred significant amounts of input tax on refurbishing a building two years ago. At that time your client had not opted to tax because the existing tenant was not able to recover any input tax it incurred on rent. Your client now has a new tenant who is able to recover VAT on rent and who has taken a 25 year lease on the building. As a result, your client has decided to opt to tax.

Your client has been told by HM Revenue & Customs that they require permission from them in order to opt to tax, and that before such permission will be given, your client must submit proposals as to how much of the input tax previously incurred they now want to recover.

You are required to summarise the advice you would give to your client.

47 Your client, Acme Builders Ltd, purchased the freehold of a public house that had lain derelict for 11 years. When the building was used as an operational pub, the pub premises were on the ground floor, and the first floor was the domestic accommodation for the manager. Acme converted the building into two semi-detached houses, the freeholds of which it intends to sell.

State the VAT treatment of the sale of the two houses, and explain whether Acme Builders Ltd can recover the input VAT in respect of this project.

Overseas and miscellaneous issues

48 Budget Ltd, which is registered for VAT, sells pine furniture. Many of Budget Ltd's customers are businesses based in France, of which some are registered for French VAT (TVA) and some are not.

Explain briefly how Budget Ltd must account for VAT on sales to its French customers. You are not required to comment on the VAT treatment to be used by the purchasers.

49 Charlie, a VAT registered trader, is selling his business assets.

State the conditions for the sale of the assets to be treated as neither a supply of goods nor a supply of services.

50 Liberty Ltd is registered for VAT and exports standard rated goods to customers in France and the US.

State the VAT treatment of the sales of goods to these customers, the evidence that must be available to support the VAT treatment, and the time period within which it must be obtained.

51 Ian is a rock guitarist who performs in gigs in Bristol, Rome and Montreal.

Ian has his home and business base in Bristol.

Ian is registered for VAT in the UK.

Explain:

(a) The place of supply of Ian's performances in each of the three cities.
(b) Whether VAT should be shown on his invoices in each case.
(c) Any other VAT implications that may arise for Ian.

52 A company registered for VAT in the UK makes the following supplies:

(a) A sale of copyright to a private individual in the USA.
(b) A sale of copyright to a private individual in France.
(c) A sale of copyright to a company which is VAT registered in Italy.

Briefly explain how the above sales will be treated for VAT purposes.

53 Your client is a celebrity chef, who is registered for VAT as a sole proprietor in the UK. He has a villa in Spain.

He has contracted with a UK based supplier of fitted kitchens to supply and install a new fitted kitchen in his Spanish villa. The kitchen suppliers have stated that they have to charge UK VAT on the supply.

Your client is not sure if this is right, but in any case, he believes that he can recover the VAT as input tax, as he often films the creation of new dishes in the kitchen of the villa, and he sells the broadcast rights of these cooking sessions to UK TV companies.

You are required to prepare brief notes on how you would advise your client.

54 A business exporting goods must have proof of export available for HM Revenue &Customs, to support zero rating.

Proof of export can be divided into two types: official evidence and commercial evidence.

You are required to give three examples of each type. You are NOT required to give examples of 'supplementary evidence' which, although supportive, is usually more circumstantial in nature.

55 Devon plc, a UK VAT registered company, manufactures poultry roasting kitchen equipment which it sells to restaurants in the UK, and to Berlin GmbH in Germany and Southern Inc in the USA.

You are required to state, giving legal references, the place of supply and the VAT liability of the supplies Devon plc makes to:

(a) UK restaurants.
(b) Berlin GmbH.
(c) Southern Inc.

56 Tapas is a Spanish manufacturer of tiles and ceramics. It set up business in the UK on 1 April 2010, having signed contracts on that date with a number of UK retailers, for the supply of tiles and other ceramic products. The aggregate monthly value of these contracts amounts to £75,000.

You are required to explain the registration implications for Tapas, including the effective date of registration.

57 Simon, a VAT registered trader, is considering selling his business. He is undecided whether he should sell his fixed assets piecemeal, or if he should sell the business as a going concern.

State briefly the VAT implications of each option, and the conditions for the transfer to be treated as the sale of a business as a going concern.

58 **Briefly explain the principle of 'direct effect' (commenting on who can and who cannot apply the principle) and direct applicability in the context of European Law.**

59 Hatter Ltd imports both children's and adult clothes from other countries within the EU.

Explain briefly how VAT on acquisitions from EU countries and on Hatter Ltd's inputs in particular should be accounted for.

60 Businesses registered for VAT in one EU Member State often incur VAT on goods or services bought in another EU Member State. Special provisions exist to allow such businesses to recover the VAT incurred from the tax authorities in the Member State in which the VAT was incurred, subject to a number of general conditions.

You are required to state the underpinning legal provision(s), and what the general principles are for recovery of the other country VAT.

VAT administration

61 **Explain how the basic VAT tax point is determined for a purchase of goods, and how this may be altered by invoicing procedures.**

62 Crest Ltd makes standard rated supplies and operates the cash accounting scheme. In the quarter ended 30 June 2010 the following transactions were recorded:

(1) 11 April – Invoice 20 issued for works completed, £5,750 inc VAT
(2) 20 April – £17,250 received from customer in relation to invoice issued in March
(3) 1 May – Deposit of £2,300 received from a customer
(4) 2 May – Goods purchased in cash for £2,000 plus VAT of £350
(5) 14 May – Invoice received from a supplier for £1,000 plus VAT of £175
(6) 3 June – Invoice 20 paid in full by customer
(7) 10 June – Invoice 21 issued for works completed £11,500 including VAT

Calculate Crest Ltd's VAT liability for the quarter ended 30 June 2010.

63 (a) Bee Ltd registered for VAT on 9 January 2009 but did not join the flat rate scheme until 1 June 2009 when the rate was 7.5%. On 1 October 2009 the business changed and the new flat rate became 9%.

State the flat rates that Bee Ltd must use from the date of joining the flat rate scheme.

(b) Wasp Ltd has turnover of £450,000 in its year ended 31 December 2009. It uses the VAT annual accounting scheme.

Explain briefly, without the aid of calculations, how payments are made under the scheme.

64 Colin's Corner Shop uses Apportionment Scheme 1 as its retail scheme to calculate its VAT liability. The scheme requires a taxpayer to calculate the value of purchases for resale at different rates of VAT and apply the proportions of those purchase values to sales. It also requires an annual adjustment. In the quarter ending 31 May 2009 Colin's corner shop had purchased £60,000 worth of standard rated items and £20,000 of zero rated items for resale. The gross takings from sales were £120,000.

(a) **Calculate the output tax liability for that quarter.**
(b) **State why an annual adjustment is included in some retail schemes.**

65 Wayward plc is a fully taxable business which has recently undergone a visit from HM Revenue & Customs. During the visit HMRC discovered that on the March 2010 VAT return, a large sales invoice for £650,000 plus VAT had been erroneously recovered as input VAT rather than accounted for as output VAT.

The March 2010 VAT return was submitted with figures as follows:

	£
VAT on sales	200,000
VAT on purchases	150,000

Explain the potential penalty which may be charged on Wayward plc.

66 Trout Ltd has a turnover in excess of £150,000 per annum. The VAT return for the quarter ended 31 December 2009 was submitted late, and the VAT due of £25,560 was not paid until 14 February 2010.

The company's VAT return for the following quarter was also submitted late, and the VAT due of £29,180 was not paid until 9 May 2010.

Explain the consequences for Trout Ltd, and what action Trout Ltd will need to take to ensure that there are no similar consequences in respect of future returns.

67 Maria, a VAT registered trader, previously always submitted returns and paid the VAT on time. The following returns and VAT payments were made late.

Quarter ended	£
30 June 2009	8,600
30 September 2009	9,000
31 December 2009	9,700
31 March 2010 (note)	9,200

The 31 March return was submitted late, but payment of £9,200 was made on 28 April 2010.

Her taxable turnover is in the region of £200,000 per year.

State the consequences.

68 Certain decisions of HMRC cannot be appealed to the Tribunal.

List five matters in respect of which an appeal can be made to the Tribunal.

69 **You are required to explain why a business may be required to settle its VAT liabilities under the Payments on Account scheme, how the scheme operates, how the payments are calculated and how they may change.**

70 VAT registered businesses will be liable to a civil penalty for not sending in their VAT returns, or paying VAT due, on time. However, if a business has a 'reasonable excuse' no such penalty will be charged.

You are required to list five of the examples that HM Revenue & Customs have indicated that they will accept as 'reasonable excuses'.

71 David Jones Yachts Ltd, a VAT registered business, has quarterly VAT periods ending 31 March, 30 June, 30 September and 31 December. The company accepted a commission to build a new private yacht for a wealthy client. After a period of discussion and the production of draft designs, the final contract to construct the yacht was signed on 1 January 2010, with a selling price for the yacht of £1.25 million plus VAT.

The client paid an initial deposit of £125,000 on 20 January 2010. A further payment of £500,000 was made on 1 August 2010 when the hull and main deck were completed. The company issued an invoice for the remaining amount due under the contract on 23 December 2010, which the client paid 40 days later, when they took delivery of the yacht on 2 February 2011.

You are required to calculate the output tax entries that the company was/is required to make in their quarterly VAT returns, for the supplies made under this contract, showing both the workings and the reasoning behind the output tax entries you have calculated.

72 In certain circumstances, errors on previous VAT returns can be corrected in the next returns submitted.

Outline the rules relating to the correction of errors on subsequent VAT returns, together with any penalty implications.

73 **Outline the conditions for entry to the cash accounting scheme.**

74 Trusting Ltd has made a number of supplies to Hardup Ltd as follows:

	Net £	VAT £	Gross £
16 April 2010	790	–	790
22 May 2010	1,022	179	1,201
18 August 2010	409	72	481
24 September 2010	1,267	222	1,489

Hardup Ltd is experiencing severe financial difficulties. Trusting Ltd received an unallocated payment on account from Hardup Ltd on 5 November 2010 for £2,200, but has been told that it is unlikely to receive any further payments.

Assuming payment is due one month after the supply, calculate the available bad debt relief on the VAT return to 30 April 2011.

75 Bungle Ltd's VAT liability for the year to 30 September 2009 is £2,400,000. For the quarter ended 31 March 2010, the company's VAT liability is £350,000.

What are substantial traders for VAT payment on account purposes, how must substantial traders account for VAT and what are the implications for Bungle Ltd in respect of the quarter ended 31 March 2010?

76 Your client is considering implementing a VAT savings idea that he has heard about from a business colleague. He has been told that schemes with certain hallmarks have to be disclosed to HM Revenue and Customs.

List the hallmarks set out in the relevant regulations which mean a scheme must be disclosed to HM Revenue and Customs

77 Karen, a trader, registered for VAT 5 months late at the beginning of June 2010. Her standard rated sales in this period are £51,750 and her standard rated purchases are £17,250 (including VAT).

Discuss the potential penalty that Karen could incur for failing to notify HM Revenue and Customs of the need to register for VAT.

Stamp taxes

78 **List five instruments which are exempt from stamp duty if properly certified.**

79 A relief is available from stamp duty which applies in the case of a reorganisation of a group of companies involving a new holding company being placed over an existing company or group, without any additional shareholders.

Outline the conditions which must be met in order to obtain this relief.

80 **State the filing date for a land transaction return, and outline the penalties and interest which may apply if a land transaction return is not filed and the stamp duty land tax is not paid.**

81 A land transaction is exempt from stamp duty land tax if these vendor and the purchaser are members of the same group of companies at the time of the transaction.

Give the circumstances in which group relief is either not available, or withdrawn.

82 Stamp duty land tax is collected under a self assessment system.

Outline the provisions under which a taxpayer may amend a land transaction return, the powers of HMRC to amend the land transaction return, and the enquiry provisions.

83 Consider the following transactions:

(a) Richard sold 2000 shares in Alpha Ltd for £81,300 to Purple plc using a stock transfer form.

(b) Pluto Ltd sold to residential land to Saturn plc, an unconnected company, for £260,000.

(c) Sun Ltd paid £80,000 for the grant of a 30 year lease of a warehouse. The net present value of the rental was £510,000 and the annual rental was £10,000. The factory was not in a disadvantaged area.

You are required to explain the stamp taxes implications of these transactions.

84 George is considering selling his shares in Blue Ltd, and has received two alternative offers.

(a) **A payment of £100,000, plus 50% of the profits of the company for the next accounting period.**

(b) **A payment of £100,000, plus 50% of the profits of the company for the next accounting period, subject to a maximum additional payment of £200,000.**

Outline the stamp duty implications in respect of the above alternative offers.

85 Stephen is the 100% shareholder in two companies, Red limited and Orange limited. Red limited transfers a small shareholding in another company, Blue Ltd to Orange limited.

Outline the relief from stamp duty that is applicable in respect of certain intra-group transfers, and comment on its application in respect of the transfer to Orange limited.

Module B
Inheritance tax, trusts and estates

Questions

Module B: Inheritance tax, trusts and estates

IHT Basics

1   Pierre inherited £100,000 on 1 January 2007 and paid £10,000 Inheritance Tax as a result.

   On 1 March 2008, Pierre made a cash gift to his son of £198,000. Pierre made no other lifetime transfers.

   On 1 February 2010 Pierre died and left an estate worth £500,000.

   Calculate the Inheritance Tax payable as a result of Pierre's death.

2   Tom and Camilla had been married for many years until Camilla sadly passed away in May 2002. Camilla's estate consisted of assets worth £260,000, £110,000 being left to Tom and the remainder to her son.

   Tom dies in December 2009, leaving an estate of £620,000.

   Calculate the IHT payable on Tom's death, assuming that neither spouse had made any lifetime transfers.

3   Richard died on 15 January 2010, leaving a death estate of £862,000. His only previous transfer had been a gross chargeable transfer of £282,000 in 2008. He left a property worth £243,000 free of tax to his son, and the rest of his estate to his wife.

   Calculate the amount of the estate that Richard's wife will receive.

4   (a)   Additional tax on chargeable lifetime transfers
    (b)   Tax on PETs becoming chargeable
    (c)   Tax on the deceased's free estate
    (d)   Tax on settled property

   Give the persons responsible for the payment of Inheritance Tax on the death of the donor for the above, and state the persons HMRC can look to where the tax remains unpaid.

5   **Give three examples of excluded property for Inheritance Tax purposes.**

6   David, who had never married, died on 1 November 2009 leaving assets of £400,000 in his free estate.

   He also had a qualifying life interest in a settlement created by his father's will. The trust assets consisted of £60,000 8% Treasury Stock quoted at 62–64p at the date of David's death.

   David had made no lifetime transfers.

   Calculate the Inheritance Tax payable on David's death, and state by whom it is payable.

7   Thomas has a salary of £100,000 per annum and lives modestly. On 1 September 2009, Thomas paid his godson's school fees for the academic year, something he has done every year since the boy started school in 1999.

   In February 2010, Thomas gave his daughter £100,000 to help her set up home with her long-term boyfriend. His daughter has told him that she believes that they do not need to be married for this gift to qualify for the marriage exemption from Inheritance Tax.

   You are required to explain briefly the Inheritance Tax consequences of these gifts.

   State the due date for payment of inheritance tax and the position as regards interest.

8   Adam owned a complete set of 12 Chippendale dining chairs. In December 2009 he gave three of these chairs to his wife and three to his son. At the date of Adam's death in January 2010, the chairs were valued as follows:

	£
Set of three chairs	40,000
Set of six chairs	120,000
Set of nine chairs	240,000
Set of twelve chairs	400,000

State the value of Adam's six remaining Chippendale chairs in his estate for Inheritance Tax purposes and calculate the IHT due on his death estate on the basis that his nil rate band has been fully utilised.

Explain who will meet the tax liabilities incurred on his death, on the basis of the information above.

9   On 1 May 2007, Sally gave shares in an investment company valued at £288,000 to her friend Anne.

On 21 October 2009, Sally died leaving an estate valued at £500,000. Anne's shares were then worth £268,000.

Calculate the Inheritance Tax payable as a result of Sally's death.

10 Natalie died on 17 February 2010. At the date of her death she owned the following assets:

(1) Main residence valued at £620,000 with an outstanding repayment mortgage of £50,000.

(2) A life insurance policy on her own life. The policy had an open market value of £75,000 immediately prior to her death; proceeds of £100,000 were received following her death. The policy was not written in trust.

(3) 10,000 £1 ordinary shares in Moon plc. On 17 February 2010 the shares were quoted at 420 – 428.

(4) Chalet in Austria, valued at €450,000. The buying exchange rate is €1.51 and the selling rate is €1.32.

Funeral expenses of £5,042 were incurred.

Calculate Natalie's estate on death.

11 Robert died on 1 January 2010 leaving assets of £400,000. He was the life tenant of an interest in possession trust created in 2001. The remainderman was his son, Daniel.

The trust assets were worth £280,000 at the time of his death.

His only lifetime gift was of £96,000 to his daughter on 31 May 2009.

Calculate the tax payable by the personal representatives and the trustees.

12 Simon has written to you as his tax adviser stating that he intends to waive his right to receive certain dividends from his family company shareholding.

Simon would also like to know the position should he choose to sell his shares to an unconnected party, at an undervalue. The company is unquoted.

Explain how a dividend waiver can avoid giving rise to a transfer of value for Inheritance Tax purposes.

Explain how the sale at an undervalue will be treated for Inheritance Tax purposes.

13 Edward owns 4,500 shares in Exams Ltd. Of the remaining shares, 2,500 are held in a trust set up in 1998 of which Edward is the life tenant and 3,000 are owned by his brother Dominic.

The shares in the company are valued as follows:

10% to 39% holding	£12 per share
40% to 49% holding	£15 per share
50% to 69% holding	£20 per share
70% to 89% holding	£25 per share
90% or more holding	£30 per share

On 20 December 2009, Edward gave 1,000 shares to his brother Dominic.

Ignoring all reliefs and exemptions, what is the transfer of value for inheritance tax purposes? Also state the value disposed of for capital gains tax purposes.

14 On 1 January 2007 Amy made a gross chargeable transfer of £350,000 to a discretionary trust. Lifetime Inheritance Tax of £13,000 was paid.

On 1 February 2007 Amy gave cash of £130,000 to her son.

On 1 March 2010 Amy died leaving a chargeable estate valued at £300,000 to her daughter.

Calculate all Inheritance Tax payable as a result of Amy's death, stating who bears any tax payable.

15 Gladys, who was domiciled within the UK, died on 7 January 2010. At the date of her death she owned the following assets.

(1) 15,000 £1 ordinary shares in Cumberland plc, a quoted investment company. On 7 January 2010 the share were quoted at 410 – 422, with marked bargains of 408, 415 and 424.

(2) Holiday house in Utopia valued at US$150,000. The cost of administering the house is £5,500. If it had been located in the UK the cost of administering would have been £1,000. The relevant exchange rate at the date of Gladys's death was £1 = US$1.48.

Funeral expenses amounted to £2,500.

Calculate the value of Gladys's estate at death for Inheritance Tax purposes.

16 Elinor made a gift of shares, in an unquoted company, to her son in February 2010. Some more of the shares are owned by a trust created in 2000, of which Elinor's husband is the life tenant.

Indicate, with reasons, whether the related property rules apply to the valuation of this gift for Inheritance Tax purposes. Explain how the related property rules work in relation to shares.

17 In January 2007, Francesca died leaving her entire estate, worth £500,000, to her brother Glen. The tax payable on her estate was £100,000.

Glen died in March 2010 leaving an estate valued at £1 million to his brother. Glen had made a gross chargeable transfer of £243,000 in February 2008.

Calculate the Inheritance Tax payable by Glen's executors.

18 **Briefly explain what may be related property for Inheritance Tax purposes and how shares are valued using the related property rules.**

19 Stephen died on 1 May 2009 and his estate comprised:

	£
6,000 £1 ordinary shares in Timber plc, a quoted company, (representing a 60% holding)	300,000
Villa in Lithuania	100,000
Matrimonial home	250,000
Personal chattels	5,000

Additional costs in administering the villa in Lithuania amounted to £6,250 and the solicitor's fee for administering the estate was £5,100.

Stephen made a gift of quoted shares valued at £400,000 in July 2006, to his son Simon. He owned 3% of the company.

Stephen left all his assets to his children with the exception of the matrimonial home which was left to his wife.

Calculate Stephen's chargeable estate and the inheritance tax chargeable in respect of the estate.

20   Queenie died on 1 February 2010. Her estate comprised the following:

	£
Cash	200,000
Life assurance proceeds (qualifying policy)	50,000
House in Surbiton, Surrey – main residence	500,000
Stamp collection	180,000
Holiday home – Faro, Portugal	120,000
Additional costs of administering foreign property	8,000

The stamp collection was a specific legacy from her father who died on 3 December 2008. At that time the collection was worth £150,000, and the average estate rate was 30%.

Calculate the Inheritance Tax payable on Queenie's death estate.

21   Ursula, who had made no previous transfers, made the following gifts in December 2009:

(a)   1 December: £5,000 to Uganda Aid – an overseas registered charity.
(b)   3 December: £20,000 to Ula, her civil partner. The couple are currently estranged and living apart.
(c)   6 December: a painting, valued at £9,000, to The National Gallery in London.
(d)   8 December: a car valued at £19,000 to her friend Olga.

Without calculating any tax, state briefly which exemptions from Inheritance Tax (if any) apply to each gift, and why. Ignore the annual exemption.

22   Sasha inherited £300,000 on 1 January 2007 and paid Inheritance Tax of £20,000 as a result.

On 1 May 2009, Sasha made a cash gift to his son of £250,000. Sasha made no other lifetime transfers. On 1 August 2010 Sasha died and left an estate worth £650,000.

Calculate the Inheritance Tax payable as a result of Sasha's death.

23   Gillian's death estate includes the following assets, which have all been held since 1995:

	£
Free estate	
3% shareholding in Gamma plc, a trading company listed on the Alternative Investment Market (AIM)	132,000
40% shareholding in Delta Ltd (see below)	364,000
Settled property (subject to an interest in possession in favour of Gillian)	
Factory used in the trade carried on by Gillian's nephew Lee, who is the remainderman of the trust, set up in 1985	264,000

Delta Ltd is an unquoted trading company, with total assets of £1.2 million at the date of Gillian's death, including an investment property worth £300,000 and plant and machinery worth £200,000 (made up of items each worth less than £6,000).

Calculate, with brief explanations, the value of these assets in Gillian's estate assuming all available reliefs are claimed.

APR, BPR and post mortem sales

24 Quentin died on 1 March 2010 owning the following assets:

Asset	Purchase date	Value £
100% of the shares in Rory Ltd, an unquoted manufacturing company	1 January 2006	50,000
An office used by Quentin in his sole trade	1 February 2006	250,000
1% of the shares in Superco Ltd, a manufacturing company listed on the Alternative Investment Market	1 December 2007	120,000
Factory let by Quentin to Rory Ltd	1 February 2008	280,000
Share in a car repair business run in partnership with his brother	1 July 2008	70,000

Based on the above information, calculate the value of Quentin's death estate.

25 Clive and his family owned shares in an unquoted company for many years as follows:

	Number of shares
Clive	5,000
Sarah (Clive's wife)	3,000
Lincoln (Clive's son)	2,000
	10,000

On 10 October 2009 Clive gave away half of his holding to his son.

Estimated values for different sizes of shareholding on 10 October 2009 were as follows:

Number of shares	Pence per share	Value £
2,000	60	1,200
2,500	80	2,000
5,000	100	5,000
5,500	125	6,875
8,000	175	14,000
10,000	250	25,000

Calculate Clive's transfer of value.

Discuss whether the gift will qualify for business property relief and explain the position regarding investments held by the company.

26 Adrian makes the following transfers.

1 May 2009

His entire holding of 1,000 voting shares in a quoted trading company owned since 1990 to a relevant property trust. His wife owns 500 and his nephew owns 1,250 of the 5,000 shares in issue.

Valuations are as follows:

Holding	£ per share
0 – 25%	12
More than 25% – 50%	16
More than 50% – 75%	28
More than 75%	32

1 June 2009

10,000 shares in an unquoted investment company to a relevant property trust. The shares were purchased in 1997 and the holding is now valued at £20,000.

Calculate the value of the quoted shares transferred, for both IHT and CGT purposes. State the business property relief available in respect of both transfers, if any, giving your reasons.

27 N Ltd owns Fuddle Farm, which has a market value of £750,000 and an agricultural value of £420,000. Other net assets of the company, consisting of farm machinery, are worth £200,000.

Patrick transferred his 60% holding of ordinary shares in N Ltd (valued at £570,000) to a discretionary trust for his nephew in January 2010.

N Ltd purchased the farm in 1986, and Patrick had purchased the shares in 1994. Patrick has not made any other lifetime gifts.

Calculate the value of Patrick's chargeable transfer in January 2010, showing any reliefs available.

28 Richard, a sole trader, gifted the following assets in November 2009:

    (a)   Freehold property used in Richard's business.
    (b)   40% shareholding in a trading company quoted on the stock exchange.
    (c)   25% shareholding of the non-voting preference shares in an unquoted trading company.
    (d)   Loan stock in an unquoted trading company of which Richard holds 52% of the share capital.
    (e)   Interest in a partnership in which Richard has held an interest since 1 December 2008.

State the business property relief, if any, applicable to each of the above transfers.

29 On 1 September 2007, Frazer died leaving his 30% interest in Apple Ltd, a trading company, to his wife Gaynor. He had set up the company in 1980.

Gaynor gave the shares in Apple Ltd to their son Charles on 1 February 2008.

On 1 October 2009, Charles was killed in a car accident. He left his entire estate to his fiancée, Ann.

Explain briefly any Inheritance Tax reliefs available for these gifts.

30 **State three examples where business property relief will be available even though the transferor has not owned the property transferred for at least two years.**

31 Leonard purchased a fish shop on 1 April 2007, which he ran until his death on 1 October 2008. The shop then passed to his wife, Lily, who continued to run it until her death on 1 February 2010.

Explain the availability of Business Property Relief on the death of:

    (a)   **Leonard**
    (b)   **Lily**

32 Priscilla owned 6,000 shares in Q Ltd, a trading company, and gifted 1,250 shares to her niece in October 2009. She had bought the shares in March 2007 for £30 per share.

Q Ltd has an issued share capital of 10,000 £1 ordinary shares. A holding of 51–75% is worth £160 per share, a holding of 26–49% is worth £100 per share and a holding of 0–25% is worth £50 per share.

Give the value transferred for Inheritance Tax purposes and calculate Priscilla's capital gains tax liability on the gift of the shares.

33. Noble ran the family trading company, N Ltd, for many years owning 100% of the shares.

On 1 June 2006 he gave 30% of the shares to Nigel, his eldest son (share values: 100% £500,000, 70% £250,000, 30% £100,000).

On 1 March 2010 N Ltd became listed on the London Stock Exchange, and Noble died of a heart attack the next day. Nigel still owned the shares given to him by his father.

Noble left his remaining shares, worth £10million, to Oxfam, and his house, worth £1million, to Noreen, his long term partner (sometimes described as a 'common law' wife).

Noble made no other gifts or transfers of any kind.

Calculate any Inheritance Tax arising as a result of Noble's death.

34. For many years, Oscar has been farming at Otters End. He is 87 years old when he dies. He owned the following :

(a) Farmland at Otters End worth £20,000 at current agricultural value, but with recent planning permission, now worth £500,000.

(b) 5 acres of farming land at Open Ditch, a town 10 miles from Otters End. This land is rented to another farmer on a 10 year lease, which has 8 years remaining, and has an agricultural value of £25,000.

(c) The farmhouse at Otters End worth £600,000 for all purposes. It is agreed that a normal sized farmhouse for a similar farm would be half the size and value.

(d) Cattle farm at Shotley farmed by Oscar and his wife in partnership, worth £125,000 with current agricultural value £100,000.

(e) Cattle herd valued at £55,000.

Calculate the value of the above assets to be included in the death estate after APR. Ignore BPR.

35. Brian owned 20% of the shares in Box Ltd, a trading company. His shares were valued at £128,000. The balance sheet of Box Ltd showed the following on 31 December 2009, the date on which Brian died:

	Net book value £	Market value £
Factory	361,000	864,000
Goodwill	Nil	200,000
Sundry investments	124,000	112,000
Net current assets	21,000	21,000
	506,000	1,197,000

Brian also left a house in Utopia valued at £410,000, which cost £23,000 to administer because of its location.

The investments are not connected with the trade of Box Ltd.

You are required to calculate Brian's chargeable estate showing how any reliefs will be given.

Overseas aspects and anti-avoidance

36. Walter is domiciled in Zanzibar for all purposes. He owns the following assets:

(a) Bearer shares in a company registered in Zanzibar. Document of title is kept in his flat in London.

(b) A debt of £100,000 lent to his friend from Zanzibar whilst he was on holiday in London. His friend is resident in Zanzibar.

(c) £150,000 deposited in the London branch of the Zanzibar National Bank.

(d) Family home in London.

(e) Personal assets kept in storage in Zanzibar.

State where each of the above assets is treated as located for Inheritance Tax purposes.

37 Paul is domiciled in Utopia. On 18 February 2010, he died leaving the following assets to his children:

	£
House in London	414,000
Shares in Utopian companies (registered in Utopia)	82,000
Cash in UK bank account	15,000
Bearer shares in UK company (share certificates are kept in Utopia)	29,000

Calculate the Inheritance Tax payable on Paul's estate.

38 Tom, who is UK domiciled, has paid his grandson's school fees for the past five years. In June 2006 he gave £40,000 to Mavis, his wife, who is domiciled in Jersey. In June 2009, he gave Mavis a further £60,000, shortly before his death in September 2009.

Tom had always used his Inheritance Tax annual exemption.

Explain briefly whether any of these gifts will be liable to Inheritance Tax. Calculations are not required.

39 Bill runs a cheese business importing and exporting cheese to and from Europe. On his death, his estate included the following assets:

(1) Branch located in Holland. There is substantial goodwill associated with this part of the business.

(2) A considerable sum owed by debtors living in Spain. No court proceedings had been initiated in relation to the debts.

(3) Shares in a French supplier quoted on the French stock exchange.

Explain briefly how you would determine where each of these assets is located for the purposes of Inheritance Tax on Bill's chargeable estate.

40 Harry gave his house to his daughter, Sue, in June 2006. It was then worth £350,000. He continued to live in the house until his death on 31 December 2009. The house was then worth £470,000.

Explain the Inheritance Tax consequences of this gift and explain briefly how the position would differ were Harry not to live in the property but visit just twice a year for a week.

41 Olivia was born in Brazil, and lived there until 1 March 1990, when she became resident in the UK on her marriage to an Englishman.

He is in poor health, and she intends to return to Brazil on his death.

Define deemed domicile for Inheritance Tax purposes, and state if Olivia will be deemed domiciled in the UK if she made a chargeable transfer on 1 November 2009.

Explain the rules regarding capital transfers between Olivia and her husband for the purposes of IHT.

42 **Briefly define a gift with reservation of benefit, and give three exceptions when such a transfer is not treated as a gift with reservation.**

43 Douglas (who has a domicile within the UK) and Sue (who is domiciled in Utopia) are married and live in the UK. Douglas has made the following gifts:

		£
1 October 2003	Gift of Farm in Utopia to Sue	175,000
1 November 2007	Gift to Utopian charity	100,000

The only other gifts made by Douglas were £3,000 each year to utilise his annual exemption.

Douglas died on 1 May 2009, leaving his chargeable estate of £270,000 to Sue.

Calculate the Inheritance Tax payable as a result of Douglas's death.

44 Henry is domiciled in Neverland. His estate contains the following assets:
   (a) House in Neverland.
   (b) House in Richmond, Surrey.
   (c) Cash balance at the Neverland branch of UK building society.
   (d) Cash balance at the Richmond branch of UK building society.
   (e) Goodwill relating to a mail order business based in Surrey.
   (f) Various antiques kept in the Richmond house.

   Explain how these assets will be treated for the purposes of calculating Henry's chargeable estate.

45 Andrew, domiciled in the UK, is married to Louise, who is domiciled in Mexico. Louise first came to the UK in June 1995, and has been here since that time.

   Andrew is in ill-health and is expected to live for only another two years. Andrew intends to give Louise a house that he owns in Mexico valued at £450,000. He is undecided whether to give the house to her in June 2010 or whether to leave it to her on his death. Andrew made gifts in 2009 that have used up his nil rate band.

   State, with explanations whether, for Inheritance Tax purposes, Andrew should make the gift in June 2010 or on his death in two years time.

46 In December 2009 Neil gifted the matrimonial home worth £800,000, to his son, Oliver. Oliver did not take up residence in the house but continued to live in his own home. Neil and his wife continued to live in the matrimonial home until March 2012 when they both died in an accident. At that date the house is worth £950,000.

   Explain the Inheritance Tax and Capital Gains Tax implications of the gift.

   You are not expected to produce calculations.

47 Antonia made the following lifetime gifts:

   1 May 2007   £115,000 to her friend Brian, on the occasion of his marriage
   1 June 2007 £200,000 to a charity in Estonia
   1 July 2007 £300,000 to her husband, Charlie who is domiciled in Canada

   Antonia died on 1 August 2009 leaving her estate of £750,000 to a political party.

   Calculate the Inheritance Tax payable as a result of Antonia's lifetime gifts and on the death estate.

48 Shirin died on 23 November 2009 and was not domiciled for any tax purposes in the UK. Her assets were:
   (a) Discovered in a UK bank safe deposit box: 2,000 share certificates in Satha Steel, registered in India, and normally dealt there. Shirin bought the shares in a one off, placed transaction in London, several years ago.
   (b) Her Picasso painting, usually hanging in her aunt's house in Calcutta, but temporarily at the National Portrait Gallery, London, being cleaned.
   (c) $15,000 US dollars held at the London branch of the Bank of India (exchange rate 1.95 USD = £1).
   (d) Debt owed to Shirin by Sarah, who resides in Alaska.

   State, with brief reasons, whether each of these items will be chargeable to UK Inheritance Tax.

49 On 20 July 2002, Victoria-Rose gave her house to her daughter Veronica but continued to live in it rent-free. At this time, the house was valued at £150,000.

   On 20 July 2005, Victoria-Rose moved into a retirement flat and Veronica immediately moved into the house, which was then valued at £390,000.

   On 21 July 2009, Victoria-Rose died, leaving her remaining estate to the Red Cross, a registered charity.

   Calculate any Inheritance Tax arising from the above events, briefly giving reasons for your answer.

50 Jacob, who is non UK domiciled, has lived with his wife Harriet, who is domiciled within the UK, in London for the last 10 years. Prior to moving to London, the family lived in Spain. He has made the following lifetime gifts:

		£
1 October 2004	Gifts of shares in Alpha plc, listed on the London stock exchange, equal amounts to his six grandchildren totalling	1,320
10 October 2005	Gifts of shares in Beta plc, listed on the London stock exchange, equal amounts to his four children totalling	3,200
15 June 2007	Gift of his home in Spain to his daughter, Grazia	156,000
20 April 2009	Gift of an antique diamond necklace to Harriet	75,000

Briefly explain the value of each gift falling within the charge to Inheritance Tax, if Jacob were to die in December 2010.

51 Zoe, who has always been domiciled in the UK, decided to emigrate to Abbeyland in January 2005. She immediately settled in Abbeyland and acquired residence and domicile there.

Zoe subsequently died owning the following assets:

House in Abbeyland
Personal chattels held in storage in the UK
Ordinary shares in Balloon plc, a UK quoted company (certificates located in Zoe's house in Abbeyland)
Bank account held at Abbeyland branch of UK bank

Explain which assets form part of Zoe's estate for Inheritance Tax purposes if Zoe died in:

(a) January 2007.
(b) January 2010.

52 **Explain when a settlor can be assessed on the income of a trust even though he is not a beneficiary of that trust.**

IHT and trusts

53 Oliver made a cash gift of £500,000 to a discretionary trust on 1 January 2005, and paid the Inheritance Tax arising. Oliver died on 1 May 2009, owning no assets and having made no other lifetime transfers.

Calculate the Inheritance Tax payable at the time of the gift and on Oliver's death.

54 Shares in Riga Ltd, an unquoted investment company with an issued share capital of 100 ordinary shares of £1 each, are held as follows:

	Shares
Charles	40
Fiona – his wife	35
Donald – his son	15
Mary – his daughter	10
	100

Current values for the shares in Riga Ltd are:

	£
75%	480,000
60%	336,000
45%	144,000
15%	35,000

On 1 December 2009 Charles gifted 15% of the shares in Riga Ltd to an interest in possession trust for his son.

(a) **Calculate the transfer of value on this disposition.**

(b) **Calculate the IHT due on the transfer on the basis that Charles had made a gross chargeable transfer of £350,000 in December 2005.**

(c) **State the value of the shares for Inheritance Tax purposes for the trustees.**

55 Viv owns 4,000 shares in Tiger Ltd, a company that has issued share capital of 5,000 £1 ordinary shares.

On 1 April 2010, she gave 3,000 shares to a discretionary trust. The shares are valued as follows:

Total shares owned	Value per share £
75% or more	30.00
50% or more, but less than 75%	27.50
25% or more, but less than 50%	18.00
Less than 25%	12.50

Viv had set up a similar trust in 2006 with a gross chargeable transfer of £500,000.

You are required to state the value of Viv's gift, before any reliefs, for the purposes of Inheritance Tax and Capital Gains Tax, and calculate the Inheritance Tax due on the transfer on the basis that the trustees pay the tax.

56 On 1 March 2004, Petula transferred land valued at £352,000 into a discretionary trust, Petula paying any Inheritance Tax due.

On 1 August 2009, Petula died. The land was now worth £410,000.

Petula had made no other lifetime gifts and left her entire estate to charity.

You are required to calculate the Inheritance Tax payable in connection with this gift.

57 Monique makes the following gifts:

(a) A business asset to Rachel, a friend, on 1 July 2009.
(b) A painting into a discretionary trust on 1 November 2009.
(c) An investment property to Kim, her daughter, on 1 January 2010.

Monique wishes to claim gift relief, if possible.

State the Capital Gains Tax claims available, by whom they must be made, and by what date.

58 Sebastian has made the following gifts into a discretionary trust and in each case, he has paid the tax due:

	£
20 March 1999	240,000
1 March 2003	160,000
1 October 2009	160,000

Show the Inheritance Tax due on the above transfers.

59 Sam transfers his shares in Tobo Ltd (representing 1% of the company) to a discretionary trust. Of the net assets owned by Tobo Ltd, 80% are chargeable business assets, the remaining 20% are chargeable assets.

Explain briefly how the chargeable gain on the transfer of the shares to the trust may be deferred and how any claims should be made.

Explain how the base cost of the asset is adjusted on deferral of the gain.

60 At the beginning of October 2009, the shares in Marvel Ltd, a property investment company, were owned as follows:

	£
David	4,000
Maria, David's wife	3,000
Peter, their son	2,000
Jane, David's sister	1,000
	10,000

The values per share of the shares in Marvel Ltd are:

	£		£
90%	100	50%	30
80%	80	40%	20
70%	60	30% and under	15
60%	50		

On 10 October 2009, David gave 1,000 of his shares to a discretionary trust. David had made a transfer to this same trust in December 2006, amounting to £400,000.

Calculate the value transferred by David and the inheritance tax arising. Also state the value transferred by David for CGT purposes.

61 Megan put £160,000 into a discretionary trust on 30 November 1999 and she paid any tax due. Up to that date she had made gross chargeable transfers of £233,000. In September 2009 the trustees advanced capital of £40,000 to one of the beneficiaries.

Calculate the Inheritance Tax payable in relation to the September 2009 advance assuming the tax is not paid out of the £40,000.

62 Pat Plumber died on 1 March 2000. Her will created a discretionary trust, The PP Trust, which was initially worth £100,000. She also left £75,000 in trust to her sister Pauline for life.

Her only previous gift was a gift of £109,000 in 1996 to a friend.

On 2 January 2009 the PP Trustees advanced £40,000 (gross) of capital to a beneficiary.

The PP Trust property was worth £330,000 on 1 March 2010.

Compute the 10 year anniversary charge to Inheritance Tax.

63 The trustees of the Poplar Discretionary Trust pass a property worth £550,000 out of the trust to one of the beneficiaries on 1 September 2009. The trust had been set up by Toby Poplar on 12 July 2003 with cash of £400,000.

Toby's only other lifetime gift had been a gift of £100,000 to his goddaughter on 1 April 2001.

You are required to calculate the exit charge when the property leaves the trust, assuming the trustees pay any Inheritance Tax due.

64 Pamela set up a discretionary trust on 1 July 2001, transferring in cash of £575,000. The trustees agreed to pay any tax due. Her only other lifetime transfers had been a transfer to a discretionary trust on 1 May 1998 of £100,000.

A payment of £50,000 was made to a beneficiary in August 2009, the trustees agreeing to pay any tax due.

You are required to calculate the exit charge in August 2009.

Trust income tax and CGT

65 Joe, the life tenant of a qualifying interest in possession trust, died on 1 October 2009. On his death, a house, which had been let commercially, passed to his daughter. A chargeable gain, which arose on the creation of the trust, had been held over at that time.

Explain briefly the likely Capital Gains Tax consequences of Joe's death.

66 The MacPherson Family Trust received rental income of £35,000 and UK dividend income of £9,000 (net) in 2009/10.

Stella is the only life tenant of the trust. There were expenses relating to the rental property of £3,000 for the year. Trustee management expenses amounted to £3,600 for 2009/10.

What amounts will be certified by the trustees as Stella's trust income for the year 2009/10?

67 Imogen set up a discretionary trust several years ago. The trust records show the following income and payments in 2009/10:

	£
UK dividend income (inclusive of tax credit)	6,150
Trustees management expenses paid	360

The trustees distributed income of £2,000 in 2009/10. There is no balance brought forward on the tax pool at 6 April 2009.

Calculate the Income Tax Liability of the trustees for 2009/10, including any additional tax due.

68 Hubert died on 1 January 1999. Under the terms of his will, the Hubert Will Trust was set up in 1999, holding a portfolio of quoted shares. Charles, Hubert's son, is the sole life tenant, entitled to the income for life, with the residuary capital going to Albert, Hubert's grandson.

The trust made capital losses of £2,250 on the sale of shares in 2000, but had no other capital transactions from 1999 until 2010.

During 2009/10, the Hubert Will Trust made capital gains of £17,500 and capital losses of £2,000. Hubert had created one other trust in his lifetime, in 1996 and this trust still existed in 2009/10.

Calculate the Capital Gains Tax payable by the trustees of the Hubert Will Trust for 2009/10.

69 Marley died in 2004. Under the terms of his will, a discretionary trust was created for the benefit of immediate family members, containing property and investments up to the value of the then nil rate band for Inheritance Tax purposes. He made no other gifts or settlements in his life or on his death.

During 2009/10, the trust received rents of £850, net building society interest of £480, and net UK dividends of £900.

The trustees made a distribution of income in the year of £1,500 (net of taxes). There was a nil balance brought forward in the tax pool at 6 April 2009.

Calculate the Income Tax liability of the trustees for 2009/10 (including any additional tax due) and state when it must be paid.

70 Yvonne set up a discretionary trust many years ago. The following income and expenses arose during 2009/10:

	£
Rental income received	22,000
Dividends received (inclusive of tax credit)	2,000
Trust expenses paid (net)	3,000
Rental expenses paid	2,000

Calculate the Income Tax payable by the trustees for 2009/10.

71 Heather bought a five hectare field on 1 June 1994 for £8,000.

She sold one hectare on 1 June 1996 for £5,000. The value of the remaining four hectares on 1 June 1996 was £30,000.

Heather gifted the remaining four hectares to a discretionary trust on 1 February 2010 when they were worth £45,000.

Calculate Heather's capital gains tax liability for 2009/10, assuming all possible claims for relief are made, and state the base cost of the land for the trustees.

General CGT

72. In 2009/10 Toby sold his shoe making business for £2 million realising a gain of £1 million. He had traded since 1997. He also sold his 6% shareholding in SUV Ltd an unquoted trading company, realising a gain of £300,000. He had held all the shares since 2003 and was also an employee of the company since that date.

    The gain on the disposal of Toby's business arose as follows:

	£
Goodwill	700,000
Factory	100,000
Warehouse	(50,000)
Investments	250,000

    Calculate Toby's Capital Gains Tax liability for 2009/10.

73. Simon bought 20 acres of land for £30,000 in January 2004. On 1 February 2010 he sold three acres for £18,000 incurring disposal costs of £360. The market value of the land immediately prior to the part-disposal was £190,000. This was his only sale during 2009/10.

    Calculate Simon's Capital Gains Tax position for 2009/10 assuming that any available claim to defer the gain is made, stating the date by which the claim is required and the cost of the land retained.

74. Lorrie inherited some land from his father in 1975 at a probate value of £12,000. The value of the land at March 1982 was £27,000. Lorrie received an offer of £19,000 for a quarter of the land, in January 2010. The remaining land was worth £85,000 at that date. Lorrie has no other capital transactions and intends to sell the remainder of the land next year.

    (a) **Calculate Lorrie's Capital Gains Tax payable on the sale of the land in January 2010, assuming no elections are made.**

    (b) **Calculate Lorrie's Capital Gains Tax payable on the sale of the land in January 2010, assuming that he makes all favourable elections.**

75. On 1 February 2010, Peter gave away his holiday home to his son and realised a capital gain of £150,000. Gift relief is not available.

    State the due date for the capital gains tax liability and explain briefly how Peter could delay paying the Capital Gains Tax on this disposal.

76. On 1 June 2003, Frank bought a farmhouse in Wales costing £130,000. On 1 June 2006, when the farmhouse was valued at £155,000, he settled the farmhouse on trust for his wife, Susan, with remainder to their daughter, Tania, absolutely. The gain on the settlement was held over and at no time was the farmhouse used for business purposes or as a principal residence.

    On 1 January 2010 Susan died. The farmhouse was then worth £128,000.

    Calculate the capital gain or loss arising on Susan's death, explaining any relief available.

77. Eric bought a painting for £50,000 in December 1975. It was worth £80,000 on 31 March 1982.

    On 1 December 2008, the painting was damaged during a flood at Eric's house. On 1 January 2010, Eric received insurance proceeds of £130,000 for restoration. The unrestored value of the painting was £150,000 and its restored value was £290,000.

    Eric did not make any elections under s.23 TCGA. Eric had capital losses brought forward of £5,000 at 6 April 2009

    Calculate Eric's Capital Gains Tax liability for 2009/10.

78 During August 2009 one of Matilda's properties was damaged by a fire. She received compensation from the insurance company of £350,000 in November 2009.

Matilda used £315,000 to restore the property. The market value of the restored property was £420,000.

The property had originally cost £80,000 in 1979 and had a market value in March 1982 of £120,000.

Calculate the gains arising as a result of the insurance proceeds assuming Matilda makes all beneficial claims and elections and show the base cost of the property for any future CGT disposal.

Estates in administration

79 Sonia died on 5 December 2009. She owned 20,000 shares in Warlock Plc. On 13 February 2010 Warlock plc paid a dividend of 4.5 pence per share in respect of the year ended 31 January 2010.

The residue of the estate was left to her daughter, Gail, absolutely. IHT was charged on the estate at an average rate of 18%. Jemima is a higher rate tax payer.

Calculate the income tax payable on this dividend by Gail when it is paid out to her.

80 Steve died on 18 August 2009. His son William was the executor of his will. William borrowed £100,000 to pay the inheritance tax due and was granted probate. The estate income and outgoings for 2009/10 were as follows:

	£
Dividends received	1,800
Bank Interest received	160
Loan interest paid.	1,250

Calculate the income tax payable by or repayable to the estate for 2009/10.

81 Lionel died on 5 December 2008 owning some shares in Blair Ltd, an unquoted trading company. These were valued for probate purposes at £37,000. The executors sold the shares on 13 February 2010 for £57,000.

Calculate the capital gains tax payable by the executors for 2009/10.

82 Carolyn died on 20 June 2008. She left the residue of the estate to her daughter, Tania.

The administration was complete on 28 February 2010.

The estate accounts showed the following income and expenditure

	£
Rental income	28,000
Interest income	4,800
Solicitors fees	320
Payment on account of income to Tania (Paid 20 December 2008)	5,000

Calculate the amounts that would be shown on the R185 provided to Tania for 2009/10.

83 Amelia died on 2 January 2010. Amelia's estate is currently being administered by her executors. The executors have received the following income during the year ended 5 April 2010:

		£
Dividends from Skye Ltd shares	Received 27 February 2010	2,300
Untaxed interest from loan stock	Received 31 March 2010	250
Interest received from cash ISA	Received 1 April 2010	700

Calculate the Income Tax payable by the estate for 2009/10.

84 (1) **State the date that the personal representatives must file the estate's Income Tax return for 2009/10.**

(2) **State the due date for the estate's 2009/10 Income Tax liability to be paid, and the implications of late payment.**

Module C
Corporation tax

Questions

Module C: Corporation tax

The corporation tax computation

1. Gerald Ltd incurred the following expenditure in the year to 31 March 2010.

	£
Donation to the Labour Party	2,000
Patent royalty (amount paid)	780
Legal expenses relating to the creation of a 40 year lease	1,500
Legal fees incurred defending title to land	3,200
Hire of car (BMW, list price £25,000, CO_2 emissions 181g/km, lease entered into 1.12.07)	4,200

   What expenditure will be disallowed in arriving at income taxed as trade profits?

2. B Ltd was incorporated on 25 July 2007.

   The company opened a building society account on 6 September 2007, and commenced trading 9 October 2008.

   The company prepared its first accounts to 30 November 2008 and annually thereafter.

   The company appointed a liquidator on 28 February 2010. The liquidator sold the trade and assets of the company on 31 January 2011. The final distribution to shareholders was made on 14 March 2011.

   List B Ltd's accounting periods, with brief explanations.

3. Tournament Ltd has been trading for several years. It has now changed its accounting date and during the nine months to 31 March 2010, it incurred the following expenditure on plant and machinery:

		£
1 August 2009	Car for sales director (20% private use; CO_2 emissions 191g/km)	18,000
1 February 2010	Computer	3,800
12 February 2010	Teleconferencing equipment	35,000

   The tax written down value of expenditure in the plant pool brought forward was £11,500.

   Calculate the capital allowances for the period to 31 March 2010.

4. Brighton Ltd received trading income of £124,500 in its 16 month accounting period to 30 September 2009. In addition it received a dividend of £80,000 (gross) from an unconnected UK company on 1 August 2009. It also made a chargeable gain of £1,480,000 on 1 October 2008.

   The tax written down value of the main pool on 1 June 2008 was £140,000. The company purchased plant and machinery costing £30,000 on 1 September 2009.

   Calculate the Corporation Tax payable on these profits.

5. Tractor Ltd has the following results for the nine months ended 31 December 2009:

	£
Adjusted trading profits before capital allowances	4,200,000
Chargeable gain	150,000

   The TWDV at 1 April 2009 was £157,000.

   The company acquired £30,000 of plant on 1 July 2009.

   Calculate Tractor Ltd's Corporation Tax liability and state the amounts and due dates for payment, assuming Tractor Ltd has always been a large company.

6. Roger Ltd is a large company that pays its Corporation Tax in quarterly instalments. It has a Corporation Tax liability of £900,000 for the ten-month period to 31 October 2009.

   State the dates and amounts of the required payments of Corporation Tax and state how long the company should retain its records.

7   Spider Ltd prepares accounts to 31 March each year.

   In the year ended 31 March 2010, the company's adjusted trading loss before capital allowances is £70,000.

   The tax written down value of the main pool on 1 April 2009 is £200,000.

   The company purchased some energy saving plant and machinery on 1 June 2009 for £75,000.

   The company's PAYE and NIC liabilities for the year ended 31 March 2010 are £87,500.

   Show the tax credit available.

8   Belan Ltd operates a theme park and incurs the following expenditure in the year ended 31 December 2009:

	£
Electric train to drive passengers around the park site	60,000
Movable partitions	7,000
False ceiling in the restaurant to hide the wiring for the lighting	12,000
Moving walkway in the aquarium	27,000

   Explain which, if any, of this expenditure qualifies for plant and machinery capital allowances.

9   Rotter Ltd made a trading profit of £782,500 for its year ended 31 December 2009.

   This trading profit includes a director's bonus of £38,000 which was not paid until 4 October 2010. During the period, the company also decided to set up a pension scheme for its employees and an actuarial valuation had shown that £27,200 should be paid into the scheme on account of salaries for the year ended 31 December 2009. A provision was included in the accounts for this sum. Of this, £20,000 was paid on 31 December 2009 and the remaining £7,200 was paid on 31 March 2010.

   Also included in the profit was an accrued amount of £15,000 relating to the company's approved share option scheme. The options cannot be exercised until the year ended 31 December 2010. Costs of running the scheme of £1,200 were also incurred in the year.

   Calculate the adjusted trading income for tax purposes, explaining briefly any adjustments which you make.

10 Clock Ltd, which was incorporated and commenced trading on 1 April 2009, prepared its first accounts for the nine months to 31 December 2009. It purchased cars for Andrew Time, the company's only director, and employees, as follows:

   (1) Car costing £36,000 for use by Andrew (CO_2 emissions 158gms/km). His private use has been agreed as 25%.

   (2) Car for Andrew's wife to use privately costing £11,000 (CO_2 emissions 105 gms/km).

   (3) A second hand car for the new sales man, costing £13,000 and with CO_2 emissions of 108 gms/km.

   (4) A new car for the sales manager, costing £18,000 and with CO_2 emissions of 176g/km.

   Calculate the capital allowances for the period.

11 Peach Ltd made a trading profit of £390,000 in its 18 month accounting period to 30 September 2010. It realised a chargeable gain on 1 September 2010 of £28,000. The company received interest on a 12 month bond deposit of £18,000, on 30 June 2010.

   You are required to calculate the Corporation Tax payable on these results. Assume FA09 rates continue in future years.

12 Tap Ltd was incorporated on 1 February 2009 and one subscriber share was issued to Bob Spanner. The company began to trade on 1 September 2009 and issued 100 shares each to the two working directors of the company, Bob Spanner and his wife Maud.

   Explain whether notifications are required to be made to HM Revenue & Customs in respect of the issue of shares to Bob and Maud and on Tap Ltd's commencement to trade.

13 Calax Ltd, a manufacturer of hunting horns, incurred the following expenditure in the year to 30 June 2009:

	£
Political donation to the Green Party	300
Donation to the Society Against Hunting (not a charity)	50
Gift to employee on exam success	75
Legal expenses defending an employee in connection with a speeding offence	200
Costs of unsuccessful business rating appeal	175
Loss on sale of machine	50
Costs of seconding an employee to NSPCA for three days	450
Accrued pension contributions (due to be paid on 1 June 2010. The equivalent amount for the year ended 30 June 2008 was £650 and was paid on 1 June 2009).	800
Legal fees on the acquisition of new office premises	320

Calculate the total allowable deduction for trading income purposes for the above items, explaining briefly your reasons for allowing or disallowing the item.

14 Bangalla Ltd draws up accounts for the 19 months ended 31 October 2010. Trading profit for the period is £4,750,000. The company disposed of an asset on 28 February 2010, realising a gain of £250,000. Interest of £380,000 accrues evenly over the period.

Calculate the corporation tax payable and state the due dates for payment, assuming Bangalla Ltd has previously paid tax at the small companies' rate.

15 **Outline the penalty regime for incorrect CT returns due to be filed on or after 1 April 2009.**

16 Damson plc was incorporated on 1 April 2007. It rented out the top floor of its head office from 1 May 2007 to 31 July 2008. Damson plc commenced to trade on 1 September 2007 and drew up its first set of accounts for the period to 31 December 2008 and annually thereafter. Damson plc appointed a liquidator to wind up the company on 31 August 2010 and ceased to trade on 30 September 2010. The liquidator completed the winding up on 30 November 2010.

Identify all taxable accounting periods, with explanations.

17 **State the time limits for HM Revenue & Customs to commence an enquiry into the tax return of a company, with a year end of 30 April 2010 and which is not part of a large group, the possible scope of an enquiry, and how a company can bring a protracted enquiry to an end.**

18 Holmes Ltd prepares accounts to 31 May. It has been late in filing Corporation Tax returns for the last two years and, as at 1 November 2010, has still not filed its return for the year ended 31 May 2009.

The directors of Holmes Ltd expect a Corporation Tax liability of approximately £50,000, for the year ended 31 May 2009. However, they have not yet made any payments in respect of this period because they have not finalised the tax computation. They accept that an interest charge will arise as a result of late payment, but say that they are too busy running the company's business to worry about this.

Briefly advise the directors of Holmes Ltd of the possible implications and HM Revenue & Customs' power in this situation. Suggest the best course of action. Assume the FA 2009 penalty provisions apply.

Loan relationships, intangibles and R&D

19 Azure Ltd patented a new cutting process on 1 May 2008. The costs of creating the patent of £120,000 were capitalised and the company expects to write off these costs over a 15 year period. The cost of registering the patent was £3,000. Azure Ltd receives patent royalties in arrears on 30 April as follows:

	£
30 April 2009	15,960
30 April 2010	23,100

For accounting purposes, the company accrues for these royalties on a monthly basis.

Explain briefly how the above items will be reflected in the company's tax computation for the year ended 31 December 2009.

20 **Explain briefly what is meant by the term 'trading loan relationship' and explain how tax relief may be given for any loss arising for an accounting period ended 31 December 2010.**

21 Graham Ltd prepares accounts to 31 March.

In February 2010 the company sold goodwill for £600,000; it had been purchased for £480,000 in April 2008. The written down value at 1 April 2009 was £460,800. The company has elected to write-off the cost of intangibles at 4% per annum. New goodwill was purchased in December 2009 for £700,000.

The company borrowed £100,000 on 1 December 2009 at 4% pa from Chuck Ltd, its parent company resident in the US (a qualifying territory), to finance the acquisition. The first payment is due on 1 May 2011.

State the tax consequences of the sale and purchase of goodwill in the year to 31 March 2010, assuming that all available reliefs are claimed.

22 **State the type of expenditure that qualifies for relief as Research and Development expenditure for a small company.**

23 Omelette Ltd (a small company) made profits of £400,000 in the year ended 31 March 2010 before adjusting for the following expenditure.

	£
Software used by the admin team supporting the R&D department	26,000
R&D salaries and NIC	102,000
Electricity for building containing R&D activities	14,000

Approximately 10% of the floor space of the building is used for the R&D activity.

Calculate the corporation tax liability for Omelette Ltd for the year ended 31 March 2010.

24 Biodec Ltd has incurred expenditure on designing a new website to market a new fertiliser which it has been researching and developing. The company has also been employing two researchers on the project full time during the past 12 months. They have purchased specialist computer software to support their activities.

The company has also used some part time agency staff in connection with the R&D expenditure.

You are required to explain briefly how tax relief will be given for this expenditure.

25 **State the reliefs available for a net deficit on a non-trading loan relationship.**

26 Datco Ltd, which prepares accounts to 31 December, purchased a business on 1 January 2007. The goodwill arising was £100,000 and this was amortised, in accordance with generally accepted accounting principles, at £15,000 per annum.

On 1 January 2009, Datco Ltd sold the goodwill to an unconnected party for £120,000, together with fixed plant for £45,000, which had cost Datco £30,700 on the acquisition of the business.

Datco also made the following purchases:

- 30 June 2009 – fixed plant used in Datco's trade – £65,000
- 30 March 2010 – further goodwill – £115,000

Explain with supporting calculations, the tax consequences of the sale of the goodwill and plant assuming that all possible claims are made. You should ignore indexation.

27 Cherry Ltd has an accounting profit for the year ended 31 March 2010 of £1,445,000. This figure includes the following items:

Trade related patent royalties paid of £145,000 including a closing accrual of £25,000.

Patent royalties (non trade) of £102,000 were receivable in the period, and £132,000 of non-trade patent royalties were payable.

Leased car for new finance director. The car has a list price of £28,945, CO_2 emissions of 178g/km and an annual operating lease charge of £6,400. The car was first leased and made available to the finance director on 1 October 2009. The lease agreement is for three years.

The theft of £140,000 by the previous finance director has been included in the accounting profit as an expense.

Calculate, with annotated workings, the tax adjusted trading profit for Cherry Ltd for its year ended 31 March 2010. You should ignore VAT.

28 Pumpkin Ltd is a trading company with 100 employees and a turnover of £2 million per annum. In its year ended 31 March 2010 it spent £500,000 on research and development. Pumpkin Ltd has a tax adjusted trading loss of £100,000 before taking account of its research and development expenditure of £500,000.

Total PAYE and NIC for payment periods ended during the year to 31 March 2010 were £345,000. Pumpkin Ltd has no other income for either the current or previous year and also made a trading loss in the previous year.

Calculate the amount of research and development tax credit that can be claimed by Pumpkin Ltd for the year ended 31 March 2010. Identify the amount of any remaining loss to be carried forward.

29 **Explain the provisions relating to the deferral of a profit on the disposal of an intangible fixed asset. Your answer should include a reference to partial reinvestment, time limits and group aspects.**

30 **Explain how relief is given for expenses incurred in connection with an intangible fixed asset, and give three examples of such expenditure.**

Capital gains and companies with investment business

31 H Ltd prepares accounts to 31 March. The company purchased a furnished property on 1 July 2009, which it rented out from that date under a 20 year lease for a premium of £35,000 and an annual rental of £120,000 per annum payable in advance. A wear and tear allowance is claimed. H Ltd took a loan on 1 July 2009 of £1,000,000 to purchase the property. The interest on the loan is 10% per annum, payable on 31 December and 30 June.

Give the taxation implications of the above transactions.

32 E Ltd is an investment company, preparing accounts to 31 March. In the year to 31 March 2010 E Ltd had:

(1) Interest paid on loans taken out to finance investments.

(2) Unrelieved charges on income.

(3) Unrelieved property income expenses.

(4) Capital loss arising on sale of shares in I-pex Ltd (E Ltd subscribed for the 5% holding in the company five years ago. I-pex Ltd is a small, unquoted trading company.)

State briefly how relief may be given for each of the above.

33 **What relief is available for the management expenses of a company with an investment business and in what circumstances might relief for these expenses be restricted?**

34 **Give three situations where excess management expenses of an investment company may not be carried forward following a change in ownership.**

35 Polo Ltd is an investment company. During its year to 31 December 2009 it purchased an investment property using a loan. Interest charged to its profit and loss account for the year amounted to £233,000 and included £13,000 which was unpaid at the year end.

Rental income received in the year was £142,000.

The company received bank interest of £40,000 during the year, with a further £4,000 accrued at the year-end.

The company received a dividend from Golf Ltd of £8,000. Golf Ltd operates as a real estate investment trust and the dividend was paid from its tax exempt income.

Polo Ltd owns 8% of the shares in Golf Ltd.

Calculate the profit chargeable to Corporation Tax of Polo Ltd for the year, giving brief explanations of the treatment of the dividend income and stating what relief is available for any surplus amounts paid.

36 Bromide Ltd owned a freehold factory which was damaged in an explosion in October 1997. Bromide Ltd spent £115,000 restoring the factory in November 1997. Insurance proceeds of £120,000 were received in February 1998.

In December 2009 the company sold the factory for £1 million. Bromide Ltd had paid £210,000 in June 1987 to purchase the property.

Calculate Bromide Ltd's chargeable gain on disposal of the factory in December 2009, assuming a claim is made under s.23(1) TCGA 1992.

37 Good Ltd has been a wholly owned subsidiary of Heavens Ltd since they were both incorporated in January 1985. Good Ltd has a capital loss brought forward of £200,000.

In March 2010, Heavens Ltd makes a disposal of an office building for £420,000 that was acquired in January 2004 for £180,000. The building replaced the original office space, which was acquired in January 2001 at a cost of £94,000, but which was destroyed by fire in November 2003. Insurance proceeds of £175,000 were received in January 2004. All available reliefs were claimed.

Calculate the gains arising in the year ended 31 March 2010, and explain how the gains may be mitigated, giving the time limits for any elections.

38 **State the conditions that must exist for a disposal of shares in one qualifying company by another qualifying company, to be treated as a disposal of a substantial shareholding. Your answer should include a reference to the level of investment activity within a company and group.**

39 Sarrat Ltd owns 65% of Hoyle Ltd, a trading company. Sarrat Ltd has the following income for the nine months ended 31 March 2010:

	£
Trading income	125,000
Chargeable gain	150,000
Dividends received from quoted companies	8,000
Dividend received from Hoyle Ltd	12,000

The chargeable gain arose on the disposal of some surplus land which has been sold to a property developer as the site for a new shopping complex. Under the terms of sale, payment of the £450,000 proceeds is deferred as follows.

	£
Paid on completion (20.1.10)	90,000
Paid once planning permission granted (30.6.10)	180,000
Paid 12m after completion	90,000
Paid 30 days after opening (31.08.12)	90,000
	450,000

Calculate the Corporation Tax payable by Sarrat Ltd for the nine months ended 31 March 2010 and state the payment date(s), assuming all available claims and elections are made.

40 Hagan Ltd had the following property transaction in its year ended 31 December 2009.

On 1 July 2009 the company granted a 10 year sublease for a premium of £30,000 and an annual rent of £10,000 payable annually in advance. Several years ago Hagan Ltd had paid a premium of £40,000 for a 30 year head lease on this property to an unconnected party.

The company also incurred ground maintenance fees in the year of £120.

Calculate the property income that Hagan Ltd must include on its Corporation Tax computation for the year ended 31 December 2009.

41 Granatia Ltd sold a building for £550,000 on 30 September 2009. Legal fees of £5,000 were incurred. The building was acquired for £120,000 on 12 April 1978, and was extended at a cost of £12,000 on 31 July 1981, and again in August 1985 for a cost of £19,500. The building's market value at 31 March 1982 is estimated at £140,000.

Granatia has capital losses brought forward of £15,750.

Calculate the net chargeable gain arising.

42 Zalaga Ltd disposed of a piece of land in January 2010 for £190,000. The land was originally acquired in August 1988 for £50,000. Part of the land was sold in September 2001 for £18,000, when the remaining land was valued at £75,000. All available reliefs were claimed.

Calculate the chargeable gain arising.

Single company losses

43 The following information relates to A Ltd, a company preparing accounts for the 10 months to 31 March 2010:

	£
Trading profits before capital allowances	1,362,223
Capital gain	20,000
UK dividend received (non-group)	27,000

As at 1 June 2009 A Ltd had a trading loss of £80,000 and a capital loss of £30,000 brought forward.

The tax written down value of the main pool on 1 June 2009 was £50,000. The company made the following purchases in the period:

	£
Integrated air conditioning system for office building	35,000
Thermal insulation of office building	8,000
Plant and machinery	12,000

Calculate A Ltd's Corporation Tax liability for the period ended 31 March 2010.

44 F Ltd prepares accounts to 31 March each year. Recent results are as follows:

	Year ended 31 March			
	2007	2008	2009	2010
	£	£	£	£
Trading income profit/(loss)	100,000	60,000	(150,000)	160,000
Profit on non-trading loan relationship	10,000	10,000	10,000	10,000
Capital gains/(losses)	Nil	15,000	(12,000)	9,000
Property income/(loss)	Nil	12,000	13,000	(7,000)

Show how the capital loss and property income loss are relieved, and give three options for relieving the trading loss for F Ltd.

45 K Ltd started to trade on 1 April 2009 and prepared accounts to 31 March. The following information is provided.

	Year ended 31 March	
	2010	2011 (est)
	£	£
Trading loss	(100,000)	320,000
Property income/(loss)	(80,000)	5,000
Profit/(loss) on non-trading loan relationship	(30,000)	8,000
Gift aid	(10,000)	(10,000)
Credit on non-trading intangible fixed assets	95,000	40,000
Chargeable gains/(losses)	(5,000)	15,000

Show how the losses are relieved.

46 Juniper Ltd has the following results:

	Year ended 30 June 2009	Six months ended 31 December 2009	Year ended 31 December 2010
	£	£	£
Trading profit/(loss)	60,000	20,000	(100,000)
Profit on non-trading loan relationship	10,000	10,000	10,000
Gift Aid	5,000	5,000	5,000
Capital gain/(loss)	(15,000)	NIL	20,000

Trading profits for the year ended 31 December 2011 are estimated at £120,000.

Calculate the PCTCT for the periods ended 31 December 2010, assuming loss relief is taken as early as possible and state how any loss unrelieved will be utilised.

47 Robin Ltd started trading on 1 April 2006 and has had the following results:

	Year ending 31 March			
	2007	2008	2009	2010
	£	£	£	£
Trading profit/(loss)	120,000	50,000	(200,000)	250,000
Property income	4,000	4,000	4,000	4,000
Gains/(losses)	(10,000)	nil	nil	15,000
Gift aid	15,000	11,250	15,000	15,000

Illustrate Robin Ltd's options for relieving the trading loss, stating how relief is given for the gift aid and capital loss.

48 Obelix Ltd had the following results in the accounting periods prior to cessation of its trade.

	Trading profit/(loss)	Profit on non-trading loan r/ship	Gain/(loss)
	£	£	£
Year ending 31 December 2006	40,000	10,000	70,000
Year ending 31 December 2007	17,000	10,000	
Year ending 31 December 2008	20,000	10,000	
Year ending 31 December 2009	(100,000)	10,000	
3 months ending 31 March 2010	1,000	2,500	(15,000)

Describe, with supporting calculations, how Obelix Ltd will relieve its losses, assuming that earliest possible loss relief is required.

49 Lago Ltd prepared accounts for the nine months ended 31 December 2009, showing the following results:

	£
Adjusted trading profit	180,000
Interest receivable	15,000
Gain	45,000
Dividend received from a 10% investment in a UK resident company	22,500
Gift aid payment	7,000

The company has a deficit on non-trading loan relationships brought forward at 1 April 2009 of £25,000, a capital loss brought forward of £40,000, and a brought forward trading loss of £9,000

Calculate the Corporation Tax liability of Lago Ltd for the period ended 31 December 2009.

50 **Contrast the reliefs available for a non-trading loan relationship deficit and a loss on non-trading intangibles.**

51 Lggle Ltd prepared accounts for the year ended 31 December 2009, showing the following results:

	£
Adjusted trading profit	30,000
Property income	20,000
Gift Aid payment	3,000

The company has a trading loss brought forward at 1 January 2009 of £35,000 and a deficit on a non-trading loan relationship brought forward at 1 January 2009 of £18,000.

Calculate the Corporation Tax liability of Lggle Ltd for the year ended 31 December 2009. State any unrelieved amounts to be carried forward at 31 December 2009, assuming all beneficial elections are made.

52 Tremain Ltd's results for recent years are as follows.

	Year ended 30 June 2007	Year ended 30 June 2008	18 months ended 31 December 2009
	£	£	£
Trading income/(loss)	265,000	290,000	(320,000)
Property income	36,000	36,000	54,000

The company expects the rental income to continue at the same rate and trade profits of £150,000 in the year ended 31 December 2010.

Calculate PCTCT for all relevant years assuming that all reliefs are claimed as early as possible.

53 Silver Ltd has the following results.

	Year ended 30 June 2007	Period ended 31 December 2007	Year ended 31 December 2008	Year ended 31 December 2009	Year ended 31 December 2010
	£	£	£	£	£
Trading income/(loss)	52,000	(120,000)	80,000	(70,000)	15,000
Gains/(losses)	(15,000)	8,000	NIL	(5,000)	20,000
Profit on non-trading loan relationship	NIL	10,000	10,000	NIL	40,000

Mr Smith, the controlling shareholder, sold his shares to Mr Jones on 1 July 2008. Mr Jones changed the business operations immediately, selling to distribution companies instead of the general public.

Calculate the PCTCT assuming all available reliefs are claimed as early as possible.

Groups of companies

54 D Ltd owns 80% of E Ltd; both companies prepare accounts to 31 March 2010.

The following information is provided.

	£
D Ltd	
Trading loss	(100,000)
Profit on non-trading loan relationship	20,000
Property income loss	(50,000)
E Ltd	
Trading income	140,000
Gift Aid payment	(25,000)
Profit on non-trading loan relationship	(27,000)

State the maximum loss that can be surrendered by D Ltd.

55 I Ltd (an investment company) purchased 100% of the ordinary share capital of J Ltd for £500,000 in June 1995. Both companies prepare accounts to 31 March. On 1 June 2006 I Ltd sold a building to J Ltd (also an investment company) for £100,000, when its market value was £250,000. I Ltd had bought the building in April 1999 for £80,000. On 1 March 2010, I Ltd sold its entire shareholding in J Ltd for £35,000,000.

Calculate any gains arising as a result of the above transactions, stating the company that the gain is charged to and the accounting period of charge in respect of the gains arising on the building.

56 Bull Ltd is a very successful investment company that has a substantial capital gain built up in one of its properties. The directors are considering the purchase of Ring Ltd. Ring Ltd has brought forward trading losses of £240,000, although recent changes to the product line mean that the company is expected to return to profit next year.

Ring Ltd has brought forward capital losses of £26,000 and is soon to dispose of an asset acquired in 2002 for £120,000 for its current market value of £45,000, although the directors are prepared to delay this disposal if advantageous to either company.

What points should be made to the directors in relation to the relief that may be available for Ring Ltd's losses?

57 Dog Ltd purchased 100% of the ordinary share capital of Cat Ltd on 1 October 2009.

Dog Ltd prepares accounts for the year to 31 March 2010, Cat Ltd for the nine-month period to 31 March 2010.

The results for the period to 31 March 2010 are as follows.

	Dog Ltd Year ended 31 March 2010 £	Cat Ltd 9 months ended 31 March 2010 £
Trading profit	800,000	(150,000)
Gains	200,000	200,000
Deficit on non-trading loan relationship	(30,000)	NIL

Dog Ltd's PCTCT in the year ended 31.3.09 was £500,000 of which £65,000 was from a profit on a non-trading loan relationship. Cat Ltd is the company's only subsidiary.

Show the maximum and the optimum claims in respect of the trading losses, and explain how best to relieve the non-trading loan relationship deficit in Dog Ltd.

58 A Ltd owns 100% of B Ltd and 100% of C Ltd. All companies prepare accounts to 31 March. C Ltd was acquired on 1 April 2006.

In January 2006 A Ltd transferred a chargeable asset to B Ltd for £100,000 when its market value was £220,000. The asset had been bought in May 1999 for £400,000.

On 1 April 2009 C Ltd sells an asset for £320,000. The asset cost £370,000 on 31 March 2004 and was estimated to be worth £355,000 on 1 April 2006.

B Ltd is sold in December 2009.

State the taxation consequences of the above transactions, and describe any claim available when B Ltd leaves the group.

59 Inspace Ltd had carried on its domestic interior design business in Scotland for many years, making profits averaging £80,000 per year. Having identified a huge new marketing opportunity in the South West of England, the directors decided to relocate the company on 1 January 2009, selling a 51% interest in the company to Snuggle Ltd, a company already based in the area at the same time.

The new business gives advice on energy saving heat insulation to local businesses in Cornwall.

Unfortunately they suffered a trading loss of £300,000 in their first year. They have now made substantial cuts to their running costs which should ensure a profitable future.

The directors sold a further 28% of their shares to Snuggle Ltd on 1 September 2009.

Explain briefly how relief for Inspace Ltd's losses may be given.

60 The structure of the Ivy plc group is as follows:

Ivy plc purchased an asset in 2003 for £100,000. In 2005 it sold the asset for £150,000 to Fern Ltd when its market value was £180,000.

In 2007 Fern Ltd transferred the asset to Leaf Ltd when its market value was £205,000.

In 2009, Ivy plc sells 30% of its shareholding in Fern Ltd, for £4.2m (the 30% holding originally cost £1.4m in 1999.)

State the tax implications of the above transfers (ignore indexation).

61 Shares in the Hat Ltd group are owned as follows:

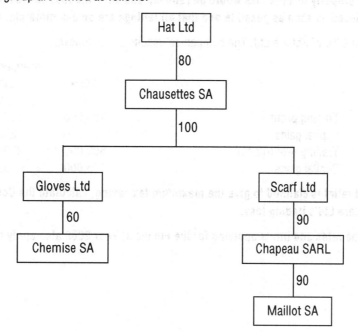

Chemise SA and Chausettes SA are incorporated and resident in Ruritania. Chapeau SARL has been dormant since 2007. Maillot SA is resident in a country in the EU which allows losses to be carried forward against all forms of locally generated income.

State, with explanations, which companies are:

(a) **Associated**
(b) **In a chargeable gains group**
(c) **In a loss relief group (giving any restrictions on the use of losses that may apply).**

62 Hound Ltd and Fox Ltd (its 100% subsidiary) have the following results for the year ended 31 March 2010:

	Hound £	Fox £
Trading profit before CAs	320,000	90,000
Chargeable gains	45,000	15,000

The companies incurred the following expenditure on assets qualifying for capital allowances:

	Hound £	Fox £
TWDV b/f	150,000	40,000
Plant and machinery additions	20,000	30,000
Integral features additions	60,000	75,000

Calculate PCTCT for both companies, assuming all beneficial claims are made.

63 Hawk Ltd and its 100% owned subsidiary, Falcon Ltd have the following results:

	Year ended 31 March 2009 £	2010 £
Hawk Ltd		
Trading income	40,000	75,000
Property income profit/(loss)	(200,000)	50,000
Falcon Ltd		
Trading income	20,000	20,000

In addition to the above, in the year ended 31 March 2009, Falcon Ltd stopped using some fixed plant and machinery in its trade. The company had acquired the plant for £230,000 in April 2003, to replace some plant and machinery which had been sold for £255,000, realising a gain of £85,000. A claim was made under s.152 TCGA 1992.

Show how the property income loss would be relieved and state the loss carried forward (if any) assuming the loss is relieved as soon as possible and that all lettings are on a commercial basis.

64 Circle Ltd owns 80% of Square Ltd. The companies' results are as follows.

		Year ended 31 March		
		2009 £	2010 £	2011 (est) £
Circle Ltd:	Trading profit	105,000	160,000	100,000
	Capital gains	–	25,000	–
Square Ltd:	Trading profit/(loss)	500,000	(70,000)	950,000
	Capital gains	175,000	5,000	–

Assuming that relief is claimed to give the maximum tax saving, calculate the Corporation Tax saved in respect of Square Ltd's trading loss.

Assume that the rates and limits applying for the Financial Year 2009 also apply for 2010.

65   Land Ltd is an investment company. Its recent results were as follows:

	Nine months ended 31 December 2009 £
Rental income receivable	100,000
Interest payable on loans to purchase property	(175,000)
Bank interest receivable	25,000

Path Ltd, which prepares accounts to 31 March acquired 80% of Land Ltd on 1 July 2009. For the 12 months ended 31 March 2010, Path Ltd made a trading profit of £210,000 and had no other profits, gains or expenses.

State, with calculations, the maximum amount that can be surrendered by Land Ltd to Path Ltd as group relief and explain how the balance will be relieved if no claims are made.

66   Shares in the Colours Group are owned as follows.

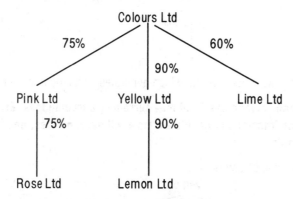

All companies prepare accounts to 31 March and are resident in the UK.

Colours Ltd intends to sell some land on 10 January 2011. 100 acres of undeveloped land was acquired for £570,000 in anticipation of planning permission being granted, but a chemical spill has made inhabiting the land impossible.

Colours Ltd has found a buyer for part of the site. They are prepared to pay £24,000. The value of the remaining site is estimated to be £48,000.

Quantify the capital loss and explain how it may be used by group members, which companies this capital loss may be passed to, the amount of the loss that may be passed, and the date by which any election must be made.

67   The Footy plc group is comprised as follows:

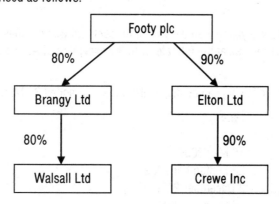

All companies have a year end of 31 December, with the exception of Brangy Ltd which has a year end of 31 March. All companies are resident in the UK except Crewe Inc, which is not resident in the European Economic Area and carries on all of its trade overseas. The companies only have ordinary share capital.

Elton Ltd has made a trading loss in its year end 31 December 2009.

Explain how you would calculate the maximum amount of Elton Ltd's loss for the year ended 31 December 2009 that could be surrendered to each of the other group companies.

68   On 1 June 2009, Lily Ltd transferred a capital asset to Maxi Ltd. Lily Ltd owns 80% of Maxi Ltd.

Lily Ltd has owned the share in Maxi Ltd since 2005. Both companies are trading companies.

Explain 1) the capital gains consequences of the above and 2) the capital gains position if Lily Ltd subsequently sells 10% of its shareholding in Maxi Ltd, including an explanation of future transfers from Lily Ltd to Maxi Ltd.

69

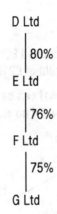

All companies are trading companies except G Ltd, which generates all its income from letting property.

Briefly explain to which company/companies E Ltd may surrender a trading loss. Explain to which company/companies F Ltd may transfer chargeable assets at nil gain, nil loss, and where replacement of business asset relief is available.

70   The Veg plc group has the following structure:

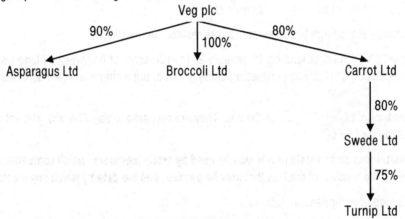

All group companies have a year ended 31 March. Broccoli Ltd was purchased by Veg plc on 1 January 2010. All companies pay Corporation Tax at the full rate, with the exception of Asparagus Ltd which pays tax at the small companies' rate.

The companies had the following capital disposals in the year ended 31 March 2010.

	Date	Gain/(loss) £
Asparagus Ltd	10 May 2009	49,000
Broccoli Ltd	22 September 2009	(14,000)
Turnip Ltd	3 December 2009	(15,000)
Carrot Ltd	10 February 2010	(11,000)

Asparagus Ltd has a brought forward capital loss of £3,000 at 1 April 2009.

Explain how much tax the group will pay for the year ended 31 March 2010 on the gain made by Asparagus Ltd. Assume all beneficial elections are made.

71 Dee plc has two wholly owned subsidiaries, Evans Ltd and Gregory Ltd. All companies prepare accounts to 31 December.

On 1 November 2009 Dee plc sold its shares in Gregory Ltd to an unrelated UK resident company.

At this date Gregory Ltd owned a property transferred to it four years earlier by Evans Ltd, worth £600,000. At the date of transfer it had an indexed cost of £130,000 and was worth £400,000.

Explain the Corporation Tax consequences, in relation to the property, of the sale of the shares in Gregory Ltd by Dee plc. Outline any possible reliefs that are available.

Personal service companies and overseas aspects

72 Aster plc owns 100% of the shares in Drake Ltd, Snake Ltd and Gunter Inc.

Aster plc, Drake Ltd and Snake Ltd are all UK resident, but Gunter Inc is resident in America.

Aster plc and Gunter Inc are trading companies. Drake Ltd is dormant and Snake Ltd is an investment company.

Croc Ltd is a 60% subsidiary of Gunter Inc. The other 40% of that company's shares are owned by three other unconnected non UK-resident companies.

Croc Ltd is resident in the Cayman Islands, where it pays tax of 5% of its profits.

(a) **Which companies must be taken into account when determining profits for the purposes of the small companies' rate of Corporation Tax?**

(b) **Is Croc Ltd a controlled foreign company?**

73 Spade Ltd (a small company) owns 100% of Club Ltd, 4% of Diamond Ltd and 7% of Heart SARL. Spade Ltd prepares accounts for the ten months to 31 March 2010 and receives the following income:

	£
Trading profit	1,220,000
Dividend from Diamond Ltd (amount received)	16,200
Dividend from Club Ltd (amount received)	22,500
Dividend from Heart SARL (amount received)	15,000
Overseas property income (net of 10% withholding tax – no double tax treaty)	45,000

Heart SARL is resident in Thalos, a country which has a double tax treaty with the UK containing a non-discrimination clause. A 25% withholding tax is deducted on all dividends paid to non-residents.

Calculate Spade Ltd's Corporation Tax liability for the period to 31 March 2010.

74 On 1 October 2008, Door plc owned all of the shares in Stover Gmbh, a company resident in Germany, which in turn owned 45% of the shares in Hinge Ltd. All are trading companies. The group meets the definition of a large enterprise.

On 1 February 2009, Stover Gmbh purchased the remaining shares in Hinge Ltd, and also acquired all of the shares in Foerster Gmbh, another German trading company.

Door plc also owns all of the shares in Mouse Ltd which has been dormant for many years.

Door plc has profits chargeable to Corporation Tax for its year ended 30 September 2009 of £712,000, from which it paid a dividend of £150,000.

Included within the profit is the sale of some raw materials to Hinge Ltd on 30 June 2009. The cost of these items was £30,000 and they were sold for £33,000.

Door plc's standard mark up on goods is 20% on cost.

Calculate the mainstream Corporation Tax of Door plc for its year ended 30 September 2009, stating which companies are associated for this purpose and any assumptions you have made.

75 Milne Ltd's profits are increasing steadily each year. Mr Milne owns 99% of the ordinary share capital of the company. Milne Ltd's income is derived entirely from a single IT contract, which is performed exclusively by Mr Milne at the company's own premises and using their equipment. Milne Ltd has a year end of 31 March 2010 and has paid a dividend to Mr Milne during the accounting period. No salary or bonus was paid during the accounting period.

Explain:

(a) **The tax risks arising from the above arrangement.**

(b) **Why the accounting date of 31 March may not be the most tax efficient, and suggest an alternative accounting date.**

(c) **Whether any action can be taken regarding the dividend payment.**

76 Both of the following workers provide personal services to clients via an intermediary. The contract exists between the intermediary and the client in both cases.

(1) Jack is both an employee and 25% shareholder of Jack Medical Ltd which provides medical services to Venture Unknown plc. Venture Unknown plc in turn owns 75% of Jack Medical Ltd. Jack has no shares in Venture Unknown plc.

(2) Harry is in a partnership which provides services to 3B plc. Harry receives 35% of the profits of the partnership. Harry's wife is also a partner and receives 30% of the profits of the partnership.

State whether Jack and Harry could fall within the scope of the rules governing the provision of services through an intermediary. In each case state why the rules do or do not apply. Outline any additional information you need to determine if the rules apply.

77 Quasar Ltd (a small company) received the following income in its year ended 31 March 2010:

	£
Adjusted trading profits	1,000,000
Chargeable gains	50,000
Dividends received from a 10% holding in a UK resident company	8,000
Dividends received from a 7% investment in an overseas resident company	6,000
Overseas property income (net of 30% withholding tax – no double tax treaty)	5,600
Gross income distribution received from the tax-exempt business of a Real Estate Investment Trust (gross)	9,000

The dividends received from overseas are net of 25% withholding tax. There is a double tax treaty with the overseas country containing a non-discrimination clause. Quasar Ltd has three associated companies and has trading losses brought forward of £90,000 and capital losses brought forward of £60,000.

Calculate the Corporation Tax liability for Quasar Ltd for the year ended 31 March 2010.

78 **List the criteria that a company must meet in order to be considered a managed service company, and give a brief explanation of the impact of the rules.**

79 It is not necessary to apportion profits in respect of an overseas subsidiary in certain situations.

List five exceptions to the CFC apportionment rules.

80 A business can obtain certainty over its transfer pricing through the use of an advance pricing agreement.

List five items of information which should be included when a company first expresses an interest in entering into an APA.

81 Coldon Ltd is an overseas incorporated company, treated as UK resident by virtue of UK central management and control. On 1 July 2009, central management and control of the company moves overseas, when the company owned the following chargeable assets.

	Cost £	MV 31 July 2009 £
UK assets	200,000	250,000
Overseas trading assets	190,000	420,000
Overseas investment assets	310,000	500,000

Coldon Ltd is a 90% subsidiary of Aphos Ltd, a UK resident company.

Calculate, with explanations, the chargeable gains arising if all available elections are made. You should ignore indexation.

82 **Give two circumstances where a company which is incorporated overseas may be subject to UK corporation tax. In each case, outline the scope of charge to UK corporation tax.**

83 **Outline the factors that will be considered in order to determine whether or not an engagement is a 'relevant engagement' for the purposes of the personal service company rules.**

84 Utopia Ltd has the following structure for the year ended 31 March 2010.

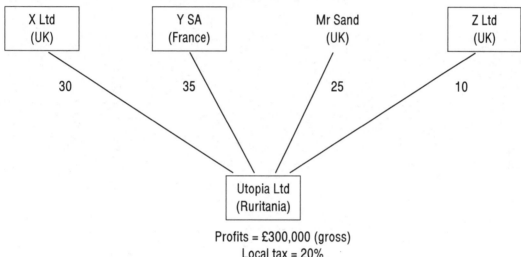

(a) **Is Utopia Ltd a controlled foreign company?**
(b) **Would your answer differ if Utopia Ltd's profits were £3,000,000?**

85 A Ltd and B Ltd are UK resident members of the Alphabet group of companies. A Ltd sells goods to B Ltd for £500,000, and the same goods to Purple Ltd, for £750,000.

(a) **Outline any potential transfer pricing adjustment.**
(b) **In what circumstances would this adjustment not be applied?**
(c) **State any recommendations you would give to B Ltd if the adjustment is made in A Ltd's return.**

Module D
Taxation of individuals

Questions

Module D: Taxation of individuals

The income tax computation and property income

1. On 1 December 2009, Jonah took out a five year loan to buy new machinery for use in his employment.

   Explain briefly how, and for which years, relief will be given for interest paid on this loan.

2. Robert has the following income in 2009/10:

	£
Gross salary	36,000
Dividends received	9,990
Loan interest received from Trading Co Ltd	1,600

   Calculate Robert's tax liability for 2009/10.

3. Stephen and Jane are married and Stephen is entitled to a full Married Couple's Age Allowance. Unfortunately their relationship is deteriorating, and they intend to separate and then divorce.

   Indicate from what point they are treated as single people, and explain the availability of the Married Couple's Age Allowance in the year of separation.

4. Tony granted a 30 year lease to Cherie on 1 February 1996 for a premium of £20,000. On 1 May 2009 Cherie granted a sublease to Gordon for 10 years, for which Gordon paid a premium of £50,000.

   Calculate the amount taxable as property income in 2009/10.

5. Mandy has decided that she would like to rent out one or two rooms in her own home.

   Explain how any income will be taxed.

6. In September 2009, Tom gave his friend a cheque made payable to a registered charity, for £312. His friend presented this to the charity having completed a sponsored cycle ride. Tom is a self employed higher rate taxpayer.

   Explain how Gift Aid relief will be given on Tom's donation.

7. On 12 December 2009, two weeks before her birthday, Kath Turner died aged 74.

   Her income since 6 April 2009 had been:

	£
State retirement pension	4,720
Pension from deceased husband's former employer (gross)	13,430
Building society interest received (net)	5,240

   Calculate Kath's Income Tax liability for 2009/10.

8. In 2009/10, Humphrey, who is 61 and single, received:

   (a) Building society interest of £19,200 net of tax deducted at source
   (b) UK dividends of £18,900, net of tax credit

   He had no other income or expenses.

   Calculate the tax repayment which Humphrey is due.

9 David owns Greenfields, a house which he lets fully furnished.

David's first tenant moved in on 26 April 2009 and paid rent, monthly in advance, of £500. At 5 April 2010 the tenant had not yet paid the rent which was due on 25 March 2010.

During the letting period David had the following expenses:

	£
Interest paid on mortgage taken out to purchase Greenfields	2,000
Council tax	1,000
Water rates	500
Other allowable expenses	3,000

Calculate David's rental loss for 2009/10, assuming that all beneficial reliefs and deductions are claimed. Work to the nearest day.

State the possible uses of this loss.

10 Vincent, a higher rate taxpayer, purchased a 'buy to let' property in 2009/10. He made a profit of £2,800 on letting the property. Vincent has not previously been required to complete a self assessment return.

He notified HM Revenue & Customs of the new source of income on 31 October 2010, and his tax return was issued on 17 November 2010. He submitted his tax return and made the correct payment of Income Tax on 15 February 2011.

Briefly explain:

(a) **The penalty(ies) which may be payable by Vincent, and/or**
(b) **Whether any interest may be charged, and if so for what time period.**

11 Mary's only income in 2009/10 was a salary of £48,000. During the year she made the following charitable donations.

(a) £30 per month to NSPCC via the payroll giving scheme, and
(b) A gift aid donation of £936 (net) to her local hospice, a registered charity.

Calculate Mary's total Income tax payable for 2009/10.

12 **State the conditions which must be met if a property in the UK or EEA is to qualify as a 'Furnished Holiday Let' in 2009/10.**

13 Eric and Bertram registered their relationship as a civil partnership on 21 December 2007. Eric was 75 in July 2009 and had net income of £13,000 for 2009/10. Bertram was 66 in August 2009 and had net income of £24,800 for 2009/10. Eric and Bertram have made no elections as to how the married couple's allowance should be allocated between them. Bertram made a cash donation of £200 in February 2010 and made a gift aid declaration in respect of this.

Calculate Bertram's entitlement to allowances for 2009/10.

Do not calculate his Income Tax liability.

14 **List four types of interest which are deductible from income as qualifying interest and state how tax relief is given for the loan interest paid.**

15 Cary, who is a higher rate taxpayer, visited a charitable property and purchased a daily admission ticket. The normal admission price was £20, but Cary chose to make an extra payment so that his purchase qualified for Gift Aid relief.

Assuming that Cary makes the minimum extra payment required by the Gift Aid rules, calculate, to the nearest penny:

(a) **Cary's tax relief.**
(b) **The tax refund which the charity can reclaim including the transitional relief.**

Calculate the relief to the nearest penny.

16. Sidney, who is 77 and has been married to Joan for 40 years, received total employment income during 2009/10 of £30,000. He had no other income or expenses. Joan had taxable income for 2009/10 of £15,000.

    Calculate Sidney's entitlement to personal allowance and married couple's allowance for 2009/10. You are not required to calculate his Income Tax liability.

    State (without calculations) the possible options, for Sidney and Joan, in relation to the married couple's allowance.

Employment income & NIC

17. Kevin is employed, earning a salary of £30,000 per annum.

    He drives 14,000 business miles in 2009/10 and is paid 35 pence per mile by his employer.

    Calculate Kevin's taxable income for 2009/10.

18. On 10 February 2006, Cassie, a higher rate taxpayer, was granted 10,000 share options in her employer's company, Tobler Ltd (a trading company), under its Enterprise Management Incentive scheme. At this time, the shares were valued at £4.20 each.

    The exercise price was £4.50 each.

    Cassie exercised her options on 15 October 2009, by which time the shares were worth £12.90 each. She immediately sold the shares. She made no other chargeable gains during the year 2009/10.

    State the income tax implications of receiving and exercising the EMI options and calculate any CGT liability for 2009/10.

19. Daphne is employed in the administration department of a manufacturing company and earns £20,000 a year.

    All administration staff are offered free meals in the works canteen, whereas employees working on the shop floor are offered free tea and coffee, but have to pay full price for any meals.

    In addition, Daphne receives vouchers worth £50 a week from her employer with which to pay an approved childcarer. These vouchers are available to all employees.

    Daphne also received a loan from her employer on 6 February 2010 of £8,000, on which she paid interest of 1% per annum.

    Explain briefly the Income Tax position of these benefits for 2009/10.

20. On 1 January 1991 Victoria began working for Harris plc in the UK. On 2 January 1992 she moved to the company's branch in France. She returned to work for the UK office on 1 January 1997.

    Victoria continued to work at Harris plc's UK office until 1 January 2000 when she moved to the US branch.

    On 1 January 2009 Victoria retuned to work at the UK branch. On 1 January 2010 Victoria was forced to leave Harris plc due to increased automation of the company's operations. She received an ex gratia redundancy payment of £50,000.

    Explain, with calculations, how much (if any) of Victoria's redundancy payment is taxable.

    You are not expected to consider double tax relief.

21. Jones Ltd set up an Enterprise Management Incentive scheme. In February 2004 options over shares with an actual market value of £25,000 were granted to Tony, the sales director with an exercise price of £23,000. At the time of the grant the shares were subject to a restriction which only allowed a future sale of the shares to be to other directors, and without the restriction the shares would have been worth £35,000.

    In May 2010 Tony exercised his options. At that time the shares had an actual market value of £26,000.

    The restriction on disposal was lifted in July 2010 and immediately after the restriction was lifted the shares were worth £50,000.

    Explain, with supporting calculations, the Income Tax implications of the events taking place in 2010. You are required to consider whether an election under s.431 ITEPA 2003 would have been beneficial.

22 John earns a salary of £15,000 a year from Orion Ltd. John's only benefit is to be provided with job related accommodation by his employer. The accommodation has an annual value of £1,000.

When the property was first provided to John, Orion Ltd also provided new furniture costing £4,000. The company also paid the following costs relating to the property in 2009/10:

	£
Heating and lighting	400
Cost of a new kitchen extension	10,200
Redecoration	500
	11,100

Calculate John's total employment income for 2009/10.

23 Harry's employer pays him a mileage allowance of 30p per mile to use his own car for business purposes. During 2009/10 he travelled 14,000 miles on business. He also carries a colleague as a passenger for 2,120 miles in total. Harry's employer does not have a policy of making payments to employees for carrying passengers.

Explain the Income Tax implications of Harry's use of his own car with supporting calculations showing the additional benefit or allowable expenditure for Harry in 2009/10.

24 Jack started working for Window Ltd on 6 October 2009. He was immediately provided with a new petrol engine car with a list price of £25,000, and CO_2 emissions of 232g/km. Window Ltd paid for all expenses of running the car including fuel. Jack made monthly contributions towards private use of the car and private petrol of £20 and £10 respectively

Calculate Jack's taxable benefit(s) relating to the car for 2009/10.

25 In 2009/10 Amelia commenced in a new employment 300 miles from her previous job. Her employer paid the following amounts during the year in relation to her employment:

(a) Relocation costs of £8,200 to Amelia relating to the cost of selling her old house and buying her new house.

(b) Incidental overnight expenses of £6 per night paid to Amelia for a period when she was required to work away from home elsewhere in the UK.

(c) Insurance premium paid to an insurance company to indemnify Amelia against liability for acts or omissions.

Explain the treatment of these items in working out Amelia's employment income for 2009/10.

26 In January 2007, Patrick was granted the option to buy 10,000 shares in his employer's company at any time up to 31 December 2018. The cost of the option was 10p per share and the exercise price was £1.00 per share. At the time of the grant, the shares had a market value of £1.20 per share. In June 2009 he exercised his option at a time when the market value was £1.80 per share. The shares are not subject to restrictions. Patrick is a higher rate taxpayer and is resident, ordinary resident and domiciled within the UK.

Patrick sold the shares on the day after exercise for £1.80 per share.

Calculate any Income Tax payable on exercise and any capital gains tax payable on the subsequent disposal of the shares.

27 Qimat, a director of Beret plc, moved into a house owned by Beret plc on 6 April 2009. This was not job-related accommodation. Beret plc built the house in January 2006 at a total cost of £668,000. In April 2009 it was valued at £965,000. The annual value of the house is £4,800.

The house was built in the garden of a bungalow also owned by Beret plc. Qimat's parents have lived in the bungalow since 6 July 2009. The bungalow was purchased in 1979 for £15,300 and was valued at £345,000 in July 2009. The annual value of the bungalow is £3,400. Qimat's parents pay Qimat rent of £200 per month.

The official rate of interest on 6 April 2009 was 4.75%.

Calculate, with workings, the amount to be included as accommodation benefit in Qimat's employment income for 2009/10. Very briefly explain your treatment of the bungalow.

28 Isabella earns a salary of £46,000 per annum. Isabella has made the following payments in relation to her employment during 2009/10:

   (a) Personal pension contributions of £4,500 deducted via the payroll and paid to a group personal pension scheme.

   (b) A laptop computer used wholly, exclusively and necessarily for business purposes purchased at a cost of £2,000 in July 2009. Isabella's employer does not provide a computer for her use.

   (c) Business suits for work use costing £489.

   (d) Isabella's employer deducted £25 each month under the Payroll Giving Scheme.

   Calculate Isabella's employment income for 2009/10.

29 **For employment income purposes, money earnings are assessable on a receipts basis. Explain how the date of receipt is determined.**

30 Peter, aged 67, started work at Ridings Ltd on 6 November 2009. Peter is an employee earning a salary of £46,992 per annum and is paid monthly. Prior to joining Ridings Ltd, Peter had been unemployed for a year.

   Calculate the Class 1 primary and secondary National Insurance Contributions for 2009/10.

31 **State five of the conditions for a Company Share Option Plan to be approved and for the full tax benefits to be available.**

32 Robin is a director of Robco Ltd. A car was made available for Robin's private use on 5 October 2009. The list price is £95,000 and the car's CO_2 emissions are 212 g/km. The car runs on diesel.

   Robin makes a non-refundable contribution of £6,000 towards the purchase of the car.

   Free fuel is provided by Robco Ltd for both business and private use.

   Robco Ltd also pays £500 plus VAT for legal fees on the sale of Robin's house. The engagement letter for this work is between Robin's solicitor and Robin personally.

   Assuming that Robco Ltd's payroll has been correctly operated throughout 2009/10, calculate the Class 1A National Insurance contributions payable by Robco Ltd and state the date on which they are payable.

33 Gerald and Arthur are both employed by Portugal Ltd. Arthur is a director of the company.

   Their payments in 2009/10 are as follows:

	Gerald £	Arthur £
Weekly wage	1,000	100
Annual bonus (paid March 2009)	–	41,000

   Arthur is the only director of Portugal Ltd.

   Calculate the Class 1 National Insurance Contribution primary liability for Gerald and Arthur.

   State by whom and on what Class 1B National Insurance Contributions are payable?

34 (a) Bonny and Clyde are both employed earning an annual salary of £29,520 and are paid a bonus of £5,000 in December.

   Bonny is an employee, Clyde is a director; they are both paid monthly.

   Calculate the National Insurance Contributions payable by Bonny and Clyde and their employer for 2009/10.

   (b) Gerald is an employee earning £12,000 per annum. His employer provided him with a loan on which the taxable value was £5,000 in 2009/10.

   Calculate the National Insurance Contributions payable on the benefit, state who is liable to pay them, and give the date they are due.

35   Emma, Fiona and Gillian are all participators in their employer's approved Share Incentive Plan. On 1 June 2008 they were each awarded free shares worth £3,000.

Assume they withdraw their shares as follows:

	Date withdrawn	Value when withdrawn £
Emma	1 May 2011	3,500
Fiona	1 July 2012	3,650
Gillian	1 July 2013	4,000

Which withdrawals will suffer an Income Tax charge and on what value? Give your reasons.

36   Willis plc enters into a PAYE Settlement Agreement in respect of benefits provided during 2009/10 to certain of its employees (all of whom are higher rate taxpayers). The total value of the benefits is £6,000.

Calculate the total settlement payable by Willis plc, state the class of National Insurance Contribution payable and the due date of payment.

37   **List five distinct payments or benefits an employer could give to an employee which are not classified as earnings for Class 1 primary or secondary National Insurance Contributions purposes.**

38   Jade is a 30 year old IT manager and is one of 500 employees of Karp Ltd. During October 2010, Jade's employment package included the following:

	£
Salary (after deduction of £20 into an approved payroll giving scheme)	1,980
Payment by Karp Ltd of employer contributions into a registered pension scheme	75
Payment of Jade's annual subscription to Loopysports, an extreme sports club. This was under an agreement whereby Karp Ltd contracted directly with Loopysports and had legal responsibility for paying Jade's subscription.	200

State whether, and if so how, each of the above items will be subject to National Insurance Contributions.

Investments and pensions

39   **Explain the following in relation to pensions:**

   (a)   Annual allowance (you may ignore the special annual allowance)
   (b)   Treatment of contributions in excess of the annual allowance
   (c)   Lifetime allowance
   (d)   Treatment of a pension fund worth more than the lifetime allowance on retirement.

40   During 2009/10, Oliver subscribed for shares worth £5,000 in each of the following companies:

   (a)   Apple Ltd, which does not trade but holds shares in several other companies which carry on manufacturing businesses. Oliver's sister is a director of Apple Ltd.

   (b)   Pear Ltd, which is an IT consultancy business. Oliver's wife is an employee of Pear Ltd.

   (c)   Orange Ltd, whose trade is the sale of motor bikes to the general public. Before the share issue, Orange Ltd had total assets of £20 million and total liabilities of £10 million.

State, with reasons, whether the above investments could potentially qualify for relief under the Enterprise Investment Scheme.

41   Emily, who was 56 on 5 July 2009, decided to retire for pension purposes on 5 November 2009. On 5 November 2009 Emily's registered pension fund was worth £1.865 million. Emily elected to take the maximum tax free lump sum possible. She then used £1,337,500 to purchase an annuity to provide pension income benefits. The balance of the fund was then taken as a further lump sum.

Calculate the tax payable as a result of Emily's retirement.

42 Parminder is 33 and single. During 2009/10 Parminder received dividends of £1,530 from Water Ltd. She also received a distribution of £3,471 from the tax-exempt business of a Real Estate Investment Trust and had trading income of £45,000.

Calculate the Income Tax payable by Parminder for 2009/10.

43 Debbie has received the following amounts in 2009/10:

(a) £9,000 dividends from shares held in an enterprise investment scheme company. Debbie purchased £250,000 worth of shares in May 2006.

(b) £3,000 received from Debbie's lodger who rents a furnished room in her home.

(c) £100 interest on a National Savings & Investments Easy Access Savings Account and £92 building society interest.

(d) Interest on a cash ISA account with a building society of £150.

(e) A stock dividend of shares worth £1,800.

For each source of income state the amount which should be included in Debbie's Income Tax computation for 2009/10.

44 Andy, a higher rate taxpayer for many years, estimates that his Income Tax liability for 2009/10 was approximately £7,300. In September 2009 he used an inheritance to invest £64,000 in shares, qualifying for relief under the Enterprise Investment Scheme.

Explain, with supporting calculations, the maximum tax relief in respect of the investment.

Explain what would happen if Andy sold the shares in September 2011.

CGT basics

45 Prudence sold the following assets on 1 June 2009

		Cost 1 May 2004 £	Proceeds 1 June 2009 £
(1)	Painting	4,200	7,800
(2)	Antique table	8,200	5,200
(3)	Plant and machinery (business asset)	12,000	8,600

Calculate Prudence's chargeable gains, before annual exempt amount, for 2009/10.

46 Beryl bought a field of four hectares for £10,000 in January 2004.

In January 2010 she sold one hectare for £5,000, the value of the remaining three hectares being £19,000 at the time of the sale.

Beryl sold no other land in 2009/10.

Explain briefly if Beryl may claim that there is no part disposal on the sale of the land.

47 Charles's only disposals in 2009/10 were in December 2009 when he realised the following gains and losses:

Asset	Purchase date	Gain/(loss) £
(1)	10 June 2007	40,000
(2)	9 November 2002	15,000
(3)	16 August 2005	(10,000)

Charles had capital losses brought forward at 6 April 2009 of £8,000.

Calculate Charles's capital gains tax liability for 2009/10.

48 Nigel, a self-employed architect who has always claimed the maximum available capital allowances, disposed of the following assets in 2009/10:

Vintage car, which had cost £28,000 on 1 February 2003, was sold for £22,000 on 1 December 2009.

Camera equipment used in his business was sold for £9,000 on 1 February 2010. It had cost £15,000 on 1 June 2005.

Antique vase bought for £20,000 on 1 May 2006, was sold for £1,000 on 1 March 2010, having discovered that it was a fake.

Explain briefly which losses will be available for relief against capital gains.

49 Reginald made the following disposals in 2009/10:

	Date of acquisition	Date of sale	Cost £	Proceeds £
Greyhound	June 2004	November 2009	4,000	7,500
Painting	May 2001	February 2010	8,500	4,050 (net of 10% commission)
Antique table	June 2003	March 2010	5,000	9,000

Calculate his chargeable gains or allowable losses for 2009/10.

50 Simon bought 20 acres of land for £30,000 in January 2003. On 1 February 2010 he sold three acres for £18,000 incurring disposal costs of £360. The market value of the land immediately prior to the part-disposal was £190,000. This was his only sale during 2009/10.

Calculate Simon's Capital Gains Tax position for 2009/10 assuming that any available claim to defer the gain is made, stating the date by which the claim is required and the CGT base cost of the land retained.

51 Naomi died on 1 December 2009. Between 6 April 2009 and the date of her death, she had made disposals giving rise to capital losses of £16,100.

Her chargeable gains and allowable losses for recent years have been:

	Gains £	Losses £	Annual exemption £
2008/09	15,000		9,600
2007/08	2,400	(1,300)	9,200
2006/07	17,000		8,800
2005/06	8,900		8,500

Calculate Naomi's net chargeable gains for the years 2005/06 to 2009/10 inclusive.

52 On 31 July 2009, Amy sold the entire share capital of Conway & Son Ltd, an unquoted trading company, to an unconnected company; she had purchased the 1,000 £1 shares at par in June 1991.

Amy received an immediate payment of £400,000. A further sum will be paid in September 2010. This further payment will be £1 for every £2 by which accounting profits of the year ended 31 July 2010 exceeds £800,000. The initial value of the further payment was estimated to be £45,000.

It is now estimated that accounting profits for the year ended 31 July 2010 will be approximately £900,000.

State, with supporting calculations, the Capital Gains Tax implications of the share disposal.

53 Albert sold two paintings in September 2009

Details were as follows:

	Purchase date	Purchase price £	Incidental disposal costs £	Disposal proceeds £
Painting 1	June 1981	6,400	200	5,250
Painting 2	January 1997	4,800	–	6,600

Painting 1 was valued at £8,000 on 31 March 1982.

Calculate Albert's capital gains tax liability for 2009/10 and show any losses carried forward at 5 April 2010.

54 Eric bought a painting for £10,000 in December 1975. It was worth £25,000 on 31 March 1982.

On 1 December 2008, the painting was damaged during a flood at Eric's house. On 1 January 2010, Eric received insurance proceeds of £130,000 for restoration. The unrestored value of the painting was £150,000 and its restored value was £290,000.

£110,000 of the insurance proceeds were used in restoring the asset. All possible elections under s.23 TCGA 1992 were made to reduce the CGT payable immediately.

Eric had no other capital gains in 2009/10.

Calculate Eric's Capital Gains Tax liability for 2009/10 explaining the tax treatment of the insurance proceeds.

55 Jeeves had owned 100% of the shares in Korvac Ltd, an unquoted trading company, since its incorporation in 2003. In January 2009 he sold his entire shareholding for £500,000 cash plus 10% of the profit before tax for the next financial year.

When the accounts were prepared recently, the profit before tax was £250,000 and Jeeves therefore received a further payment of £25,000 in March 2011.

Explain the Capital Gains Tax consequences of the above.

56 Nadia purchased three non-wasting chattels (which did not form part of a set) in January 1995 and sold them in January 2010. Details are as follows:

Chattel	Cost	Gross proceeds
	£	£
A	3,500	9,000
B	9,000	3,000
C	4,000	5,800

Nadia incurred £80 expenses in disposing of each of the above assets.

Assuming that Nadia had no capital losses brought forward and made no other chargeable disposals during the year, calculate her capital gains tax for 2009/10.

57 **Explain the consequences of an individual making a negligible value claim, including when any relief is deemed to crystallise.**

58 Graham made the following disposals in 2009/10:

(a) On 22 October 2009, he sold a franchise for £116,500. Graham had acquired the franchise, with 15 years left to run on 23 July 2001, when it cost £45,000. The franchise was always used for business purposes.

(b) On 15 March 2010, he sold a watch at auction for £7,200, after deducting auctioneer's fees of £300. The watch had cost him £4,100 in August 2000.

Calculate Graham's capital gains tax payable for 2009/10.

59 Yasmin purchased 2,000 shares in Red plc on 1 January 1990 for £3,500. Red plc made a one for two rights issue and Yasmin sold her rights for £1,600 on 10 June 2000, when the market value of the remaining shares was £2.50 per share.

On 1 February 2010 Yasmin sold all of her shares for £16,000. She made no other chargeable disposal in 2009/10.

Calculate Yasmin's capital gains tax payable on disposal of the Red plc shares in 2009/10.

CGT reliefs

60 State four periods of absence (excluding the last 36 months of ownership) which are deemed to be periods of occupation for the purposes of principal private residence relief and state any conditions that need to be satisfied for the periods of absence to qualify as deemed periods of occupation.

61 Carla purchased a house called Darklands on 31 March 1980. Darklands was her main residence until 28 February 1995, when she purchased a second property which she immediately elected to be her main residence.

Darklands was let as residential accommodation from 28 February 1995 until 31 March 2008. It was then vacant until sold by Carla on 31 March 2010 for a gain of £130,000.

Calculate Carla's chargeable gain.

62 On 10 February 2010, Mr Wong sold a factory for £325,000. It had cost Mr Wong £53,000 in October 1979 and was extended at a cost of £108,000 in April 1996. The factory had a market value of £64,600 at 31 March 1982.

Mr Wong has always used the factory in a partnership business, in which Mr Wong was a partner. Mr Wong's partnership share was also sold on 10 February 2010, realising gains of £150,000.

Calculate Mr Wong's capital gains tax payable for 2009/10 assuming all available reliefs are claimed.

63 James worked for Yellow Ltd, an unquoted trading company, from 1 June 1985 until his retirement on 6 April 2009. In October 1997 he had purchased a 6% shareholding in Yellow Ltd. On 6 April 2009 he sold his shares in Yellow Ltd realising a chargeable gain of £56,292.

Calculate James's capital gains tax liability for 2009/10 on the disposal of the Yellow Ltd shares, assuming all available reliefs are claimed. Explain the conditions that must be satisfied for any relief to be claimed.

Overseas aspects of IT and CGT

64 An individual is usually resident or not resident in the UK for a complete tax year.

State briefly five occasions when HM Revenue and Customs will split a tax year for determining residence status for income tax purposes.

65 Anthea, Beryl, Candice and Daphne have employment income for duties performed wholly abroad in 2009/10 as follows:

Anthea, who is resident, ordinarily resident and domiciled in the UK, £20,000.

Beryl, who is resident but not ordinarily resident in the UK, £28,000.

Candice, who is resident, ordinarily resident but not domiciled in the UK, £42,000. Her employer is not resident in the UK.

Daphne who is non-resident in the UK, £30,000.

Each of them remits £10,000 to the UK.

Give the amount, if any, chargeable to UK Income Tax for each of them, assuming all possible claims are made.

66 Nigel is resident in Thailand and a citizen of Tanzania.

Oliver is a UK citizen currently working as a missionary in China.

Paul lives in, and is a citizen of, Monaco.

Sergei is resident in the UK, but domiciled in Russia and claims the remittance basis of taxation in the UK (having more than £2,000 of unremitted income and gains in each tax year).

All four have rental income from property in the UK.

State which of them is or are able to claim personal allowances for 2009/10, and give a brief explanation.

67 Edwina and Cordelia are both resident and ordinarily resident in the UK. Edwina is also domiciled in the UK but Cordelia is domiciled in Holland.

Edwina receives a foreign pension of £10,000 per annum and remits £5,000 per annum to the UK.

Cordelia receives foreign dividend income of £8,000 per annum and remits £6,500 per annum to the UK. Cordelia has no other unremitted foreign income or gains.

Edwina and Cordelia each have taxable income of £50,000 excluding their foreign income.

State how much of their foreign income is assessed in the UK, explaining the basis of assessment used and the rate of tax applicable.

You are not expected to consider double tax relief.

68 **State how foreign pension, dividend and interest income are taxed on an arising basis and how they are taxed on a remittance basis.**

69 Paolo was born in Canada in 1970 to a French father and an Italian mother who were on holiday in Canada at the time. In 1980 Paolo and his parents moved to Australia and became Australian citizens, all three then held only Australian passports. In 2000 Paolo moved to the UK renouncing all ties with any other country intending to make the UK his permanent home.

Explain the terms domicile of origin and domicile of choice and state with explanations, the nature of Paolo's domicile in 1970, 1980 and 2000.

70 During 2008/09 and 2009/10, Tabitha let two furnished rooms in her main home and she also let a property in Spain as a long term let. Details are as follows:

	Rental income £	Allowable expenses £
Spanish property		
2008/09	7,000	9,000
2009/10	8,000	7,000
Tabitha's home		
2008/09	4,000	4,500
2009/10	6,000	3,000

Explain (with appropriate calculations) Tabitha's tax position for 2009/10 regarding the above, assuming that Tabitha makes all advantageous elections.

71 Lola is resident and ordinarily resident in the UK but domiciled in Poland.

In 2009/10 she received the following income:

UK employment income (taxed under PAYE)	£12,000
UK bank interest (net)	£5
Foreign employment income (net of 15% tax)	£5,000

She made no disposals of capital assets during the year.

Lola remitted £4,000 of foreign employment income to the UK.

Briefly explain Lola's UK tax position for 2009/10 and state whether the position would be different if she had received foreign rental of £4,000.

Administration of IT and CGT

72 Omar, having notified HMRC of his chargeability on time, is issued with a tax return for 2009/10 on 31 December 2010.

In June 2011, having submitted his return on time, Omar discovers a mistake.

State the date by which Omar should have submitted his original return, and the date by which amendments to the return must be made.

73 Edward is employed as a salesman with an annual salary of £22,000. He has use of a company car, which has a list price of £8,000 and CO_2 emissions of 142g/km. Private petrol is not provided.

Edward's 2007/08 tax due under self assessment was £180. This is to be collected through his notice of coding for 2009/10.

Calculate Edward's 2009/10 tax code.

74 On 1 February 2010, Peter gave away his holiday home to his son and realised a capital gain of £150,000. Gift relief is not available.

Explain briefly how Peter could delay paying the Capital Gains Tax on this disposal.

75 Arnold, Barry and Charles had income and gains for 2009/10 as follows:

Arnold: Employment income of £12,000 and a chargeable gain of £25,000.

Barry: Patent royalty income of £16,000 (amount received).

Charles: Dividend income of £45,000 (amount received).

None of them has received a notice to file a return.

State which of the three, if any, has to give notice of chargeability to HM Revenue & Customs, giving your reasons.

76 Lucy filed her self assessment tax return for the year 2008/09 on 15 December 2009. She amended the return on 20 February 2010.

Give the time limits for HMRC to commence enquiries.

77 Martin was issued with a tax return for 2009/10 in April 2010. He submitted his tax return for 2009/10 on 15 August 2011.

State the penalties which may apply for late filing. Assume FA 2009 penalty provisions apply.

78 Chas and Bill both received a tax return for their 2009/10 income in early May 2010. Chas is an employee but also receives a pension from his former employer. Bill is an employee and also receives letting income.

State the period of time for which Chas and Bill are each required to keep records relating to their 2010 tax return and the penalty for failure to comply.

79 Mark filed his tax return for 2009/10 on 20 February 2011. On 12 March 2011 he realised that he had forgotten to include a deduction for pension contributions which he had paid and he filed an amended return. On 1 June 2011 he amended his return again for some investment income which he had omitted.

State the period within which HM Revenue & Customs may correct obvious errors or mistakes in his tax return and the period within which they can open an enquiry.

80 Sharon made two capital disposals in the year to 5 April 2010:

(a) Gift of her tenanted farmland to her sister realising a chargeable gain of £120,000.

(b) Sale of her furniture restoration business realising a chargeable gain of £428,000. The proceeds from this sale will be payable in six annual instalments commencing on 1 December 2009.

Sharon is concerned that having made these disposals, she may not have enough cash to pay the capital gains tax.

State the due date for the payment of CGT on the above transactions, assuming no elections are made to defer paying the tax and explain briefly what elections Sharon can make to defer paying this tax.

81 George's self assessment liability for 2008/09 was £4,000. In January 2010 he had initially expected his liability for 2009/10 to be £2,500. He made a claim to reduce his payments on account accordingly, and made the first payment on account of the reduced amount on the due date

In June 2010 he revised his estimate of the 2009/10 expected liability to £2,800. On the due date, he made the second payment on account based on this figure. He also paid the appropriate additional tax which would have been paid had this estimate been used when the first payment on account was made.

He has now calculated his actual liability for 2009/10 to be £3,600. He will make the balancing payment on 16 November 2010.

State the amount(s) of underpaid tax, if any, and the date(s) during which interest will accrue. You are not required to calculate any interest payable.

82 PAYE must be accounted for on income provided to an employee in the form of a 'readily convertible asset'.

State five examples of items that will be treated as 'readily convertible assets'.

83 Saorise, aged 43 and single, is an employee of Trilby plc earning £15,000 per annum. On 6 December 2009 Trilby plc loaned Saorise a painting with a market value of £15,000. The painting hangs on the wall in Saorise's home. Saorise personally paid £89 for a subscription to her trade association (an approved body). Saorise also has uncollected tax of £156 from 2007/08.

Calculate Saorise's PAYE code for 2009/10, assuming that all of the above items are included in the computation of her 2009/10 tax code.

84 Anton, who is 33 and single, received the following income during 2009/10:

(a) Self employment income of £40,000, and

(b) Property income distributions from the tax exempt business of a Real Estate Investment Trust (REIT) of £6,800 (amount of cash received).

He had no other income or expenses. He has made payments on account for 2009/10 totalling £5,000.

Calculate Anton's balancing payment which will be due on 31 January 2011.

85 Iwona received a notice to deliver a 2009/10 tax return on 30 November 2010.

Assuming that she files her return online, give the due date for Iwona to submit her 2009/10 tax return to HM Revenue & Customs, and explain the consequences if the return is delivered one week after that date.

86 Blogitt & Co, an accountancy firm, has devised a range of tax planning schemes which aim to save its clients tax. It is aware that the schemes are potentially subject to compulsory notification to HM Revenue & Customs if any of the 'hallmarks' of avoidance are present.

State any five of these hallmarks.

Module E
Taxation of unincorporated businesses

Questions

Module E: Taxation of unincorporated business

Trading income

1. Becki commenced trading on 1 November 2008, preparing accounts to 30 April each year. Her trading profits before capital allowances are as follows:

	£
Period to 30 April 2009	42,000
Year ended 30 April 2010	94,800

   Becki purchased the following assets for her business:

		£
1 November 2008	Van	12,000
1 January 2010	Car; CO_2 emissions 146g/km	13,000

   Becki uses the car 50% for private purposes.

   Show her taxable profits for the years 2008/09 to 2010/11 inclusive, identifying any overlap profits.

2. Bill and Ben began trading on 1 September 2007 and prepared their accounts as follows:

	£
1 September 2007 to 30 June 2008	40,600
1 July 2008 to 30 June 2009	67,200
1 July 2009 to 31 March 2010	35,940

   Thereafter, they will prepare accounts to 31 March.

   Bill and Ben share profits equally after allocating Ben a salary of £1,000 per month.

   Calculate Bill's taxable profits for the years 2007/08 to 2009/10 inclusive, indicating any overlap relief arising or used.

3. Sam started to trade on 1 May 2009, preparing her first accounts to 31 March 2010. Her adjusted trading profit for the period was £79,510. This takes no account of a computer costing £48,000 purchased on 1 July 2009, a car costing £9,500 purchased on 1 December 2009 with CO_2 emissions of 148g/km, which is used only for business purposes, and a car costing £13,000 purchased new on 1 February 2010 with CO_2 emissions of 109g/km.

   Calculate her trading income profit for 2009/10.

4. Marcus, who had been trading for many years, incurred the following expenses in his year ended 31 March 2010:

	£
Repairs required to a new machine before it could be used	387
Christmas party for his secretary and two sales staff	385
Food hampers for his five largest clients	550
200 fountain pens bearing his business logo for distribution at a conference	400
Donation to a local hospice	628

   Explain briefly whether any or all of these expenses are allowable deductions for the purposes of calculating Marcus' taxable profits.

5   Candice started trading on 1 January 2008, preparing accounts to 30 April 2009 and annually thereafter. She ceased trading on 30 June 2012.

Her results were as follows:

	£
Period to 30 April 2009	48,000
Year to 30 April 2010	50,400
Year to 30 April 2011	63,000
Period to 30 June 2012	51,000

State her trading income assessment for all relevant tax years.

6   Dorian, a sole trader, has prepared accounts to 31 October each year.

The following capital expenditure was incurred in the year to 31 October 2009:

		£
1 November 2008	Water recycling plant	12,500
1 January 2009	Van	8,000
1 June 2009	Computer	3,200
1 July 2009	Plant	1,600
1 September 2009	Car (emissions 105g/km, private use 30%)	12,500
1 October 2009	Car (emissions 176g/km, 100% business use)	15,000

Calculate the maximum capital allowances that may be claimed for the year to 31 October 2009.

7   Maggie joined a partnership on 1 January 2010, having previously been an employee for many years and never having completed a tax return. The partnership accounts are prepared for calendar years, and figures are usually available within three months of the year end.

State what action Maggie should take in relation to declaring her share of the taxable profits for 2009/10, what figures should be used, and the basis upon which these figures will be taxed.

8   Frank started to trade on 1 October 2008, preparing his first accounts to 31 December 2009. His adjusted profits for the 15 month period, before capital allowances, were £21,781. He bought machinery costing £3,000 on 1 October 2008 and £2,880 on 1 May 2009. He purchased a car costing £16,000 (CO_2 emissions 156g/km) on 1 November 2008. The car is used 25% for private use. He also purchased a car for use by an employee for £14,500 (CO_2 emissions 154g/km) on 1 June 2009.

Calculate his taxable profits for 2008/09 and 2009/10.

9   Angie has been in business for many years. On 1 January 2008, she admitted Billy into partnership and henceforth they began sharing profits equally after allocating herself a salary of £10,000 and Billy interest at 2% on his capital of £15,000. The accounts showed taxable profits as follows:

	£
Year ended 31 December 2007	31,000
Year ended 31 December 2008	42,000
Year ended 31 December 2009	65,000

Calculate Angie's and Billy's taxable trading profits for the tax years 2007/08, 2008/09 and 2009/10. You are not required to consider overlap profits carried forward.

10   Sam has been trading for many years preparing accounts for years ended 30 April. He ceased trading on 30 September 2009 having made profits as follows:

	£
Year ended 30 April 2008	61,000
Year ended 30 April 2009	43,000
Five months to 30 September 2009	11,000

He has overlap profits brought forward of £1,700.

Calculate his assessable profits for the year 2008/09 and 2009/10. By what date(s) will he need to submit his final tax return as a self employed individual for 2009/10 and how long will he need to keep his trading income records for?

11   List six key features of a working relationship that indicate that the individual concerned is likely to be self-employed rather than employed.

   What are the implications for NIC purposes of an individual being treated as self employed rather than employed?

12   Alice and Christopher started trading on 1 May 2009 and will prepare accounts to 31 August 2010 and annually thereafter. They will share profits and losses equally after Alice is allocated a salary of £10,000 per annum. Estimated results are as follows:

	£
1 May 2009 to 31 August 2010	40,000
Year to 31 August 2011	42,000

   Calculate Alice's trading income for 2009/10 to 2011/12 and identify any overlap profits.

13   Beryl prepares accounts to 31 October each year. The tax written down value of the main pool at 1 November 2008 was £10,000.

   She had the following transactions in the year to 31 October 2009:

   12 February 2009   Sold plant for £4,250 (original cost in 1999 £4,000)

   13 February 2009   Purchased plant for £20,000

   16 March 2009   Part exchanged a pool car. She was given a part exchange allowance of £2,800 on the old car, and paid an additional £6,200 for the new car (CO_2 emissions 165g/km). Original cost of old car was £6,000.

   14 June 2009   Bought plant under a hire purchase agreement. She paid an initial deposit of £3,000 then 18 monthly instalments of £100. The cash price of the plant was £4,000.

   Calculate the maximum capital allowances available to Beryl for the year to 31 October 2009.

14   Charles, who manufactures hunting horns, incurred the following expenditure in the year to 30 June 2009.

	£
Political donation to the Green Party	300
Donation to the Society Against Hunting (not a charity)	50
Gift to employee on exam success	75
Legal expenses defending Charles in connection with a speeding offence	200
Costs of unsuccessful business rating appeal	175
Loss on sale of machine	50

   Explain briefly whether or not each of the above items is an allowable expense for trading income purposes.

15   Delia commenced business as a sole trader on 1 January 2009 and prepares accounts to 31 December each year.

   She incurred the following expenditure:

			£
(1)	15.1.09	New Car, CO_2 emissions 150g/km; 100% business use	20,000
(2)	15.1.09	New Car, CO_2 emissions 140g/km; 100% business use	9,000
(3)	15.4.09	New Car CO_2 emissions 110g/km; 100% business use	15,000
(4)	15.6.09	New Car, CO_2 emissions 130g/km; 60% business use	10,000
(5)	15.7.09	Energy saving plant	12,000
(6)	15.8.09	Machinery	4,000
(7)	15.8.09	General lighting	10,000

   Calculate Delia's capital allowances for the year to 31 December 2009.

16 Graham prepared accounts to 31 December each year until 31 December 2008 when he changed his year end to 31 March and prepared accounts for the 15 months period to 31 March 2010.

Profits for the period to 31 March 2010, before capital allowances, were £39,750. The balance on the main pool at 1 January 2009 was £12,000. Graham incurred the following capital expenditure:

	£
May 2009 – plant	10,000
June 2009 – car for employee; CO_2 emissions 143g/km.	8,000

Transitional overlap profits brought forward are £2,000 (representing three months).

Calculate Graham's taxable trade profits for the 2009/10 tax year.

17 Rhian is in business and prepares accounts to 31 January. On 1 February 2008 she decided to change year end to 30 June. Her accounts show the following tax adjusted profit:

	£
Year ended 31 January 2007	30,000
Year ended 31 January 2008	36,000
17 months ended 30 June 2009	68,000

Unrelieved overlap profits at 1 February 2008, representing two months' trading, were £5,000.

Calculate:

(a) Rhian's assessable trading profits for the tax years 2006/07 to 2009/10.

(b) Rhian's unrelieved overlap profits after the change of accounting date and state the period of time to which any additional overlap profit relates.

(c) Explain the conditions to be met for a change of accounting date to be effective for tax purposes.

18 Holly has been trading as a sole trader for many years and prepares accounts to 5 April. Her business has tax written down values brought forward at 6 April 2009 as follows:

	£
Main pool	15,000
Mercedes	14,000
Porsche	20,000
Short life asset acquired December 2004	3,000

Holly uses the Porsche for private purposes 25% of the time. One of Holly's employees uses the Mercedes for private purposes 5% of the time.

During the year ended 5 April 2010, Holly bought and sold the following items:

3 May 2009	Sold a van, which had cost £5,000 for £1,000
10 June 2009	Purchased a replacement van for £2,400
15 December 2009	Sold the Mercedes for £12,000

Calculate the maximum capital allowances available for the year ended 5 April 2010, including the tax written down values carried forward.

19 Bertie commenced trading on 1 February 2006. He prepared his first accounts to 30 July 2007 and annually thereafter. He stopped trading on 30 April 2010. His tax adjusted trade profits were as follows:

	£
1 February 2006 to 31 July 2007	54,000
Year to 31 July 2008	40,000
Year to 31 July 2009	20,000
9 months to 30 April 2010	30,000

Calculate Bertie's assessable trading profits for all relevant years.

20 Claudia is in business as a carpet maker. During the year ended 31 March 2010, her accounts show a profit of £60,000. The profit and loss account contains the following expense items:

	£
Lease payments for a car (with CO_2 emissions of 195 g/km) costing £25,000; used 50% for business purposes; lease taken out 1.6.08	5,000
Interest on late payment of PAYE deductions	45
Legal fees relating to the purchase of new business premises	3,500
Legal fees relating to debt collection	500
Donation to the National society for the Protection of Horses	750
Subscription to 'Carpet Makers' monthly magazine	50
Subscription to 'Heat' magazine	60

Calculate Claudia's tax adjusted profit for the year ended 31 March 2010.

21 Yuri has been in business for many years preparing accounts to 30 April.

His adjustment income arising following the implementation of Urgent Issues Task Force Abstract 40 (UITF 40) in his year ended 30 April 2006 was £79,800.

His adjusted trading profits are as follows. Yuri makes all beneficial claims and elections.

	Trading profits £	Capital allowances £
Year ended 30 April 2007	156,600	12,600
Year ended 30 April 2008	78,900	6,200
Year ended 30 April 2009	120,500	10,800

Calculate the additional Income Tax and/or National Insurance Contributions payable by Yuri for 2007/08 to 2009/10.

22 Saloni is a sole trader preparing accounts to 30 June. The tax written down values of her plant and machinery at 1 July 2008 are:

	£
Main pool	3,000
Motor car (used 70% for business by Saloni)	8,000
Short life asset	5,000

In the year ended 30 June 2009 she made the following additions and disposals of plant and machinery:

		£
Additions		
10 October 2008	Furniture	1,600
15 May 2009	Computer equipment	1,500
Disposal		
16 May 2009	Short life asset	400
27 June 2009	Machine (original cost £11,000)	3,300

Calculate Saloni's capital allowances for the year ended 30 June 2009.

23 Jacinta has been trading for many years preparing accounts to 30 June each year. Her overlap profits on commencement of trade were £2,000.

Her accounts to 30 June 2009 are expected to show adjusted trading profits of £64,000. Her business is then likely to make adjusted trading profits of £6,000 per month. She intends to incorporate her business on either 1 April 2010 or 1 May 2010.

State her trade profits, if any, for 2009/10 and 2010/11 under the two options, and when she will settle her tax liability for her trading income under each option.

24 It can sometimes be difficult to distinguish between a hobby and a trade.

You are required to list six of the main indicators which may be taken into account in determining whether a trade is being carried on, with a brief explanation for each one.

25 Jack has been trading for many years and has always used 31 December as his year end.

Jack's adjustment income arising following the implementation of Urgent Issues Task Force Abstract 40 (UITF 40) in his year ended 31 December 2005 was £84,000. Jack's year ended 31 December 2005 was the first year ending after the introduction of UITF 40. Jack's trading profits for the year ended 31 December 2005 to 31 December 2010 were:

	Trading profits before capital allowances £	Capital allowances £
Year ended 31 December 2005	115,890	12,000
Year ended 31 December 2006	133,446	13,200
Year ended 31 December 2007	205,340	10,870
Year ended 31 December 2008	60,100	9,810
Year ended 31 December 2009	81,200	3,600
Year ended 31 December 2010	75,400	2,750

Jack has made no elections regarding his adjustment income.

Calculate, with supporting workings, the adjustment income for 2005/06 to 2009/10.

26 Samuel commenced trading on 1 January 2009 and drew up his first set of accounts to 31 March 2010. On 1 January 2009 he purchased a car (CO_2 emissions 159g/km) for £14,000 and agreed business usage at 65%. He also bought a second hand car (CO_2 emissions 146g/km) for £8,000 for use by an employee. Also on 1 January 2009 he purchased fixtures, fittings and office equipment for £2,400. On 1 July 2009 he purchased machinery for £5,000 and on 30 April 2010 machinery for £51,000.

Calculate the maximum capital allowances available to Samuel for the period from commencement to 31 March 2010 and year ended 31 March 2011.

27 **Explain what is meant by a 'short-life asset election', how it operates, when it might be beneficial to make such an election and when it should not be made. Assume the AIA is not available.**

28 Eleanor commenced trading on 1 September 2007. She prepared her first accounts to 31 December 2007 and annually thereafter. Her tax adjusted trade profits were as follows:

	£
1 September 2007 to 31 December 2007	5,200
Year ended 31 December 2008	21,600
Year ended 31 December 2009	28,800

Calculate Eleanor's assessable trading profits for 2007/08 through to 2009/10 and clearly identify any overlap profits and the period(s) to which they relate.

Eleanor is considering changing her year end to 31 March. What conditions need to be satisfied for the new accounting period to be valid for tax purposes and what will the effect be of changing her accounting year end date.

29 Yasmin is in business as a beautician. Her accounts for the year ended 30 June 2009 show a net profit of £67,000 after deducting the following items:

	£
Legal fees relating to debt collection	230
Legal fees relating to the negotiation of a loan to buy an investment property	500
Gifts of moisturising cream to customers, containing a business advert, each costing £5.50	1,650
Subscription to the National Beautician Association	200
Membership of local health spa	600
Repairs to a spray-tan booth before it could be used	560
Cost of re-decorating the main salon	1,200

Calculate Yasmin's tax adjusted trading profit for the year ended 30 June 2009, briefly explaining the tax treatment of each of the above items.

30 Antonia is in business and prepares accounts to 31 January. On 1 February 2008 she decided to change her accounting date to 31 May. Her accounts show the following tax adjusted trading profits:

	£
Year ended 31 January 2008	23,400
16 months ended 31 May 2009	38,000
Year ended 31 May 2010	31,000

Unrelieved overlap profits at 1 February 2008, representing two months' trading, were £7,200.

You may assume that the requirements for the change of accounting date to be recognised by HM Revenue & Customs are met.

You are requirement to:

(a) Calculate Antonia's assessments for 2007/08 through to 2009/10.

(b) **Quantify the amount of unrelieved overlap profits after the change of accounting date stating the number of months they represent.**

(c) **State the date by which Antonia must notify HMRC of her change of accounting date and the due dates for paying her income tax liability for her year of change.**

31 Jacob, a caterer, prepared accounts for the year ended 31 March 2010. The tax written down values brought forward at 1 April 2009 were:

	£
Main pool	NIL
BMW car (40% private use by Jacob)	10,500

Jacob made the following purchase during the accounting period:

	£
Car for use by an employee (50% private use) (CO_2 emissions 108g/km)	14,000

Additionally, Jacob part exchanged the BMW for a newer model (CO_2 emissions 130g/km). The cash price of the new car was £27,000 but Jacob paid only £22,000.

Jacob also has 40% private use of the new car.

Jacob ceased trading on 31 March 2011 due to personal problems. During the year he had purchased a new oven for £5,000 on 31 March 2011. He sold all his equipment for £12,000. He kept the BMW (market value £16,700) and sold the car used by the employee for £8,000.

Calculate the maximum capital allowances available for the year ended 31 March 2010 and 31 March 2011.

32 James decided to incorporate his business on 31 December 2009. During the period ended 31 December 2009 he had purchased equipment costing £16,000.

At 1 April 2009 the tax written down value brought forward on the main pool was £65,000.

At 31 December 2009 the assets in the pool were worth £37,000.

Calculate the maximum capital allowances to be claimed by James for the period to 31 December 2009 assuming:

(a) No succession election is made.
(b) A succession election is made.

By what date does James need to make a succession election and in what other circumstances could an individual make a succession election?

33 Give five examples of loan interest that may be deductible in arriving at net income.

Trading losses

34 Hilda, who has been trading for many years, incorporated her business on 1 December 2009. The consideration consisted entirely of shares. Hilda is employed by the company and continues to own the shares. Hilda incurred a trading loss in her final period as a sole trader.

State four loss reliefs available to Hilda, and indicate how the trading loss is relieved in each situation.

35 Ian, a sole trader, sold his business to a company, I Ltd, on 1 June 2009. Ian and his wife, Joan, each own 50% of the shares in I Ltd. They each receive a salary of £20,000, interest of £5,000 and dividends of £4,680 from the company in the period to 5 April 2010.

Ian's business had unrelieved trading losses of £30,000 in the final accounting period.

Show how these losses will be set-off against income from the company and state the other options available for using the loss.

36 Harry had been an employee earning a salary of £50,000 for several years. On 6 April 2009 he set up his own graphic design business but suffered a trading loss of £110,000 in his first year. Harry has no other income.

State briefly how Harry could claim relief for his loss and explain which loss relief option may be the most beneficial.

37 Amy commenced trading on 1 January 2009 and made a trading loss in her year ended 31 December 2009.

Briefly explain Amy's basis of assessment and the loss relief options available to her, for relief against income.

38 Freddy commenced trading on 1 August 2008 and prepared his first set of accounts for the 11 months to 30 June 2009 making a tax adjusted trading loss of £43,400. He made a further loss of £23,000 for the year ended 30 June 2010. Freddy sold a painting in 2008/09 for £50,000, generating a gain of £40,000.

Calculate the amount of loss which relates to 2008/09 and the amount which relates to 2009/10. Briefly explain how the losses could be relieved.

39 Hamid's business ceased on 30 September 2009. His recent adjusted trading profits/(losses) are as follows:

	£
Eight months ended 30 September 2009	(20,000)
Year ended 31 January 2009	12,000
Year ended 31 January 2008	5,000
Year ended 31 January 2007	4,000
Year ended 31 January 2006	8,000

Unrelieved overlap profits from the commencement of trade are £8,000.

Hamid has gross dividend income of £1,000 per annum.

Compute Hamid's terminal loss and show how it can be relieved.

40 Anya's business ceased on 30 June 2009. Her recent adjusted trading profits/(losses) are as follows:

	£
Year ended 30 September 2007	30,000
Year ended 30 September 2008	8,000
Nine months ended 30 June 2009	(27,000)

Unrelieved overlap profits from the commencement of trade are £1,500.

Calculate Anya's terminal loss and show how it will be relieved.

41 **Explain the additional relief available where a trading loss is incurred in 2008/09 or 2009/10 and a claim is made under s.64 ITA 2007.**

42 **Explain the loss relief options available to a sole trader who has been trading for many years if a loss is incurred in 2009/10.**

CGT basics

43 Give six occasions when a capital gain could arise and state how the date of a chargeable disposal is determined.

44 Jessica has the following gains and losses in 2009/10:

	£
Gain on sale of painting to her uncle	15,000
Gain on gift of antique to charity	11,000
Loss on sale of shares to her father	6,000
Gain on sale of a holiday cottage	34,000
Capital losses brought forward	33,000

Calculate Jessica's Capital Gains Tax liability, and state the date by which it must be paid.

45 On 31 July 2009, Amy sold the entire share capital of Conway & Son Ltd, an unquoted trading company, to an unconnected company; she had purchased the 1,000 £1 shares at par in June 1990.

Amy received an immediate payment of £400,000. A further sum will be paid in September 2010. This further payment will be £1 for every £2 by which accounting profits of the year ended 31 July 2010 exceeds £800,000. The initial value of the further payment was estimated to be £45,000.

It is now estimated that accounting profits for the year ended 31 July 2010 will be approximately £900,000.

State, with supporting calculations, the Capital Gains Tax implications of the share disposal and if there are any reliefs available to Amy on the sale of the shares, giving the conditions that need to be satisfied in order to claim any relief(s).

46 During August 2009 one of Matilda's properties was damaged by a fire. The following month she received compensation from the insurance company of £350,000.

Matilda used £315,000 to restore the property. The market value of the restored property was £420,000.

The property had originally cost £80,000 in 1979 and had a market value on March 1982 of £120,000.

Calculate the gains arising as a result of the receipt of the insurance proceeds assuming Matilda makes all beneficial claims and elections. State the revised base cost of the property.

47 (a) Jeeves had owned 100% of the shares in Korvac Ltd, an unquoted trading company, since its incorporation in 2003. In January 2009 he sold his entire shareholding for £500,000 cash plus 10% of the profit before tax for the next financial year.

His accountants anticipate that when the accounts are prepared the profit before tax will be £250,000 and Jeeves will therefore receive a further payment of £25,000 in March 2011.

Explain the Capital Gains Tax consequences of the above.

(b) One of Jeeves' friends told him that because he is receiving his consideration in instalments he can pay his capital gains tax by instalments.

Explain when capital gains tax can be paid by instalments.

48 Simon bought 20 acres of land for £30,000 in January 2003. On 1 February 2010 he sold three acres for £18,000 incurring disposal costs of £360. The market value of the land immediately prior to the part disposal was £190,000. This was his only sale during 2009/10.

Calculate Simon's Capital Gains Tax position for 2009/10 assuming that any available claim to defer the gain is made, stating the date by which the claim is required and the cost of the land retained.

49   Beryl bought a field of four hectares for £10,000 in January 2003.

In January 2010 she sold one hectare for £5,000, the value of the remaining three hectares being £19,000 at the time of the sale.

Beryl sold no other land in 2009/10.

The remaining three hectares were sold in 2010/11 for £60,000.

Explain briefly if Beryl may claim that there is no part disposal on the sale of the land. Calculate the gains arising in 2009/10 and 2010/11, assuming she makes any beneficial claims and elections.

50   **State the conditions for the gain on a small part disposal of land to be deferred when the disposal:**

(a)   **Is not a compulsory purchase.**
(b)   **Is to an authority as a compulsory purchase.**

Explain how the gain is deferred and by what date must a claim to defer a gain be made?

51   Alan bought a building that was damaged in a fire. He received £100,000 insurance proceeds; of this, £98,000 was used to restore the building. Alan elects to avoid a part disposal calculation.

State the conditions for claiming this relief. State how Alan's election would differ if he only used £93,000 to restore the building.

52   Eric bought a painting for £50,000 in December 1975. It was worth £80,000 on 31 March 1982.

On 1 December 2008, the painting was damaged during a flood at Eric's house. On 1 January 2010, Eric received insurance proceeds of £130,000 for restoration. The unrestored value of the painting was £150,000 and its restored value was £290,000.

Eric did not make any elections under s.23 TCGA and had no other capital gains or losses during 2009/10.

Calculate Eric's Capital Gains Tax liability for 2009/10.

Explain the election that Eric could make if he is planning to use all or some of the proceeds to restore the asset.

Partnerships

53   Ursula, Vernon and Walter are in partnership preparing accounts to 31 March each year. Their capital sharing ratio was 1:1:1.

On 1 February 2010 a non-business partnership asset was distributed to Ursula, when its value was £100,000. The asset had cost £70,000 in November 2006. Ursula sold the asset on 10 March 2010 for £108,000.

State the tax implications of these transactions. Briefly show how the tax implications would change if instead of the asset being distributed to Ursula the partners changed their capital profit sharing ratio to 2:2:1.

54   Peter, Paul and Mary share profits in the ratio of 2:2:1 after allowing a salary of £10,000 each for Paul and Mary.

The taxable profits of the partnership for the year to 31 March 2010 were £18,000 and £50,000 for the year to 31 March 2011.

Calculate the shares of assessable profits for Peter, Paul and Mary for 2009/10 and 2010/11.

55   Edith, Fiona and Geraldine have been in partnership for many years, preparing accounts to 31 January each year.

The profit sharing arrangement until 31 October 2009 was a salary of £10,000 each per annum, with the balance of the profit being shared in the ratio of 3:2:1. On 1 November 2009 the arrangement was changed when Geraldine retired to profits being shared 60:40 with salaries of £5,000 each to Edith and Fiona.

The trading profit for the year to 31 January 2010 was £82,500.

Geraldine had overlap profits of £2,230.

Calculate each partner's share of assessable profits for 2009/10.

56 (a) Explain the Capital Gains Tax effect of the introduction of a new partner to a partnership, resulting in a change in the profit sharing ratio, including where an upward revaluation of an asset in the accounts has taken place prior to the change.

(b) How is a payment outside the accounts treated for tax purposes where there is a payment between partners on a change of the profit sharing ratio?

57 Aaron, Mark and Zoë have been trading as a partnership for many years, preparing accounts to 30 June. The partnership receives the following income.

Trading income for the year ended 30 June 2009: £68,000

Bank interest received gross

	£
31 December 2008	500
30 June 2009	1,000
31 December 2009	2,000

Bank interest received net

	£
31 December 2008	50
30 June 2009	100
31 December 2009	200

The profit sharing arrangement was that Aaron received a salary of £8,000, Mark a salary of £12,000 and then any remaining trading profits were split in the ratio 1:2:3 for Aaron, Mark and Zoë. This arrangement changed on 1 April 2009, from then on profits were shared equally after salaries.

Based on the above information, calculate the amounts on which Aaron, Mark and Zoë will be taxed for 2009/10.

58 Debbie and Cath had been trading in partnership for many years until they decided to retire on 31 July 2009. Debbie and Cath's final accounts were:

	£
Year ended 30 April 2008	144,000
Period ended 31 July 2009	251,000

Debbie and Cath had always shared profits equally and drew salaries of £20,000 and £10,000 respectively. Both Debbie and Cath had originally made capital investments of £30,000 into the partnership and charged interest on capital invested at 7.5%. Debbie has transitional overlap profits of £15,000.

Calculate Debbie's and Cath's assessable trading profits for all relevant tax years.

59 Isabel, Jessica and Katie have been in partnership for many years, preparing accounts to 30 April each year. Profits are shared equally.

On 1 August 2008 the partnership agreement was changed so that Katie receives a salary of £24,000 per annum, and the profit sharing ratio changed so that profits are shared in the ratio 2:2:1.

On 31 July 2009 Katie retired from the partnership. From this date Isabel and Jessica split profits equally after allocating Jessica a salary of £10,000. Katie had overlap profits of £3,000.

The taxable trading profit for the partnership for the year ended 30 April 2009 was £90,000 and for the year ending 30 April 2010 £85,000.

Calculate the taxable trading profits for all the partners for 2009/10 and 2010/11.

60. Kim and Mick have been in partnership for many years. They have always shared profits in the ratio 2:1 respectively, after allocating Kim a salary of £15,000.

On 1 January 2009 Roz joined the partnership. From that date Kim, Mick and Roz share profits in the ratio 2:2:1 respectively, Kim continues to be allocated her salary. The recent adjusted trading profits of the partnership are:

	£
Year ended 30 June 2008	115,000
Year ended 30 June 2009	120,000
Year ended 30 June 2010	200,000

Allocate the profits for all years between the partners, and calculate the assessable trading profits for all partners for the relevant tax years.

61. Nadine and Oberon have been in partnership for many years sharing profits and losses equally. Their recent adjusted trading profits/(losses) are as follows:

	Nadine £	Oberon £
2007/08	NIL	NIL
2008/09	(10,000)	(10,000)
2009/10	25,000	15,000

Nadine also has another business which generated adjusted trading profits of nil, £25,000 and £25,000 in 2007/08, 2008/09 and 2009/10 respectively.

Calculate the National Insurance Contributions for Nadine and Oberon for 2009/10 and state the due dates for payment (assuming losses are relieved as early as possible).

CGT reliefs

62. Stephen incorporated his business in May 2009 by transferring his entire business to S Ltd. He transferred the following assets to the company:

	Cost £	Market value £
Building	120,000	360,000
Goodwill	–	160,000
Plant	4,000	2,000
Debtors		13,000

The consideration for his business was:

	£
Cash	200,000
Shares	800,000
	1,000,000

Stephen sold his shares in February 2010 for £950,000.

Calculate Stephen's taxable gains for 2009/10. Assume no claims or elections are made.

63. On 1 November 2008, Gary sold a factory for £650,000, which had cost him £350,000 exactly three years earlier.

On 1 December 2008, Gary reinvested the proceeds in a new factory costing £710,000.

Gary uses the factories for a trade.

On 1 April 2010, Gary sold his entire business. The proceeds included £795,000 for the factory.

Calculate and explain the minimum overall chargeable gains that Gary would be taxed on from the above transactions.

64 Gregory and Bill have been in partnership for many years sharing profits and losses equally. They transferred their farming business to a company on 28 February 2010 in exchange for shares and £20,000 cash each.

The value of the business at incorporation was £350,000.

Two chargeable assets were transferred to the company:

	MV @ incorporation £	Cost £
Goodwill	250,000	–
Freehold property	50,000	10,000

Bill sold his shares in January 2011 for £250,000.

You are required to:

(a) **Explain the conditions for incorporation relief to apply.**

(b) **Calculate each partner's gain in February 2010 assuming incorporation relief is not disapplied and assuming all other beneficial claims and elections are made.**

(c) **Calculate Bill's gain in January 2011.**

65 **State the conditions required for assets and shares to qualify for gift relief and explain the restrictions on gift relief if the shares gifted are held in a company which holds both business and non-business assets.**

66 (a) **State the conditions that must be met for incorporation relief to apply automatically.**

(b) **Give reasons why an individual might elect not to receive incorporation relief.**

(c) **Give the date by which the election must be made if incorporation is in June 2009 and the shares are still held in June 2011.**

67 Since 1 January 2003, George has owned the business premises from which ABC Ltd trades. George owns 10% of the shares in ABC Ltd.

On 1 March 2010, he sold the property to his son for £100,000 realising a gain of £175,000. The property had originally cost £60,000 and had a market value in March 2010 of £235,000.

Explain if payment of Capital Gains Tax could be deferred on this disposal, stating the time limit for making any necessary claims and by whom they should be made.

68 In 2009/10 Toby sold his shoe making business for £2 million realising a gain of £1 million. He had traded since 1997. He also sold his 6% shareholding in SUV Ltd, an unquoted trading company, realising a gain of £300,000. He had held all the shares since 2003 but has never worked for SUV Ltd.

The gain on the disposal of Toby's business arose as follows:

	£
Goodwill	700,000
Factory	100,000
Warehouse	(50,000)
Investments	250,000

Calculate Toby's Capital Gains Tax liability for 2009/10.

69 **State the conditions for chargeable gains to be deferred on the incorporation of a sole trader's business.**

If a sole trader does not satisfy the conditions for incorporation relief what other reliefs are available?

70 On 1 June 2003 John purchased a leasehold factory with 55 years left to run on the lease for £300,000.

In December 2003 he sold a freehold factory for £200,000. John had purchased the freehold factory in March 2000, for £37,500.

John purchased an additional leasehold factory for £180,000 in October 2009. At the time of the purchase there were 85 years left to run on the lease.

Explain with supporting calculations, the Capital Gains Tax implications of these events. You should assume that all beneficial claims and elections are made.

71 Jack has been running a successful business for several years. He intends to transfer his business to a company on 30 June 2010 in exchange for shares.

State what options are available to Jack to defer any gains arising on incorporation and any conditions he must satisfy.

72 In August 2009, John sold 1,000 shares (representing a 10% holding) in Pigpen Ltd, a trading company, to his son Charlie for £200,000. The shares cost £75,000 in 1976, and had a market value of £140,000 on 31 March 1982 and £395,000 at the date of sale. At the date of the gift Pigpen Ltd's net assets consisted of the following:

	£
Freehold property	700,000
Investment property *	620,000
Goodwill	70,000
Stock	15,000
Plant and machinery (each item bought and sold for <£6,000)	10,000
Debtors	120,000
Creditors	(75,000)
	1,460,000

* Assume the company's non-trading activities are not significant.

John has worked full time for Pigpen Ltd since 1976. A claim for gift relief was made.

Calculate John's chargeable gain and Charlie's allowable expenditure, assuming John makes all available claims.

73 David commenced trading in November 1998. On 9 November 2009 he transferred his business to a company in exchange for shares and cash. The market value of the chargeable assets transferred was £200,000 and the gains were £120,000.

David made no other chargeable gains in 2009/10. He had capital losses brought forward at 6 April 2009 of £20,000. The conditions for incorporation relief were met.

Calculate the optimum non-share consideration on incorporation and explain the conditions to be satisfied for incorporation relief to be available.

74 Derek and David are brothers. Derek owned 800 shares in Donald Ltd, which he bought at par in January 2004. He made the following gifts of Donald Ltd shares to David:

	Shares
April 2009	200
July 2010	400

Share values were as follows:

	200 shares £	400 shares £	600 shares £	800 shares £
April 2009	10,000	27,000	48,000	70,000
July 2010	12,000	30,000	60,000	95,000

Calculate the chargeable gain at each of the following dates:

(a) April 2009 (original)
(b) April 2009 (revised)
(c) July 2010.

Explain the conditions for the disposals to qualify for entrepreneurs' relief.

75 (a) Herman purchased a factory on 1 April 2001. He then sold it for £300,000 on 1 January 2010, generating a gain of £200,000.

Herman purchased a new factory on 1 April 2010 for £250,000. Both factories have been used 90% for the purposes of his sole trader business.

Assuming that all possible elections will be made, calculate 1) the chargeable gains, before the annual exempt amount, arising on the sale of the first factory and 2) the base cost of the second factory.

(b) Herman owns another factory, acquired in July 1997 that he is planning to give to his son.

Explain the relief(s) available in respect of the chargeable gain that is likely to arise.

76 On 10 October 2001 Henry bought a factory costing £63,000 for use in his business. He spent £50,000 on an extension in October 2004. He sold it for £293,000 on 10 December 2009 and reinvested £210,000 in a new factory. One quarter of the old factory was let to tenants for the entire period of ownership.

You are required to calculate Henry's chargeable gain after all available reliefs, state the base cost of his replacement factory and state the date by which he must claim any reliefs.

NIC and administrative aspects of IT and CGT

77 Omar is issued with a tax return for 2009/10 on 31 December 2010.

In June 2011, having submitted his return on time, Omar discovers a mistake.

State the date by which Omar should submit his original return, the date by which amendments to the return must be made, the date by which HMRC can correct an error and the date by which HMRC must notify their intention to enquire into his return.

78 Lucy filed her self assessment tax return on line for the year 2008/09 on 15 December 2009. She amended the return on 20 February 2010.

Give the time limits for HMRC to commence enquiries and the possible scope of the enquiry.

79 Martin received his tax return form for 2009/10 in April 2010 and filed it online on 29 April 2011.

His income tax and Class 4 NIC was paid as follows:

	£
31 January 2010 – first POA	10,000
30 November 2010 – second POA	10,000
30 April 2011 – balancing payment	5,000

State the penalties which will apply to Martin.

State two factors which the legislation states are not reasonable excuses to avoid a penalty for late payment of tax.

Assume FA 2009 penalty provisions apply.

80 On 1 February 2010, Peter gave away his holiday home to his son. It had a market value at the date of the gift of £200,000.

The holiday home had originally cost £75,000 in June 1985. In May 1986 he had an extension built for £55,000 and in 1992 he had the whole property redecorated for £20,000.

Calculate Peters gain and explain briefly how Peter could delay paying the Capital Gains Tax on this disposal.

81 Which of the following transactions qualify for payment of capital gains tax by instalments and if so, how many instalments will be due and will any interest be due?

    (a)   Theresa gave away a piece of land realising a chargeable gain. The land is not used in her trade.

    (b)   Cathy sold an investment property for which the consideration is receivable over a 2 year period.

    (c)   Beth sold a 2% holding in a quoted trading company for £10,000 (when its market value was £30,000) to her cousin. This was her entire shareholding.

    (d)   Gerard sold an asset realising a considerable chargeable gain. The consideration is receivable over 10 years.

    (e)   Richard gave away his entire holding of shares in an unquoted trading company and chose not to claim gift relief.

82 Amber has been in business for many years making up her accounts to 31 December. Her trading profit/(losses) for the two years to 31 December 2009 were:

	£
Year ended 31 December 2008	(3,000)
Year ended 31 December 2009	50,000

She received a dividend (including tax credit) of £8,000 in June 2008 and of £6,000 in June 2009.

She made an election under s.64 ITA 2007 to relieve the trading loss against her non-trading income. She also has trading loss brought forward from 2007/08 of £1,000.

Calculate Amber's Class 4 National Insurance Contributions payable, if any, for 2008/09 and 2009/10. Also explain when the contributions are payable.

83 Jerome and Karen are both chargeable to Capital Gains Tax for 2008/09.

Jerome has not received a notice to file a tax return and has not given notice of his chargeability. He paid the Capital Gains Tax due on 10 January 2010.

Karen notified her chargeability on 25 September 2009 and notice to file a tax return was issued on 10 November 2009.

Explain the maximum penalty that Jerome may incur and give, with explanation, the due date for payment of Karen's capital Gains Tax.

Explain when gains are not required to be reported via self assessment.

84 Patrick's payments on account required for 2009/10 were originally £6,000 each. However, Patrick made a claim to reduce his payments on account for 2009/10 to £4,500 each. He paid £4,500 on 31 January 2010 and £4,500 on 30 September 2010. He made a balancing payment of £13,000 for 2009/10 on 28 February 2011 which was made up as follows: Income Tax £4,000, Class 4 National Insurance Contributions £800, Capital Gains Tax £8,200.

State the due date(s) for payment of the above tax, the time periods for which interest will be charged and the amounts of tax on which interest will be charged.

Assuming an interest rate of 2.5%, calculate the interest due to the nearest month.

85 Stefan is self employed. His statements of account for 2009/10 showed tax and Class 4 national insurance due as follows:

		£
31 January 2010	First payment on account for 2009/10	5,000
31 July 2010	Second payment on account for 2009/10	5,000

The tax and National Insurance had been paid on these demands on the due dates.

Stefan submitted his tax return on 31 January 2011, which after processing showed that his total tax and national insurance liability for the year was £14,150. He paid this in full on 12 March 2011.

Stefan had previously claimed to reduce his payments from £7,000 each.

Assume the interest rate on tax paid late is 2.5%.

You are required to calculate the interest and penalties which will arise in respect of the above.

Module A
VAT

Answers

Module A: VAT

VAT basics and treatment of supplies

1. (a) Any person making taxable supplies is required to register for VAT if the total value of the taxable supplies exceeds the registration threshold. A person includes a limited company and so both companies must register separately for VAT. They cannot form a VAT group as there is no common control.

    Michael must also register, but both of his businesses must be covered by a single registration since a person's registration covers all of his business activities.

   (b) Pre registration input tax is recoverable in the first return period on all goods purchased within the previous 3 years provided they are still held at registration.

    Therefore VAT on the printer can be recovered, but not on the computer.

    VAT paid on services within the six months prior to registration can be recovered, so 6 × £80 = £480.

2. If a supply cannot be split into two components, there is a composite (or compound) supply to which one rate of VAT must be applied. The rate used will depend on the nature of the supply involved as a whole.

    In this type of supply, one element is likely to be merely incidental to the main element, or the customer perceives what they receive as a single supply.

    In other circumstances, individual supplies may simply be bundled together, but charged at a single price. In these circumstances, the VAT treatment will be determined using a fair apportionment.

    In the case of the air travel, this is not a mixed supply since that would require the two elements to be the subject of separate negotiation and choice. The supply will be zero rated as a supply of air travel (*British Airways v CCE*).

    In the case of the cruise liner, the supply will be treated as a mixed supply because the supply of catering is not considered to be incidental to the main supply (*Sea Containers Ltd v C&E Commrs*).

3. (a) Where a discount is offered for prompt payment, VAT is chargeable on the net amount regardless of whether the discount is taken up.

    Where a quantity discount is offered VAT is charged on the reduced price.

    The VAT charged on the invoice is therefore:

    £3,200 × 95% = £3,040 × 17.5% = £532

   (b) Gifts for business purposes are not taxable supplies if the cost of gifts to the same person does not exceed £50 in any 12 month period.

    Since each barbeque set costs £80, all are taxable and output tax must be accounted for by Blythe in full.

    Gifts of trade samples are specifically not taxable supplies so there is no VAT payable on the wine coolers.

4. Even though Carla's sales do not exceed the registration threshold, Carla can and should voluntarily register for VAT, as she is making zero rated supplies.

    Advantages

    (1) Can recover input VAT suffered of £10,000 × 17.5% = £1,750 pa
    (2) Hides the size of her business
    (3) Administration – more up to date accounts

    Darla may also voluntarily register for VAT, as she is making a combination of standard rated and zero rated supplies.

    If she registers for VAT, she too will be able to hide the size of her business, receive any administrative benefits, and recover the input VAT suffered.

    However, Darla will also have to either charge VAT on any standard rated sales, or maintain her current prices and accept a lower profit margin.

    The benefits to Darla of a voluntary VAT registration will therefore depend on the extent to which she can pass on the VAT increase to her customers.

5

		£	£
	April	8,000	8,000
	May	8,000	16,000
	June	8,000	24,000
	July	8,000	32,000
	August	8,000 + 13,000	53,000
	September	8,000	61,000
	October	8,000	69,000

Gaby exceeds the £68,000 limit in October and must request registration within 30 days of 31 October 2009, ie 30 November 2009. Her registration will be effective from 1 December 2009.

6   Advantages include any of the following:

    (a)   Supplies between group members are normally disregarded for VAT purposes.

    (b)   Only one consolidated VAT return needs to be declared.

    (c)   Centralisation of VAT affairs.

    (d)   Can include exempt companies which otherwise would not be able to register and therefore possibly allow greater input tax recovery (see disadvantage).

Disadvantages include any of the following:

    (a)   Joint and several liability

    (b)   Inclusion of an exempt business will make the group partially exempt, which may reduce the input tax recovery.

    (c)   Cash flow advantages may be lost (eg loss of repayments if zero rated companies are included)

    (d)   Centralisation of VAT affairs to allow production of one return may create problems with timing and collection of the separate figures.

7   (a)   (i)   The group has to nominate one company as the representative member to submit returns.
         (ii)   Invoices between group members do not attract VAT.
         (iii) All members of a group have joint and several liability.

    (b) (i)   Companies must have a fixed establishment in the UK
         (ii)   Companies must be under common control

8   (a)   A child's car seat – reduced rate 5%
    (b)   Medical care provided by a registered doctor – exempt
    (c)   A train ticket – zero rated
    (d)   A newspaper – zero rated
    (e)   An educational CD-Rom – standard rated

9   Features of a mixed supply may include:

- There is more than one supplier
- Separate pricing or invoicing
- Components are available separately
- There is a time differential between the parts of the supply
- Components are not interdependent or connected.

Features of a composite supply may include:

- The different components are not available separately
- Goods are physically packaged together
- It would not normally make sense to supply part of the package independently (eg a new fridge and its delivery from the warehouse)
- The customer perceives what they receive as a single supply not independent elements
- The different components are aspects of the quality or grade of the overall supply

- The different elements are integral to one overall supply and if one or more is removed, the nature of the supply would be affected
- Some components are clearly incidental or ancillary to an identifiable main supply, and for customers these are a means of better enjoying the main supply
- The separation of elements, on an invoice or otherwise, is artificial.

10 Is the activity an occupation or function which is actively pursued with reasonable or recognisable continuity?

Does the activity have a certain measure of substance in terms of the quarterly or annual value of supplies made?

Is the activity a serious undertaking earnestly pursued?

Is the activity predominantly concerned with making taxable supplies for a consideration?

Is the activity something others commonly do by way of business?

Is the activity conducted in a regular manner and on sound and recognised business principles?

11 Hot food, for consumption off the premises on which it was supplied, is a standard rated supply of catering. Such food will therefore be liable to VAT – as a supply of catering – whether it is consumed off or on the premises.

Cold or ambient temperature foods bought for consumption off the premises may be zero rated, according to the normal VAT liability rules on foods.

But when consumed on the premises, even these cold foods will be liable to VAT as consumption on premises means that their supply is also a standard rated supply of catering services.

12 (a) It is compulsory to cancel the VAT registration of a company ceasing to make taxable supplies within 30 days of cessation.

HM Revenue and Customs will issue a formal cancellation of registration notice.

A VAT charge is made on the final return on assets on which VAT had previously been recovered which are still held at deregistration. Output tax is payable on this deemed supply if the tax exceeds £1,000.

Input tax cannot be recovered on inputs after the date of deregistration except where they relate to the business before that date.

(b) A person is eligible for voluntary deregistration if HMRC are satisfied that the value of his taxable supplies in the following 12 month period will not exceed £66,000.

However voluntary deregistration will not be allowed if the reason for the expected fall in value of the taxable supplies is the future cessation of the business (or the suspension of taxable supplies for a period of 30 days or more).

HMRC will cancel a person's registration from the date the request is made or from an agreed later date.

13 The sale of both donated and bought in goods, by charities (including trading subsidiaries) is always a business activity.

If the charity, or the trading subsidiary, is not already registered, then it will have an obligation to register for VAT, if the taxable supplies made in selling the goods, exceeds the current VAT registration limits.

For donated goods, the sale or hire of such goods is zero rated (Item 1 Group 15 of Schedule 8 VATA 1994)

For bought in goods, the supplies are standard rated unless they fall under the general zero rate or reduced rate or exempt provisions, of the VAT legislation

14 Very Fry Ltd knows on 14 May 2010 that its supplies in the next 30 days will exceed the VAT registration threshold, so HMRC must be notified within 30 days, ie by 13 June 2010.

HMRC will register Very Fry Ltd with effect from 14 May 2010.

Steamy limited will have taxable turnover of £72,000 after nine months of trading. This means that the registration threshold of £68,000 will be exceeded by the end of October 2010. The company must notify HMRC by 30 November 2010, and the registration will be effective from 1 December 2010.

15 India Ltd will be required to register for VAT at the end of March 2010, when its turnover reaches £69,250. The company will have 30 days to notify HMRC, and the registration will be effective from 1 May 2010.

Pre-registration VAT may be recovered as follows:

Input tax on goods purchased prior to registration:

- The goods must be acquired for business purposes, and not be sold or consumed prior to registration.
- The goods were not acquired more than three years prior to registration.

Input tax on services supplied prior to registration

- The services must be supplied for business purposes
- The services were not supplied more than six months prior to registration.

The normal evidence must be held, ie tax invoice.

16 The VAT group should contain H and B. The VAT group will be partially exempt, but as the input VAT relating to exempt supplies is £7,000 it can be recovered anyway as the de minimis provisions will apply.

A should be excluded as a repayment trader, to retain the cash flow benefit of monthly repayments of VAT.

17 This is a mixed supply as each component can be provided separately. The notes – on their own – would be zero rated. The tuition – on its own – would be standard rated.

There are no legislative rules as to how to calculate the VAT on a mixed supply. This can be done on the basis of the cost of each individual element or on the basis of the market value of each individual item.

Using the costs given in the question, the VAT that should be charged is $^{200}/_{300} \times 17.5\% \times £500 = £58$

18 (a) Cultural, artistic, sporting, scientific, educational or entertainment services
    (b) Services relating to exhibitions, conferences or meetings
    (c) Services ancillary to the services in (a) and (b), including those of organising
    (d) Valuation of or work carried out on any goods
    (e) Ancillary transport services.

19 (a) Such consideration in money (excluding VAT) as would be payable by the person making the supply if he were, at the time of the supply, to purchase goods identical in every respect to the goods supplied.

    (b) Where the value cannot be determined under a) above, such consideration in money (excluding VAT) as would be payable by that person if he were, at that time, to purchase goods similar to, and of the same age and condition as, the goods concerned.

    (c) Where the value cannot be determined under a) or b) above, the cost of producing the goods concerned if they were produced at that time.

(**Tutorial note.** The focus is not on historic cost, but on a "real time" value, being the value at the precise time that the actual or deemed supply takes place.)

Input tax

20

	Recoverable input tax £
Taxable supplies	34,000
Partly attributable to taxable supplies	
$9,500 \times \dfrac{215,500}{(215,500 + 59,780)}$ (78.3%) round up to 79%	7,505
Recoverable	41,505

Exempt input tax is 5,600 + (9,500 − 7,505) = £7,595

This is more than £625 per month on average so cannot be recovered.

The VAT on the new car is not recoverable as there is some element of private use. The client entertaining is also irrecoverable. Both items are therefore excluded from the above calculation.

21 VAT on the cost of buying the car is not recoverable.

All VAT on the cost of repairing and maintaining the car will be recoverable. There is no apportionment for private use.

Martin can recover all of the input tax on fuel purchases through his quarterly return but output tax on the deemed sale to himself of private fuel must be accounted for based on the value of the supply. This is determined using scale charges depending on the CO_2 emissions level of the car.

Martin can avoid output tax on the scale charge if he does not reclaim any VAT on car fuel or if he claims back the VAT relating to the business mileage only.

22

	£
Wholly attributable to taxable supplies	1,725
Partly attributable to taxable supplies £1,380 × 83% (W1)	1,145
	2,870
Exempt input tax is de minimis (W2)	1,270
	4,140

Workings

(1) $PE\% = \dfrac{36,400}{36,400 + 7,800} = 83\%$ (rounded up to nearest %)

Exempt input tax is (£1,380 − 1,145) + £1,035 = £1,270

(2)

	£
Monthly average	1,270/3 = £423 (<£625), and
Proportion of total	$\dfrac{1,270}{4,140}$ = 31% (< 50%)

Therefore exempt input tax is all recoverable

The annual adjustment is as follows:

Recoverable input tax is calculated for the VAT year to 31 March, using the same method and tests as for the quarterly returns.

The result for the year is compared with the sum of the results for the individual VAT quarters.

Any excess output tax is accounted for or any excess input tax is either claimed on the return for the next period after the end of the year or (for tax years ending on or after 30 April 2009) on the final VAT return of the tax year, if the trader so chooses.

23 A less detailed invoice must contain:

(a) The name and address of the supplier
(b) The registration number of the supplier
(c) The time of supply
(d) A description of the goods or services
(e) The total amount payable including VAT
(f) For each rate of VAT, the gross amount payable and the rate of VAT applied.

The maximum value for which a less detailed tax invoice can be issues is £250 (including VAT).

24 Significant known or anticipated non-business use of the van would mean that full deduction of input tax on the purchase, without any adjustments to account for the non-business use at any stage, would be incorrect.

One option would be to make an initial reasonable adjustment to the input tax to account for the anticipated personal use by employees.

As an alternative, the Lennartz mechanism would allow the business to keep all the original input tax, but account for output tax on the non-business use of the van as a supply of services (usually based on straight-line depreciation over 5 years).

25 (a) The company's partial exemption percentage is:

$^{100}/_{120}$ = 83.3%. This must be rounded up to 84%.

Exempt input tax

£7,500 × 16% = £1,200

Directly attributable = £350

Total potentially irrecoverable = £1,550

So long as the relevant input tax in any period is less than both:

(i) £625 per month on average, and
(ii) One half of all the input tax for the period concerned,

all such input tax in that period is treated as attributable to taxable supplies.

All the exempt input tax is de minimis, therefore the total input tax is recoverable = £37,850

(b) The annual adjustment can either be completed on this return ie the final VAT return of the tax year or on the first return of the next VAT year, which in this case is the return for the period ended 30 June 2010.

26
	£
£1,200 × 50% × 17.5%	105
£320 × 17.5%	56
£180 × 70% × 17.5%	22

When a car is leased for business use, only 50% of the VAT can be reclaimed as HMRC considers there will be some private use.

The purchase of the competitor's business should be treated as a transfer of a going concern, which means that it is outside the scope of VAT.

Only VAT in respect of business phone calls can be recovered.

The VAT on the new BMW is irrecoverable, assuming there is some element of private use.

The VAT on the delivery charge for the new BMW is also blocked. The purchase of the car and the delivery is likely to be treated as a single supply, and the VAT treatment will follow from the main supply.

27 Input tax incurred on the buildings is £35,000 and £70,000.

Year of acquisition (y/e 31.12.08), input tax deduction = £35,000 × 50% = £17,500 and £70,000 × 50% = £35,000

2nd year (y/e 31.12.09) – Building A is not subject to the capital goods scheme as cost below £250,000 and therefore not liable to further adjustment

Building B adjustment = £70,000 × (40% – 50%) ÷ 10 = £700 payable to HMRC

28 Five of:
- Motor cars (excluding those used solely for business purposes)
- Business entertaining
- 'White goods' and similar items often incorporated into new dwellings.
- Domestic accommodation for directors and business proprietors
- Goods purchased under a margin scheme
- Costs incurred under TOMS (Tour Operators Margin Scheme)
- Otherwise allowable items where the input tax was not claimed and due to the passage of time, the VAT is now subject to the '4 year cap'.

29 In general, in order to claim any credit for input tax:
- A supply must have been made
- The supply must be to the claimant
- The supply must be for a business purpose
- The claimant must hold the required evidence
- The input tax must have been correctly charged
- The claimant must be a taxable person when the supply is made
- The supply must be linked to the making of taxable supplies.

30 The following supplies are disregarded when calculating the partial exemption percentage:
(1) Supplies of capital goods used in the business
(2) Incidental property transactions
(3) Incidental financial transactions
(4) Self supplies
(5) Reverse charge services.

31 *Year ended 31 March 2010*

Recover £9,000 × 60% = £5,400.

Year ended 31 March 2011

Taxable usage 80%

Adjustment $\frac{9,000 \times (60\% - 80\%)}{5 \text{ years}}$ = £360 additional recovery

Year ended 31 March 2012

Taxable usage 80%

Adjustment $\frac{9,000 \times (60\% - 80\%)}{5 \text{ years}}$ = £360 additional recovery

As the computer is sold in the year ended 31 March 2012 there is a final adjustment for the remaining complete years.

As sale is taxable then assume taxable usage in remaining years would have been 100%.

Adjustment 2 years × $\frac{9,000 \times (60\% - 100\%)}{5 \text{ years}}$ = £1,440 additional recovery

However, the sale adjustment is restricted to the amount of VAT charged on sale: the VAT recovered under the sale adjustment is therefore restricted to £6,000 × 17.5% = £1,050.

Total VAT recovery under the capital goods scheme in year ended 31 March 2012 = £1,410

32 (1) Capital assets included in the scheme are: computers/computer equipment with a value of £50,000 or more (VAT-exclusive); land and buildings (including certain extensions) with a value of £250,000 or more (VAT exclusive). Also included is the cost of refurbishing existing properties where the refurbishment cost exceeds £250,000.

(2) Annual adjustments are 5 years for computers and 10 years for land and buildings.

(3) Adjustment made on 2nd VAT return after the VAT year end.

33 If the company used contractors to do the work, only 80% of the VAT suffered would be recoverable, ie 20% × 17.5% × £200,000 = £7,000 irrecoverable

However if the company offers employment contracts to the contractors they would be paid a salary totalling £200,000 which is outside the scope of VAT.

So it would appear that the company would be in a better situation by taking the second option.

However HMRC will treat this as a self supply and the company will be required to charge itself output tax of £200,000 × 17.5% = £35,000. Using the P/E fraction, 20% of this would be recoverable, ie 20% × £35,000 = £7,000, putting the company in the same position as if it had used contractors.

34 Alternative methods possible by agreement with HMRC:

(a) Number of transactions
(b) Areas occupied by staff
(c) Time spent on transactions
(d) Management accounts.

HMRC can impose a special method if unallocated input tax > £50,000 and the standard method does not give a fair and reasonable reflection of use.

35 The input tax suffered on the purchase of the car (£2,625) is blocked as there is an element of private use.

The input tax on the CD player (£17.50) is not recoverable as although it is an accessory which is added at a later stage, it does not have business use.

As Rafi is opting to apply the fuel scale charge, all of the input VAT suffered in respect of the fuel (£74) is recoverable. However Rafi must account for output tax of £441 × $^{7}/_{47}$ = £66.

36 Exam setting fees are exempt from VAT.

A taxable person making partly taxable (standard and zero rated) and partly exempt supplies is partially exempt and may reclaim part, but not necessarily all input tax suffered.

All VAT relating to sales of clothes is recoverable in full.

Input tax relating to exam fees is not recoverable.

Input tax not directly related to either type of supply is apportioned.

If the total irrecoverable VAT does not exceed a de minimis limit all VAT can be recovered in full.

De minimis limit is:

- £625 per month on average
- 50% of all input tax for the period.

37 A good case can be made for recovering the VAT as input VAT.

HMRC may well seek to challenge the recovery, as they tend to regard such expenditure as being incurred for the individual's benefit, rather than the business's.

But although HMRC have won some of the many VAT Tribunal cases over the years on this very point, the Tribunal does tend to decide on the facts of each case.

Provided that publicity is generated in the local press and in other media, I would argue that following decisions in similar cases, eg the case of Myatt & Leason, (but there are others) where a family partnership purchased a racing car and the business received significant publicity and was able to show that new business had been generated as a result, that Input VAT is recoverable in this case.

One key point is that the car must be a business asset – if it is the private property of the senior partner, the VAT on its purchase will not be recoverable.

38 (a) The requirement is for a Declaration by the business, that the method being proposed is fair and reasonable.

(b) There is no official form designated for the purpose but HM Revenue & Customs have published a specimen Special Method Declaration template which businesses can use, on their own business stationery.

(c) The declaration should be submitted to HM Revenue & Customs at the same time as, and accompanying, the actual partial exemption special method proposal.

(d) The legal basis is paras (9) and (10) of Regulation 109, of the VAT General Regulations (SI 1995/2518)

Land and buildings

39 Any supplies made in connection with the building will be standard rated.

Input tax paid by Frump Ltd will be recoverable.

The election applies to the whole site and not just to certain floors.

Any output tax charged to the tenants will be recoverable by them but only if they are registered and make VAT-able supplies. If they do not, the input tax they pay will be a cost borne by them.

This means that the building will become effectively more expensive for the bank, because the VAT will not be recoverable as they only make exempt supplies.

The clothes retailer should be able to recover the VAT on the building in accordance with normal VAT recovery rules.

40 (a) Exempt (but the option to tax can be made)
    (b) Zero rated
    (c) Standard rated
    (d) Exempt (but the option to tax can be made)
    (e) Zero rated

41 (a) (i) Sale of a house by the present owner is an exempt supply.

(ii) Hire of a hotel conference room for a meeting is an exempt supply.

(iii) A two year old commercial building is considered to be a new building therefore its sale is a standard rated supply.

(iv) The grant of an eight year lease in a commercial building is an exempt supply.

(b) An option to tax could be exercised only on the hire of a hotel conference room and the eight year lease of a commercial building. It would change the VAT liability of these supplies to standard rated.

42 The option to tax is a two stage process:

(a) The decision to opt to tax must be made by a suitably authorised person within Alpha – ideally the date of this decision should be recorded in writing, eg in minutes of a meeting.

(b) The option to tax must be notified to HM Revenue & Customs ('HMRC') in writing no later than 30 days from the date on which the decision to opt to tax is made

The notification must clearly state the land and buildings the company is opting to tax.

If any exempt supplies have previously been made by Alpha in respect of the site, it will be necessary to determine whether or not permission will need to be sought from HMRC before the option to tax can be exercised.

If the conditions for automatic permission are not able to be met, it will be necessary to write to HMRC for permission to opt to tax stating the date from which Alpha would like its option to tax to be effective, and giving details of what, if any, input VAT previously incurred that Alpha would now like to recover as a result of opting.

43 The default position is that VAT will apply to all repairs & maintenance, and alterations, unless a relief exists in the law.

VAT Law allows a relief – in the Zero Rate schedule, Group 6 of Schedule 8 to the 1994 VATA.

That relief only applies to 'approved' alterations – not to repairs & maintenance, which are always liable to VAT.

The relief also only applies to 'protected' buildings that are designed to be used as, or remain used as:

(a) Dwellings
(b) For certain defined ('relevant') charitable purposes
(c) For certain other defined ('relevant') residential purposes.

(For historic listed buildings that are used for commercial purposes, there is no relief from VAT.)

44 Use for any relevant residential purpose means use as:

(a) A home or other institution providing residential accommodation for children

(b) A home or other institution providing residential accommodation with personal care for persons in need of personal care by reason of old age, disablement, past or present dependence on alcohol or drugs or past or present mental disorder

(c) A hospice

(d) Residential accommodation for students or school pupils

(e) Residential accommodation for members of any of the armed forces

(f) A monastery, Nunnery or similar establishment

(g) An institution which is the sole or main residence of at least 90% of its residents, except use as a hospital, prison or similar institution or a hotel, inn or similar establishment

45 The subcontractor fees on the construction of a building will be zero rated for VAT purposes. The zero rating provisions however do not extend to the services of an architect. The architect must therefore standard rate the supplies to Penguin Limited. Penguin Limited will recover the VAT on the architects fees in their VAT return, as the sale of a new freehold dwelling will be zero rated.

The subcontractors in respect of the charitable building will not be able to zero rate their invoices to Penguin Limited. Accordingly, these invoices will be standard rated and Penguin Limited will have to recover the VAT so charged in its VAT return.

The sale of a freehold building to a charity for use entirely for a charitable purpose is a zero rated supply, so Penguin Limited will be able to recover the VAT charged in full in its VAT return.

46 Whilst it might be tempting to suggest to your client that they should propose recovery of $^{25}/_{27}$ of the VAT incurred on the refurbishment (on the basis that the current lease will expire 27 years after the refurbishment took place, and there will be 25 years of taxable rent) HM Revenue & Customs policy is not likely to accept such proposals.

It is HM Revenue & Customs policy that following the Tribunal case of The Trustees of R&R Pension Fund, even if the refurbishment is not a capital item, the VAT recovery must be calculated as if it was, ie on the basis of a 10 year period.

Therefore it is unlikely that HMRC would accept any recovery greater than $^{8}/_{10}$ of the VAT, on the basis that there has already been 2 years of exempt income.

47 The freehold sale of a non-residential commercial building converted into residential properties, sold by the person who has converted them, will be zero rated as per Item 1(b) of Group 5 Schedule 8, 1994 VAT Act.

As the whole pub has been derelict for more than 10 years, the whole building qualifies as a non-residential property under Note 7 to Group 5, Schedule 8 1994 VAT Act.

Note 9 requires that additional dwellings be created in order for the final supply of the major interest to be zero-rated.

As two houses have been created, this condition is met.

The sale will be zero rated and hence input tax incurred, other than any VAT blocked on white goods, can be recovered.

Overseas and miscellaneous issues

48 Where EU customers are VAT registered, VAT is accounted for using the destination system.

The sales are zero rated in the UK (being the country of origin) and are chargeable at the appropriate rate in force in France.

Budget Ltd does not have to account for any output tax.

Budget Ltd should obtain these customers' VAT registration number.

Where customers are not VAT registered, VAT is accounted for using the origin system and Budget Ltd must charge VAT at the standard rate of 17.5%.

49 (1) Business is sold as a going concern.
    (2) Transferee must use the assets to carry on essentially the same kind of business.
    (3) Transferee must be VAT registered or become VAT registered.
    (4) There should be no significant break in trading.
    (5) Where only part of a business is transferred it must be capable of separate operation.

50 The sale of otherwise standard rated goods to a customer in the US is zero rated.

The sale of otherwise standard rated goods to a customer in France is zero rated if the customer has provided their VAT registration number.

Evidence of export is also required:

(1) Commercial documentation (such as sea waybill or air waybill)
(2) Official evidence (normally a Single Administrative Document stamped by HMRC).

Evidence must be obtained within three months of the date of the supply.

51 The place of supply for a performing artist is where the performances are given (Sch 4A VATA 1994). The place of supply is therefore Bristol, Rome or Montreal as appropriate.

Ian's performances in Rome and Montreal are therefore outside the scope of UK VAT. He should add VAT to his invoices only for performances in Bristol.

Depending upon how successful Ian actually is, there may be an Italian VAT registration issue in connection with his performance in Rome.

52 Copyright is a Schedule 5 service.

- For customers outside the EU, Schedule 5 services are supplied where the customer belongs, so the place of supply of copyright to a customer in the USA is the USA. No UK VAT is therefore charged on this supply.

- For customers based in the EU, the place of supply is where the customer belongs if they are using the supply for business purposes, but reverts to the normal rule of being supplied where the supplier belongs if not for business purposes. The supply to France is not for business purposes so the supply is made in the UK, and UK VAT should therefore be charged on the supply.

- The supply to Italy is to a EU recipient for business purposes so is made in Italy. The Italian company will account for Italian VAT under the reverse charge mechanism.

53 The place of supply is Spain, as this is a supply and installation of goods.

Thus, the UK kitchen supplier would be incorrect to charge UK VAT.

The UK kitchen supplier will be liable to register for VAT in Spain if their supply exceeds the Spanish VAT registration limit, and hence they would charge Spanish VAT.

The UK kitchen supplier would be unable to take advantage of any simplification procedures the Spanish VAT authorities have implemented, unless the Chef is VAT registered in Spain, and the Spanish VAT authorities have accepted that the supply was received by the chef in the course or furtherance of his business activities.

54 *Official Evidence* – any document, electronic or hard copy, produced by HM Revenue & Customs, such as a Goods departed notice generated under the New Export System, or a SAD – Single Administrative Document – endorsed by HM Revenue & Customs at the point of exit or confirmation of electronic discharge of an New Computerised Transit System movement.

Commercial Evidence – authenticated sea or air waybill, International consignment notes, bills of lading; certificates of shipment which contain full details of the consignment and how it left the EC; International Consignment notes fully completed by the consignor, the haulier and the recipient; FTA (Freight Transport Association) own account transport document fully completed and signed by the receiving customer.

55 (a) *Supplies to UK Restaurants* – the place of supply is the UK, as per s.7(2) VATA 1994. The liability is standard rated as per s.1(1) & 2(1) VATA 1994 as there is no zero rate or exemption available under s.30 or s.31.

(b) *Supplies to Berlin GmbH* – the place of supply is the UK as per s.7(7)(a) VATA 1994. The liability is zero rated, as per Reg 134, SI 1995/2518.

(c) *Supplies to Southern Inc* – the place of supply is the UK as per s.7(7)(a) VATA 1994. The liability is a zero rated export, as per s.30(6) VATA 1994.

56 The provisions of Schedule 1 VATA 1994, covering the liability, notification and registration for VAT will apply to Tapas in respect of its taxable supplies and lays down that a person incurs a liability to register for VAT in one of 2 ways – the backward (or historic) test or the forward (or future) test.

The forward look test – if at any time there are reasonable grounds for believing that the value of taxable supplies in the period of 30 days then beginning will exceed £68,000.

The backward look test – if at the end of any month the value of taxable supplies in a period of one year then ending exceeded £68,000.

The backward look test will not apply as Tapas had reasonable grounds for believing that its taxable supplies would exceed £68,000 in the 30 days beginning 1 April.

Schedule 1 para 6(10) requires Tapas to notify its liability to be registered by the end of the period when the liability arises – ie by 30 April 2010.

Under the forward look test, the HM Revenue & Customs are required to register Tapas from the beginning of the period when the liability arises – so the effective date of registration will therefore be 1 April 2010.

57 *Assets sold piecemeal*

Each asset will be subject to VAT at the appropriate rate.

Business sold as a going concern

The supply of assets is outside the scope of VAT.

Conditions

- The assets are to be used by the transferee to carry on essentially the same kind of business as the transferor
- The purchaser of the business must also be VAT registered or become registered as a result of the transfer
- Where only part of a business is transferred that part must be capable of separate operation
- There should be no significant break in trading.

58 Member States are required to implement the EC Directive(s), then if the domestic legislation is flawed or otherwise does not implement the EC Directives, taxpayers have the right to take the view that they will rely on the EC Legislation, and "ignore" the domestic legislation.

The Revenue Authorities in Member States cannot take this position, and if their domestic legislation is flawed, they must stand by it until it is amended.

The above is "vertical" direct effect (in an action between a taxpayer and the member state). "Horizontal" direct effect – issues between two taxpayers – is also possible but unlikely to apply in VAT.

Direct applicability means that a regulation automatically becomes part of national law, without intervention by the authorities of the Member States.

59 No VAT is payable at the border on EU acquisitions by a supplier registered for VAT in their own country.

Hatter Ltd must account for VAT in the UK on the acquisition of the goods at the same rate as would apply to a supply of identical goods in the UK. VAT must be accounted for in the period when the tax point occurs and may be recovered in the usual way.

The VAT on the adult clothing will be included in the VAT return, both as an amount owed to HMRC, and an amount recoverable from HMRC.

No VAT will be due on the acquisition of goods that are currently zero-rated in the UK, such as children's clothes.

60 The underpinning legal provision is the EC 8th Directive and the general principles are:

- The business must not be registered, or liable to be registered in the EC country in which it incurred the VAT
- The business must have no place of business or residence in the EC country in which it incurred the VAT
- It must not make supplies in the EC country in which it incurred the VAT
- The VAT incurred would be deductible as input tax if the business was registered in the EC country in which it incurred the VAT.

VAT administration

61 The basic tax point is the date on which goods are removed or made available to the purchaser.

If a VAT invoice is issued or payment is received before the basic tax point, the earlier of these dates is automatically taken as the tax point.

If the 'earlier' rule' does not apply, and if a VAT invoice is issued within 14 days after the basic tax point, the invoice date becomes the tax point.

This 14 day period may be extended to accommodate the invoicing procedures of the seller.

62 *Output tax*

	£
20 April – payment received ($7/_{47} \times £17,250$)	2,569
1 May – payment received ($7/_{47} \times £2,300$)	343
3 June – payment received ($7/_{47} \times £5,750$)	856
Total output tax	3,768

Invoice 21 issued – no VAT to pay as no cash received

Input tax

	£
2 May – cash purchase	350
14 May – invoice received but no payment made	–
Total input tax	350

VAT liability £(3,768 – 350) = £3,418

63 (a)

	%
1 June 2009 – 30 September 2009	6.5
1 October 2009 – 8 January 2010	8.0
9 January 2009 onwards	9.0

Note A reduction of 1% off the normal flat rate applies to businesses in the first VAT year of registration.

(b) Under the annual accounting scheme, 90% of the estimated liability must be paid by direct debit in nine equal instalments.

The first is due on the last day of the fourth month of the current accounting year, ie 30 April 2009.

One VAT return is then submitted by the end of the second month after the VAT year, ie 28 February 2010, together with any balancing payment.

64 (a) Proportion of standard rated purchases = $\frac{£60,000}{(£60,000 + £20,000)} = 75\%$

Proportion of standard rated sales = $75\% \times £120,000 = £90,000$

Output tax liability = $£90,000 \times {}^{3}/_{23} = £11,739$

(b) An annual adjustment is required as it ensures that any distortions in the expenditure pattern in individual quarters is smoothed out by calculating the figures over a full year.

65 The penalty will be calculated as a percentage of the potential lost revenue. The percentage will depend on the behaviour giving rise to the error as follows:

Careless error	30%
Deliberate but not concealed	70%
Deliberate and concealed	100%

The potential lost revenue is the additional VAT payable of $£650,000 \times 17.5\% = £113,750$.

There is no reduction for disclosure as the error was discovered by HMRC.

66 *Quarter ended 31 December 2009*

First default. Surcharge liability notice issued. No penalty.

Quarter ended 31 March 2010

First default within the surcharge period.

Surcharge penalty of $£29,180 \times 2\% = £584$ payable

Surcharge period extended to 31 March 2011.

In order to ensure that there are no future penalties arising, Trout Ltd must make payments of the VAT due on or before the due date.

In order to be removed from the SLN surcharge period, Trout Ltd must submit and pay the tax due by the due date for four consecutive returns.

67

30 June 2009	Surcharge liability notice served extending to 30 June 2010. No penalty.
30 September 2009	Surcharge liability period extended to 30 September 2010. Potential penalty of 2%, but waived as less than £400.
31 December 2009	Surcharge liability period extended to 31 December 2010. Penalty 5% (£485).
31 March 2010	Surcharge liability period extended to 31 March 2011. No penalty as no tax paid late

68 Any five from:
- Registration or cancellation of registration
- Refusal of a group registration application
- Assessments for VAT and/or penalties
- VAT chargeable on the supply of any goods or services
- Input VAT reclaimable
- Use of special schemes, eg retail schemes.

69
- If a business has an annual VAT liability which exceeds £2 million then it will have to make payments on account.
- HMRC monitor businesses' VAT payments due, and will notify businesses if they exceed the threshold over a particular 12 month period known as the basis period.
- The business will have to make two monthly payments of $1/_{24}$ of the VAT liability calculated for the basis period and then:
- The remainder – the balancing payment – will therefore be the remaining actual VAT liability, for that particular VAT period, and is paid when the VAT return is submitted. HMRC can increase the payments due if the actual VAT liability for the current year exceeds the basis period liability by 20% or more
- Similarly, if the current year liability is less than 80% of the basis period liability, HMRC should notify the business that the payments due have decreased.
- Payments can change if the business still has quarterly return periods but elects to pay the actual monthly VAT liability, rather than the imputed $1/_{24}$ of the basis period liability.
- Payments will change if the business asks to be put on monthly VAT returns.

70
- Computer breakdown where the essential records are held on a computer and it breaks down either just before or during the preparation of the return, and the business can also demonstrate that reasonable steps to correct the fault have been taken.
- Illness of the person normally responsible for preparing the return provided it can be shown that no-one else was capable of completing the return.
- Loss of key personnel responsible for preparing the return at short notice where there is no-one else to complete it on time.
- Unexpected cash crisis where funds available to pay the VAT are unavailable because of a sudden reduction or withdrawal of overdraft facilities, sudden non-payment by a usually reliable customer, insolvency of a large customer, fraud, burglary, or act of God such as fire.
- Loss of records – but only if the records for the current VAT period are stolen or destroyed.

71
- £125,000 received 20 January 2010. An Actual Tax Point created on that date.
- So treating the payment received as VAT inclusive, VAT of £18,617 (£125,000 × $7/_{47}$) due on March 2010 VAT return.
- £500,000 received 1 August 2010. An Actual Tax Point created on that date.
- So treating the payment received as VAT inclusive, VAT of £74,468 (£500,000 × $7/_{47}$) due on September 2010 VAT return.
- Balance due is £843,750 (total due = £1,250,000 + VAT = £1,468,750 less amounts paid of £125,000 and £500,000 leaves a balance of £843,750 which is £718,085 plus VAT of £125,665).
- Invoice issued 23 December 2010 creates a basic tax point and the liability to account for VAT falls in period to December 2010.
- This is not over-ridden by the fact that the customer did not pay till 2 February, 40 days later. The delivery of the goods to the customer creates a basic tax point, but this basic tax point does not apply as the invoice is issued before the basic tax point, and the issue of the invoice always creates the actual tax point.

- The 14 day tax point rule also cannot apply – not only are there more than 14 days between the actual and the basic tax points, but the 14 day rule only applies when the basic tax point comes first – which it does not, in this case.
- So the VAT of £125,665 is due to be paid by David Jones Yachts Ltd in VAT period to December 2010 and has to be paid to HMRC no later than 31 January, which is before they receive the final payment from the client.

72   Errors on previous VAT returns not exceeding the greater of:

- £10,000 (net under declaration minus over declaration), and
- 1% × net VAT turnover for return period (maximum £50,000),

may be corrected on the next return. Other errors should be notified to HMRC on form VAT652 or by letter.

In both cases, a penalty for the error may be imposed. Correction of an error on a later return is not of itself an un-prompted disclosure of the error and fuller disclosure is required for the penalty to be reduced under the common penalty regime.

73   A taxable person is eligible to begin to operate the cash accounting scheme from the beginning of any prescribed accounting period if:

(a) He has reasonable grounds for believing that the value of taxable supplies to be made by him in the period of one year then beginning will not exceed £1,350,000

(b) He has made all the returns which he is required to make

(c) He has paid all of the amounts owed in respect of those returns or in respect of any assessment that has been made

(d) He has not in the period of one year preceding been convicted of any offence in connection with VAT.

74   The £2,200 payment is allocated on a FIFO basis therefore:

	Net £	VAT £	Gross £	Payments on account £
16 April 2010	790	–	790	790
22 May 2010	1,022	179	1,204	1,204
18 August 2010	409	72	481	206
24 September 2010	1,267	222	1,489	

18 August 2010   £(481 – 206) × 7/47 = 41
24 September 2010   £1,489 × 7/47 = £222

Total claimed in VAT return period to 30 April 2011 = **£263**

75   (1) Substantial traders are those with a VAT liability exceeding £2 million pa.

(2) They must make monthly payments on account based on the previous year's VAT liability, generally to the previous 30/9, 31/10 or 30/11.

Each payment is 1/24 of that annual figure. Two POA are required each quarter, followed by the balance with the return.

(3) Bungle Ltd must pay £100,000 on 28.2.10, £100,000 on 31.3.10 and the balance of £150,000 on 30.4.10 when the return is submitted.

76   The hallmarks are:

- Confidentiality agreements
- Agreements to share a tax advantage
- Contingent fee arrangements
- Prepayments between connected parties
- Funding by loans, share subscriptions or subscriptions in securities
- Offshore loops
- Property transactions between connected persons
- Issue of face value vouchers.

77 Penalty is a percentage of the potential lost revenue as a result of failure, ie the net VAT due from the date Karen was required to be registered up to the date of notification.

Supplies in period are treated as VAT inclusive, so VAT due in period = ($£51,750 \times {}^7/_{47}$) − ($£17,250 \times {}^7/_{47}$) = £5,138.

The percentage depends on the type of behaviour leading to the failure. If deliberate and concealed, the maximum percentage is 100%. The penalty can be reduced if there is disclosure. If the failure is not deliberate and there is unprompted disclosure, the penalty can be reduced to nil as the failure was rectified within 12 months.

Stamp taxes

78 Any five of the instruments listed in the stamp duty (exempt instruments) regulations 1987, such as:

- The vesting of property subject to a trust in the Trustees of the trust on the appointment of a new trustee, or in the continuing Trustees on the retirement of a trustee
- The conveyance or transfer of property the subject of a specific legacy to the beneficiary named in the will (or his nominee)
- The conveyance or transfer of property out of the settlement in or toward satisfaction of the beneficiaries' interest, not being interest acquired for money or money's worth
- The conveyance or transfer of property on and in consideration only of marriage to a party to the marriage
- The conveyance or transfer of property on and in consideration only of the formation of a civil partnership to a party to the civil partnership
- The conveyance or transfer of property in connection with divorce or dissolution of civil partnership
- The conveyance or transfer by the liquidator of property which formed part of the assets of the company in liquidation to a shareholder of that company
- Outright gifts
- Variations of dispositions on death

79 The conditions that must be met for this relief to apply (FA 1986, s.77):

(a) The transfer must take place as part of an arrangement under which the whole of the issued share capital of the target company will be acquired

(b) The acquisition must be for bona fide commercial reasons and not part of a tax avoidance scheme

(c) The consideration for the acquisition must consist entirely of the issue of shares in the acquiring company to the target company's members

(d) After the acquisition, the acquiring company must have the same classes of shares and each class must form nearly the same proportion of the total number of shares as the target company's share capital prior to the acquisition

(e) After the acquisition, each former shareholder in the target company must be a shareholder in the acquiring company and hold the same percentage of each class of shares in the new company as in the old.

80 The filing date for a land transaction return in respect of a land transaction which is not exempt is 30 days from the transaction date. There is an immediate late filing penalty of £100, then penalties of 5% if the return is more than six months late and a further 5% if more than 12 months late. Note that there are no daily £10 penalties if more than three months late as these only apply to annual returns.

Higher penalties of 70% of the tax due apply where a person fails to submit the return for over 12 months and they have deliberately withheld information necessary for HMRC to assess the tax due (100% penalty if deliberate with concealment).

The stamp duty land tax is payable within 30 days of the transaction. Late payment interest is charged on late paid tax. There are penalties for late payment as follows:

- 5% × tax unpaid one month after the payment date
- 5% × tax still unpaid at 6 and 12 months.

Tutorial note: The CIOT examine prospective legislation passed more than five months before the examination even where it is not yet in force. The above late filing and payment penalties are contained in *Sch 55 & Sch 56 FA 2009*.

81 Group relief is not available if:

(a) At the date of the transaction there are arrangements under which some person could, then or subsequently, obtain control of the purchaser but not the vendor.

(b) All part of the consideration is provided by a third party (who is not a group member), and the purchaser is to cease to be in the same group as the vendor by ceasing to be a 75% subsidiary.

Group relief is withdrawn if the purchaser and vendor cease to be members of the same group within three years, or if arrangements to leave the group are made within that period, and the purchaser or an associated company which is also leaving the group still owns the land.

82 The taxpayer may amend a land transaction return within 12 months of the filing date.

HMRC may amend the return to correct obvious errors within nine months of the actual filing date.

HMRC may raise enquiries into the return within nine months of the later of the due and actual filing dates. On completion of the enquiry they must issue a closure notice stating their conclusions and making any necessary amendments to the return.

83 The stamp taxes implications are:

(a) Stamp duty of 0.5% × £81,300 rounded to the nearest five pounds is payable by purple plc, ie £410. No stamp duty reserve tax will be payable if the stamp transfer document is presented within six years of the contract date.

(b) Stamp duty land tax of £7,800 (£260,000 × 3%) is payable by Saturn plc.

(c) Stamp duty land tax is payable by Sun Ltd as follows:

Premium: £80,000 × 1% equals £800. The zero rate is not available as the annual rent exceeds £1,000 and the property is non-residential.

Stamp duty land tax is also payable on the net present value of the rentals as follows:

£(510,000 − 150,000) × 1% = £3,600

84 When the consideration payable under instrument is uncertain and depends upon a contingency happening, the contingency principle applies to ascertain the stamp duty payable. To the extent that the consideration is unascertainable, no percentage duty is payable.

However, if there is a maximum possible payment the stamp duty is charged upon this.

In this case therefore, the stamp duty payable in respect of option (a) will be £100,000 × 0.5% = £500 and the stamp duty payable in respect of option (b) will be £300,000 × 0.5% = £1,500.

85 Relief from stamp duty may be given in respect of certain intra-group transfers. The conditions that must be met are:

(a) The effect of the instrument must be to transfer the beneficial interest in property from one body corporate to another

(b) Those bodies corporate must be associated at the time the instrument is executed, i.e. one must be the parent of the other or they must have a common parent.

For the associated companies test, one company is regarded as the parent of another if it has:

- Beneficial ownership of at least 75% of the ordinary share capital
- A 75% interest and dividends and assets are winding up
- There must not be arrangements for a non associated person to acquire control of the transferee.

In this case, because Blue Ltd and Orange limited are not under the control of a common parent company, the relief does not apply and stamp duty may be payable.

Module B
Inheritance tax, trusts and estates

Answers

Module B: Inheritance tax, trusts and estates

IHT basics

1

	£	£	£
Pierre's death estate			500,000
Less: NRB		325,000	
failed PET	198,000		
	(6,000)		
		(192,000)	
			(133,000)
Chargeable estate			367,000
IHT payable @ 40%			146,800
Less: QSR 3–4 years 40% × £10,000 × $\frac{100-10}{100}$			(3,600)
IHT payable			143,200

2 Camilla's chargeable estate 2002/03:

	£
Total	260,000
Less: exempt	(110,000)
	150,000
NRB £250,000	(150,000)
	NIL

NRB remaining: $^{100}/_{250} \times 100\% = 40\%$

Tom's chargeable estate 2009/10:

	£
Total	620,000
Less: NRB (W)	(455,000)
Taxable	165,000

Tax at 40% = £66,000

WORKING

NRB 2009/10	325,000
Plus 40% × £325,000	130,000
	455,000

3 Single grossing

	£
Tax free legacy to son	243,000
Inheritance tax on this: £(243,000 – 43,000) (W) × $^{40}/_{60}$	133,333
	376,333

Hence the amount available to Richard's wife is: (£862,000 – 376,333) = £485,667

WORKING

Remaining nil rate band £(325,000 – 282,000) = £43,000

4 (a) Additional IHT arising on chargeable lifetime transfers made within seven years of death is paid by donee.
(b) IHT arising on PETs becoming chargeable is paid by donee.
(c) IHT on the deceased's free estate is paid by the personal representatives out of the estate assets.
(d) IHT on settled property is paid by the trustees out of the capital of the trust.

Where IHT remains unpaid, HM Revenue & Customs can look beyond those primarily responsible for the tax.

For example:

- Personal representatives can become liable in respect of any of the IHT liabilities arising as a result of death.

  Their liability will, however, be limited to the estate assets in their possession.

- Beneficiaries under the deceased's Will can become liable if the personal representatives do not pay the IHT on the estate.

  Their liability is limited to the IHT on the assets that they have inherited.

5   Three out of:

- Property situated outside the UK which is owned by a non-UK domiciled person
- Property located outside the UK held in a settlement created by a non-UK domiciled individual
- Reversionary interest (ie remainderman's interest) in a settlement situated outside the UK
- Reversionary interests unless:
   (i)   It was acquired for a consideration in money or money's worth
   (ii) It is an interest to which either the settler or his spouse is/has been beneficially entitled
   (iii) It is expectant on the determination of a lease for life
- Holdings in authorised unit trusts owned by a non-UK domiciled person
- Shares in open-ended investment companies owned by a non-UK domiciled person
- Certain Government securities owned by individuals not ordinarily resident in the United Kingdom
- Specified National Savings products held by persons domiciled in the Channel Islands or the Isle of Man
- Emoluments and tangible movable property of members of overseas forces posted to the UK
- Money which could have been paid to a deceased's personal representatives but instead is converted into an annuity for his dependants.

6

	£
Free Estate	
Assets	400,000
Settled property	
£60,000 Treasury stock at $62\tfrac{1}{2}$p	37,500
	437,500

IHT

$40\% \times £(437{,}500 - 325{,}000) = £45{,}000$

Paid by:

Personal representatives $£45{,}000 \times \dfrac{400{,}000}{437{,}500} = £41{,}143$

Trustees $£45{,}000 \times \dfrac{37{,}500}{437{,}500} = £3{,}857$

7   Gift of school fees represents normal expenditure out of income, ie:

- Habitual nature
- Taking one year with another the payments are made out of his income
- The gifts leave him with sufficient income to maintain his usual standard of living.

and is therefore exempt.

The £100,000 to his daughter is a PET and will not be chargeable unless Thomas dies within 7 years. If he does, then the annual exemption for 2009/10 and 2008/09 will be available to set off, although the marriage exemption could not apply as the gift must have been in consideration of actual marriage.

8   Value of chairs in Adam's estate

$$\left(240{,}000 \times \frac{120{,}000}{120{,}000 + 40{,}000}\right)$$ £180,000

Tax at 40% = £72,000

Death estate: Paid by personal representatives – suffered by residuary legatees

Failed PET to son: paid by son

9   The PET becomes chargeable

	£
Value of gift	288,000
Less: AE 2007/08	(3,000)
AE 2006/07	(3,000)
Transfer of value	282,000
Fall in value: £288,000 – £268,000	(20,000)
	262,000

No IHT as covered by NRB

	£	£
Death estate		500,000
NRB	325,000	
GCT	(282,000)	
		(43,000)
		457,000

Tax at 40% = £182,800

10

	£
House £(620,000 – 50,000)	570,000
Life policy	100,000
10,000 £1 ordinary shares in Moon plc (W)	42,200
	712,200
Austrian Chalet $\frac{450{,}000}{1.51}$	298,013
	1,010,213
Less: funeral expenses	(5,042)
Net estate	1,005,171

Working
¼ (428 – 420) + 420 = 422p
10,000 × 422p = £422

11 Death Estate

	£
Free estate	400,000
Settled property (as qualifying IIP trust)	280,000
	680,000
IHT	
£(680,000 – (325,000 – 90,000(W))) × 40%	178,000
PR's liability	
£178,000 × $\frac{400{,}000}{680{,}000}$	104,706
Trustees' liability	
£178,000 × $\frac{280{,}000}{680{,}000}$	73,294

Working

Gift	96,000
Less: AE × 2	(6,000)
	90,000

12 No transfer of value takes place provided that Simon waives his dividend within the 12 months before the right to the dividend accrues.

An interim dividend accrues when it is actually paid.

A final dividend accrues when it is declared in general meeting of the company.

Sale at an undervalue: no transfer of value as long as it is freely negotiated at the time of sale.

13 The value of Edward's shares will be calculated using the related property rules, taking into account the shares in the trust, ie 70% before transfer and 60% after transfer.

	£
Before the transfer his interest is 4,500 × £25	112,500
After the transfer his interest is 3,500 × £20	(70,000)
Transfer of value	42,500

For capital gains tax purpose (10%): 1,000 × £12 = £12,000

14 *1 January 2007 gift at death rates*

Gross transfer = £350,000

	£
Death tax £(350,000 – 325,000) × 40%	10,000
Less: taper relief 3 – 4 years @ 20%	(2,000)
	8,000
Less: lifetime tax	(13,000)
	NIL

No refund available

1 February 2007 gift to son

PET now chargeable (no AEs left) = £130,000

	£
Death tax at 40%	52,000
Less taper relief (3–4 years) of 20%	(10,400)
IHT suffered by Amy's son	41,600

Death estate

Tax on estate of 40% × £300,000 = £120,000

NRB fully utilised

Payable out of the estate so suffered by the daughter.

15 Gladys' death estate at 7 January 2009

	£	£
Cumberland plc Lower of: 1/4 up = 410 + 1/4 (422 – 410) = 413 Mid bargain = 1/2 (408 + 424) = 416 15,000 × 4.13		61,950
No BPR as an investment company		
House in Utopia $\frac{150,000}{1.48}$	101,351	
Less lower of: (i) 5% × £101,351 = £5,067, and (ii) Additional costs of administering £(5,500 – 1,000) = £4,500	(4,500)	
		96,851
		158,801
Less: funeral expenses		(2,500)
		156,301

16 Shares in unquoted companies are worth more as a whole than in their constituent part, hence can be treated as related property under s.161(1) IHTA 1984.

Related property rules will apply to this gift. The rules apply if the share would be in the estate of Elinor's spouse.

As Elinor's husband is the life tenant of a qualifying IIP trust, the shares would be in his estate.

How to value the shares

Individual's own shares are valued in relation to the larger related holding, ie $\frac{A\%}{A\% + B\%}$ × (value of (A% + B%)).

17 *March 2010 – Tax on Glen's death*

	£	£
Estate		1,000,000
NRB	325,000	
Previous 7 years	(243,000)	
Remaining NRB		(82,000)
		918,000
		£
Tax @ 40%		367,200
Less: QSR (3 – 4 years) $\frac{\text{Increase in Glen's estate}}{\text{Decrease in sister's estate}}$ × tax on 1st gift × 40% $\frac{500,000 - 100,000}{500,000}$ × £100,000 × 40%		(32,000)
Tax on Glen's estate		335,200

18 Property is related to that held by:

- A spouse/civil partner

- A trust in which the individual or their spouse/civil partner has a qualifying interest in possession, and

- A charity, political party or other exempt body to which an exempt transfer was made by the transferor or his spouse/civil partner (or owned by such an exempt body within the five years before the present event and transferred to that body by the person or his spouse/civil partner).

How to value shares for related property purposes – individual's own shares are valued in relation to the larger related holding, ie:

$\frac{A\%}{A\% + B\%}$ × (value of (A + B)%)

19

		£
Transfer July 2006		400,000
Less: AEs 2006/07		(3,000)
AEs 2005/06		(3,000)
PET		394,000

No BPR as Stephen did not control the company.

	£	£
6,000 ordinary shares in Tiber plc		300,000
Less: BPR (50%)		(150,000)
		150,000
Villa in Lithuania	100,000	
Less: additional costs – max (£100,000 × 5%)	(5,000)	
		95,000
Matrimonial home	250,000	
Less: spouse exemption	(250,000)	
Personal chattels		–
Chargeable estate		5,000
		250,000
NRB	325,000	
GCT	(394,000)	
		(NIL)
		250,000

Tax at 40% = £100,000

Solicitors' fee excluded.

20

	£	£
Cash		200,000
Life assurance proceeds		50,000
House		500,000
Stamp collection		180,000
Holiday home	120,000	
Less: expenses – max 5% × £120,000	(6,000)	
		114,000
		1,044,000

	£
£325,000 at 0%	
£719,000 at 40%	287,600

QSR: 1 – 2 years $\dfrac{\text{Increase in Queenie's estate}}{\text{Decrease in father's estate}} \times$ tax on 1st gift × 80%

(£150,000 × 30%) × $\dfrac{150,000}{150,000 + 45,000}$ × 80%   (27,692)

IHT payable   259,908

21 (a) No exemption. UK charities only are covered by s.23(1) IHTA 1984.

(b) Exempt s.18(1). Transfer between civil partners. Living apart is not relevant, as it would be for Capital Gains Tax: s.58 TCGA 1992

(c) Exempt: s.25(1), Sch 3 IHTA 1984. Gift for national purpose.

(d) PET

22

	£	£	£
Sasha's death estate			650,000
Less: NRB		325,000	
failed PET (below nil rate band)	250,000		
	(6,000)		
		(244,000)	
			(81,000)
Chargeable estate			569,000
IHT payable @ 40%			227,600
Less: QSR 3–4 years 40% × £20,000 × $\frac{300-20}{300}$			(7,467)
IHT payable			220,133

23 Death estate

	£	£
Free estate		
Gamma plc – AIM companies are treated as unquoted for BPR purposes		132,000
Less: 100% BPR		(132,000)
		NIL
Delta Ltd shares	364,000	
Less: 100% BPR (W)	(273,000)	
		91,000

(W) BPR is not available on non business assets but plant and machinery is a business asset (*Note.* Not chargeable for CGT)

	£	£
Settled property		
Factory – not used in a trade carried on by the life tenant (Gillian) hence no BPR		264,000
Chargeable estate		355,000

Working

$$^{BA}/_A = \frac{(£1.2m - 300,000)}{1.2m}$$

$$\frac{900,000}{1.2m} \times £364,000 = £273,000$$

APR, BPR and post mortem sales

24

	Value for IHT purposes £
Shares in Rory Ltd – Unquoted trading company, therefore 100% Business Property Relief available	NIL
Office used in sole trade – no BPR generally available	250,000
Shares in Superco Ltd – AIM companies count as unquoted, therefore also 100% BPR	NIL
Factory used by Rory Ltd, a company controlled by Quentin, in its business, therefore 50% BPR	140,000
Interest in a business not owned for two years, therefore no BPR	70,000
Total	460,000

25

		£
Before transfer $\frac{5,000}{8,000} \times £14,000$		8,750
After transfer $\frac{2,500}{5,500} \times £6,875$		(3,125)
Transfer of value		5,625

If the company is an investment company no BPR available. If the company is a trading company BPR will be available at a rate of 100%. If the trading company holds investments they will be 'excepted' assets and BPR is only available in respect of the value of the shares relating to the business assets, calculated by applying the fraction

$$\frac{\text{Total value of assets} - \text{excepted assets value}}{\text{Total value of assets}}$$

26 Value of shares transferred for IHT

Valued as part of a 30% holding

Adrian's transfer of value for IHT 1,000 × £16 = £16,000

CGT value: market value 1,000 × £12 = £12,000

1 May 2009 transfer: No BPR as Adrian does not have control of quoted company.
1 June 2009 transfer: No BPR as the company is an investment company.

27

	£
Total company	950,000
Agricultural value	420,000
'Other assets'	200,000

His share: 60%

	£
Shares	570,000
APR 100% × $^{420}/_{950}$ × £570,000	(252,000)
	318,000
BPR on other assets 100% × $^{200}/_{950}$ × £570,000	(120,000)
	198,000

28 (a) NIL – not an interest in a business. Relief only applies for land and buildings where they are used in a partnership, or a company that the individual controls. *Note.* Possible 100% BPR available if it can be shown that the transfer of the property actually reduces the net value of the business (Nelson Dance (2009)).

 (b) NIL – quoted company, no control.

 (c) 100% – any holding in an unquoted company.

 (d) 100% – securities in an unquoted co where donor has control.

 (e) NIL – 2 years ownership not satisfied.

29 *Frazer – 1 September 2007*

Exempt as to spouse. (*Note.* If left to anyone else, 100% BPR for gift. Unquoted shares in a trading company owned for more than 2 years.)

Gaynor – 1 February 2008

PET. 100% BPR potentially available for gift. Unquoted shares in a trading company owned for less than 2 years, but acquired on the death of a spouse so combine the shareholding periods.

Charles – 1 October 2009

100% BPR for shares. Unquoted shares in a trading company owned for less than 2 years, but there was a transfer in the last two years which itself qualified for BPR and that or the second transfer (in this case) was on death so no ownership requirement on the second transfer.

30 BPR is available on the disposal of qualifying property owned for less than 2 years by the transferor if:

The property replaced other business property, and together they were owned for periods which together total at least two years out of the last 5 years. There must have been full reinvestment of the proceeds on disposal of the first property.

The transferor became entitled to the property on the death of his spouse/civil partner, and the combined ownership of the transferor and his spouse/civil partner was at least 2 years.

The property was entitled to BPR on an earlier transfer, and either the earlier transfer or this one is a transfer due to death.

31 *Death of Leonard*

BPR is not available as the shop has been owned for less than two years. However, the spouse exemption would mean that no IHT was payable.

Death of Lily

BPR is available as the ownership by herself and her spouse exceeds two years. The period can be combined because Lily acquired the shop on the death of her spouse.

32

	£
IHT	
Before transfer 6,000 × £160 per share	960,000
After transfer 4,750 × £100 per share	(475,000)
Value transferred	485,000

	£
CGT	
Disposal proceeds (MV) 1,250 × £50	62,500
Less: cost 1,250 × £30	(37,500)
Gain	25,000
Less: AE	(10,100)
Taxable gain	14,900

Tax at 18% = £2,682

33 (a) 1 June 2006 – transfer of value

	£
Before (100%)	500,000
After (70%)	(250,000)
TOV	250,000

BPR = 100%

(b) 2 March 2010 – death within 7 years: PET becomes chargeable

   (i)   Still owned by donee, but
   (ii) Shares now listed, therefore not relevant business property
   (iii) Therefore BPR lost

Therefore

	£
PET chargeable	250,000
Annual exemptions	(6,000)
Total	244,000

Below nil rate band of £325,000

			£
	Therefore tax on estate		1,000,000
	Nil rate band £(325,000 – 244,000)		(81,000)
			919,000

Tax at 40% = £367,600

34 Possible estate at death.

			£	£
(a)	APR available on agricultural value only as vacant possession and farmed himself		500,000 (20,000)	480,000
(b)	Open Ditch: no vacant possession within 1 year, but let after 1 September 1995 Therefore 100% APR		25,000 (25,000)	–
(c)	Farmhouse £(600,000 ÷ 2) – although this is a subjective test.			300,000
(d)	Cattle farm Less: APR 100%		125,000 (100,000)	25,000
(e)	Cattle herd (no APR)			55,000

35 Brian's estate:

	£	£
Shares		128,000
BPR 100% × £128,000 × $\frac{(1{,}197{,}000 - 112{,}000)}{1{,}197{,}000}$		(116,023)
		11,977
House		410,000
Less: lower of		
Administration costs £23,000		
5% × £410,000 = £20,500	(20,500)	
		389,500
Chargeable estate		401,477

Overseas aspects and anti-avoidance

36 (a) London
    (b) Zanzibar
    (c) London
    (d) London
    (e) Zanzibar

37 Utopian shares and bearer shares are excluded property

Chargeable estate is therefore £429,000 (414,000 + 15,000)

IHT thereon is 40% × £(429,000 – 325,000) = £41,600

38 *Grandson's school fees*

It is probable that the gifts will be covered by the normal expenditure out of income rules:

- Habitual nature
- Taking one year with another, gift is out of income
- Gifts leave transferor with sufficient income to maintain usual standard of living.

Otherwise these would have been PETs that becomes chargeable following Tom's death within 7 years.

Gift to non-domiciled wife

First £55,000 is exempt therefore covers whole £40,000. £15,000 of the £60,000 is exempt. If there are no other gifts within 7 years, still within nil rate band, otherwise it will be chargeable on his death.

39 Goodwill is located where the trade is carried on. If this is a separate part of the business based in Holland, then it will be located there. Otherwise it will be the UK.

For IHT, the debt is located where the debtor resides, therefore Spain. No court judgements have been made in relation to the debts.

Shares are located where the register is kept, therefore in France.

40 This is a PET valued at £350,000 and is also a gift with reservation of benefit (GWROB). The PET becomes chargeable on his death within 7 years in 2009.

In addition, the house continues to form part of Harry's estate, now valued at £470,000.

To prevent a double charge to tax, regulations apply to ensure that IHT is only paid on the event that gives the greatest amount of tax.

If visits only:

Virtual exclusion of benefit. No GWROB. PET valued at £350,000 becomes chargeable on his death within 7 years in 2009. The house does not form part of Harry's estate at death.

41 An individual is deemed domiciled in the UK:

- If resident in the UK for at least 17 out of the last 20 tax years ending with the year in which any chargeable transfer is made.
- For 36 months after ceasing to be domiciled in the UK under general law.

Olivia is deemed domiciled in the UK on 1 November 2009.

Transfers from Olivia to her husband are exempt from IHT in lifetime or on death, because they are both UK domiciled.

42 A gift with a reservation of benefit is made when an individual disposes of any property by way of gift, but continues to have beneficial use of the property.

Exceptions:

- Incidental use only
- Full consideration paid for use
- For land, unforeseen change in circumstances of transferor that means the donee, who is his relative, needs to maintain the donor due to old age or infirmity.

Any others listed in Para 6(1) Sch 20 FA 1986 would be awarded marks.

43 Lifetime gift:

	£
1 October 2003	
Farm to Sue	175,000
Less: exempt to non domiciled wife	(55,000)
Chargeable transfer (within NRB)	120,000
1 November 2007	
Gift to charity (overseas so not exempt)	100,000
Cumulative total at death	220,000

Tax on chargeable estate: £325,000 − £220,000 = £105,000 at 0%

Balance of estate: £165,000 (£270,000 − £105,000) at 40% = £66,000

44 Property owned by a person non domiciled in the UK, which is situated outside the UK is excluded property and so not included in his chargeable estate.

- House in Neverland – situated in Neverland – excluded
- House in Richmond – situated in UK – chargeable
- Cash balance at the Neverland branch of UK building society – situated in Neverland – excluded
- Cash balance at the Richmond branch of UK building society – situated in UK – chargeable
- Goodwill relating to a mail order business based in Surrey – situated in UK – chargeable
- Various antiques kept in the Richmond house – situated in UK – chargeable

45 Transfers by a UK domiciled spouse to a non UK domiciled spouse are exempt provided total transfers do not exceed £55,000.

Hence £395,000 would be treated as a PET, chargeable at 40% on his death in 2 years time if Andrew were to gift the house in June 2010.

There will be no reduction for taper relief, as there is less than three years between the gift and death.

By June 2012, the date of Andrew's anticipated death, Louise will have been resident in the UK for at least 17 out of the last 20 tax years. Hence she will be treated as deemed UK domiciled. All transfers between two UK domiciled spouses are exempt.

Andrew should therefore wait until his death to transfer the Mexican house to Louise as the transfer will then be exempt, in full.

46 *IHT*

December 2009

This is a PET but is also a gift with reservation.

March 2012

PET becomes chargeable as dies within 7 years.

Property also included in Neil's estate at market value.

Double charges relief available. The event remaining in charge is the one which gives the highest IHT charge.

CGT

December 2009

Gain realised on gift of house so principal private residence relief potentially available. Oliver acquires the house at a deemed base cost of £800,000. When Neil disposes of the house in the future, no principal private residence relief available for the period December 2009 to March 2012.

47 *In lifetime*

	£
1 May 2007 PET	115,000
Less: marriage exemption	(1,000)
AE 2007/08 and 2006/07	(6,000)
	108,000

No IHT due

	£
1 June 2007 Charity (non-UK) PET	200,000
No AE available (used)	–
	200,000

No IHT due

	£
1 July 2007 PET	300,000
Less: non-domiciled spouse exemption	(55,000)
	245,000

No IHT due

On death

	£	£
1 May 2007 failed PET		108,000
NRB £325,000		(108,000)
		NIL

No tax due

	£	£
1 June 2007 failed PET		200,000
NRB	325,000	
Less	(108,000)	
	217,000	(200,000)
		NIL

No tax due

	£	£
1 July 2007 failed PET		245,000
NRB	325,000	
Less	(108,000)	
	(200,000)	
	17,000	(17,000)
		228,000

Tax at 40% = £91,200

Death estate: exempt (transfer to political party, therefore exempt).

48   (a)   Not chargeable – situs depends on place where shares are registered

     (b)   Not chargeable – chattels situated where physically kept – but ESC F7 applies (temporary presence in UK for cleaning or restoration)

     (c)   Chargeable – branch bank accounts sited where the branch is sited

     (d)   Not chargeable – where debtor resides (not under court order)

49   (1)   20 July 2002 PET £150,000, also gift with reservation

     (2)   20 July 2005 release of the reservation – also a deemed PET £390,000

     (3)   Death 21 July 2009

           First PET £150,000 escapes – over 7 years from death, thus preventing a double charge

           Second PET chargeable: 20 July 2005

7 year gifts b/f	NIL
This gift	£390,000

£325,000 at 0%
£65,000 at 40% = £26,000

Taper relief (4 – 5 years: 40%)

60% chargeable = £15,600

Tutorial Note: The AE is not available to reduce the value of a deemed PET (IHTM14343).

50

	£
Alpha plc shares	1,320
Small gifts as each one an outright gift of less than £250. Hence exempt	(1,320)
	NIL
Beta plc shares	3,200
Not small gifts as each is in excess of £250	–
Annual exemption is unused for 2005/06	(3,000)
Plus part of the annual exemption for 2004/05	(200)
	NIL
Home in Spain	
As Jacob is non-UK domiciled overseas property is excluded property and not subject to UK inheritance tax	NIL
Necklace to Harriet	75,000
Gift from a non-domiciled spouse to a domiciled spouse is fully exempt	(75,000)
	NIL

Note. The £55,000 restriction only applies to gifts from a UK domiciled spouse to their non-UK domiciled spouse.

51 (a) Zoe was UK domiciled less than 3 years before her death and is therefore deemed to be UK domiciled for Inheritance Tax purposes.

Therefore all of the assets form part of her chargeable estate

(b) Because Zoe was domiciled in Abbeyland for Inheritance Tax purposes, any property situated outside the UK is excluded property and does not form part of her chargeable estate. UK situated assets are included in her estate.

   (i) House in Abbeyland – situated in Abbeyland – excluded
   (ii) Personal chattels held in the UK – included
   (iii) Shares in UK company – not bearer shares, therefore situated in the UK and included
   (iv) Bank account – situated at Abbeyland branch – excluded

52 A settlor will be assessed on the income of a trust if the income is payable to or for the benefit of the settlor's spouse. It will also be assessed on the settlor if the income will or may become payable to or for the benefit of the settlor's spouse. The whole of the trust income will be assessed on the settlor.

In addition, the settlor will be assessed on the income where it is paid to or for the benefit of his minor children, unless the gross income distributed does not exceed £100 per annum.

IHT and trusts

53

	£
Chargeable lifetime transfer made on 1 January 2005	500,000
Less: AE for 2004/05 and 2003/04	(6,000)
	494,000

Therefore tax at £(494,000 – 263,000) × $^{20}/_{80}$ = £57,750

On death

	£
Gross chargeable transfer = £(494,000 + 57,750)	551,750
Less: nil rate band 2009/10	(325,000)
	226,750
Tax at 40%	90,700
Less: taper relief (4 – 5 years) = 40%	(36,280)
	54,420
Less: tax already paid	(57,750)
Balance	NIL

No refund available

54 Charles's transfer

	£	£
Before $\frac{40}{40+35}$ × £480,000		256,000
After $\frac{25}{25+35}$ × £336,000		(140,000)
Transfer of value		116,000
Less: AE's (2 × £3,000)		(6,000)
		110,000
Less: NRB	325,000	
Less: GCT	(350,000)	
		(NIL)
Taxable transfer		110,000

Tax at $^{20}/_{80}$ (assume settlor pays the tax as question is silent) = £27,500

Value of trustee's shares:

15% holding = £35,000

55

(a) Inheritance tax using diminution in value:

		£	£
Value before transfer	4,000 × £30		120,000
Value after transfer	1,000 × £12.50		(12,500)
Value transferred			107,500
Less: AEs			(6,000)
			101,500
NRB		325,000	
Less: GCT		(500,000)	
			(NIL)
			101,500

Tax at 20% = £20,300

(b) Capital gains tax:

Value of shares gifted = 3,000 × £27.50 = £82,500

56

	£
Value transferred 1 March 2004	352,000
Less: AE 2003/04	(3,000)
AE 2002/03	(3,000)
	346,000
Nil rate band remaining 1 March 2004	(255,000)
Taxable	91,000

Tax at $^{20}/_{80}$ = £22,750

Gross chargeable transfer £(346,000 + 22,750) = £368,750

Death tax

	£
Gross chargeable transfer	368,750
Less: Nil rate band at death	(325,000)
	43,750
Tax at 40%	17,500
Less: Taper relief (5 – 6 yrs @ 60%)	(10,500)
	7,000
Less: Lifetime tax paid	(22,750)
	NIL

No refund of lifetime tax paid.

57 (a) *Gift to Rachel*

Joint gift relief election (s.165) by Monique and Rachel, by 5 April 2014

(b) *Gift to trust*

Gift relief election (s.260) by Monique only, by 5 April 2014

(c) *Gift to Kim*

No gift relief available as:

- Not a business asset (no s.165)
- Not an immediate charge to IHT as gift is a PET (no s.260)

58

20 March 1999

	£
CLT	240,000
Less: AE 1998/99, 1997/98	(6,000)
	234,000
Nil rate band available	(223,000)
	11,000

IHT × $^{20}/_{80}$ = £2,750

Gross chargeable transfer = £236,750

1 March 2003

	£
CLT	160,000
Less: AE 2002/03, 2001/02	(6,000)
	154,000
Nil rate band available £(250,000 – 236,750)	(13,250)
	140,750

IHT × $^{20}/_{80}$ = £35,188

Gross chargeable transfer = £189,188

	£
1 October 2009	
CLT	160,000
Less: AE 2009/10, 2008/09	(6,000)
	154,000
Nil rate band available £(325,000 – 189,188)	(135,812)
	18,188

IHT × $^{20}/_{80}$ = £4,547

Gross chargeable transfer = £158,547

59 The gain computed in the normal way may be deferred by a claim for gift relief under s.260 TCGA. A claim is required to be signed by Sam alone, within 4 years of the end of the tax year of the disposal.

The CBA/CA assets restriction does not apply for gift relief claims made under s.260.

	£
Market value of asset at transfer	X
Less: gain held over	(X)
Adjusted cost for trustees	X

60 *David's gift*

		£
Value before (part of 70% holding) £60 × 4,000		240,000
Value after (part of 60% holding) £50 × 3,000		(150,000)
Value transferred		90,000

	£	£
Transfer		90,000
Less: AEs 2 × £3,000		(6,000)
		84,000
NRB	325,000	
GCTs £(400,000 – 6,000)	(394,000)	
		(NIL)
		84,000

Tax at $^{20}/_{80}$ = £21,000

Capital gains tax value (10%)

£15 × 1,000 = £15,000

61 September 2009 Exit charge

	£	£
Initial value of settled property		160,000
Nil rate band	325,000	
Transfers in 7 years before creation	(233,000)	
		(92,000)
		68,000

Notional tax @ 20% = £13,600

Effective tax rate $\frac{13,600}{160,000} \times 100\% = 8.5\%$

Number of quarters since creation = 39

Actual rate $^{39}/_{40}$ × 30% × 8.5% = 2.486%

IHT payable $\frac{2.486}{100 - 2.486} \times £40,000 = £1,020$

62

		£	£
Current value			330,000
Related settlement			75,000
			405,000
NRB at PC		325,000	
Less: GCTs £(109,000 – 6,000)		(103,000)	
Exits		(40,000)	
			(182,000)
			223,000

Tax at 20% = £44,600

Effective rate $\dfrac{44,600}{405,000}$ = 11.01234%

Actual rate 11.01234% × 30% = 3.3037%

Therefore principal charge: £330,000 × 3.3037% = £10,902

63

Exit charge	£
Transfer to trust	400,000
Less: nil rate band (Note)	(325,000)
	75,000

Tax @ 20% = £15,000

Effective rate:

$\dfrac{15,000}{400,000} \times 100 = 3.75\%$

Actual rate:

3.75% × 30% × $^{24}/_{40}$ = 0.675%

Grossed up (trustees paying tax) 0.675/100 – 0.675 × 100 = 0.67958%

Exit charge:

0.67958% × £550,000 = £3,738

Note. The PET to Toby's goddaughter does not use up any of his nil rate band as it is exempt during lifetime.

64 August 2009 Exit charge

	£	£
Initial value of settled property(W)		490,800
Nil rate band	325,000	
Transfers in 7 years before creation £(100,000 – 6,000)	(94,000)	
		(231,000)
		259,800

Notional tax @ 20% = £51,960

Effective tax rate $\dfrac{51,960}{490,800} \times 100\%$ = 10.5868%

Number of quarters since creation = 32

Actual rate $^{32}/_{40}$ × 30% × 10.5868% = 2.5408%

IHT payable 2.5408% × £50,000 = £1,270

Working

Transfer 7/01 £(575,000 – 6,000)	569,000
NRB £(242,000 – 94,000)	(148,000)
Chargeable transfer	£421,000
Tax payable by trustees @ 20%	£84,200
Initial value £(575,000 – 84,200)	£490,800

Trust income tax and CGT

65 An asset leaving a qualifying interest in possession trust, due to the death of a life tenant, is a deemed disposal at market value, but the gain is usually exempt.

However, in this case, a gain was held over on the creation of the trust so the gain that is now chargeable is the lower of:

- Actual gain to the date of death
- Gain held over when the asset was placed in the trust.

This gain can be held over again (under s.260 TCGA 1992) as the assets will enter Joe's death estate as his settled property for IHT purposes.

66

	Non savings £	Dividend £
Income £(35,000 – 3,000)	32,000	
Dividends £9,000 × 100/90		10,000
Less: tax at 20%	(6,400)	
Less: tax at 10%		(1,000)
Net income	25,600	9,000
Less: expenses		(3,600)
Distributable to Stella	25,600	5,400

R185

	Net £	Tax £	Gross £
Non savings	25,600	6,400	32,000
Dividends	5,400	600	6,000
	31,000	7,000	38,000

67 2009/10 income tax computation

	Dividends £	Expenses £
UK dividend income £6,150 – (£360 × 100/90)	5,750	
Income used for expenses £360 × 100/90		400
	5,750	400

	£
Tax 1,000 × 10%	100
4,750 × 32.5%	1,544
400 × 10%	40
	1,684
Less: dividend tax credits £6,150 × 10%	(615)
	1,069

S.497 liability: tax pool

	£
Balance brought forward	NIL
Add in tax liability (less dividend tax credits)	1,069
Distribution £2,000 × 40/60	(1,333)
Additional tax due	(264)

68

	£
Net chargeable gains £(17,500 – 2,000)	15,500
Losses b/fwd	(2,250)
Net gains	13,250
Less: AE $\frac{5,050}{2}$	(2,525)
	10,725

£10,725 × 18% = £1,930

69

	NS £	S £	Dividends £
Rent	850		
BSI £480 × $^{100}/_{80}$		600	
Dividends £900 × $^{100}/_{90}$			1,000
Total income	850	600	1,000

	£
Tax 850 × 20%	170
150 × 20%	30
450 × 40%	180
1,000 × 32.5%	325
Tax liability	705
Less: tax at source dividend tax credits	(100)
	605
BSI tax @ source	(120)
	485

Payable 31 January 2011

Tax pool

	£
Brought forward	NIL
Add: trustees' tax	605
Distribution: £1,500 × $^{40}/_{60}$	(1,000)
Additional tax due	(395)

70

	£	Dividends £	Expenses £
Rental income £(22,000 – 2,000)	20,000		
Dividends		2,000	
Expenses against dividends (£1,800 × $^{100}/_{90}$)		(2,000)	2,000
Expenses against rent £(3,000 – 1,800) × $^{100}/_{80}$	(1,500)		1,500
	18,500	NIL	

	£
Tax 1,000 × 20%	200
17,500 × 40%	7,000
2,000 × 10%	200
1,500 × 20%	300
	7,700
Less: tax credits 2,000 × 10%	(200)
Tax payable	7,500

71 June 1996 disposal

Market value before part disposal = (A + B) = £(30,000 + 5,000) = £35,000

20% × (A + B) = £35,000 × 20% = £7,000

⇒ proceeds of £5,000 are 'small', so reduce the base cost for future disposals

No disposal in June 1996.

February 2010 disposal

	£	£
Proceeds (MV)		45,000
Less: Cost	8,000	
Less: small part disposal proceeds	(5,000)	
		(3,000)
Chargeable gain		42,000
Less: gift relief		(42,000)
		NIL

Base cost of land for trustees

	£
MV	45,000
Less: deferred gain	(42,000)
Cost c/f	3,000

General CGT

72

	Relevant business assets £	Other assets £	Total £
Shoe making business			
Goodwill	700,000		
Factory	100,000		
Warehouse	(50,000)		
Investments		250,000	
SUV Ltd shares	300,000		
	1,050,000	250,000	
Entrepreneurs' relief £1,000,000 × 4/9	(444,444)		
	605,556	250,000	855,556
Less: AE			(10,100)
			845,456

CGT × 18% = £152,182

73
The consideration is less than £20,000 and less than 20% of market value (£38,000). Aggregate proceeds from all sales of land during the year are less than £20,000, so a claim can be made such that no chargeable disposal takes place (before 31 January 2012).

	£
Original cost	30,000
Less: net proceeds of part disposal £(18,000 – 360)	17,640
Allowable expenditure of land retained	12,360

74 (a) No claim to avoid part disposal

	£
Proceeds	19,000
Less: MV 1982 × $\dfrac{A}{A+B}$	(4,933)
£27,000 × $\dfrac{19}{19+85}$	
Chargeable gain	14,067
Less: AE	(10,100)
Taxable gain	3,967

Tax at 18% = £714

(b) Small part disposal of land:

20% × (A + B) = 20% × £(19,000 + 85,000) = £20,800

Therefore 'small'

If a claim is made, under s.242(2) TCGA 1992, no disposal in January 2010.

Cost carried forward of £27,000 is adjusted for the small part disposal proceeds ⇒ additional tax to pay on future disposal

75 Due date 31 January 2011.

Where a disposal of land, the taxpayer can elect to pay CGT by ten equal instalments.

The first instalment is due when the full amount would otherwise be due, ie 31 January 2011.

The unpaid balance accrues interest from this date.

If the recipient disposes of the asset, the balance of tax outstanding becomes payable immediately.

76 1 June 2006 Settlement

	£
Deemed proceeds	155,000
Less: cost	(130,000)
Gain held over	25,000

1 January 2010 Susan's death

	£	£
Disposal at market value		128,000
Less: market value at settlement	155,000	
Gain held over	(25,000)	
		(130,000)
Loss on Susan's death		(2,000)

The loss on the farmhouse is transferred to Tania who may only use the loss against a gain subsequently arising from the future sale of the farmhouse.

77

	£
Insurance proceeds received	130,000
Less: MV 1982 × $\dfrac{A}{A+B}$	(37,143)
£80,000 × $\dfrac{130}{130+150}$	
Chargeable gain	92,857
Less: Losses brought forward	(5,000)
	87,857
Less: AE	(10,100)
Taxable gain	77,757

Capital gains tax liability £77,757 × 18% = £13,996

78 Property

<95% of proceeds were used in restoration, therefore election for a part disposal only to apply to the proceeds not used in restoring the property.

	£
Proceeds £(350,000 − 315,000)	35,000
MV 1982 £120,000 × $\dfrac{35,000}{35,000 + 420,000}$	(9,231)
Enhancement £315,000 × $\dfrac{35,000}{35,000 + 420,000}$	(24,231)
Capital gain	1,538

Base cost of property:

	£
MV 1982	120,000
Enhancement	315,000
Part disposal – cost	(9,231)
Part disposal - enhancement	(24,231)
Proceeds used in restoration	(315,000)
Base cost	86,538

Estates in administration

79 Gail is assessed on the dividend when it is paid out to her.

However since part of the dividend accrued prior to Sonia's death, Gail is entitled to relief under s.669 ITTOIA 2005 for higher rate purposes.

	£
Dividend income (20,000 × 4.5p)	900
Pre death element – taxed twice (10/12 × £900)	750
Average IHT rate = 18%	
£750 × 18% (only liable at the basic rate)	135
Dividend liable to tax at the higher rate £(900 − 135)	765
Gross up @ 100/90	£850
Income tax @ 32.5%	276
Less: Tax credit	(85)
Higher rate tax payable	£191

80 Estate income tax computation

	SI £	Divs £
Interest £160 × 100/80	200	
Dividends £1,800 × 100/90		2,000
Less qualifying loan interest	(200)	(1,050)
	NIL	950
Tax:		
£950 × 10% =		95
Tax liability		95
Less tax credits:		
Taxable dividend £950 × 10%		(95)
Less tax on interest £200 × 20%		(40)
Repayable		40

81

	£
Proceeds	57,000
Probate value	(37,000)
Gain	20,000
Less: annual exempt amount	(10,100)
Taxable gain	9,900
CGT @ 18%	£1,782

82

	NS £	S £
Rental income	28,000	
Interest £4,800 × 100/80		6,000
	28,000	6,000

Tax:

	£
28,000 × 20% =	5,600
6,000 × 20% =	1,200
Tax liability	6,800

Income available for distribution:

	NS £	S £
Gross income	28,000	6,000
Less tax	(5,600)	(1,200)
Less expenses		(320)
	22,400	4,480
Distribution 2008/09 (from NS income first)	(5,000)	
	17,400	4,480

R185

	NSI £	SI £
Net	17,400	4,480
Tax	4,350	1,120
Gross	21,750	5,600

83

	Savings £	Dividends £	Tax due £
Untaxed interest	250		
ISA interest no longer exempt and will have been received net of tax £700 × 100/80	875		
Dividends from Skye Ltd £2,300 × 100/90		2,556	
Taxable	1,125	2,556	

	£
Tax liability	
Savings all at 20%	225
Divs at 10%	256
Total liability	481
Less tax paid	
Interest £875 × 20%	175
Dividends £2,556 × 10%	256
	(431)
Tax payable	50

84 Personal representatives are subject to the normal self assessment rules and therefore:

(1) The 2009/10 estate income tax return would need to be filed with HMRC by 31 October 2010 if filing this in paper format. The deadline is 31 January 2011 if the return is filed online.

(2) The due date for the 2009/10 income tax liability is

31 January 2011.

The implications of the late payment of tax are:

- Interest will accrue from the due date.
- A penalty of 5% will be payable if the tax remains unpaid at 2 March 2011.
- A further 5% will be payable if there is any tax still unpaid at 31 July 2011.
- A further 5% will be payable if there is any tax still unpaid at 31 January 2012.

Module C
Corporation tax

Answers

Module C: Corporation tax

The corporation tax computation

1

	£
Political donation	2,000
Legal expenses	1,500

If the patent royalty is trade related, it is deductable from trade profits. Otherwise it should be added back, and instead treated as a deficit on a non-trading intangible fixed asset.

The allowable element on the hire of the expensive car (lease taken out pre 1.4.09) is as follows:

$$£4,200 \times \frac{£25,000 + £12,000}{2 \times £25,000} = £3,108$$

Therefore the adjustment (add back) is £1,092.

2

6.9.07 – 5.9.08	source of income acquired 6.9.07 ceases 12 months after start
6.9.08 – 8.10.08	trade commences 9.10.08
9.10.08 – 30.11.08	end of period of account
1.12.08 – 30.11.09	end of period of account
1.12.09 – 27.2.10	appointment of liquidator starts new AP
28.2.10 – 27.2.11	cessation of trade in liquidation does not end an AP, so 12 months from start
28.2.11 – 14.3.11	end of liquidation

3

	AIA/FYA	Pool	Special Rate Pool	Allowances
	£	£	£	£
9 m/e 31.03.10				
TWDV b/f		11,500		
Additions: P&M £(35,000 + 3,800)	38,800			
Additions: car (>160 g/km)			18,000	
	38,800	11,500	18,000	
AIA (£50,000 × 9/12)	(37,500)			37,500
	1,300			
FYA @ 40%	(520)			520
	780			
WDA @ 20% × 9/12		(1,725)		1,725
WDA @ 10% × 9/12			(1,350)	1,350
Transfer to pool	(780)	780		
TWDV c/f	NIL	10,555	16,650	41,095

4

	12 months to 31 May 2009 £	4 months to 30 September 2009 £
Trading profit 12:4	93,375	31,125
Less: capital allowances (W)	(28,000)	(29,467)
	65,375	1,658
Chargeable gains	1,480,000	NIL
PCTCT	1,545,375	1,658
Gross dividend	NIL	80,000
Profits for SCR purposes	1,545,375	81,658
Limits		
Upper limit	1,500,000	500,000
SCR	300,000	100,000
Tax:		
£1,545,375 × 28%	432,705	
£1,658 × 21%		348

Working

Capital allowances

	AIA/FYA £	Main pool £	Allowances £
12 m/e 31.05.09			
TWDV b/f		140,000	
WDA @ 20%		(28,000)	28,000
TWDV c/f		112,000	
4 m/e 30.09.09			
Additions	30,000		
AIA (max = £50,000 × 4/12 = £16,667)	(16,667)		16,667
	13,333		
FYA @ 40%	(5,333)		5,333
	8,000		
WDA @ 20% × 4/12		(7,467)	7,467
Transfer to pool	(8,000)	8,000	
TWDV c/f		112,533	
Total allowances			29,467

5

	£
Adjusted trade profits before CAs	4,200,000
Capital allowances:	
AIA: £30,000 × 100% (max AIA = £50,000 × 9/12 = £37,500)	(30,000)
WDA: £157,000 × 20% × 9/12	(23,550)
Trading Income	4,146,450
Gain	150,000
	4,296,450

CT @ 28% = £1,203,006

Each instalment is: $3 \times \dfrac{£1,203,006}{9} = £401,002$

		£
14.10.09		401,002
14.01.10		401,002
14.4.10	Balance	401,002
		1,203,006

6   Each instalment is

$$3 \times \frac{£900,000}{10} = £270,000$$

Payments are due:

	£
14 July 2009	270,000
14 October 2010	270,000
14 January 2010	270,000
14 February 2010 (balance)	90,000

The company should retain its records until the later of :

- Six years from the end of the accounting period
- The date after which enquiries may not be commenced
- The date any enquiry is complete.

HMRC may shorten the period for which records need to be retained.

7
	£
Adjusted trading loss before CAs	(70,000)
CAs:	
Energy saving plant (100% enhanced CAs)	(75,000)
WDA: £200,000 × 20%	(40,000)
Trading loss	(185,000)

Eligible to surrender:

Lower of (a)   Trading loss = £185,000
          (b)   Enhanced CAs = £75,000

          ie £75,000

Tax credit:

Lower of (a)   £75,000 × 19% = £14,250
          (b)   PAYE + NIC = £87,500
          (c)   Upper maximum = £250,000

          ie £14,250

The remaining trading loss of £110,000 (£185,000 – £75,000) is carried forward.

8   Plant and machinery includes all assets used to carry on the business, but will exclude expenditure on the setting, which is deemed to be part of the cost of the building.

The electric train and movable partitions (List C, 23(4) CAA 2001) will both qualify for plant capital allowances.

The expenditure on the false ceiling is likely to be considered part of the building *(Hampton v Fortes Autogrill)*. Under the integral features rules, lighting systems do qualify for allowances at the 10% rate, but there is no indication here that this cost is linked to the installation of lighting. Allowances are unlikely to be available.

Moving walkways qualify for plant and machinery allowances. The 10% rate will apply as this is an 'integral feature'.

9
	£
Trading profit	782,500
Add: Director's remuneration not paid within 9 months of the year end	38,000
Pension contributions not actually paid in the year	7,200
Accrued amount relating to options not yet exercised	15,000
Trading income	842,700

10
	FYA/ECA £	Main pool £	SR pool £	Allowances £
Additions:				
Car 1 & 3		49,000		
Car 2	11,000			
Car 4			18,000	
ECA @ 100%	(11,000)			11,000
WDA: @ 20% × 9/12 (<160 g/km)		(7,350)		7,350
WDA @ 10% × 9/12 (>160 g/km)			(1,350)	1,350
				19,700
	NIL	41,650	16,650	

Note. No ECAs on second hand low emission cars (car 3).

11
	12 months ended 31 March 2010 £	6 months ended 30 September 2010 £
Trading income (12:6)	260,000	130,000
Chargeable gain		28,000
Profit on non-trading loan relationship (accruals basis)	13,500	4,500
	273,500	162,500
Upper limit	£1,500,000	£750,000
Lower limit	£300,000	£150,000
		£
CT @ 21%	57,435	
CT @ 28%		45,500
7/400 (750,000 − 162,500)		(10,281)
		35,219

12 The issue of the subscriber shares do not need to be reported on Form 42 if:
- The initial subscriber shares are acquired at nominal value, and
- No form of security other than shares is acquired, and
- The shares are not acquired by reason of another employment, and
- The shares are acquired by a person who is a director or prospective director.

The issue of 100 shares each to Bob and Maud will not need to be reported to HMRC (before 7 July 2010) using Form 42 if:
- The shares are issued before the start of trade and,
- The shares are acquired by the initial subscriber or a director or a prospective director, and
- The shares are acquired at nominal value, and
- The shares are not acquired by reason of another employment

When Tap Ltd comes within the charge to corporation tax for the first time s.55 Finance Act 2004 requires the company to notify HMRC and to provide prescribed information about the company and its directors by completion of Form CT41G. The form has to be filed within three months of the beginning of the company's first accounting period, ie before 1 December 2009.

13

	£
Political donations not allowable	–
Donations only allowed if small, local charity and benefits the trade	–
Gift to employee on exam success	75
Legal expenses are not trade-related	–
Costs of unsuccessful business rating appeal trade related	175
Loss on sale = capital item	–
Charitable secondment staff costs allowable	450
Pension contributions:	
Prior year now paid allowable	650
Current year accrual unpaid - not allowable	–
Legal fees relate to capital acquisition so not allowable	–
Total allowable trading deduction	1,350

14

	Year ended 31 March 2010 £	7 months ended 31 October 2010 £
Trading profit 12:7	3,000,000	1,750,000
Gain	250,000	
Profit on non-trading loan relationship (12:7)	240,000	140,000
	3,490,000	1,890,000
Upper limit	1,500,000	875,000
CT @ 28%	977,200	529,200

Due dates and amounts:

14.10.10	3/7 × £529,200		226,800
01.01.11		977,200	
14.01.11	3/7 × £529,200		226,800
14.02.11	Balance re 7 m/e 31.10.10		75,600
		977,200	529,200

15

A penalty will not be charged if the taxpayer took reasonable care.

In other cases the penalty is a percentage of the potential lost revenue as a result of the error. The percentage depends on the behaviour giving rise to the error. The penalty can be reduced by disclosure to HMRC.

The maximum penalty percentage where the error is deliberate and concealed is 100%. If the behaviour is not deliberate and there is unprompted disclosure to HMRC, the penalty can be reduced to nil.

16

1 May 2007 – 31 August 2007 (acquires first source of income)

1 September 2007 – 31 August 2008 (commences to trade)

1 September 2008 – 31 December 2008 (balance of long period of account)

1 January 2009 – 31 December 2009 (12 month period of account)

1 January 2010 – 31 August 2010 (entered liquidation)

1 September 2010 – 30 November 2010 (company wound up – cessation is irrelevant if subsequent to the commencing of winding up the company, ie a liquidation)

17   If the return was filed on time, HMRC can enquire at any time up to 12 months from the date of the actual submission.

If the return is filed late, then the deadline extends to the quarter day following the anniversary of the actual filing date.

HMRC can enquire into anything in the tax return, eg claims and elections, loss relief and surrender to group companies.

A company may apply to the Tribunal requesting a direction that a closure notice must be issued by HMRC within a specified period. HMRC must show reasonable grounds for continuing the enquiry or the notice will be issued.

18   The return for the year ended 31 May 2009 should have been filed by 31 May 2010. As the return is late, a £100 penalty will have been automatically charged. As the return has been outstanding for more than 3 months, daily penalties of £10 per day can be imposed for a maximum of 90 days.

If the return is outstanding for more than 6 months, a penalty of 5% of the tax due for the period will be charged, so the return should be filed before 30 November 2009 to avoid this penalty.

The penalty for late payment of corporation tax is 5% of the tax unpaid 30 days after the payment due date of 1 March 2010. If the tax is still unpaid 6 months after the due date an additional 5% penalty will be charged. The tax should be paid by 31 August 2010 to avoid this further 5% penalty. A further 5% penalty applies if the tax still outstanding 12 months after the due date.

HM Revenue & Customs can make a determination of the tax payable to the best of their knowledge and ability. They could then enforce this by legal proceedings including distraint. The determination can only be displaced by Holmes Ltd making a self assessment of its corporation tax liability on its tax return and so the company should be encouraged to submit the return as soon as possible.

Loan relationships, intangibles and R&D

19   The tax treatment of 'new' intangibles, including patent royalties, follows their accounting treatment.

The taxable income in the year ended 31 December 2009 will be:

(£15,960 × 4/12) + (£23,100 × 8/12) = £20,720

This will be taxed as trading income or as a profit on a non-trading intangible fixed asset, after deducting the amortisation of the patent (£120,000 ÷ 15 = £8,000).

The costs of registering the patent should be capitalised and amortised on the same basis (ie a deduction of £200 pa).

20   A trading loan relationship occurs where a company takes out a loan to fund its trading activities.

Tax relief for interest paid will be given by a deduction in arriving at trading income on an accruals basis.

To the extent that this creates a loss, trading loss relief will be allowed, as follows:

(a)   Current year offset vs total profits before charges
(b)   Prior year offset vs total profits before charges (after (a) above)
(c)   Carry forward vs trade profits
(d)   Group relief.

21   Gain of £139,200 (600,000 – 460,800) in Profit and Loss account.

If relief is claimed, £120,000 (£600,000 – £480,000) of this gain can be deducted, leaving £19,200 in trading income.

Cost of the new goodwill is £580,000 (£700,000 – £120,000).

New goodwill is written off at £23,200 pa (£580,000 × 4%).

The loan interest is payable to a connected party resident in a qualifying territory therefore is allowed on the accruals basis, giving a deduction of £100,000 @ 4% × 4/12 = £1,333.

22 Small companies can claim R & D on the costs of:
- Employing staff directly and actively engaged in carrying out R & D, and
- Software + consumable stores including water, fuel and power used for R & D.
- Agency staff
- R&D costs incurred in connection with R&D activity sub-contracted to the small company by a large company
- Payments to subcontractors in connection with R&D carried out on behalf of the small company
- Relevant payments to subjects of clinical trials.

23

	£	£
Trade profits before additional R&D relief		400,000
Less electricity cost not related to R&D (£14,000 × 90%)		(12,600)
Qualifying R&D:		
R&D salaries and NIC	102,000	
Electricity: £14,000 × 10%	1,400	
	103,400	
Relief for qualifying R&D		
£103,400 × 175%		(180,950)
Software (used indirectly for admin purposes, so not eligible for R&D relief)		(26,000)
		180,450

CT @ 21% = £37,895

24 Website design costs and expenditure on software are likely to be treated as an intangible fixed asset. In these circumstances relief is given by following the accounts treatment. For specialist software, if it is for the R&D activity it is potentially eligible for extra R&D relief. Otherwise it is possible to elect for capital allowances treatment to apply.

Researchers' employment costs will be eligible as research and development expenditure, and additional relief at either 75% or 30% will be deductible in arriving at taxable profits depending on the size of the company.

65% of the costs of the agency staff also qualify for R&D relief (or, by election, the actual staff costs paid by the agency may be used).

25 (1) Set against profits of the same accounting period before charges and s 393A loss relief
    (2) Surrender as group relief
    (3) Set against non-trade loan relationship profits of the previous 12 months
    (4) Set against any future non-trading profits of the company

26
- Tax written down value of original goodwill at 1 January 2009 = £100,000 less 2 years @ £15,000 = £70,000.
- Taxable credit before reinvestment relief = £120,000 less £70,000 = £50,000.
- Proceeds not reinvested in qualifying intangible assets = £120,000 less £115,000 = £5,000. Therefore reinvestment relief = £120,000 − £100,000 (excess of proceeds over original cost]) − £5,000 = £15,000.

Therefore Datco Ltd's taxable credit for the year ended 31 December 2009 will be £50,000 less £15,000 = £35,000.

The base cost to be carried forward of the goodwill purchased in March 2010 will be £115,000 − £15,000 = £100,000.

The credits in respect of intangible assets cannot be rolled over into the fixed plant.

The gain on the sale of the plant of £14,300 can be deferred against the fixed plant. The gains will crystallise when the fixed plant is sold, no longer used in the trade, or at a maximum 10 years from 30 June 2009, ie 30 June 2019.

27

		£	£
Accounting profit			1,445,000
Trade related patent royalties are allowable			0
Non-trading royalties (net)			30,000
Leased car (CO_2 emissions >160g/km)			
Amount included in accounting profit = £6,400 × 6/12		3,200	
Disallowed = £3,200 × 15%			480
Theft by director is disallowed			140,000
Tax adjusted trading profit			1,615,480

28 R&D expenditure £500,000

Total relief £500,000 × 175% = £875,000

Surrenderable loss = lower of:

(a) Unrelieved trading loss £100,000 + £875,000 = £975,000
(b) R&D relief = £875,000

Tax credit = lower of:

(a) £875,000 × 14% = £122,500
(b) PAYE + NIC = £345,000

ie £122,500

Surrender £875,000 of loss, carry forward £100,000 balance.

29 Where an intangible fixed asset (IFA) is sold:

- The maximum deferral = proceeds – cost
- Where all of the proceeds are reinvested in a new IFA, the profit is deferred by deducting from the acquisition cost of the new IFA
- Where the proceeds are not fully reinvested, the retained proceeds remain chargeable
- The new IFA must be acquired in the period running from 12 months before the IFA sale to 36 months after
- IFA rollover is available on a group-wide basis within a 75% chargeable gains group.

30 Relief is given for tax purposes in accordance with the accounts treatment.

Trade related IFA income (credits) and expenditure (debits) are taken into account in arriving at trading income.

Non-trade IFA debits and credits are pooled and treated as profits/losses on non-trade intangible fixed assets.

Examples of IFA expenditure include:

- Costs of bringing IFAs into existence
- Losses on disposal
- Royalties payable
- Amortisation.

Capital gains and companies with investment business

31 *Property income*

	£
Rental income: £120,000 × 9/12	90,000
Premium taxed as income: £35,000 − [2% × (20 − 1) × £35,000](Note)	21,700
Less: wear and tear allowance 10% × £90,000	(9,000)
	102,700
Deficit on non-trading loan relationship	
£1,000,000 × 10% × 9/12	75,000

A claim can be made to offset the non-trading loan relationship deficit against the company's other income for the year.

Note: Alternative working: $£35,000 \times \frac{50-19}{50} = £21,700$

32 (1) Treated as non-trading loan relationship deficit. Claims can be made to offset against current year profits, prior year non-trading loan relationship income, or group relieve. Balance is carried forward against non-trading income

(2) Treated as management expenses in the following accounting period

(3) Treated as property income loss

(4) Loss arising may be treated as a capital loss or a claim can be made to offset against income in the current and preceding year.

33 (a) Set off against other income and gains of the same accounting period
(b) Excess management expenses may be group relieved
(c) C/f and treat as management expenses of the following accounting period.

Management expenses may not be carried forward beyond the date of change of ownership of an investment company where:

(a) There is a major change in the nature or conduct of the business
(b) The activities before the change were small but are revived after the changes
(c) There is a significant increase in the investment company's share capital after the change in ownership.

34 (1) Change in ownership and there is a significant increase in the company's share and loan capital, ie the company's share and loan capital is increased by at least £1,000,000, or at least doubled, within three years after the change

(2) There is a major change in the nature or conduct of the company's business within the period of six years commencing three years before the change

(3) The company's business becomes small or negligible, the ownership changes and there is then a considerable revival.

35

	£
Property income: £142,000 + £8,000 (from REIT)	£150,000
Non trading loan relationship:	
Interest received	40,000
Accrued at year end	4,000
	44,000
Interest payable	(233,000)
Deficit on non-trading loan relationship	(189,000)

A claim may be made to set this against the PCTCT of £150,000 and, if made, the surplus of £39,000 will be automatically carried forward against non-trading profit of the next year unless an election is made to the contrary.

Dividends from the tax exempt income of a REIT are taxed as property income. Payments to UK companies are made gross.

36 Under s.23(1) TCGA 1992 compensation is rolled over against the cost of the factory as follows:

	£	£
Sale proceeds		1,000,000
Less allowable cost		
Original cost	210,000	
Restoration cost	115,000	
Less s.23(1) insurance proceeds	(120,000)	(205,000)
Unindexed gain		795,000
Less indexation allowance		
$= 1.033 \times £210,000$ (6/87 – 12/09)	216,930	
$= 0.298 \times £115,000$ (11/97 – 12/09)	34,270	
$= 0.293 \times £(120,000)$ (2/98 – 12/09)	(35,160)	
		(216,040)
		578,960

37

	£	£
Heavens Ltd gain:		
Proceeds		420,000
Cost	180,000	
Less: gain deferred (W)	(74,420)	
		(105,580)
		314,420
Less: IA Jan 2004-March 2010 $\frac{206.2 - 183.1}{183.1}$ (0.126) $\times £105,580$		(13,303)
Chargeable gain		301,117

Working

Deferred gain (January 2004)

	£
Proceeds	175,000
Cost	(94,000)
Less: IA $\frac{183.1 - 171.1}{171.1}$ (0.070) $\times £94,000$	(6,580)
	74,420
Deferred (compensation spent in full)	(74,420)
Gain	NIL

An election can be made to deem the gain (or part thereof) made by Heavens Ltd, to have been made by Good Ltd to use the brought forward capital losses. The election must be made within 2 years of the end of the accounting period in which the gain was made, ie by 31 March 2012.

38 A disposal of shares in one qualifying company by another is a disposal of a substantial shareholding if:

- The investing company has, for at least 12 months out of the 2 years preceding the date of disposal
    - Held not less than 10% of the ordinary share capital
    - Been entitled to not less than 10% of the profits available for distribution, and
    - Been entitled to not less than 10% of the asset on a winding up.

- The investing company must be a trading company or member of a trading group throughout the qualifying period.

- The investee company must be a trading company or holding company of a trading group throughout the qualifying period.

- Investment activities up to 20% may be disregarded for the purposes of the trading company definition.

39 Limits:

PCTCT: £125,000 + £150,000	£275,000
Profits: £275,000 + (£8,000 × 10/9)	£283,889
£300,000/2 × (9/12)	£112,500
£1,500,000/2 × (9/12)	£562,500

∴ marginal relief applies

	£
PCTCT at full rate = £275,000 × 28%	77,000
Less marginal relief =	
(7/400) × (£562,500 − £283,889) × (£275,000/£283,889)	(4,723)
Corporation tax payable	72,277

As the proceeds are received over a period of more than 18 months, the tax can be paid on the gain by instalments as received.

Tax on gain = $\dfrac{£150,000}{£275,000} \times £72,277 = £39,424$

Payments made by normal due date of 1.1.11:

	£
20.1.10	90,000
30.6.10	180,000
	270,000
Due on 1.1.11 $\dfrac{270,000}{450,000} \times £39,424$	23,654
Balance of tax £72,277 − 39,424	32,853
	56,507
Due on 20.1.11 $\dfrac{90,000}{450,000} \times £39,424$	7,885
Due on 31.08.12 $\dfrac{90,000}{450,000} \times £39,424$	7,885
	72,277

40 Hagan Ltd – Property income

	£
Property income re premium received	
£30,000 − [2% × (10 − 1) × £30,000] or (£30,000 × $\dfrac{50-9}{50}$)	24,600
Property income re premium paid	
£40,000 − [2% × (30 − 1) × £40,000] or (£40,000 × $\dfrac{50-29}{50}$) × 10/30	(5,600)
	19,000
Rental income (£10,000 × 6/12)	5,000
Less: expenses	(120)
Total property income	23,880

41

	Cost £	MV82 £
Proceeds	550,000	550,000
Legal fees on sale	(5,000)	(5,000)
	545,000	545,000
Less: Cost	(120,000)	
Enhancement 1981	(12,000)	
MV82		(140,000)
Enhancement 1985	(19,500)	(19,500)
	393,500	385,500

Less: IA

$$\frac{208.3 - 79.44}{79.44} \ (1.622) \times £140,000 \qquad (227,080) \quad (227,080)$$

$$\frac{208.3 - 95.49}{95.49} \ (1.181) \times £19,500 \qquad (23,029) \quad (23,029)$$

	143,391	135,391
Use MV82, as lower		
Capital loss b/f		(15,750)
Net gain		119,641

42 September 2001: (a) Proceeds £18,000 < £20,000

(b) $\dfrac{18,000}{18,000 + 75,000} = 19.4\%$

Small part disposal of land, no gain in 2001, deduct proceeds from base cost carried forward.

January 2010

	£	£
Proceeds		190,000
Cost (August 1988)	50,000	
Less: small part disposal proceeds (Sept 2001)	(18,000)	
		(32,000)

Less: IA
August 1988 to Jan 2010

$$\frac{206.8 - 107.9}{107.9} \ (0.917) \times £50,000 \qquad\qquad 45,850$$

Sept 2001 to Jan 2010

$$\frac{206.8 - 174.6}{174.6} \ (0.184) \times £18,000 \qquad\qquad (3,312)$$

		(42,538)
		115,462

Single company losses

43

	£
Trading income (W)	1,307,312
Less: trading loss b/f	(80,000)
	1,227,312
Capital gain (£20,000 − £(20,000) b/f)	–
PCTCT	1,227,312
FII (£27,000 × 100/90)	30,000
'Profits'	1,257,212

Upper Limit £1,500,000 × 10/12 = £1,250,000

£1,227,312 × 28% = £343,647

WORKING

Capital allowances for 10 months ending 31 March 2010

	AIA/FYA £	Main pool £	SR pool £	Allowances £
TWDV b/f		50,000		
Additions:				
Air conditioning	35,000			
Insulation	6,667		1,333	
	41,667	50,000		
AIA (£50,000 × 10/12)	(41,667)			41,667
P&M	12,000			
FYA @ 40%	(4,800)			4,800
	7,200			
WDA @ 10% × 10/12			(111)	111
WDA @ 20% × 10/12		(8,333)		8,333
Transfer to pool	(7,200)	7,200		
TWDV c/f	NIL	48,867	1,222	54,911

Trading Income:	
Trading profits before CAs	1,362,223
CAs	(54,911)
	1,307,312

Note. Thermal insulation of an office building qualifies for a 10% WDA.

44

	2007 £	2008 £	31 March 2009 £	2010 £
Trading income	100,000	60,000	NIL	160,000
Profit on non-trading loan relationship	10,000	10,000	10,000	10,000
Capital gains		15,000	NIL	NIL
Property income		12,000	13,000	NIL
Total profits	110,000	97,000	23,000	170,000
Property Income loss	NIL	NIL	NIL	(7,000)
	110,000	97,000	23,000	163,000

The remaining capital loss is carried forward (£12,000 – £9,000 = £3,000). Property income losses are automatically offset against total profits for the accounting period.

The options for relieving the trade loss of £150,000 are as follows:

		£
(1)	s.393A y/e 31.03.09 (CY)	23,000
	s.393A y/e 31.03.08 (CB)	97,000
	s.393A (extended CB loss relief) y/e 31.03.07	30,000
		150,000
(2)	s.393A y/e 31.03.09 (CY)	23,000
	s.393(1) y/e 31.03.10 (CF)	127,000
		150,000
(3)	s.393(1) y/e 31.03.10 (CF)	150,000

45

	Year ended 31 March	
	2010 £	2011 £
Trading income	NIL	320,000
Less: trade loss c/fwd		(100,000)
		220,000
Property income	NIL	5,000
Profit on a non-trading intangible fixed asset	95,000	40,000
Profit on non-trading loan relationship		8,000
Chargeable gains (net of b/f losses)	NIL	10,000
Deficit on non-trading LR c/fwd vs non-trade income		(25,000)
Total profits	95,000	258,000
Property income loss CY offset	(80,000)	
Deficit on non-trading LR – CY claim	(5,000)	
Gift aid	(10,000)	(10,000)
	NIL	248,000

46

	Year ended 30 June 2009 £	Six months ended 31 December 2009 £	Year ended 31 December 2010 £
Trading income	60,000	20,000	–
Chargeable gains £(20,000 – 15,000)	NIL	NIL	5,000
Profit on non-trading loan relationships	10,000	10,000	10,000
	70,000	30,000	15,000
Less: s.393A	(35,000)	(30,000)	(15,000)
Gift Aid	(5,000)	–	–
PCTCT	30,000	–	–

Trade loss to c/f £20,000 – offset vs trading income of y/e 31.12.11 (120,000 – 20,000 = £100,000)

Loss memo	£
Loss	100,000
s.393A – CY	(15,000)
	85,000
s.393A – PY	
6 m/e 31.12.09	(30,000)
y/e 30.6.09	
£70,000 × 6/12	(35,000)
C/fwd	£20,000

The gift aid payments are deducted from total profits. Unrelieved gift aid payments are wasted, as there is no scope for group relief.

The capital loss is offset against the capital gain in 2010.

47

	£
Option 1	
y/e 31.3.09 (wastes gift aid of £4,000)	4,000
y/e 31.3.08 (wastes gift aid of £11,250)	54,000
y/e 31.3.07 Max £50,000	50,000
y/e 31.3.10	92,000
	200,000
Option 2	
y/e 31.3.09 (wastes gift aid of £4,000)	4,000
y/e 31.3.10	196,000
	200,000
Option 3	
y/e 31/3/10	200,000

The gift aid payments are deducted from total profits. Unrelieved gift aid payments are wasted, as there is no scope for group relief.

The capital loss is offset against the capital gain in 2010.

48 *Loss relief*

Loss of last 12 months carried back 36 months before the beginning of the accounting period of the loss, ie from the start of the loss period, not just the start of the final 12 months, therefore can carry back to 1.1.06.

Loss of y/e 31.12.09 falling within last 12 months £(75,000) carried back LIFO to y/e 31.12.06.

Non terminal loss – other £25,000 of y/e 31.12.09 carried back 12 months to y/e 31.12.08 after current year relief. This relief is claimed first to avoid losing the relief.

	2006 £	Year ended 31 December 2007 £	2008 £	2009 £	3 months ended 31 March 2010 £
Available profit	120,000	27,000	30,000	10,000	3,500
Less: non terminal loss £25,000			(15,000)	(10,000)	
Less: terminal loss £75,000	(33,000)	(27,000)	(15,000)		
PCTCT	87,000	NIL	NIL	NIL	3,500

No relief is possible in respect of the capital loss arising in 3 m/e 31.3.10.

49 **Lago Ltd**

Corporation Tax computation

9 months ended 31 December 2009

	£	£
Trading income £(180,000 – 9,000)		171,000
Profit on non-trading loan relationship	15,000	
Gain £(45,000 – 40,000)	5,000	
	20,000	
Deficit on non-trading loan relationship b/f	(20,000)	NIL
Gift aid		(7,000)
PCTCT		164,000
PCTCT		164,000
FII (£22,500 × 100/90)		25,000
Profits		189,000
Upper limit (× 9/12)		1,125,000
Lower limit (× 9/12)		225,000
PCTCT @ 21%		34,440

50

	Current year	Carry-back	Carry-forward	Group relief
Non-trading loan relationships	Total profits	12m vs non-trading loan relationship income	vs non-trade income	in full
Non-trading intangible fixed assets	Total profits	not available	vs future non-trading intangible fixed asset income	excess only

51 **Lggle Ltd**

Corporation tax computation

Year ended 31 December 2009

	£	£
Trading income	30,000	
Loss brought forward	(30,000)	
		–
Property income	20,000	
Deficit on non-trading loan relationship	(17,000)	
		3,000
Gift Aid payment		(3,000)
Profits chargeable to Corporation Tax		–
CT liability		NIL

Unrelieved amounts carried forward at 31 December 2009:

	£
Trading loss	5,000
Deficit on non-trading loan relationship	1,000

Election made to carry forward the non-trading deficit against non-trading profits of a succeeding accounting period. This claim can be made for all or any part of the deficit (*s.458 CTA 2009*).

52

	Year ended 30 June 2007 £	Year ended 30 June 2008 £	2009 £	6 months ended 31 December 2009 £	Year ended 31 December 2010 £
Trading income	265,000	290,000	NIL	NIL	150,000
Trade loss c/f					(63,667)
Property income	36,000	36,000	36,000	18,000	36,000
Total profits	301,000	326,000	36,000	18,000	122,333
CY loss relief			(36,000)	(18,000)	
PY loss relief		(177,333)			
		(25,000)			
PCTCT	301,000	123,667	NIL	NIL	122,333

	£
Loss allocations:	
12 m/e 30.6.09: £320,000 × 12/18	213,333
Current year vs total profits	(36,000)
	177,333
Carry back vs total profits of y/e 30.6.08	(177,333)
	NIL
6 m/e 31.12.09: £320,000 × 6/18	106,667
Current yr vs total profits	(18,000)
	88,667
Carry back vs y/e 30.6.09	NIL
Vs y/e 30.6.08 (extended carry back claim – maximum £50,000 × 6/12)	(25,000)
	63,667
Vs y/e 30.6.07	
Carry forward vs trade profits	(63,667)
	NIL

53

	Year ended 30 June 2007 £	Period ended 31 December 2007 £	Year ended 31 December 2008 £	Year ended 31 December 2009 £	Year ended 31 December 2010 £
Trading income	52,000	NIL	80,000	NIL	15,000
Less: trade loss b/f			(40,000)		(15,000)
Gains (Note)	NIL	NIL	NIL	NIL	8,000
Profit on non-trade LR	NIL	10,000	10,000	NIL	40,000
Total profits	52,000	10,000	50,000	NIL	48,000
CYR loss relief		(10,000)		NIL	
PYR loss relief	(52,000)		(45,000)		
PCTCT	NIL	NIL	5,000	NIL	48,000

Note. Capital losses carried forward without restriction against capital gains.

Loss relief

	£
P/e 31.12.07 Trade loss	120,000
CY relief	(10,000)
PY relief	(52,000)
	58,000

Carried forward: max = 6/12 × £80,000 as change in ownership on 1 July 2008 and major change in conduct of trade

	(40,000)
	18,000
y/e 31.12.09 Trade loss	70,000
CY relief	NIL
PY relief: max = 6/12 × £90,000 as change in ownership	(45,000)
C/f vs trade profits y/e 31.12.10	(15,000)
C/f	10,000

Groups of companies

54 Amount surrendered:

	£
Trading loss	100,000
Excess property income loss £(50,000 – 20,000)	30,000
	130,000
Restricted to available profit of E Ltd (assumes all current year claims are made) £(140,000 – 25,000 – 27,000)	88,000

55 *1 June 2006*
No gain no loss transfer

1 March 2010
Sale of J Ltd
1 June 2006 transfer becomes chargeable

	£
Proceeds (MV)	250,000
Less cost	(80,000)
	170,000

Less IA

$£80,000 \times \dfrac{198.5 - 165.2}{165.2} = 0.202$ (16,160)

	153,840

Gain chargeable on J Ltd in y/e 31.03.10
Gain on sale of shares:

	£
Proceeds	35,000,000
Less: cost	(500,000)
IA: $\dfrac{206.2 - 149.8}{149.8} \times £500,000$	(188,251)
Chargeable gain	34,311,749

Gain is not exempt as trading company requirements are not met.

56 Ring Ltd will only be able to carry forward its capital losses of £26,000 and relieve them against its own future capital gains.

Ring Ltd's losses will be ring fenced which will prevent it from relieving gains realised after joining the group.

Bull Ltd will therefore not be able to set the losses against the gain on its property.

These rules will also apply to the loss arising on the asset acquired in 2002, even if it is sold after Ring Ltd joins the group.

The trading losses are likely to be restricted as it appears there has been a major change in Ring Ltd's trade. These losses will not be available to carry forward beyond the change of ownership.

57

Maximum surrender
Lower of:
Cat Ltd's available loss
£150,000 × 6/9   £100,000
Dog Ltd's available profits
£970,000 × 6/12   £485,000
ie £100,000

Optimum surrender based on small companies' limits for 2 associated companies:

Dog Ltd	£1,500,000 × $^1/_2$	£750,000
	£300,000 × $^1/_2$	£150,000
Cat Ltd	£1,500,000 × $^1/_2$ × 9/12	£562,500
	£300,000 × $^1/_2$ × 9/12	£112,500

Reduce Cat Ltd's profits to £112,500, so use £87,500 of loss, and surrender the balance of £62,500 to Dog Ltd.

The deficit on the non-trading loan relationship should be carried back and offset against the non-trading loan relationship income in Dog Ltd in the previous 12 months. This saves tax at the marginal rate of 29.75%.

58 *January 2006*

Transfer to B Ltd is at no gain/no loss.

April 2009

The loss arising in C Ltd is as follows:

	£
Proceeds	320,000
Cost	(370,000)
	(50,000)

A proportion of the loss is pre-entry and can only be used in C Ltd, not against gains in A Ltd:

£50,000 × 2/5 = £20,000

An election to recalculate the pre-entry loss as if it were based on market value when C Ltd joins the group would give a capital loss of £355,000 – £370,000 = £15,000, so would be beneficial.

December 2009

A de-grouping loss of £180,000 (£220,000 – £400,000) arises in B Ltd in the year ended 31 March 2010.

B Ltd may jointly claim with A Ltd or C Ltd to have the de-grouping loss attributed to A Ltd or C Ltd.

59 A trading loss can be carried back only to accounting periods in which the loss making trade was carried on.

S.768A applies where there is a change in ownership of the company, preventing the carry back of losses under s.393A. In this case there has been a major change in the nature or conduct of the trade within a three year period including a change of ownership.

The losses can be carried forward against first available trading profits of Inspace Ltd in the future.

Following the sale of the 28% on 1 September 2009, losses can be group relieved to Snuggle Ltd.

60 Ivy plc sale to Fern Ltd: This is a no gain/no loss transfer

Fern Ltd transfer to Leaf Ltd: This is a disposal outside the 75% group

	£
Market value of transfer	205,000
Less cost to Ivy plc	(100,000)
Gain to Fern Ltd	105,000

When Fern Ltd is sold, a gain of £2.8m arises. Assuming all companies are trading companies, this should be exempt under the substantial shareholding exemption.

61 (a) All companies are associated except Chapeau SARL, which is excluded as it is dormant.

(b) Hat Ltd, Gloves Ltd and Scarf Ltd are included in the chargeable gains group. Non resident companies are not included except where they carry on activities which are chargeable to UK corporation tax.

(c) Hat Ltd, Gloves Ltd and Scarf Ltd are in a group relief group.

Scarf Ltd and Maillot SA may also be separately grouped, as EU companies may now be included. However, as the losses in Maillot SA can be used locally, they are ineligible for group relief.

62

	Hound	Fox
	£	£
Trade profit before CAs	320,000	90,000
Less: CAs (W)	(85,000)	(21,500)
Trading Income	235,000	68,500
Chargeable gain (note)	NIL	60,000
PCTCT	235,000	128,500

Note: Gain transferred to Fox as Fox pays tax @ 21%.

Workings

CAs: Hound Ltd, y/e 31.3.10

	AIA/FYA	Main pool	SR pool	Allowances
	£	£	£	£
TWDV b/f		150,000		
Additions:				
Integral features	50,000		10,000	
AIA @ 100%	(50,000)			50,000
P&M	20,000			
FYA @ 40%	(8,000)			8,000
	12,000			
WDA @ 20%		(30,000)		30,000
WDA @ 10%			(1,000)	1,000
Transfer to pool	(12,000)	(12,000)		
TWDV c/f	NIL	108,000	9,000	89,000

CAs: Fox Ltd, y/e 31.3.10

	AIA/FYA	Main pool	SR pool	Allowances
	£	£	£	£
TWDV b/f		40,000		
Additions	30,000		75,000	
FYA @ 40%	(12,000)			12,000
	18,000			
WDA @ 20%/10%		(8,000)	(7,500)	15,500
Transfer to pool	(18,000)	18,000		
TWDV c/f		50,000	67,500	27,500

Note. One AIA per group. Allocated to Hound as that company pays tax at the highest marginal rate.

63

	£
Property income loss	200,000
Hawk Ltd y/e 31.3.09	(40,000)
Falcon Ltd y/e 31.3.09 (note)	(80,000)
Hawk Ltd y/e 31.3.10	(80,000)
Property income loss c/f	NIL

Note. The gain of £85,000 in 2003 was deferred in part due to the acquisition of the fixed plant. As £25,000 of proceeds were not reinvested, the frozen gain is £60,000 (£85,000 – £25,000).

The gain becomes chargeable when Falcon Ltd ceases to use the asset in its trade, bringing PCTCT to a total of £80,000.

64 Limits

£1,500,000 ÷ 2 = £750,000
£300,000 ÷ 2 = £150,000

Loss relief options:

		£
1	Carry forward	
	Saves £70,000 × 28%	19,600
2	Group relieve to Circle Ltd in full	
	Saves £35,000 × 29.75%	10,413
	Saves £35,000 × 21%	7,350
		17,763
3	Group relieve to Circle Ltd to SCR, carry forward balance	
	Saves £35,000 × 29.75%	10,413
	Saves £35,000 × 28%	9,800
		20,213
4	Current year claim, carry back balance	
	Saves £5,000 × 21%	1,050
	Saves £65,000 × 32.5%	21,125
		22,175
5	Group relieve to Circle Ltd to SCR, current year claim, carry back balance	
	Saves £35,000 × 29.75%	10,413
	Saves £5,000 × 21%	1,050
	Saves £30,000 × 32.5%	9,750
		21,213

Option 4 is the best option.

65 Land Ltd

	9 months ended 31 December 2009 £
Non-trading credits	(175,000)
Non-trading debits	25,000
Non-trading deficit	(150,000)

Note. This non-trading deficit does not need to be set off against Land Ltd's rental income for the current or future periods if Land Ltd does not wish this.

Path Ltd was a member of the group from July 2009 to 31 December 2009 (6 months) therefore the maximum group relief is the lower of:

6/9 × £150,000 = £100,000
6/12 × £210,000 = £105,000

Therefore £100,000.

The balance of the loss will be carried forward and automatically offset against future non-trading income.

66

	£
Proceeds	24,000
Cost £570,000 × $\frac{24,000}{24,000 + 48,000}$	(190,000)
Capital loss	(166,000)

- A joint election may be made to transfer the loss to another group member.
- ie to Pink Ltd, Rose Ltd, Yellow Ltd or Lemon Ltd.
- Any amount of the loss up to £166,000.
- Election by 31 March 2013.

67 Walsall Ltd is not in the loss group as Footy plc has an effective holding of 64%, which is less than 75%. Hence Walsall Ltd cannot accept any of the losses.

Crewe Inc. is resident outside of the EEA with no permanent establishment in the UK, therefore it cannot claim any UK losses.

Losses arising in Elton Ltd can be surrendered to Footy plc in the year ended 31 December 2009 up to a maximum of the lower of:

- The trading loss of Elton Ltd, and
- The available profits of Footy plc.

The losses in Elton Ltd can also be surrendered to Brangy Ltd in its years ended 31 March 2009 and 2010, up to a maximum of:

To year ended 31 March 2010, the lower of:

- 3/12 × trading loss of Elton Ltd, and
- 3/12 × available profits of Footy plc

To year ended 31 March 2009, the lower of:

- 9/12 × trading loss of Elton Ltd, and
- 9/12 × available profits of Footy plc.

68 Lily Ltd owns at least 75% of Maxi Ltd so the companies are in the same capital gains group.

This means that an asset is deemed to be transferred at a value which produces neither a gain nor a loss for Lily Ltd.

If Lily Ltd sells 10% of its shareholding in Maxi Ltd within 6 years of the date of the transfer, then Maxi Ltd will no longer be part of the capital gains group (since the holding will have fallen below 75%) and a gain will arise in Maxi Ltd on the first day of the accounting period in which it leaves the group.

The calculation of the gain will be based on a notional disposal of the asset at market value at the time of the original no gain/ no loss transfer.

A gain will arise in connection with the disposal of shares. The substantial shareholding exemption appears to apply, so this gain will be exempt.

If Lily Ltd owns 70% of Maxi Ltd, the companies will no longer be in the same capital gains group, but they will still be connected parties since Lily Ltd will still control Maxi Ltd. This would mean that the consideration for any assets transferred will be deemed to be at market value regardless of the amount actually paid.

If a capital loss arises, this can only be offset against capital gains arising on other disposals to Maxi Ltd (whilst Lily Ltd and Maxi Ltd are still connected).

69 E Ltd may surrender losses to either D Ltd or F Ltd. To be in a loss group a company must have a direct holding of at least 75% and an effective interest of at least 75%. There are thus three separate losses groups: D Ltd and E Ltd; E Ltd and F Ltd; and F Ltd and G Ltd.

F Ltd may transfer assets at no gain/ no loss to D Ltd and E Ltd. A gains group is formed where all direct holdings are at least 75% and effective interests are > 50%. A company may only be in one gains group at a time, ie F Ltd and G Ltd cannot form a second gains group.

Replacement of business asset relief is available on a group wide basis for D, E and F. G Ltd is not in a group and not carrying on a trade, so rollover relief is not available for G Ltd.

70 Veg plc is the principal company of the capital gains group. The other group members are Asparagus Ltd, Broccoli Ltd, Carrot Ltd and Swede Ltd since these are "75% subsidiaries" and indirect holdings by Veg plc are more than 50%. Turnip Ltd is not in the group as the indirect shareholding is not more than 50% (80% × 80% × 75% = 48%). None of the Turnip Ltd loss can be utilised.

The brought forward capital loss of £3,000 in Asparagus Ltd is automatically offset against the gain in Asparagus Ltd, so a gain equivalent to at least £3,000 should remain in that company.

Asparagus Ltd can elect to treat part of the gain as made by Carrot Ltd. £11,000 of the gain should be relieved in Carrot Ltd so that this gain and Carrot's £11,000 loss can be offset. The taxable gain in Asparagus Ltd is therefore reduced to £35,000 £(46,000 − 11,000). The tax on the gain is therefore £7,350 (£35,000 × 21%).

The loss in Broccoli Ltd cannot be offset against the gain in Asparagus Ltd since Broccoli Ltd was not a member of the group when either of these two disposals made.

71 Dee plc

A degrouping charge will arise:

- When Gregory Ltd leaves the 75% group on 1 November 2009
- As this is within 6 years of the no gain no loss transfer and the asset is still owned by Gregory Ltd
- The degrouping charge will be £270,000 (£400,000 − £130,000)
- And it will be assessed as if arising in the accounting period ending 31 December 2009.

The degrouping charge can be allocated to Dee plc or to Evans Ltd. A joint election would be required within 2 years of the end of the accounting period in which Gregory Ltd leaves the group, ie 31 December 2011 (TCGA 1992 s.179A).

Degrouping charges are also eligible for business assets rollover relief provided the property was used for trade purposes by Gregory Ltd and Evans Ltd (TCGA 1992 s.179B).

Personal service companies and overseas aspects

72 (a) Associated companies include overseas and investment companies but exclude dormant companies.

Aster plc, Snake Ltd, Gunter Inc and Croc Ltd must be taken into account.

(b) Croc Ltd is controlled from the UK (indirect control is sufficient), resident overseas and subject to a lower level of tax. Croc Ltd is a CFC.

73

		£	£
Trading Income			1,220,000
Overseas property income			
Net:		45,000	
Add: withholding tax @ 10/90 × £45,000		5,000	
			50,000
PCTCT			1,270,000
FII £(16,200+15,000) × 100/90			34,667
			1,304,667
Limits: £1,500,000 × 10/12 ÷ 2 = £625,000			
£300,000 × 10/12 ÷ 2 = £125,000			
CT @ 28% × £1,270,000			355,600
DTR @ lower of (a) £50,000 × 28% = £14,000			
(b) £50,000 × 10% = £5,000, ie			(5,000)
			350,600

74 All companies under common control at any point in the year are associated unless they are dormant (ie Mouse Ltd). Overseas companies are included.

There are therefore four associates and the upper and lower limits are therefore £75,000 and £375,000 respectively. Large company rate applies.

Door plc must also self assess for any transfer pricing advantage:

	£
Standard sales price:	
Cost	30,000
Mark up @ 20%	6,000
	36,000
Sales price to Hinge	(33,000)
Transfer pricing adjustment	3,000
PCTCT	712,000
Revised PCTCT	715,000
£715,000 × 28%	£200,200

75 (a) It is likely that the entire income in Milne Ltd will be caught by the personal service company rules, because amongst other indicators it appears:

(i) There is no right of substitution
(ii) Mr Milne appears to be integrated into the company's organisation
(iii) Mr Milne does not provide his own equipment.

A deemed employment payment should be calculated.

(b) The deemed employment payment is treated as paid to Mr Milne on 5 April. Hence the deemed payment (and related NI contributions) on 5 April 2010 will be a deduction in Milne Ltd's accounting period to 31 March 2011. As the company's profits are steadily rising, there will be profits chargeable to corporation tax each year which would not otherwise have arisen due to the deduction for the deemed payment. A more appropriate accounting date would be 5 April.

(c) Where dividends are paid by Milne Ltd out of profits that are treated as a deemed employment payment, Milne Ltd can claim to set the deemed payment against the dividend in order to reduce the amount of the taxable dividend.

76 Jack – Yes

Jack holds at least 5% of the intermediary. The intermediary and client are not associated for this purpose as they are not both under the worker's control (s.51 ITEPA 2003).

Harry – Yes

Harry together with his associates is entitled to at least 60% of the profits of the partnership (s.52 ITEPA 2003).

Further information would be required to determine whether or not, in the absence of the intermediary, the workers would be treated as employees of the respective clients.

77 Quasar Ltd – Year ended 31 March 2010

	£
Trading income	1,000,000
Less: losses brought forward	(90,000)
Gain £(50,000 – 60,000)	NIL
Overseas property income (£5,600 × 100/90)	8,000
Property income – from REIT	9,000
PCTCT	927,000
PCTCT	927,000
FII (£14,000 × 100/90)	15,556
Profits	942,556

	£
Corporation tax:	
£927,000 × 28%	259,560
Less DTR on overseas property income at lower of:	
(a) £8,000 × 30% (overseas tax) = £2,400	
(b) £8,000 × 28% (UK tax) = £2,240	
ie	(2,240)
CT	257,320

78 A company is a managed service company if (s.61B ITEPA 2003):

- Its business is wholly/mainly providing services of an individual to other persons
- Payments are made to the individual equal to all or most of the payment received for the services
- The after tax amount received by the individual is higher than it would be if the payments were treated as employment income.

If a company is a managed service company, an amount of deemed employment income must be calculated, and taxed on the employee.

79 The exceptions are:

- Where chargeable profits do not exceed £50,000 per year
- Companies in jurisdictions on the excluded countries list
- Where the company pays 90% of its income profits up by dividend within 18 months of the end of the accounting period
- Where the company carries on exempt activities
- Where the motive of setting up overseas was not to avoid UK taxation.

80 The following information should be included in an APA expression of interest (SP3/99):

- Nature, value of transfer pricing issues and parties involved
- Description of the parties' business activities
- Proposed transfer pricing method
- Details of current transfer pricing enquiries, or other APAs
- Whether a unilateral or bilateral APA is required.

81 Assuming that the UK assets are in use in a UK trade, there is an exit charge arising based on market value at migration on overseas assets only as follows.

	o/s trading assets £	o/s investment assets £
MV 1.7.09	420,000	500,000
Cost	(190,000)	(310,000)
	230,000	190,000

A joint election can be made by Coldon Ltd and Aphos Ltd to defer the £230,000 only, until the following:

- Coldon Ltd sells the trading assets within 6 years of migration
- Coldon Ltd ceases to be a 75% subsidiary of Aphos Ltd
- Aphos Ltd becomes non-UK resident.

82 Overseas incorporated companies which are managed and controlled from the UK are treated as UK resident. These companies are chargeable to UK corporation tax on their worldwide income and gains.

Overseas incorporated companies which are managed and controlled from outside the UK are subject to UK corporation tax on any income arising from a UK permanent establishment ('PE').

These companies are chargeable on (s.19 CTA 2009).

- Trading income arising directly or indirectly through or from the PE
- Gains on assets used for the UK PE's trade

83   An engagement is likely to be a relevant engagement if (any five of):
- The individual has to do the work themselves
- The individual is told where, when and how to do the work
- The individual works set hours
- The individual uses equipment provided by the client
- The individual works mainly or exclusively for one client
- The individual bears little or no financial risk
- The individual is integrated into the organisation
- The individual has no opportunity to profit by organising their work effectively.

84 (a) Utopia Ltd is:
   (i)   Overseas resident
   (ii) Controlled from the UK
   (iii) Not subject to a lower level of taxation as the company would pay tax at 21% if UK resident, so not a CFC.

   (b) Utopia Ltd would now pay tax at 28%, so the 20% rate is 71% of the UK rate. As this is less than 75%, Utopia Ltd is a CFC.

85 (a) Potential adjustment = £250,000 increase in profits for A Ltd, based on third party sales price to Purple Ltd.

   (b) Transfer pricing adjustments will not be required if the Alphabet group is a small enterprise. No adjustments are required if the Alphabet group is a medium sized enterprise, unless HMRC issue a transfer pricing notice.

   (c) B Ltd can make a claim to correspondingly reduce their profits in respect of the adjustment. B Ltd must claim within two years of the date of submission of A Ltd's return.

Module D
Taxation of individuals

Answers

Module D: Taxation of individuals

The income tax computation and property income

1   Relief is given for the loan interest for up to three years after the end of the tax year in which the loan was granted.

Interest paid in the years 2009/10 up to and including 2012/13 will be deductible from total income.

2

	Non savings £	Savings £	Dividends £
Income	36,000	2,000	11,100
PA	(6,475)		
	29,525	2,000	11,100

		£
Tax	29,525 × 20%	5,905
	2,000 × 20%	400
	5,875 × 10%	587
	5,225 × 32.5%	1,698
IT liability		8,590

3   They are taxed as single people from the date of separation.

Stephen will receive a full MCAA in the tax year of separation.

Half or all of the £2,670 minimum amount may be transferred to Jane.

4

	£
Premium	50,000
Less: £50,000 × 2% × (10 – 1)	(9,000)
(or £50,000 × 50 – 9/50)	41,000
Less allowance for premium paid (20,000 – (20,000 × 2% × (30 – 1))) × $^{10}/_{30}$	(2,800)
(or £20,000 × 50 – 29/50 × $^{10}/_{30}$)	
	38,200

5   The income is taxable as property income. However, rent-a-room relief may be available.

If gross rental income is not more than £4,250 per tax year:

- Ignore both income and expenses relating to the letting and no property income assessment arises.
- There will similarly be no loss unless the taxpayer elects to set aside the exemption for the year, so claiming to use the loss instead.

If gross rental income is more than £4,250 per tax year:

- A normal property income assessment arises, or
- The taxpayer can elect instead to be taxed on gross rental receipts in excess of £4,250 (so ignoring any expenses incurred).

6   Tom is deemed to have made a gift aid donation of £312 net of basic rate income tax assuming that he signed the necessary gift aid declaration regarding his own position as a taxpayer. The charity reclaims the tax deducted at source of £312 × $^{20}/_{80}$ = £78. Donations from 6 April 2008 to 5 April 2011 are eligible for transitional relief. An extra 3p per £1 donated is given to the charity by HMRC.

Tom is given tax relief at the higher rate of 40% by entering the payment on his 2010 Tax Return. Relief is given by extending the basic rate band by the gross payment. He may claim relief in the year 2009/10 or he may claim to carry it back for relief in 2008/09.

7

	Non savings £	Savings £
State pension	4,720	
Pension from deceased husband's former employer	13,430	
Building society interest × $^{100}/_{80}$		6,550
Less age allowance £(9,640 – 900)	(8,740)	
(Abatement: ½ × £(24,700 – 22,900) = £900 and use 75 + rate)		
Taxable income	9,410	6,550

Income tax liability
£15,960 × 20%   £3,192

8

	Savings £	Dividends £	Tax £
Income (£19,200 × $^{100}/_{80}$)/(£18,900 × $^{100}/_{90}$)	24,400	21,000	
PA	(6,475)		
	17,525		
10%	2,440		244
20%	15,085		3,017
10% £(37,400 – 17,525)		19,875	1,987
32.5%		1,125	366
			5,614
Tax credits (dividends)			(2,100)
Tax deducted at source (interest)			(4,800)
Tax repayable			(1,286)

9

	£	£
Rental income = £6,000 – ($^{20}/_{30}$) × £500		5,667
Less expenses:		
Mortgage interest	2,000	
Council tax paid	1,000	
Water rates	500	
Other allowable expenses	3,000	
Wear and tear allowance = 10% × (£5,667 – £1,000 – £500)	417	
		(6,917)
Property loss		(1,250)

This rental loss may be offset against any other net property income for 2009/10 which David may have. Any remaining loss is then carried forward and offset against David's net rental income for 2010/11.

Note. Taxable rental income is calculated on an accruals basis.

An alternative calculation of rental income would be 345/365 × £6,000 = £5,671. Either is acceptable

10 (a) Notice of chargeability was not given by 5 October 2010.

Amount of penalty depends on behaviour leading to failure to notify. If the behaviour is deliberate and concealed, the maximum penalty is 100% of the tax outstanding as a result of the failure at 31 January 2011. If the behaviour is deliberate but not concealed, the maximum penalty percentage is 70%, reducing to 30% in any other case. The amount of the penalty will be reduced where there is disclosure. As the failure in this case is rectified within 12 months, if the failure was not deliberate, the penalty can be reduced to nil with unprompted disclosure.

(b) Interest on late payment of tax
Runs from 31 January 2011 to 15 February 2011.

The time limit for payment of tax is not extended because HMRC were notified late of chargeability.

Note: The tax return was filed on time – within 3 months, hence no late filing penalty.

11

	£
Salary	48,000
Less payroll giving (12 × £30)	(360)
	47,640
Less personal allowance	(6,475)
	41,165
Basic rate band	37,400
Extended (£936 × 100/80)	1,170
	38,570
Income tax payable	
38,570 × 20%	7,714
2,595 × 40%	1,038
Total income tax payable	8,752

12 Let on a commercial basis with a view to making profit.

The person entitled to use the FHL is also entitled to use the furniture.

The FHL must be available for commercial letting to the public as FHL for at least 140 days a year.

The FHL must actually be let for 70 days within the 140 days.

Not more than 155 days may fall during periods of 'longer term occupation'. Longer term occupation is a continuous period of more than 31 days during which the FHL is in the same occupation.

All in ss.322–328 ITTOIA 2005

13

	£
Income restriction (£24,800 – (£200 × 100/80) – £22,900) × ½	825
PAA	
Age 66	9,490
Less: restriction	(825)
	8,665
MCAA – allocated to higher earner	
– based on Eric's age at any point in tax year	6,965
MCA given as a tax reduction at 10%, ie	697

14 Any four from:

- Loan to buy an interest in a close company if minimum holding of 5% or work for greater part of time in management of company.
- Loan taken out in order to lend money to a close company.
- Loan to buy into a partnership.
- Loan to buy an interest in a co-operative or employee controlled company.
- The first four years' interest on a loan by an employee to provide plant and machinery for his employment (excludes cars).
- Loan to pay inheritance tax.
- The first four years interest on a loan by a partner to provide plant and machinery for the business (can include cars).

All in Chapter 1 part 8 ITA 2007

Tax relief is given by deducting the interest paid from total income.

15   The normal price of a ticket is £20. This must be increased by at least 10%, ie to £22, for the donation to qualify for Gift Aid relief.

The £22 payment will then be grossed up by $^{100}/_{80}$ to give £27.50

(a)   Cary's higher rate tax relief equals (40 – 20)% × £27.50 = £5.50

(b)   Due to the availability of transitional relief, from 6 April 2008 to 5 April 2011, the charity can reclaim an additional 2%, as they can gross up the donation using the old basic rate of 22%.

£22 × $^{100}/_{78}$ = £28 × 22% = £6.16

(HMRC's website explains that this represents an additional 3 pence for every £1 donated to compensate for the reduction in the basic rate band from 22% to 20%. The charity would therefore receive 22 × 3p = 0.66p, making a total receipt of 0.66p + £5.50 = £6.16).

16   Total abatement = $^1/_2$ × (£30,000 – £22,900) = £3,550

Age PA (over 75) = £9,640 – £3,165 = £6,475 (normal PA)

Age MCA (over 75) = £6,965 – £(3,550 – 3,165) = £6,580

The MCA may be used as follows:

- All relieved against Sidney's tax liability for 2009/10 at a rate of 10%
- Half of the basic MCA of £2,670 may be claimed by Joan
- All of the basic MCA may be transferred to Joan with Sidney's consent.

Employment income & NIC

17

	£	£	£
Earnings			30,000
Amount received from employer			
14,000 × 35		4,900	
Less authorised mileage allowance			
10,000 × 40p	4,000		
4,000 × 25p	1,000		
		(5,000)	
			(100)
			29,900

18   Providing all other relevant conditions are satisfied there are no income tax implications of receiving options under the EMI scheme, as the option price ≥ MV of shares at grant.

	£
Proceeds (10,000 × £12.90)	129,000
Cost (10,000 × £4.50)	(45,000)
Gain	84,000
Less annual exempt amount	(10,100)
	73,900

CGT at 18% = £13,302

19   Free meals are only exempt if the meals are available to employees generally. The meals therefore constitute a taxable benefit, as not all employees are entitled to them.

Child care vouchers of up to £55 per week are exempt.

The loan was received at a rate of interest below the market rate. A taxable benefit of the loan × official rate of interest (4.75%) less the interest actually paid (loan × 1%) would be charged on Daphne. As the loan was only available for two months, the benefit would be restricted to 2/12 of the full yearly amount.

20 (a) Total years spent in foreign service = 5 years in France + 9 years in the US = 14.

Total length of service = 19 years.

Therefore proportion of time spent in foreign service = $^{14}/_{19}$ = 73.7%. Therefore the 75% test for complete exemption of the redundancy payment is not met.

(b) Not all of the last 10 years have been spent in foreign service and therefore this test for complete exemption is not met.

(c) The total period of service is less than 20 years and therefore the 'half of total period of service including 10 of the past 20 years' test is not met.

Therefore the foreign service proportion of the redundancy payment is exempt from tax.

	£
Redundancy payment	50,000
Less tax-exempt amount	(30,000)
	20,000
Less foreign service proportion: $^{14}/_{19}$ × £20,000	(14,737)
Taxable amount	5,263

21 *Without a s.431 election*

May 2010: As the option was granted at a discount there is a charge to income tax equal to the difference between the price paid and the market value of the shares at the time of the GRANT.

Employment income = £2,000 (£25,000 − 23,000)

July 2010: The removal of the restriction is a chargeable event. A charge to income tax arises on the increase in value on the chargeable event on the untaxed proportion of the restricted securities.

Employment income = £14,286 (£50,000 × (35,000 − 25,000)/35,000) (ss.427 and 428 ITEPA 2003)

This gives a total employment income figure of £16,286 for 2010/11.

With a s.431 election

May 2010: On exercise an election is made to ignore any restrictions on the shares acquired.

Employment income = Unrestricted MV at exercise − exercise price
= £35,000 − 23,000 = £12,000

There is no further charge on the lifting of the restriction.

The s.431 election would have been beneficial as £4,286 less would be charged to income tax in 2010/11.

22

	£	£
Salary		15,000
Job related accommodation		
Annual value – exempt		−
Property expenses		
Heating and lighting	400	
Cost of extension – capital	−	
Redecorating	500	
Provision of furniture (20% × £4,000)	800	
	1,700	
Restricted to 10% of other employment income		1,500
Total employment income		16,500

23 Harry is provided with income of £4,200 (14,000 × 30p) by his employer.

As he is using his own car he can set off expenses based on the HMRC authorised mileage rates, equal to £5,000 ((10,000 × 40p) + (4,000 × 25p)).

Hence Harry will be able to claim an additional allowable expense of £800 (£4,200 – £5,000).

Exemption from income tax is given for passenger payments made by an employer, but no claim may be made for a deduction where no payment is received. As Harry's employer does not make payments for carrying passengers, he cannot claim an additional expense.

24

	£
Car benefit: 34% (W) × £25,000 × 6/12	4,250
Less contribution (6 × £20)	(120)
	4,130
Fuel benefit: 34% × £16,900 × 6/12	2,873
No relief for contribution towards private use of fuel	–
Total benefit	7,003

WORKING

	%
230g/km – 135g/km = 97/5	19
Base percentage	15
Car and fuel benefit %	34

25 *Relocation costs*

Reasonable relocation costs are tax free up to a limit of £8,000. The excess relocation costs of £200 are taxable employment income.

Incidental overnight expenses

Incidental overnight expenses are exempt up to £5 per night. However, as the amount paid has exceeded the limit, the whole of the reimbursed expenses are taxable.

Insurance premium

As Amelia's employer pays the cost of the insurance, she will be taxed on the premiums as a benefit. However, she can claim a corresponding deduction on her self assessment tax return to reduce the value of the benefit to NIL.

26 *Income tax on exercise (unapproved as exercisable >10 years after grant)*

	£	£
Income tax		
Market value at exercise £1.80 × 10,000		18,000
Less costs of acquiring the shares		
option cost 10p × 10,000	1,000	
exercise cost £1 × 10,000	10,000	
		(11,000)
Employment income		7,000

£7,000 @ 40% = £2,800

The base cost of the shares for future disposal is £18,000 (market value at exercise).

Capital gains tax

	£
Proceeds (£1.80 × 10,000)	18,000
Less base cost (£11,000 + £7,000)	(18,000)
	NIL

27

	£
Annual value – house	4,800
Annual value – bungalow £3,400 × 9/12	2,550
	7,350
Rent paid by parents is to Qimat not employer	
Additional charge – house (£668,000 – £75,000) × 4.75%	28,167
Additional charge – bungalow	Nil
	35,517

Note. Although the bungalow has been owned more than 6 years and is now worth more than £75,000, it originally cost less than £75,000 and therefore there is no additional charge (s.107 ITEPA 2003).

28

	£
Salary	46,000
Less: allowable deductions	
Personal pension contributions (note)	
Capital allowances on laptop – Annual investment allowance	(2,000)
Business suits	–
Payroll giving (£25 ×12)	(300)
	43,700

Note. The pension contribution will be deducted from net pay. Higher rate tax relief will be obtained by extending the basic rate band by the gross amount of the contribution.

29

Date of receipt is the earliest of the time when:

- The payment is made
- A person becomes entitled to payment.

For directors only, it is the earliest of:

- The time when earnings are credited in the company's accounts or records
- If the amount of the earnings for a period is determined by the end of the period, the time when the period ends
- If the amount of the earnings for a period is not determined until after the period has ended, the time when the amount is determined

All in s.18 ITEPA 2003

30

Class 1 primary

As Peter is above retirement age no primary Class I NIC is due

	£
Class 1 secondary	
£46,992 × 5/12	19,580
Less earnings threshold = £5,715 × 5/12	(2,381)
	17,199

NIC due at 12.8% = £2,201

31

Any five of the following features:

The total value of shares granted under CSOP schemes must not exceed £30,000 per employee valued as at the date of the grant.

Only full time directors may be granted options (can be granted to full or part time employees).

The scheme must provide that no individual can participate in the scheme if he (together with associates) has, at the time the option is granted or within the previous 12 months, held a material interest in a close company:

- Whose shares are the subject of the CSOP, or
- Which controls or is a member of a consortium controlling that company.

A 'material interest' in this context broadly means a 25% interest in the company.

The shares must be ordinary shares in the scheme organiser or controlling company/ consortium member.

The shares must be in a company which is either (i) listed, (ii) controlled by a listed company, or (iii) not controlled by another company.

The shares must be fully paid up, not redeemable, and not subject to certain restrictions.

The market value of the shares at the date of grant must not be less than the exercise price of the shares. (ie no discount)

The options must be exercised between 3 and 10 years after the date of grant (unless due to injury, redundancy etc)

32 Benefits reportable on Form P11D.

Emissions factor of car = $\left(\frac{15+(210-135)}{5}\right)+3 = 33\%$

Car list price £95,000 limited to £80,000

Deduct capital contribution (limited to £5,000) to give £75,000

Multiply by 33% = £24,750

Time apportion × ($^6/_{12}$) = £12,375

Fuel benefit: £16,900 × 33% = £5,577

Time apportion × (6/12) = £2,789

Legal fees – as Robco Ltd is meeting Robin's personal liability, Class 1 and NOT Class 1A National Insurance arises

Total benefits = £15,164

Class 1A National Insurance 12.8% = £1,941

This is payable by Robco Ltd by 19 July 2010

33

	£
Gerald	
(844 – 110) × 11% × 52	4,198
(1,000 – 844) × 1% × 52	81
	4,279
Arthur	
(43,875 – 5,715) × 11% =	4,198
(46,200* – 43,875) × 1% =	23
	4,221

*Use annual earnings period for directors. Total earnings ((£100 × 52) + £41,000 = £46,200

Class 1B NICs payable:

(a) By employers.

(b) On items covered by a PAYE settlement agreement which would otherwise be liable to Class 1 or Class 1A contributions.

34

		£
Bonny		
Monthly earnings threshold		476
Upper earnings limit		3,656
Regular monthly earnings (£29,520/12)		2,460

Primary
	£
$(2,460 - 476) \times 11\% \times 11$	2,401
$(3,656 - 476) \times 11\%$	350
$(7,460 - 3,656) \times 1\%$	38
	2,789

Secondary
	£
$(2,460 - 476) \times 12.8\% \times 11$	2,793
$(7,460 - 476) \times 12.8\%$	894
	3,687

Clyde
Annual earnings period as director – total earnings £34,520

Primary
$(34,520 - 5,715) \times 11\% = £3,169$

Secondary
$(34,520 - 5,715) \times 12.8\% = £3,687$

Gerald
Class 1A
$£5,000 \times 12.8\% = £640$
Payable by employer
Due 19 July 2010.

35 **Emma:** charge on £3,500
Withdrawal within 3 years

Fiona: charge on £3,000 (lower of value on award and on withdrawal)
Withdrawal 3–5 years

Gillian: no charge
Withdrawal after 5 years

36

	£
Income tax on benefits = 40% × £6,000	2,400
Gross up: £2,400 × ($^{100}/_{60}$)	4,000
Total benefits plus tax = £6,000 + £4,000	10,000
Class 1B National Insurance = 12.8% × £10,000	1,280

Payable by 19 October 2010

Note. The first two steps of this calculation can be carried out as one step by multiplying by $^{40}/_{60}$ and full credit should be given for this method.

37 Five from:

Any expense payment which is made wholly, exclusively and necessarily for the purpose of the employee's employment.

Subsistence payments with no profit element for employees working away from the office

Vouchers for childcare of up to £55 per week

Mileage payments for business miles which are less than limits set under the statutory mileage rates scheme (SMRS).

Statutory redundancy pay / redundancy pay.

Ex gratia payments, eg damages for death or injury at work.

Share options or share awards made under various approved schemes.

Any other correct answer.

38 Payroll giving is not deductible for National Insurance purposes.

Class 1 employer's and employee's contributions will be payable on the gross salary.

Payments into a registered pension scheme are not earnings for NIC purposes.

Liability for payment of Loopysports subscription was that of Karp Ltd, not that of Jade. Therefore this payment is subject to Class 1A National Insurance (payable 19 July 2011).

Investments and pensions

39 (a) The annual allowance is the amount by which pension savings can increase in a specific tax year.

(b) Any contributions in excess of the annual allowance (£245,000 in 2009/10) are subject to a tax charge at 40%.

(c) The lifetime allowance is the maximum amount of a pension fund that can benefit from tax relief. In 2009/10 the limit is £1,750,000.

(d) Again a tax charge will be levied on any excess. The rate of tax charged depends on whether the excess is taken as part of the tax free lump sum on retirement (55%) or part of the fund used to buy the annuity to pay the pension (25%).

40 Apple Ltd: This is a holding company of companies which carry on a qualifying trade and therefore this investment is potentially eligible for EIS relief. Oliver's sister is not an 'associate' for these purposes and so her directorship of Apple Ltd is not relevant.

Pear Ltd: Oliver's associate, ie his wife, is an employee of Pear Ltd and therefore this investment does **not** qualify, as Oliver's associate is connected with the company.

Orange Ltd: This company had gross assets of £20 million before the investment and therefore this investment does **not** qualify, as gross assets cannot exceed £7 million before issue.

41

	£
Pension fund	1,865,000
Taken as TFLS, ie 25% of lifetime allowance = £1,750,000 × 25%	(437,500)
	1,427,500
Invested in pension income benefits	1,337,500
Lifetime allowance less TFLS (ie £1,750,000 – £437,500)	(1,312,500)
Excess over lifetime allowance remaining	25,000
Lifetime allowance tax charge @ 25%	6,250
Further lump sum is in excess of lifetime allowance	90,000
Lifetime allowance tax charge @ 55%	49,500

42

	Non savings £	Dividends £
Trading income	45,000	
Property income dividend (REIT) = £3,471 × 100/80	4,339	
Dividend = £1,530 × 100/90		1,700
	49,339	1,700
Less: personal allowance	(6,475)	
Taxable income	42,864	1,700

	£
Income tax due	
Non-savings income £37,400 × 20%	7,480
£5,464 × 40%	2,186
£42,864	
Dividend income £1,700 × 32.5%	553
Income tax liability	10,219
Less: income tax deducted at source:	
Dividends	(170)
REIT	(868)
Income tax payable	9,181

43

(a) *Dividends*

Dividends from EIS shares are taxable £9,000 × 100/90 = £10,000

(b) *Lodger*

£3,000 is below the rent-a-room limit so is exempt = NIL

(c)

	£
NSI EASA interest is received gross	100
BSI is received net = £92 × 100/80	115
	215

(d) ISA interest is tax free

(e) A stock dividend is taxable as a dividend. Cash equivalent of shares (£1,800) is a net dividend. Therefore, dividends in the income tax computation will be £1,800 × 100/90 = £2,000

44 Andy is eligible for tax relief of £12,800 (20% × £64,000) on his investment in EIS shares.

However the relief is only a tax reduction (ie the tax liability for 2009/10 will be reduced from £7,300 to nil), and cannot create a repayment

An election can be made for the balance of the investment to be treated as if paid in the previous fiscal year (provided the maximum investment limit of that year is not exceeded).

If Andy sold the shares in September 2011 he would not have held the shares for 3 years and therefore income tax relief would be withdrawn. HMRC would issue an assessment to collect the tax due, which would need to be paid within 30 days of the issue of the assessment. Interest would accrue from 31 January following the end of the tax year for which the assessment is made.

CGT basics

45

			£
(1)	Proceeds		7,800
	Less cost		(4,200)
			3,600
	$5/3 \times £(7,800 - 6,000)$		3,000
	Gain		3,000

			£
(2)	Proceeds (deemed)		6,000
	Less cost		(8,200)
	Allowable loss		(2,200)
(3)	Allowable loss (as has already had P&M CAs)		NIL

	£
Asset 1	3,000
Asset 2	(2,200)
	800

46 Conditions for claim:

(a) Aggregate consideration from sale of land does not exceed £20,000, and

(b) The disposal is small, ie 20% or less of the MV of the land before disposal

$20\% \times £(19,000 + 5,000) = £4,800$

Therefore no claim is possible

47

	£
Total Gains £(40,000 + 15,000)	55,000
CY Loss	(10,000)
Net Gains	45,000

	£
Net Gains	45,000
Loss brought forward	(8,000)
	37,000
Less annual exempt amount	(10,100)
	26,900

CGT @ 18% = £4,842

48 Cars are exempt. No loss relief.

Camera equipment:

This is a wasting chattel, which is plant and machinery and sold at a loss. As, presumably, Nigel could have claimed capital allowances, there will be no CGT loss allowed.

Vase (no CAs, as not used in his trade) loss available for relief

However, the loss is restricted by using deemed proceeds of £6,000:

	£
Proceeds (deemed)	6,000
Cost	(20,000)
Loss	(14,000)

49 *Greyhound*
Wasting chattel – exempt

Painting

	£
Proceeds (deemed)	6,000
Less commission (£4,050 × $^{10}/_{90}$)	(450)
	5,550
Less cost	(8,500)
Allowable loss	(2,950)

Antique table

	£
Proceeds	9,000
Less cost	(5,000)
Gain	4,000

$^5/_3$ × (gross sale proceeds − £6,000)

$^5/_3$ × £(9,000 − 6,000) = £5,000

Therefore, gain of £4,000 is lower and taxed.

50 The consideration is less than £20,000 and less than 20% of market value (£38,000). Aggregate proceeds from all sales of land during the year are less than £20,000, so a claim can be made such that no chargeable disposal takes place (before 31 January 2012).

	£
Original cost	30,000
Less net proceeds of part disposal £(18,000 − 360)	(17,640)
Allowable expenditure of land retained	12,360

51

	Gains	CY losses	Loss c/b	Annual exemption	Net chargeable gain
	£	£	£	£	£
2008/09	15,000	0	(5,400)	(9,600)	0
2007/08	2,400	(1,300)	0	(9,200)	0
2006/07	17,000	0	(8,200)	(8,800)	0
2005/06	8,500	NIL	0	(8,500)	400

52 The disposal made by Amy includes consideration which is both contingent and unascertainable (*Marren v Ingles*)

The right to the deferred consideration is a separate asset s.21(1)(a) TCGA 1992.

Hence in July 2009 the gain is calculated using the initial consideration and the value of the right to receive the additional consideration.

	£
Sales proceeds £(400,000 + 45,000)	445,000
Less allowable expenditure	(1,000)
Gain	444,000

In September 2010, Amy will receive an additional amount of approximately £50,000.

The resulting gain will be:

	£
Sale proceeds	50,000
Less cost (estimated at July 2009)	(45,000)
Gain	5,000

53 Painting 1

	£
Deemed proceeds	6,000
Less : Incidental costs of disposal	(200)
: MV @ 3/82	(8,000)
Loss	(2,200)

Painting 2

	£
Proceeds	6,600
Less acquisition cost	(4,800)
	1,800
Restricted to:	
$^{5}/_{3} \times £(6,600 - 6,000)$	1,000
Less allowable loss (restricted)	(1,000)
	—

Capital gains tax liability = NIL. Balance of loss (£1,200) is carried forward

54

	£
Insurance proceeds not used in restoration £(130,000 – 110,000)	20,000
Market value 1982 = £25,000 × $\dfrac{20,000}{20,000+290,000}$	(1,613)
Enhancement = £110,000 × $\dfrac{20,000}{20,000+290,000}$	(7,097)
	11,290
Less: Annual exempt amount	(10,100)
	1,190

Capital gains tax at 18% = £214

The insurance proceeds not reinvested in restoring the asset (£130,000 – £110,000 = £20,000) are > £6,500 (5% × £130,000 insurance money).

The insurance money of £130,000 is > 5% of the value of the asset.

Therefore a part disposal calculation cannot be avoided.

However, an election can be made for the part disposal only to apply to the part of the proceeds not used in the restoration (ie £20,000).

55

The '10%' part of the disposal proceeds represents consideration which is contingent and unascertainable at the date of the disposal. Therefore *Marren v Ingles* applies as follows:

A capital gain was calculated at the time of the 2008/09 disposal. The proceeds were £500,000 plus the estimated net present value of the '10%' right.

Now that Jeeves has received the £25,000, a separate capital gain is calculated on the basis that this was a disposal of the right to receive the contingent consideration. The proceeds are £25,000 and the base cost will be the sum used as the estimated value in the earlier calculation.

If the calculation produces a capital loss then an election can be made to treat this as occurring in the same tax year as the original disposal.

56

	A £	B £	C £
Proceeds (deemed in B)	9,000	6,000	Exempt as both proceeds and cost are less than £6,000
Expenses of disposal	(80)	(80)	
Cost	(3,500)	(9,000)	
	5,420	(3,080)	
$5/3$ × (Gross proceeds – £6,000)	5,000		
Take lower figure	5,000	(3,080)	

Therefore taxable gain = £5,000 – £3,080 = £1,920.

£1,920 – annual exempt amount = £Nil, so no CGT to pay.

57 When an asset has become of negligible value, the owner of the asset can make a claim to treat the asset as having been disposed of for nil proceeds and immediately reacquired. This has the effect of crystallising a capital loss.

The deemed disposal takes place on the date of the claim unless the claimant specifies an earlier time. This earlier time:

(a) Cannot be more than 2 years before the start of the tax year in which the claim is made
(b) Must be a time when the claimant owned the asset, and
(c) Must be a time when the asset had become of negligible value.

58 *Capital gains tax*

	£
Gains Franchise (W1)	96,250
Watch (W2)	2,500
	98,750
Less annual exempt amount	(10,100)
	88,650

CGT £88,650 × 18% = £15,957

Workings

(1) *Franchise – wasting asset (not chattel)*

	£
Sale proceeds	116,500
Less allowable cost (W)	(20,250)
Chargeable gain	96,250

WORKING

$$\frac{\text{Unexpired life}}{\text{Total}} \times \text{original cost} = \text{allowable cost}$$

$$\frac{6.75}{15} \times £45,000 = £20,250$$

(2) *Watch – chattel*

	£
Gross sale proceeds	7,500
Less: auctioneers' fees	(300)
Net sale proceeds	7,200
Less: allowable cost	(4,100)
Chargeable gain	3,100

Restricted to:

$5/3 \times £(7,500 - 6,000) = £2,500$

59
	£
Sale proceeds	16,000
Less: allowable cost (W)	(1,900)
Chargeable gain	14,100
Less: annual exempt amount	(10,100)
	4,000

CGT @ 18% = £720

Share pool

	No. of shares	Cost £
January 1990 purchase	2,000	3,500
June 2000 – Rights nil paid Sale of rights ('small' as under £3,000)		(1,600)
	2,000	1,900
February 2010 Disposal	(2,000)	(1,900)
	NIL	NIL

CGT reliefs

60 (a) Any period during which the owner was employed abroad.

(b) Any period for whatever reason (not exceeding three years in total).

(c) Any periods (not exceeding four years in total) during which the owner was required by his employment to work away from home elsewhere in the UK or was self employed and forced to work away from home.

These periods are deemed periods of occupation provided the period is preceded and followed by actual occupation as the owner's only or main residence.

(d) Any period prior to taking up residence following acquisition up to a maximum of one year for alterations, decoration etc.

61

Period	Comment	Total months	Principal Private Residence (PPR) months	Not PPR months
31 March 1980 to 31 March 1982	Not relevant for PPR purposes			
1 April 1982 to 28 February 1995	PPR	155	155	
1 March 1995 to 31 March 2007	Letting period but another property = PPR so no relief	145		145
1 April 2007 to 31 March 2010	Last 36 months	36	36	—
Total		336	191	145

PPR calculation

	£
Gain before PPR relief	130,000
PPR relief = $^{191}/_{336}$ × £130,000	(73,899)
Chargeable gain	56,101

62 Mr Wong

Chargeable gain on disposal of factory

	£
Sale proceeds	325,000
Less: allowable cost	
MV 31 March 1982	(64,600)
Enhancement	(108,000)
Chargeable gain	152,400

Gains eligible for entrepreneur's relief:

	£
Gain on sale of factory (associated disposal)	152,400
Gain on sale of partnership share	150,000
Gains eligible for entrepreneurs' relief	302,400
Less entrepreneur's relief $^4/_9 \times £302,400$	(134,400)
	168,000
Less annual exempt amount	(10,100)
	157,900

CGT £157,900 × 18% = £28,422

63 6 April 2009 – Disposal by James

	£
Gain	56,292
Less entrepreneurs' relief (Note) $^4/_9 \times £56,292$	(25,019)
	31,273
Less annual exempt amount	(10,100)
	21,173

CGT £21,173 × 18% = £3,811

In order for entrepreneurs' relief to be available the shares sold must be in James' personal company (ie owns ≥ 5%) and he must have been an employee of the company, for one year before the disposal.

Overseas aspects of IT and CGT

64 (a) Permanent emigration

(b) Leave UK to take up employment for at least 2 years

(c) Permanent immigration

(d) Comes to UK to take up employment for at least 2 years

(e) Going abroad for full time service under a contract of employment lasting a complete tax year (candidates are not required to qualify this re trips back to earn full marks)

65 (a) Anthea   £20,000 (arising).

(b) Beryl   £10,000 (remittance basis. £30,000 RBC may apply).

(c) Candice   £10,000 (chargeable overseas earnings ∴ remittance basis. £30,000 RBC may apply).

(d) Daphne   £NIL (non-resident)

66 Nigel   – Yes, Commonwealth citizen (Note. Not available from 2010/11 where based solely on Commonwealth Status).

Oliver – Yes, UK citizen working as a missionary

Paul   – No, not a UK citizen, Commonwealth citizen or EEA national.

Sergei – No, claims remittance basis and therefore UK PA not available

67   *Edwina*

Basis of assessment – arising (as R/OR/UK Dom)

Pension assessable £10,000 × 90% = £9,000

Income tax rate = 40%

Cordelia

Basis of assessment – remittance (as R + OR but non-dom). No claim needed – automatic application as unremitted foreign income and gains less than £2,000.

Dividend income assessable = £6,500

Income tax rate = 40% (tax as non savings income if remittance basis applies)

68   Foreign income taxable on an arising basis is taxed in the same way as it would be if it had arisen in the UK.

Income taxable on a remittance basis is taxed as non-savings income. If the remittance basis has to be claimed no UK personal allowance is available and a remittance basis charge of £30,000 may apply (if resident in the UK for at least 7 out of the 9 previous tax years and is over 18 years old).

For income assessed on an arising basis only, there is 10% relief for foreign pensions.

69   *Domicile of origin*: A child usually takes on their father's domicile at birth and this domicile remains until displaced by a domicile of dependency or choice.

Domicile of dependency: Where a child's father (or other person on whom they are legally dependent) changes his domicile during a child's minority (until 16), then the child's domicile follows the father's.

Domicile of choice: If a person severs all ties with the domicile of origin/dependency and establishes a permanent home in a new country, he takes on domicile of choice in that new country.

1970 – Domicile of origin = French
Paolo has French domicile as at birth he is treated as having the same domicile as his father.

1980 – Domicile of dependency = Australian
As a minor, Paolo adopts his parents' domicile. Assuming they have adopted Australian domicile, so too does Paolo.

2000 – Domicile of choice = British
As an adult Paolo can choose to change his domicile. In practice it is hard to do but severing all ties with any other country indicates he has renounced his previous domicile.

70   *Spanish property*

	2008/09 £	2009/10 £
Rental income	7,000	8,000
Expenses	(9,000)	(7,000)
Loss b/fwd and offset against CY income		(1,000)
Assessable income	NIL	NIL
Loss c/fwd	(2,000)	(1,000)

Tabitha's home

	2008/09 £	2009/10 £
Rental income	4,000	6,000
Expenses	(4,500)	
Rent-a-room deduction		(4,250)
Loss b/fwd and offset against CY income		(500)
Assessable income	NIL	1,250
Loss c/fwd	(500)	NIL

The losses from the overseas rental business cannot be offset against profits from the UK rental business. They will be carried forward and offset against future rental income from other overseas properties.

Tabitha must elect to claim relief for her expenses for 2008/09 rather than rent a room relief.

Tabitha must also elect to receive the rent a room amount as a deduction, instead of her expenses, for 2009/10.

71 Lola's foreign employment income will not be subject to tax in the UK (under s.828C ITA 2007) as she meets the conditions of ss.828A and 828B ITA 2007.

Lola will not be required to file a UK tax return in 2009/10.

She will be entitled to the UK PA. The automatic remittance basis will not apply.

If Lola had foreign rental income of £4,000, she would not qualify for this exemption, as one of the conditions under .s828B ITA 2007 is that the individual can only have foreign employment or foreign interest income.

Administration of IT and CGT

72 Return submitted: 31 March 2011 (later of 31 January 2010 and 3 months after issue)

Amendments by 31 March 2012 (15 months after the date of the notice as above).

73
	£
Personal allowance	6,475
Less: car benefit (£8,000 × 16%) (W)	(1,280)
Tax underpayment £180 × 100/20	(900)
	4,295

Tax code 429L

Working

142g − 135g = 7g ÷ 5g = 1% + 15% = 16%

74 Where a disposal is of land, the taxpayer can elect to pay CGT by ten equal annual instalments.

The first instalment is due when the full amount would otherwise be due, ie 31 January 2011.

The unpaid balance accrues interest from this date.

If the recipient disposes of the asset the tax becomes payable immediately.

75 Arnold is required to give notice as although his employment income will have been subject to PAYE, he has chargeable gains in excess of his annual exempt amount.

Barry is not required to give notice as his income has had income tax deducted at source, and he is not a higher rate taxpayer.

Charles is required to give notice as he is a higher rate taxpayer and will have additional tax payable.

76 Enquiries into the return must be made within 12 months of HMRC receiving the original return, so by 15 December 2010.

However, the time limit for an enquiry is extended if the return is amended after the statutory filing date of 31 January 2010 (which it is – 20 February 2010).

The enquiry window extends to the quarter day following the anniversary of the day on which the amendment was made.

The amendment was made on 20 February 2010; the anniversary of this date is 20 February 2011. The enquiry window therefore extends to 30 April 2011.

77 As the return is late a £100 penalty will apply.

As the return is more than 3 months late, daily penalties of £10 per day can be imposed for a maximum of 90 days.

As the return is more than 6 months late, a penalty of 5% of the tax (and Class 4 NIC) outstanding at 31 January 2011 will be charged (or £300 if greater).

78 Since the tax returns have been issued in good time, records must be kept for 5 years after 31 January following the tax year that the taxpayer is in business. This includes property letting.

Bill must keep his records until 31 January 2016.

In other cases records must be kept for 1 year after 31 January following the tax year.

Chas must keep his records until 31 January 2012.

HMRC have the flexibility to shorten the periods for which records must be kept.

The penalty for failure to keep and retain records is up to £3,000 per tax year.

79 HM Revenue & Customs may correct obvious errors or mistakes within 9 months of receiving a tax return.

Since the return was filed after the due date of 31 January 2011, an enquiry may be opened at any time up to the quarter date following the first anniversary of the actual filing date. With a filing date of 20 February 2011, that means that the enquiry window extends to 30 April 2012.

Mark amended his tax return on 12 March 2011, so the enquiry date extends to the quarter date following the first anniversary of the actual amendment which is still 30 April 2012.

A further amendment on 1 June 2011 pushes the enquiry window later to 31 July 2012.

80 CGT from these disposals is normally due on 31 January 2011.

Gift of the farmland

Since this is a gift of land, Sharon can elect to pay the CGT in 10 equal annual instalments, the first being due on 31 January 2011. The unpaid balance of the tax attracts interest.

Furniture restoration business

The instalment option is available if consideration is paid in instalments, receivable over a period in excess of 18 months as in this case. Tax in respect of the first instalment (equal to 50% of the consideration due) will be payable on 31 January 2011 (unless a different date is agreed with HMRC) and on the date each subsequent instalment is received, until the liability is discharged. These instalments will be interest free.

81

Payment date	Did pay £	Should have paid (***) £	Under paid £	Interest runs between
31 Jan 2010	1,250 (*)	1,800	150	31 Jan 2010 and 31 July 2010
31 July 2010	1,550 (**)	1,800	400	31 July 2010 and 16 Nov 2010

(*) £2,500 × 50%
(**) (£2,800 × 50%) + £(1,400 − 1,250) = £1,550
(***) £3,600 × 50%

82 The following are examples of readily convertible assets (s.702 ITEPA 2003) [state five from the following]:

- Assets capable of being sold on a recognised investment exchange
- Assets capable of being sold on the London Bullion Market
- Assets capable of being sold on the New York Stock Exchange
- Assets capable of being sold on a market specified in the PAYE regulations
- Rights in relation to a money debt
- Property subject to a warehousing regime
- An asset likely to give rise to a right enabling a person to obtain money likely to be similar to the expense incurred in the provision of the expense
- An asset for which trading arrangements are in existence, or are likely to come into existence.

83

	£
Personal allowance	6,475
Less: Painting benefit	
Use of painting = 20% × £15,000 × 4/12	(1,000)
Underpaid tax = £156 × 100/20	(780)
Plus trade association subscription	89
	4,784

PAYE code 478L

84

	Income £	Tax £
Income from self employment	40,000	
Income from REIT = £6,800 × 100/80	8,500	
	48,500	
PA	(6,475)	
	42,025	
Basic rate (20%)	37,400	7,480
Higher rate (40%)	4,625	1,850
Tax liability		9,330
Deduct tax deducted at source from REIT income = £8,500 × 20%		(1,700)
Less payments on account		(5,000)
Further tax payable		2,630

85 The due date is the later of 31 January 2011 (if online submission) and three months after the date of issue of the notice, ie 28 February 2011.

Consequences of lateness:

- There will be a £100 penalty resulting from late submission of the return.
- As her return is filed late the deadline for HM Revenue & Customs to raise an enquiry into the return will be the quarter day following the first anniversary of the actual filing date. Enquiry window ends on 30 April 2012.

86 Any of the following:

- The schemes are likely to be kept confidential from other promoters/HM Revenue & Customs.
- A premium fee is expected.
- The schemes include financial products which are made available on off-market terms.
- The schemes are based on standardised documentation ('shrink wrapped'/'mass marketed' schemes)
- The schemes are designed to create an income tax or CGT loss for more than one person.
- The products include a plant and machinery lease and certain other conditions are met.

Module E
Taxation of unincorporated businesses

Answers

Module E: Taxation of unincorporated business

Trading income

1. | | | | |
    |---|---|---|---|
    | 2008/09 | Actual basis | 1 November 2008 to 5 April 2009 | $30,000 \times \frac{5}{6} = £25,000$ |
    | 2009/10 | First 12 months | 1 November 2008 to 31 October 2009 | $30,000 + \frac{6}{12} \times 93,500 = £76,750$ |
    | 2010/11 | CYB | Year ended 30 April 2010 | £93,500 |

		£
Overlap profits	1 November 2008 to 5 April 2009	25,000
	1 May 2009 to 31 October 2009	46,750
11 months		71,750

    WORKING

    (1)
	6 months to 30 April 2009 £	Year ended 30 April 2010 £
Trading profits	42,000	94,800
Less capital allowances (W2)	(12,000)	(1,300)
	30,000	93,500

    (2)
	AIA/FYA £	PU 50% £	Allowances £
6 months to 30 April 2009			
Additions – van	12,000		
AIA @ 100%(£50,000 × ⁶/₁₂)	(12,000)		12,000
Year ended 30 April 2010			
Additions – car		13,000	
		13,000	
WDA @ 20% (<160g/km)		(2,600) @ 50%	1,300
TWDV c/d		10,400	1,300

2. | | | £ |
    |---|---|---|
    | 2007/08 | 1 September 2007 to 5 April 2008 | |
    | | ⁷/₁₀ × £15,300 | 10,710 |
    | 2008/09 | 1 September 2007 to 31 August 2008 | |
    | | £15,300 + (²/₁₂ × £27,600) | 19,900 |
    | 2009/10 | 21 months to 31 March 2010 | |
    | | £27,600 + £13,470 (21m) | 41,070 |
    | | Less overlap relief £(10,710 + 4,600) (9m) | (15,310) |
    | | | 25,760 |

    No overlap remaining

Working

	Total £	Bill £
1 September 2007 to 30 June 2008	40,600	
Salary to Ben	(10,000)	
	30,600	
PSR 50:50		15,300
		15,300
Year ended 30 June 2009	67,200	
Salary to Ben	(12,000)	
	55,200	
PSR 50:50		27,600
		27,600
9 months to 31 March 2010	35,940	
Salary to Ben	(9,000)	
	26,940	
PSR 50:50		13,470
		13,470

3

	£
Adjusted trading profit	79,510
Less capital allowances (w)	(61,442)
	18,068

Working

	AIA/FYA £	ECA £	Main pool £	CAs £
11 months to 31 March 2010				
Additions				
Computer	48,000			
Car (<160g/km)			9,500	
Low emission car		13,000		
	48,000	13,000	9,500	
AIA 50,000 × $^{11}/_{12}$ = 45,833	(45,833)			45,833
	2,167			
FYA @ 40%	(867)			867
	1,300			
ECA × 100%		(13,000)		13,000
WDA × 20% × $^{11}/_{12}$			(1,742)	1,742
Transfer to pool	(1,300)		1,300	
	NIL		9,058	61,442

4 *Repairs* – disallow – capital as required before property can be used.

Christmas party

Staff entertaining is allowable

Food hampers

Gifts of food and drink to clients are not allowable

200 fountain pens

Allowable as they are gifts not costing more than £50 per donee this year, carry a prominent advertisement, and are not food, drink or tobacco.

Donation

Local donations are allowable if small and for business purposes.

5

				£
2007/08	Actual basis	1 January 2008 to 5 April 2008	$3/16 \times £48,000$	9,000
2008/09	No AP end	6 April 2008 to 5 April 2009	$12/16 \times £48,000$	36,000
2009/10	12 months to AP end	1 May 2008 to 30 April 2009	$12/16 \times £48,000$	36,000
2010/11	CYB	Year ended 30 April 2010		50,400
2011/12	CYB	Year ended 30 April 2011		63,000
2012/13	Final tax year	14 months to 30 June 2012		51,000
		Less overlap profits (W)		(33,000)
				18,000

Working

Overlap 1 May 2008 to 5 April 2009 $11/16 \times £48,000 = £33,000$

6

	£
Water recycling plant (£12,500 × 100%)	12,500
Van (£8,000) AIA @100%	8,000
Computer (£3,200) AIA @ 100%	3,200
Plant (£1,600) AIA @ 100%	1,600
Car 1 (low emission) £12,500 × 100% × 70%	8,750
Car 2 (>160g/km) £15,000 × 10%	1,500
	35,550

Note: AIA of £50,000 pa is available in total.

7

Maggie is required to register as self-employed for Class 2 NIC purposes as soon as she joins the partnership.

Maggie has a new source of income on which tax is payable for 2009/10 and must notify chargeability for income tax and Class 4 NIC purposes by 5 October 2010.

The submission date for the 2009/10 tax return is 31 January 2011. Since the partnership accounts will not be available by this date, Maggie must use provisional figures on her tax return estimating her share of her first year's profits.

She must tick a box to draw attention to the fact that the figures are provisional, explain why this is so, and state when actual figures should be available.

Her 2009/10 basis of assessment will be $3/12$ of the estimated profits for the year ended 31 December 2010 to tax the period 1 January 2010 to 5 April 2010.

8

	£
Adjusted profits	21,781
Less capital allowances (W1)	(12,317)
	9,464

2008/09	£9,464 × $6/15$ = £3,786
2009/10	£9,464 × $12/15$ = £7,571

Workings

(1) *15 months to 31 December 2009*

	AIA £	Main pool £	Private use £	Allowance £
Additions				
Machinery				
£(3,000 + 2,880)	5,880			
AIA @ 100%	(5,880)			5,880
Car 1 ('old' car)			16,000	
Car 2 (<160g/km)		14,500		
		14,500	16,000	
WDA @ 20% × $^{15}/_{12}$		(3,625)		3,625
Max £3,000 × $^{15}/_{12}$			(3,750) @ 75%	2,812
TWDV c/d		10,875	12,250	12,317

AIA available

£50,000 × $^{15}/_{12}$ £62,500

9   After Billy's admission, Angie and Billy each have profit shares of:

	Total £	Angie £	Billy £
Year ended 31 December 2008	42,000		
Salary	(10,000)	10,000	
Interest £15,000 × 2%	(300)		300
	31,700		
PSR 50:50	(31,700)	15,850	15,850
		25,850	16,150
Year ended 31 December 2009	65,000		
Salary	(10,000)	10,000	
Interest 15,000 × 2%	(300)		300
	54,700		
PSR 50:50	(54,700)	27,350	27,350
		37,350	27,650

Angie has an ongoing business and her taxable profits are:

			£
2007/08	Year ended 31 December 2007		31,000
2008/09	Year ended 31 December 2008		25,850
2009/10	Year ended 31 December 2009		37,350

Billy has a new business and his taxable profits are:

			£
2007/08	1 January 2008 to 5 April 2008	$^{3}/_{12}$ × £16,150	4,038
2008/09	Year ended 31 December 2008		16,150
2009/10	Year ended 31 December 2009		27,650

10

		£
2008/09	Year ended 30 April 2008	61,000
2009/10	Year ended 30 April 2009	43,000
Add 5 months to 30 September 2009		11,000
		54,000
Less overlap relief		(1,700)
Taxable		52,300

Sam's 2009/10 tax return will be due by:

(a)   31 October 2010 if a paper return.
(b)   31 January 2011 if filed electronically.

Sam will need to keep his records until 31 January 2016.

11 Key indicators

- Ability to send a substitute
- High degree of financial risk/ability to profit from sound management
- A relatively low degree of integration into the business, ie not 'part and parcel' of the business
- Worker has ability to decline work and the person engaging the worker is not obliged to provide work
- Paid at irregular time intervals: paid 'per job' rather than regularly weekly/monthly
- Low level of routine (ie does not necessarily work set hours and attend a set location)

A self employed individual will be liable to pay Class 2 NIC at £2.40 per week for 2009/10 if their trading profits for 6 April 2009 to 5 April 2010 exceed the small earnings exception limit. They will also be liable to Class 4 NIC on trading profits for 2009/10 over £5,715 at 8% and 1% over £43,875.

An appropriate level of credit should be given for slightly less key indicators such as:

- Provision of own equipment
- The engagement is for a relatively short period of time
- Provision of own insurance
- A relatively low level of direct supervision
- Required to correct unsatisfactory work in own time and at own expense
- Job title is 'contractor', 'consultant', etc rather than employee/officer
- Does not receive holiday pay/sick pay/pension
- Works for more than one business at the same time
- Any other relevant point not already covered

12 Alice's profit allocation:

	Total £	Alice £
16 months to 31 August 2010	40,000	
Salary £10,000 × $^{16}/_{12}$	(13,333)	13,333
	26,667	
PSR 50%		13,334
		26,667
Year ended 31 August 2011	42,000	
Salary	(10,000)	10,000
	32,000	
PSR 50%		16,000
		26,000

			£
2009/10	1 May 2009 to 5 April 2010	$^{11}/_{16}$ × £26,667	18,333
2010/11	1 September 2009 to 31 August 2010	$^{12}/_{16}$ × £26,667	20,000
2011/12	Year ended 31 August 2011		26,000
Overlap profits	1 September 2009 to 5 April 2010	$^{7}/_{16}$ × £26,667	11,667

13

	AIA £	Main pool £	Allowances £
Year ended 31 October 2009			
TWDV b/d		10,000	
Plant £(20,000 + 4,000)	24,000		
AIA @ 100%	(24,000)		24,000
Cheap car £(2,800 + 6,200)		9,000	
Disposal £(4,000 + 2,800)		(6,800)	
		12,200	
WDA × 20%		(2,440)	2,440
TWDV c/d		9,760	
Total allowances			26,440

14

	£
Political donations not allowable	–
Donations only allowed if small, to a local charity and benefits the trade	–
Gift to employee on exam success – staff cost	75
Legal expenses are not trade-related	–
Costs of unsuccessful business rating appeal – cost of trading	175
Loss on sale of machine – capital item	–

15   Capital allowances year ended 31 December 2009

		£
(1)	£20,000 × 20% = £4,000; Max £3,000 ('old' car)	3,000
(2)	£9,000 × 20% (<160g/km)	1,800
(3)	£15,000 × 100% (low emission car)	15,000
(4)	£10,000 × 20% × 60% (<160g/km)	1,200
(5)	FYA 100% (ECA)	12,000
(6)	AIA @100%	4,000
(7)	No capital allowances – not plant	
	Total allowances	37,000

16

	AIA £	Pool £	Allowances £
15 months to 31 March 2010			
TWDV b/f		12,000	
Addition – car (<160g/km)		8,000	
		20,000	
WDA @ 20% × 15/12		(5,000)	5,000
Addition – plant	10,000		
AIA £50,000 maximum	(10,000)		10,000
TWDV c/f		15,000	
Total allowances			15,000
Adjusted profit £39,750 – £15,000			24,750
2009/10 15 months to 31 March 2010			24,750
Less overlap b/f			(2,000)
Taxable trade profits			22,750

17   The year of change is 2008/09.

(a)   Assessments are as follows:

	£
2006/07	
Year ended 31 January 2007	30,000
2007/08	
Year ended 31 January 2008	36,000
2008/09	
12 months to 30 June 2008, therefore:	
7/12 (1 July 2007 to 31 January 2008) × £36,000 = £21,000	
5/17 (1 February 2008 to 30 June 2008) × £68,000 = £20,000	41,000
2009/10	
12 months to 30 June 2009, therefore	
12/17 × £68,000	48,000

(b) Overlap profits:

	£
Brought forward (2 months)	5,000
Arising during 2008/09 (7 months from 1 July 2007 to 31 January 2008)	21,000
Total (9 months)	26,000

(c) Conditions for a change of accounting date to be effective for tax purposes:

Accounting period not longer than 18 months and either:

    (i)   No change in the previous five years
    (ii)   HMRC are satisfied the change is for bona fide commercial reasons

18 Holly's capital allowances

	AIA £	Main Pool £	Mercedes £	Porsche £	SLA £	Allowances £
Balances at 6 April 2009		15,000	14,000	20,000	3,000	
Transfer to main pool		3,000			(3,000)	
Additions	2,400					
Disposals		(1,000)	(12,000)			
		17,000	2,000			
AIA @ 100%	(2,400)					2,400
WDA @20%		(3,400)				3,400
WDA limited to £3,000				(3,000)		
£3,000 × 75%						2,250
Balancing allowance			(2,000)			2,000
Total allowances						10,050
TWDV c/f	NIL	13,600	NIL	17,000		

19

			£
2005/06	1 February 2006 to 5 April 2006		
	2/18 × £54,000		6,000
2006/07	6 April 2006 to 5 April 2007		
	12/18 × £54,000		36,000
2007/08	1 August 2006 to 31 July 2007		
	12/18 × £54,000		36,000
2008/09	1 August 2007 to 31 July 2008		40,000
2009/10	1 August 2008 to 31 July 2009		20,000
2010/11	1 August 2009 to 30 April 2010	30,000	
	Less overlap profits*	(24,000)	6,000
*Overlap profits	1 August 2006 to 5 April 2007		
	8/18 × £54,000		24,000

20

	£
Accounts profit	60,000
Add: Allowable proportion of lease rentals (lease taken out pre 6.4.09):	
£5,000 × 50% = £2,500	
£2,500 × (12,000 + 25,000)/(2 × 25,000) = £1,350	
Therefore disallowable amount = £5,000 – £1,350 =	3,650
Interest on late PAYE	45
Legal fees relating to the purchase of new business premises (relate to capital)	3,500
Donation to the National Society for the Protection of Horses	750
Subscription to 'Heat' magazine	60
	68,005

21 Under the spreading provisions of para 2 Sch 15 Finance Act 2006 the adjustment income chargeable to tax is the lower of:

2007/08

$1/3$ × original adjustment income: $1/3$ × £79,800 = £26,600 and
$1/6$ × trading profits before deducting capital allowances
$1/6$ × £(156,600) = £26,100

As Yuri is a higher rate taxpayer the additional income tax payable for 2007/08, the second year of the spreading, is:

£10,440 (40% of £26,100)

2008/09

Lower of:

$1/3$ original adjustment income = £26,600
$1/6$ trading profits before capital allowances £78,900 × $1/6$ = £13,150

Income tax as a higher rate tax payer £13,150 × 40% = £5,260

2009/10

Year 4: lower of:

$1/3$ original adjustment income = £26,600
$1/6$ trading profits before capital allowances £120,500 × $1/6$ = £20,083
Untaxed adjustment income £79,800 – £26,100 – £13,150 = £40,550

Income tax £20,083 × 40% = £8,033

There are no Class 4 National Insurance contributions on adjustment income.

22 Saloni Capital allowances for year ended 30 June 2009

	AIA £	Main pool £	Private use asset (70% bus) £	SLA £	Allowances £
TWDV b/d		3,000	8,000	5,000	
Additions					
£(1,600 + 1,500)	3,100				
Disposal					
16 May 2009				(400)	
27 June 2009		(3,300)			
	3,100	(300)	8,000	4,600	
AIA @ 100%	(3,100)				3,100
Balancing charge		300			(300)
WDA × 20%			(1,600)		
£1,600 × 70%					1,120
Balancing allowance				(4,600)	4,600
Transfer					
TWDV c/f		NIL	6,400	NIL	
					8,520

23 *If Jacinta ceases to trade on 31 March 2010*

In 2009/10 she will be assessed to income tax on:

	£
Year ended 30 June 2009	64,000
9 months ended 31 March 2010 (9 × £6,000)	54,000
Less overlap relief	(2,000)
	116,000

Final payment for trading income tax liability due 31 January 2011.

If Jacinta ceases to trade on 30 April 2010

In 2009/10 she will be assessed to income tax on:

	£
Year ended 30 June 2009	64,000

In 2010/11 she will be assessed to income tax on:

	£
10 months ended 30 April 2010 (10 × £6,000)	60,000
Less overlap relief	(2,000)
	58,000

Final payment for trading income tax liability 31 January 2012.

24 *Subject matter* – for example 1 million toilet rolls are unlikely to be held as an investment, therefore held to be a trading profit.

Frequency of transactions – transactions which may be treated, in isolation, as capital will be interpreted as trading, where their frequency indicates the carrying on of a trade.

Profit motive – the presence of a profit motive is a strong indication of trading.

Supplementary work – when work is done to make an asset more marketable, or steps are taken to find purchasers, the courts are more likely to ascribe a trading motive.

Way in which asset acquired – when goods are acquired by way of a gift or inheritance it is difficult to prove a trading motive.

Length of ownership – where items are purchased and sold soon afterwards, this may infer trading.

Reason for sale – if the sale is in order to generate cash to settle personal borrowings (for example) this is unlikely to indicate trading.

Source of finance – if the purchase of an asset is via financing that then makes it necessary to sell the asset promptly, this tends to indicate trading.

25 Adjustment income spread as follows:

Lower of:

		£
2005/06	$1/3 \times £84,000 = £28,000$ or $1/6 \times £115,890 = £19,315$	19,315
2006/07	$1/3 \times £84,000 = £28,000$ or $1/6 \times £133,446 = £22,241$	22,241
2007/08	$1/3 \times £84,000 = £28,000$ or $1/6 \times £205,340 = £34,223$	28,000
2008/09	$1/3 \times £84,000 = £28,000$ or $1/6 \times £60,100 = £10,016$ or Amount untaxed (£84,000 − £19,315 − £22,241 − £28,000) = £14,444	10,016
2009/10	$1/3 \times £84,000 = £28,000$ or $1/6 \times £81,200 = £13,533$ or Amount untaxed (£14,444 − £10,016) = £4,428	4,428
		84,000

26

	AIA £	Main pool £	Expensive Car (Bus 65%) £	Allowances £
15 months ended 31 March 2010				
Additions:				
Expensive car			14,000	
Second hand car		8,000		
Fixtures & Machinery	7,400			
	7,400	8,000	14,000	
AIA @ 100%	(7,400)			7,400
WDA £8,000 × 20% × 15/12		(2,000)		2,000
WDA £14,000 × 20% × 15/12			(3,500)	
£3,500 × 65%				2,275
TWDV c/f		6,000	10,500	
Total allowances				11,675
Year ended 31 March 2011				
Addition – machinery	50,000	1,000		
(post 6.4.09 so no FYA)	50,000	7,000	10,500	
AIA @ 100% (max)	(50,000)			50,000
Addition – machinery	5,000			
FYA @ 40%	(2,000)			2,000
	3,000			
WDA × 20%		(1,400)		1,400
WDA × 20%			(2,100)	
£2,100 × 65%				1,365
Transfer to pool	(3,000)	3,000		
TWDV c/d		8,600	8,400	
Total allowances				54,765

27 A short-life asset election can be made to de-pool an asset, if it is an asset which would normally be included in the main pool.

Short-life assets automatically revert to the main pool at the beginning of the first accounting period which is more than four years after it was purchased, ie after 5 lots of WDA.

When an asset is de-pooled the allowances are calculated separately so that on its disposal within 4 years it will generate a balancing allowance on disposal if sold for less than its TWDV.

A balancing allowance on the main pool is only possible in the year of cessation so this would not happen unless the asset was de-pooled. It is therefore only suitable for assets which depreciate faster than capital allowances are awarded and which are likely to be sold within the short life asset period.

A short-life asset election should not be made if an asset is likely to be sold within 4 years for more than its TWDV as a balancing charge would arise. Instead the asset should stay in the main pool.

28 Eleanor

		£
2007/08	1 September 2007 to 5 April 2008 4 months ended 31 December 2007 and 3 months ended 5 April 2008 £5,200 + ($3/_{12}$ × £21,600)	10,600
2008/09	Year ended 31 December 2008	21,600
2009/10	Year ended 31 December 2009	28,800
Overlap period	1 January 2008 to 5 April 2008 $3/_{12}$ × £21,600	5,400

Conditions for change of accounting period to be valid for income tax purposes (s.217 ITTOIA 2005):

- The first period of account ending with the new date does not exceed 18 months
- The change is notified to HMRC by 31 January following the year of change, and
- Either:
    - There has been no change in the last five tax years, or
    - HMRC is satisfied the change is for bona fide commercial reasons.

In the year of change Eleanor will relieve the overlap profits created in her first two tax years.

29 Yasmin

	£
Net profit per accounts	67,000
Legal fees re debt collection (Allowable as related to trade)	–
Legal fees re-investment property (Disallowable as not related to the trade. Deductible from property income)	500
Gifts of moisturiser cream (Allowable as contain advert, cost less than £50 per item and not food, tobacco or alcohol)	–
Subscription to Beautician association (Allowable as related to the trade)	–
Membership of local health spa (Disallowable as not wholly and exclusively incurred in relation to the trade)	600
Spray-tan booth repairs (Disallowable as capital. Repairs required in order for the asset to be used)	560
Redecorating the main salon (Allowable as genuine revenue expense for maintaining the salon)	–
Adjusted profit	68,660

30 **Antonia**

Assessments are as follows:

			£
(a)	*2007/08*		
	Year ended 31 January 2008		£23,400
	2008/09		
	No accounting period ends in this tax year so tax the 12 months to the new accounting date: 12 months ended 31 May 2008		
	($^8/_{12}$ × £23,400 + $^4/_{16}$ × £38,000) = £15,600 + £9,500		£25,100
	2009/10		
	12 months ended 31 May 2009 ($^{12}/_{16}$ × £38,000)		£28,500

(b) Unrelieved overlap profits:

	£
2 months brought forward	7,200
8 months to 31 January 2008 (£23,400 × $^8/_{12}$)	15,600
Total of 10 months	22,800

(c) Antonia must notify HMRC by 31 January 2010 of her change of accounting date.

Her income tax will be due on the following dates:

First payment on account 31 January 2009
Second payment on account 31 July 2009

Final balancing payment 31 January 2010.

31 **Jacob**

	ECA £	Main pool £	BMW1 (60% bus) £	BMW2 (60% bus) £	Allowances £
Year ended 31 March 2010					
TWDV b/d		–	10,500		
Additions:					
Low emission car	14,000				
BMW (<160g/km)				27,000	
Disposal (27,000 – 22,000)			(5,000)		
	14,000	–	5,500	27,000	
ECA @ 100%	(14,000)				14,000
BA			(5,500)		3,300
£5,500 × 60%					
WDA @ 20%				(5,400)@60%	3,240
TWDV c/d	–	–	–	21,600	
Total allowances					20,540
Year ended 31 March 2011					
Additions		5,000			
Disposals – equipment		(12,000)			
– employee's car		(8,000)			
– BMW				(16,700)	
		(15,000)		4,900	
BC		15,000			(15,000)
BA				(4,900)	
£4,900 × 60%					2,940
Additional profit in final year	–		–		(12,060)

32 James

Without a succession election

	Main pool £	Allowances £
TWDV b/f	65,000	
Additions	16,000	
Disposal (MV)	(37,000)	
	44,000	
Balancing allowance	(44,000)	44,000

With a succession election

	Main pool £	Allowances £
TWDV b/f	65,000	
Additions	16,000	
	81,000	
Disposal (TWDV)	(81,000)	

No allowances are available in the period of cessation.

The succession election must be made within two years of the date of succession.

A succession election can be made when trade passes from one connected person to another.

James is connected with his spouse, his or his spouses brothers, sisters, ancestors and lineal descendants.

33 Any five from:

- Loan to pay inheritance tax
- Loan to buy into a partnership
- Loan to buy plant or machinery to be used by a partnership
- Loan to buy an interest in a close company
- Loan to buy an interest in an employee controlled company
- Loan to buy an interest in a co-operative
- Loan to purchase a life annuity
- First 4 years interest on loan taken out by employee to buy P&M for use in employment

Trading losses

34

(1) s.86   Against income received from the company

(2) s.64   Against net income of the tax year of the loss and/or the previous year

If a s.64 claim is made, as the loss is incurred in 2009/10, can claim to carry back loss against trade profits of the previous 3 years (LIFO). Maximum carry back to the earliest 2 years = £50,000 in total.

(3) s.89   Unrelieved trading loss of the last 12 months relieved against trading income of the final tax year and the preceding three years (LIFO)

(4) s.64   Against net income, then s.71 (s.261B TCGA) against capital gains in the tax year of the s.64 claim. The maximum s.71 claim is the lower of:

Unused trading loss after s.64, or

	£
Capital gains	X
Current year capital losses	(X)
Brought forward capital losses	(X)
	X

35 Ian's loss is relieved against Ian's income from I Ltd, as follows:

	£
2009/10	
Ian's salary	20,000
Less: loss	(20,000)
	–
Ian's interest: £5,000 × 100/80	6,250
Less: loss (£30,000 – £20,000 = £10,000)	(6,250)
	–
Ian's dividends: £4,680 × 100/90	5,200
Less: loss (£10,000 – £6,250)	(3,750)
Dividends remaining chargeable	1,450

The loss in the final accounting period could also be relieved using:

(a) s.89 terminal loss relief. Loss of the last 12 months carried back 3 tax years on a LIFO basis.

(b) s.64 offset loss against net income of final or preceding tax year. Could then extend against capital gains. If a s.64 claim is made, as the loss is incurred in 2009/10, can claim to carry back loss against trade profits of the previous 3 years (LIFO).

36 Harry could claim loss relief as follows:

- s.72 ITA 2007 – against net income as follows:

	£
2006/07	50,000
2007/08	50,000
2008/09	10,000

- s.64 ITA 2007 – against net income in 2009/10 and or 2008/09

	£
2009/10	–
2008/09	50,000

The remaining loss would be carried forward under s.83 ITA 2007

- s.83 ITA 2007 – against first available future trading profits.

A claim under s.72 is likely to be most beneficial to Harry because it will generate repayment of earlier years' income tax and use the loss as soon as possible.

37 Amy's loss in the year to 31 December 2009 will be assessed as follows:

2008/09 loss for 1 January 2009 to 5 April 2009 $3/_{12}$ × loss
2009/10 loss for year ended 31 December 2009 – less loss allocated to 2008/09

The loss relief options available to Amy are:

- Relief by carrying forward against future trading profits of the same trade (s.83 ITA 2007).

- Relief against general income of the tax year of the loss and/or the preceding tax year (s.64 ITA 2007).

- As the losses are in one of the first four tax years of trading relief against net income of the 3 tax years preceding the year of the loss on a first in first out basis (s.72 ITA 2007).

	£
2008/09	
$^8/_{11} \times £(43,400)$	(31,564)
2009/10	
Period ended 30 June 2009	(43,400)
Less: loss allocated to earlier year	31,564
$^1/_{12} \times £(23,000)$	(1,917)
	(13,753)

Options for use of the losses:

- Freddy could offset the loss against general income in the current year and/or the prior year in any order under s.64 ITA 2007.

- Alternatively Freddy could offset the loss under s.72 ITA 2007 against the total income of the preceding three years on a FIFO basis. Any remaining loss will automatically be carried forward and set against future profits from the same trade.

- Freddy could offset the loss in 2008/09 against general income using s.64 ITA 2007 and then against his gains using s.71 ITA 2007 (s.261B TCGA 1992).

The relief available under s.71 ITA 2007 is the lower of:

- Unused loss after s.64
- Capital gains minus capital losses and capital losses brought forward

39 Hamid

Calculation of the terminal loss (loss of the last 12 months of trading) (s.89 ITA 2007)

	£	£
Period 6 April 2009 to 30 September 2009		
Loss = $^6/_8 \times £20,000$		15,000
Add overlap profits		8,000
		23,000
Period 1 October 2008 to 5 April 2009		
Loss from 1 February 2009 to 5 April 2009		
$^2/_8 \times £20,000$	5,000	
Profit from 1 October 2008 to 31 January 2009		
$^4/_{12} \times £12,000$	(4,000)	
		1,000
Total terminal loss		24,000

The terminal loss can be relieved against trading income of the year of cessation and the three years of assessment prior to that of cessation on a LIFO basis, as follows:

	2006/07	2007/08	2008/09	2009/10
	£	£	£	£
Trading income	4,000	5,000	12,000	–
s.89	(4,000)	(5,000)	(12,000)	–
	–	–	–	–
Dividend income	1,000	1,000	1,000	1,000
Net income	1,000	1,000	1,000	1,000

	£	£
Loss memo: 2009/10 loss £(20,000 + 8,000)		28,000
s.89 relief available:		
2008/09	24,000	
	(12,000)	(12,000)
2007/08	(5,000)	(5,000)
2006/07	(4,000)	(4,000)
	3,000	
Total unused loss		7,000

40. Calculation of terminal loss (loss of last 12 months of trading)

	£	£
Period 6 April 2009 to 30 June 2009		
Loss = $^3/_9 \times £27,000$		9,000
Add overlap profits		1,500
		10,500
Period 1 July 2008 to 5 April 2009		
Loss from 1 October 2008 to 5 April 2009		
$^6/_9 \times £27,000$	18,000	
Profit from 1 July 2008 to 30 September 2008		
$^3/_{12} \times £8,000$	(2,000)	
		16,000
Total terminal loss		**26,500**

Relieved as follows:

	2007/08 £	2008/09 £	2009/10 £
Trading income	30,000	8,000	–
S.89	(18,500)	(8,000)	
Revised trading income	11,500	–	

41. A claim can be made under Sch 6 FA 2009 for the loss to be carried back 3 years against trading profits on a LIFO basis.

    The maximum loss that can be carried back to the earliest 2 years is £50,000 in total for each loss making year.

    If a s.64 claim is made against the net income of the previous year, then the loss is carried back against the trade profits of the two years prior to that year.

42. 2009/10 loss options

    The trader could make a s.64 claim to offset the loss against general income of 2009/10 and/or 2008/09 in any order.

    If a s.64 claim is made for a year, then a claim can be made under s.71 to offset the remaining loss against the net chargeable gains of the year.

    If a s.64 claim is made for either 2009/10 or 2008/09 a claim for extended loss relief can be made to set the loss against trading profits of the three years prior to the loss making year, setting the loss against the income of the later year first. The maximum carry back to the earliest two years is £50,000 in total.

    If no action is take the losses will be carried forward under s.83 claim to set against first available trading profits.

CGT basics

43. 6 out of:

    - Sale of asset
    - Gift of asset
    - Part disposal of an asset
    - Receipt of a capital sum in relation to an asset
    - Asset lost or destroyed
    - Asset becoming of negligible value
    - Interim and final payouts on liquidation of a company
    - Certain deemed disposals.

    A chargeable disposal occurs on the date of contract.

    Where the date of contract is conditional, the date of disposal is taken as the date the condition is satisfied.

44 2009/10

	£
Gain on painting	15,000
Gain on antique – gift to charity takes place at no gain/ no loss	–
Loss on shares – to a connected party – only usable against gains to same connected person	–
Gain on holiday cottage	34,000
	49,000
Loss brought forward	(33,000)
	16,000
Annual exempt amount	(10,100)
Taxable gains	5,900

Capital gains tax @ 18% = £1,062 payable on 31 January 2011.

45

The disposal made by Amy includes consideration which is both contingent and unascertainable (*Marren v Ingles*).

The right to the deferred consideration is a separate asset s.21(1)(a) TCGA 1992.

Hence in July 2009 the gain is calculated using the initial consideration and the value of the right to receive the additional consideration:

	£
Sale proceeds (£400,000 + £45,000)	445,000
Less allowable expenditure	(1,000)
Gain	444,000

In September 2010, Amy will receive an additional amount of approximately £50,000 $\left(\dfrac{£900,000 - £800,000}{2}\right)$.

The resulting gain will be:

	£
Sale proceeds	50,000
Less cost (estimated at July 2009)	(45,000)
Gain	5,000

Entrepreneurs' relief will be available against the £444,000 if:

- She owned at least 5% of the ordinary share capital and voting rights
- She was employed by the company
- The company is a trading company

throughout the 12 months prior to disposal.

If she satisfies these conditions, $^4/_9^{th}$ of the gain is exempt from CGT.

46 Property

<95% of proceeds were used in restoration, therefore Matilda can elect for a part disposal only to apply to the proceeds not used in restoring the property.

	£
Proceeds £350,000 – £315,000	35,000
MV 1982 £120,000 × $\dfrac{£35,000}{£35,000 + £420,000}$	(9,231)
Enhancement £315,000 × $\dfrac{£35,000}{£35,000 + £420,000}$	(24,231)
Capital gain	1,538

Base cost of property:

	£
Market value @ 3/82	120,000
Enhancement	315,000
	435,000
Proceeds not charged	(315,000)
Used in part disposal	(33,462)
Base cost	86,538

47 (a) The '10%' part of the disposal proceeds represents consideration which is contingent and unascertainable at the date of the disposal. Therefore *Marren v Ingles* applies as follows:

A capital gain was calculated at the time of the 2008/09 disposal. The proceeds were £500,000 plus the estimated net present value of the "10%" right.

Entrepreneurs' relief would have been available if he was an employee or officer of the company to reduce the gain by $4/9$.

Once Jeeves has received the £25,000, a separate capital gain is calculated on the basis that this was a disposal of the right to receive the contingent consideration. The proceeds are £25,000 and the base cost will be the sum used as the estimated value in the earlier calculation.

No entrepreneurs' relief will be available on this gain as it is not a disposal of shares.

If the calculation produces a capital loss then an election can be made to treat this as occurring in the same tax year as the original disposal.

(b) CGT can be paid by instalments if:

   (i)   Proceeds are received in instalments, and
   (ii) The proceeds are receivable over a period exceeding 18 months

   OR

   (iii) The gain arose on the gift of assets not qualifying for gift relief, and
   (iv) The gift is of land, quoted shares from a controlling shareholding or unquoted shares.

48 The consideration is less than £20,000 and less than 20% of market value (£38,000). Aggregate proceeds from all sales of land during the year are less than £20,000, so a claim can be made, before 31 January 2012, such that no chargeable disposal takes place.

	£
Original cost	30,000
Less net proceeds of part disposal (£18,000 – £360)	(17,640)
Allowable expenditure of land retained	12,360

49 Conditions for claim:

(a) Aggregate consideration from sale of land does not exceed £20,000

(b) The disposal is small, ie 20% or less of the MV of the land before disposal

   20% (£19,000 + £5,000) = £4,800

   Therefore no claim is possible as fails (b).

	£	£
2009/10		
Proceeds		5,000
Cost £10,000 × $\frac{£5,000}{£5,000 + £19,000}$		(2,083)
Gain		2,917
2010/11		
Proceeds		60,000
Cost	10,000	
Used in part disposal	(2,083)	
		(7,917)
Gain		52,083

50 (a) A claim may be made if the aggregate consideration from land in the year does not exceed £20,000 and it represents less than 20% of the value of the land before the transfer.

(b) A claim may be made if the conditions in (a) above are satisfied. Alternatively, a claim may be made if consideration is either 5% or less of the market value or less than £3,000.

The gain is deferred by deducting the 'small proceeds' from the base cost of the land.

A claim must be made by an individual, on or before the first anniversary of 31 January following the tax year of the disposal.

51 The capital sum may be deducted from the cost of the asset as:

(a) The asset is non-wasting, and
(b) The sum not used is less than the greater of 5% of the capital sum and £3,000.

If Alan only uses £93,000 to restore the building only a combination claim will be possible:

(a) Part disposal re £7,000 not used in restoration
(b) Compensation used in restoration is deferred by deduction from cost of asset, also treated as enhancement expenditure on asset.

52

	£
Insurance proceeds received	130,000
Market value 1982 £80,000 × $\frac{130,000}{(130,000 + 150,000)}$	(37,143)
Gain	92,857
Annual exempt amount	(10,100)
	82,757

Capital Gains Tax at 18% = £14,896

Eric can defer the entire gain by reducing the base cost of the asset with the £92,857 gain if all the proceeds are used to restore the painting.

If Eric used at least 95% of the proceeds in restoring the asset, again the full gain can be deferred.

If Eric uses less than 95% of the insurance proceeds to restore the asset then he can deduct the proceeds used in restoring the asset from the cost of the asset, and use the 'unused' proceeds for the part disposal calculation.

Partnerships

53

	£
Gain on asset £(100,000 – 70,000)	30,000

Vernon and Walter have a chargeable gain of £10,000 each

	£
Ursula receives the asset so her share of the gain reduces the base cost of asset: £(100,000 – 10,000)	90,000

Sale of asset

	£
Proceeds	108,000
Less cost	(90,000)
Gain	18,000

If instead of the asset being distributed to Ursula, the partners change their capital profit sharing ratio to 2:2:1 the tax implications will be as follows:

This would be a no gain/no loss transaction.

	Ursula	Vernon	Walter
	£	£	£
Cost £70,000 ⅓ each	23,333	23,333	23,334
New ratio 2:2:1 £70,000	28,000	28,000	14,000
Increase/(decrease)	4,667	4,667	(9,334)

No gain/no loss disposal by Walter

	£
Proceeds	9,334
Cost	(9,334)
No gain/loss	–

Base cost for future disposals:

	Ursula £	Vernon £	Walter £
	28,000	28,000	14,000

54

	Total £	Peter £	Paul £	Mary £
Year ended 31 March 2010				
Profit	18,000			
Salaries	(20,000)	NIL	10,000	10,000
Loss	(2,000)			
Allocate 2:2:1	2,000	(800)	(800)	(400)
		(800)	9,200	9,600
Reallocate notional loss 9,200:9,600		800	(391)	(409)
Profit share		NIL	8,809	9,191
Year ended 31 March 2011				
Profit	50,000			
Salaries	(20,000)	NIL	10,000	10,000
	30,000			
Allocate 2:2:1	(30,000)	12,000	12,000	6,000
		12,000	22,000	16,000

55

	Total £	Edith £	Fiona £	Geraldine £
Year ended 31 January 2010				
1 February 2009 to 31 October 2009				
$^9/_{12} \times £82,500$				
Salary $\times ^9/_{12}$	22,500	7,500	7,500	7,500
Balance 3:2:1	39,375	19,688	13,125	6,562
	61,875	27,188	20,625	14,062
1 November 2009 to 31 January 2010				
$^3/_{12} \times £82,500$				
Salary £5,000 $\times ^3/_{12}$	2,500	1,250	1,250	–
Balance 60:40	18,125	10,875	7,250	
	82,500	39,313	29,125	14,062
2009/10 assessment		39,313	29,125	14,062
Less overlap profits – Geraldine				(2,230)
				11,832

56 (a) When a new partner is introduced there will be a change in profit sharing ratio. This results in:

(i) A disposal of each asset with a fractional share decrease for at least one partner and
(ii) An acquisition with a fractional share increase for at least one partner.

If there has been a prior revaluation:

(i) A partner with a decreasing fractional share has an immediately chargeable gain, with sale proceeds being the fraction of the revalued amount
(ii) A partner with an increasing fractional share has a base cost for the increase being the fraction of the revalued amount.

(b) A payment outside the accounts on a change of profit sharing ratio represents consideration for the whole or part of the partners share in the partnership assets (in addition to the consideration calculated in (a)).

The partner making the payment can only deduct the payment as a capital cost in arriving at capital gains/losses when he finally disposes of his share of the asset.

57

	Total £	Aaron £	Mark £	Zoë £
Year ended 30 June 2009				
1 July 2008 to 31 March 2009				
£68,000 × $^9/_{12}$	51,000			
Salaries £8,000 × $^9/_{12}$	(6,000)	6,000		
£12,000 × $^9/_{12}$	(9,000)		9,000	
	36,000			
PSR 1:2:3	(36,000)	6,000	12,000	18,000
1 April 2009 to 30 June 2009				
£68,000 × $^3/_{12}$	17,000			
Salaries £8,000 × $^3/_{12}$	(2,000)	2,000		
£12,000 × $^3/_{12}$	(3,000)		3,000	
	12,000			
PSR 1/3 each	(12,000)	4,000	4,000	4,000
		18,000	28,000	22,000

Untaxed interest (for the *accounting period*) to 30 June 2009 = £500 + £1,000 = £1,500.

	Total £	Aaron £	Mark £	Zoë £
£1,500 × $^9/_{12}$	1,125			
Split 1:2:3	(1,125)	188	375	562
	–			
£1,500 × $^3/_{12}$	375			
Split 1/3 each	(375)	125	125	125
	–	313	500	687

Taxed interest (calculated for the *tax year*) = £100 + £200 × $^{100}/_{80}$ = £375

	Total £	Aaron £	Mark £	Zoë £
	375			
Split equally	(375)	125	125	125
	–	125	125	125

58

	Debbie £	Cath £	Total £
Year ended 30 April 2008			144,000
Salary	20,000	10,000	(30,000)
Interest @ 7.5%	2,250	2,250	(4,500)
			109,500
PSR 1:1	54,750	54,750	(109,500)
	77,000	67,000	–

Current year basis = 2008/09 for both Debbie and Cath

Year of cessation 2009/10

	Debbie £	Cath £	Total £
P/E 31 July 2009			251,000
Salaries × $^{15}/_{12}$	25,000	12,500	(37,500)
Interest @ 7.5% × $^{15}/_{12}$	2,813	2,813	(5,626)
			207,874
PSR 1:1	103,937	103,937	(207,874)
	131,750	119,250	–

Assessable profits for Debbie: £131,750 – £15,000 = £116,750
Assessable profits for Cath: £119,250

59 Isabel, Jessica and Katie

	Total £	Isabel £	Jessica £	Katie £
Year ended 30 April 2009				
3 months ended 31 July 2008	22,500			
PSR (1:1:1)	(22,500)	7,500	7,500	7,500
9 months ended 30 April 2009	67,500			
Salary $^9/_{12} \times £24,000$	(18,000)			18,000
PSR (2:2:1)	(49,500)	19,800	19,800	9,900
Assessments for 2009/10		27,300	27,300	35,400
Year ended 30 April 2010				
3 months ended 31 July 2009	21,250			
Salary $^3/_{12} \times £24,000$	(6,000)			6,000
	15,250			
PSR (2:2:1)	(15,250)	6,100	6,100	3,050
	–			
9 months 30 April 2010	63,750			
Salary $^9/_{12} \times £10,000$	(7,500)		7,500	
	56,250			
PSR (1:1)	(56,250)	28,125	28,125	
	–	34,225	41,725	9,050
Less overlap		–	–	(3,000)
Assessments for 2010/11		34,225	41,725	6,050

60 Allocate profits:

	Total £	Kim £	Mick £	Roz £
Year ended 30 June 2008	115,000			
Salary	(15,000)	15,000		
	100,000			
PSR 2:1	(100,000)	66,667	33,333	
	–	81,667	33,333	
Year ended 30 June 2009				
1 July 2008 to 31 December 2008				
£120,000 × $^6/_{12}$	60,000			
Salary £15,000 × $^6/_{12}$	(7,500)	7,500		
	52,500			
PSR 2:1	(52,500)	35,000	17,500	
	–			
1 January 2009 to 30 June 2009				
£120,000 × $^6/_{12}$	60,000			
Salary £15,000 × $^6/_{12}$	(7,500)	7,500		
	52,500			
PSR 2:2:1	(52,500)	21,000	21,000	10,500
	–	71,000	38,500	10,500
				6 months
Year ended 30 June 2010	200,000			
Salary	(15,000)	15,000		
	185,000			
PSR 2:2:1	(185,000)	74,000	74,000	37,000
	–	89,000	74,000	37,000

			Kim £	Mick £	Roz £
2008/09	CYB		81,667	33,333	
	Actual 1 January 2009 to 5 April 2009				
	£10,500 × 3/6				5,250
2009/10	CYB		71,000	38,500	
	First 12 months				
	£10,500 + 6/12 × £37,000				29,000
2010/11	CYB		89,000	74,000	37,000

61 Nadine and Oberon

Earnings for 2009/10

	Nadine £	Oberon £
Partnership	25,000	15,000
Less: loss b/f [Note]		(10,000)
Sole trader (Nadine)	25,000	
Class 4 earnings	50,000	5,000

Class 2 contributions £2.40 × 52
Payable monthly or quarterly by direct debit   125   125

Class 4 contributions

	£
Nadine	
8% × £(43,875 – 5,715)	3,053
1% × £(50,000 – 43,875)	61
	3,114
Oberon	
Below the lower profits limit	NIL

Note. Nadine's trading losses of 2008/09 are relieved against her other sole trader profits in 2008/09.

Due via self assessment – first POA 31 January 2010
– second POA 31 July 2010
– balance due 31 January 2011.

CGT reliefs

62 *Incorporation*

Chargeable gains £400,000 (W) × $\frac{£200,000}{£1,000,000}$ = £80,000

Sale of shares

	£	£
Proceeds		950,000
Less cost	800,000	
Less gain rolled over (automatic)	(320,000)	
		(480,000)
		470,000

	£
Total gains 2009/10	550,000
Less AE	(10,100)
Taxable gains	539,900

Working

	Building £	Goodwill £
Proceeds	360,000	160,000
Cost	(120,000)	–
Gain	240,000	160,000

£240,000 + £160,000 = £400,000

Plant sold at a loss – taken through capital allowances system.

Debtors are not a chargeable asset.

63 Factory 1

	£
Proceeds	650,000
Cost	(350,000)
Gain rolled over (as all proceeds reinvested)	300,000

Factory 2

	£
Proceeds	795,000
Cost £(710,000 – 300,000)	(410,000)
Gain	385,000

On cessation of his business Gary can claim entrepreneurs' relief (in respect of maximum lifetime gains of £1million):

£385,000 × 4/9 = £(171,111)

Gain after entrepreneurs relief = £213,889

64 (a) In order for s.162 TCGA 1992 incorporation relief to apply to the disposal of the business to the company all of the assets (apart from cash) must have been transferred. The consideration must be wholly or partly shares. The business must be transferred as a going concern.

(b)

	Goodwill £	Property £
MV @ incorporation	250,000	50,000
Cost		(10,000)
Gain	250,000	40,000

Total gains = £290,000

	Each partner £
Split 50:50	145,000
Incorporation relief: £145,000 × $\frac{(£350,000 \div 2) - 20,000}{£350,000 \div 2}$	(128,429)
Gain after incorporation relief per partner	16,571
Entrepreneurs' relief: £16,571 × 4/9	(7,365)
Gain after entrepreneurs' relief per partner	9,206

(c) Sale of shares by Bill

	£	£
Proceeds		250,000
Cost	155,000	
Incorporation relief	(128,429)	
		(26,571)
Gain		223,429

Note. No entrepreneurs' relief available as shares not held for at least one year.

65 Assets used in a trade, profession or vocation carried on by:
   (a) The donor
   (b) The donor's personal company (hold at least 5% of voting rights)
   (c) A trading company owned by a holding company which is the donor's personal company.

   Shares and securities in trading companies or holding companies of trading groups where:
   (a) They are not listed on a recognised stock exchange, or
   (b) The donor can exercise at least 5% of the voting rights.

   Restriction (re shares in a personal company)

   Gain held over is limited to:

   $$\text{Gain} \times \frac{\text{MV of chargeable business assets}}{\text{MV of chargeable assets}}$$

66 (a) The business is transferred as a going concern.
   (i) All assets, or all assets other than cash, are transferred.
   (ii) The consideration is wholly or partly in shares.

   (b) To obtain relief using entrepreneurs' relief on the disposal of the business. Entrepreneurs' relief would not be available on a subsequent disposal of the shares if they are held for less than 12 months.

   (c) 31 January 2013.

67 George can claim relief for gifts of business assets under s.165 TCGA 1992 because the property is used by George's personal company (owns ≥5%).

   This will defer £135,000 of gain (see below) until his son later sells the premises, at which time his son's base cost of the market value of the property at the time of the gift will be reduced by the amount of the gain held-over. The remaining gain of £40,000 will be chargeable in 2009/10.

   The time limit for making the claim is 5 April 2014 (4 years after the end of the tax year of disposal) and needs to be made by both George and his son.

	£
Gain	175,000
Gain taxed now (actual proceeds – cost)	(40,000)
Gain deferred	135,000

68 Taxable income

	Relevant business assets £	Other assets £	Total £
Shoe making business			
Goodwill	700,000		
Factory	100,000		
Warehouse	(50,000)		
Investments		250,000	
SUV Ltd shares		300,000	
	750,000	550,000	
Entrepreneurs' relief £750,000 × 4/9	(333,333)		
	416,667	550,000	966,667
Less AE			(10,100)
			956,567

   CGT × 18% = £172,182

69 The business must be transferred as a going concern.

All of the business assets, or all except cash, must be transferred to the company.

The consideration must be wholly or partly in exchange for shares in the company. The proportion of the gains attributable to consideration other than shares will be chargeable.

If the above conditions are not met then two reliefs are available:

Gift relief can be used to defer the gain on chargeable assets transferred to the company, by deducting the gain from the base cost (market value) of the asset for the company.

Entrepreneurs' relief is available to relieve $4/9^{ths}$ of up to £1 million of gains. However, this £1 million is a lifetime limit and if used on incorporation, would not be available when the shares in the company are finally sold.

70 Disposal of freehold factory in December 2003

	£
Sale proceeds	200,000
Less allowable expense	(37,500)
	162,500

The gain can be deferred on the purchase of the depreciating asset on 1 June 2003, until the earliest of:

- The disposal of the leasehold factory
- Ceasing to use the leasehold factory
- 10 years after acquisition of the leasehold factory (1 June 2013)

As a non depreciating asset (leasehold more than 60 years) is acquired before any of these events occur, an election can be made so that the gain can be rolled over against the base cost of the new asset.

	£
Gain before rollover	162,500
Proceeds not reinvested (October 2009 non-depreciating asset £200,000 – £180,000)	(20,000)
Gain eligible for rollover relief into October 2009 asset	142,500

Revised base cost of new leasehold £180,000 – £142,500 = £37,500

	£
Remaining gain	162,500
	(142,500)
	20,000

The £20,000 continues to be deferred with the original depreciating asset.

71 *Incorporation relief*

If Jack satisfies the following conditions, incorporation relief will apply automatically to his capital gains:

- Business is transferred as a going concern
- All assets (other than cash) are transferred
- Consideration is wholly or partly in shares.

Entrepreneurs' relief

If Jack elects to disapply incorporation relief (within 2 years of 31 January following the tax year of incorporation) or if incorporation relief does not apply to part or all of the gains, he could claim entrepreneurs' relief at $4/9^{ths}$ of up to £1,000,000 of gains.

He must elect for entrepreneurs' relief within two years of 31 January following the tax year of incorporation.

Jack must have owned the business for at least a year before incorporation.

72

	£
MV at date of disposal	395,000
Less: MV 31 March 1982	(140,000)
Gain	255,000

(a)

	£
Gain	255,000
Gain chargeable now (£200,000 – £140,000)	(60,000)
Remaining available for gift relief	195,000
£195,000 × $\dfrac{700,000 + 70,000}{700,000 + 70,000 + 620,000}$ Gift relief	(108,022)
Remaining chargeable	86,978

Total gain chargeable £60,000 + £86,978 = £146,978

(b) The remaining chargeable gain will be eligible for entrepreneurs' relief:

	£
Gain remaining chargeable	146,978
Less £146,978 × $^4/_9$	(65,324)
Chargeable gain	81,654

Base cost for Charlie:

	£
Market value @ gift	395,000
Gift relief	(108,022)
	286,978

73

	£
Gains	120,000
Incorporation relief (balance)	(65,820)
Gain before entrepreneurs' relief after incorporation relief (ie £30,100 (below) × $^9/_5$)	54,180
Entrepreneurs' relief £54,180 × $^4/_9$	(24,080)
Gain before loss relief	30,100 ($^5/_9$)
Capital losses b/f	(20,000)
Gain after entrepreneurs' relief = Annual exempt amount – Work upwards from here ↑	10,100

Optimum share consideration:

£120,000 × $\dfrac{\text{Shares}}{200,000}$ = £65,820 (above)

Shares = £109,700

Non-share consideration £200,000 – £109,700 = £90,300

Conditions for incorporation relief to apply:

- The business must be transferred as a going concern
- All the assets of the business must be transferred (except cash)
- The transfer must be wholly or partly in exchange for shares.

If the conditions are satisfied incorporation relief applies automatically.

74 (a)
200 shares	10,000
Cost	(200)
Gains	9,800

Assets disposed of in a series of transactions to connected person: TCGA 1992, s.19 and s.20

(b) $\dfrac{200}{600} \times £48,000 = £16,000 - £200 = £15,800$

(c) $\dfrac{400}{600} \times £60,000 = £40,000 - £400 = £39,600$

Conditions for shares to qualify for entrepreneurs' relief. In the period of 12 months up to the disposal:

- Derek must own at least 5% of the ordinary shares and votes
- Derek must be employed by Donald Ltd
- The company must be a trading company or a holding company of a trading group.

75 (a)

	£	£
Total chargeable gain on sale of first factory		200,000
Eligible for rollover:		
Gain re business £200,000 × 90%	180,000	
Restrict for proceeds not reinvested:		
(90% × £300,000) – (90% × £250,000)	(45,000)	
Rollover relief		(135,000)
Gain chargeable now		65,000

Base cost of new factory:

	£
Cost	250,000
Rollover relief	(135,000)
	115,000

(b) Gift relief will be available to defer the gain if:

(i) Herman's son is UK resident
(ii) Herman and his son make a joint claim to defer the gain
(iii) The asset has been used in Herman's trade, or in his personal company (own ≥ 5%).

The gain will be deferred by reducing the son's base cost (market value) by the gain deferred.

If Herman receives any actual proceeds from his son then the gain equal to actual proceeds less original cost cannot be deferred.

76

	£
Proceeds	293,000
Cost	(63,000)
Enhancement	(50,000)
Gain	180,000

Gain not eligible for rollover £180,000 × ¼ = £45,000

	£
Gain eligible £180,000 – £45,000	135,000
Rollover relief	(125,250)
Proceeds not reinvested £293,000 × ¾ – £210,000	9,750

Total gains chargeable £45,000 + £9,750 = £54,750

	£
Base cost of factory	210,000
Less rollover relief	(125,250)
	84,750

Rollover relief must be claimed by 5 April 2014.

NIC and administrative aspects of IT and CGT

77 Return submitted: 31 March 2011 (later of 31 January 2011 and 3 months after issue)
Amendments by 31 March 2012 (15 months after the date of the notice as above).

HMRC can correct an error in a return within 9 months of receiving it.

HMRC must formally notify Omar of their intention to enquire into his tax return by the first anniversary of the actual filing date if filed on time.

78 Enquiries into the return must be made within 12 months of the actual filing date.

However, the time limit for an enquiry is extended if the return is amended after the statutory filing date of 31 January 2010 (which it is – 20 February 2010)

The enquiry window extends to the quarter day following the anniversary of the day on which the amendment was made.

The amendment was made on 20 February 2010; the anniversary of this date is 20 February 2011; the enquiry window therefore extends to 30 April 2011.

The scope of the enquiry extends to anything contained in the return including any claim or election included in the return.

79 There will be a £100 penalty in respect of the late filing of the return.

There is no penalty for the late payment of the payments on account.

Tax of £5,000 is outstanding more than 30 days after the due date, therefore a penalty of 5% × £5,000 = £250 will be levied.

2 factors listed in the legislation which do not qualify as a 'reasonable excuse' are

– Insufficiency of funds
– Reliance on a 3rd party, unless the taxpayer took reasonable care.

80

	£
Proceeds = market value	200,000
Cost	(75,000)
Enhancement (not redecoration – revenue)	(55,000)
Gain	70,000

Where a gift is of land, the taxpayer can elect to pay CGT by ten equal annual instalments.

The first instalment is due when the full amount would otherwise be due, ie 31 January 2011.

The unpaid balance accrues interest from this date.

If the recipient disposes of the asset the tax becomes payable immediately.

81 (a) The capital gains tax can be paid in 10 equal annual instalments, commencing with the normal due date. The outstanding balance will attract interest.

(b) The consideration is receivable in instalments over more than 18 months, and therefore can be paid in instalments.

No interest is charged on the outstanding balance.

(c) Cannot be paid by instalments. It is not a controlling holding in a quoted company.

(d) The tax can be paid over instalments as the consideration is receivable over more than 18 months.

The tax can be paid over a maximum of 8 years and the outstanding balance is interest free.

(e) Although Richard chose not to claim gift relief on the gift, gift relief was available and therefore he cannot pay by instalments.

82

	2008/09 £	2009/10 £
Trade profit for the year	NIL	50,000
Less losses brought forward		(1,000)
Less losses of 2008/09		(3,000)
Class 4 profits	NIL	46,000

* Class 4 loss relief claims are independent of income tax claims
** Dividend income is not profit for Class 4 purposes

Contributions payable:

	£
2008/09 – no profits	NIL
2009/10 8% × (£43,875 – £5,715)	3,053
1% × (£46,000 – £43,875)	21
	3,074

Class 4 NIC is payable via self assessment. Therefore payments on account are due on 31 January during the tax year and 31 July after the tax year based on 50% of the previous tax years liability (in this case nil). Therefore, a final balancing payment is due by 31 January following the end of the tax year.

83 The maximum penalty where notice of chargeability is not given (assuming the failure was deliberate and concealed) is 100% of the tax not paid by 31 January 2010. However, as the tax is paid on 10 January 2010 the penalty is nil.

The normal due date for Capital Gains Tax would be 31 January 2010. However, Karen notified chargeability by 5 October 2009 and notice to file a return was not issued before 31 October 2010 so the tax is due three months after the issue of the notice, ie 10 February 2010.

Individuals do not need to report capital gains on their tax returns if:

- Total chargeable gains are less than the annual exempt amount, and
- Proceeds from all disposals are less than 4 times the annual exempt amount, or
- If losses are deducted, the gains before deducting losses are less than the annual exempt amount, and
- You do not want to claim an allowable capital loss or make any other capital gains claims or elections for the ear.

84 Patrick reduced his POAs by too much. He should have paid the original amount of £6,000 on each due date.

POA 1

On £4,500 – nil – paid on time
On £1,500 from due date of 31 January 2010 to day before payment 27 February 2011

31 January 2010 to 27 February 2011 £1,500 × 2.5% × $^{13}/_{12}$ = £40

POA 2

On £4,500 from due date of 31 July 2010 to payment on 30 September 2010
On £1,500 from due date of 31 July 2010 to payment on 28 February 2011

31 July 2010 to 29 September 2010   £4,500 × 2.5% × $^{2}/_{12}$ = £19
31 July 2010 to 27 February 2011   £1,500 × 2.5% × $^{7}/_{12}$ = £22

Balancing payment

On £10,000 from due date of 31 January 2011 to payment on 28 February 2011

31 January 2011 to 27 February 2011   £10,000 × 2.5% × $^{1}/_{12}$ = £21

85 Stefan should not have made a claim to reduce his payments on account. Interest will be payable on the under paid instalments as follows:

First payment on account

Under paid £2,000 31 January 2010 to 11 March 2011 = £2,000 × $^{13}/_{12}$ × 2.5% = £54

Second payment on account

Under paid £2,000 31 July 2010 to 11 March 2011 = £2,000 × $^{7}/_{12}$ × 2.5% = £29

Balancing payment

	£
Total tax and NIC due	14,150
Payments on account	(14,000)
	150

Interest on late payment

31 January 2011 to 11 March 2011 = £150 × $^{1}/_{12}$ × 2.5% = £Nil (< £1)

Late payment penalty

Tax outstanding more than 30 days after the due date: £14,150 − £5,000 − £5,000 = £4,150 × 5% = £207

Mock Exam 1: Questions

CTA Awareness Paper

Mock Examination 1 (Pilot Paper)

Question Paper	
Time allowed	*3 hours*

Attempt all questions

DO NOT OPEN THIS PAPER UNTIL YOU ARE READY TO START UNDER EXAMINATION CONDITIONS

Module A

1. Alpha Developments owns a number of properties which it leases to tenants. The company purchased a mainframe computer for £140,000 plus VAT on 29 June 2007, and used this for its general business purposes.

   Under Alpha Developments' partial exemption method, the level of taxable use has been determined as follows.

		Rate %
Year to 31 March	2007	80
	2008	70
	2009	85
	2010	75

   The computer was sold on 7 August 2009 for £47,000 inclusive of £6,130 VAT.

   You are required to:

   (1) **Compute the amount of input tax recoverable in respect of the purchase of the computer as well as any subsequent adjustments which must be made.** (2 marks)

   (2) **Compute the additional input tax, if any, reclaimable from HMRC following the sale of the computer.** (3 marks)

   Total (5 marks)

2. (1) The sale of the freehold in a warehouse built 18 months ago and used to store manufactured products since then.

   (2) Sale of 20 acres of land at the edge of his farm by Farmer Giles. The land has been in his family since 1800s.

   (3) Sale of the freehold of a semi-detached post WWII house by the current owner a VAT registered plumber.

   (4) 24 month lease of newly built apartment by the builder Kimple Builders to Mr Smith.

   (5) 99 year lease of a newly built office block by the builder Stats Construction.

   You are required to categorise the above supplies of land and buildings for VAT and if possible state whether the option to tax is available. (5 marks)

3. Horricks Ltd is selling its business as a going concern to a major competitor JL Industries Ltd on 1 May 2010.

   The assets of the business comprise:

	£'000
Freehold interest in a two-year old warehouse	250
Goodwill	50
Plant and machinery	50
	350

   You are required to:

   (1) **State how the transfer will be treated for VAT assuming both businesses are VAT registered.** (3 marks)

   (2) **Calculate the VAT due (if any) and state any planning points available to reduce the VAT chargeable.** (2 marks)

   Total (5 marks)

4   Lancashire Candles Ltd sells candles to both the wholesale and retail trade. The bad debts account at 30 June 2010 reflects the following:

Date of invoice	Debtor	Details	Amount £
30 June 2009	Scents Ltd	Retail sales	2,000
30 November 2009	Hope Ltd	Sale of now obsolete plant	10,000
20 December 2009	Dot Ltd (in liquidation)	Wholesale	5,000
15 April 2010	Jingle Ltd	Retail sales	3,000
			20,000

Notes

(1) No adjustment has been made for any VAT relief.
(2) Lancashire Candles Ltd has terms requiring payment within 10 days of the invoice date.
(3) On 15 May 2010, a dividend of £1,500 was received from the liquidators of Dot Ltd.

In accordance with normal accounting practice, debtors are shown inclusive of VAT in the accounts.

You are required to calculate the amount of bad debt relief for VAT that can be claimed on the quarterly return to 30 June 2010. (5 marks)

5   Charlie and Bella Royle have been in business as partners acting as Personal Trainers for over 10 years. However, due to their age, they decide to retire on 30 April 2010. On that date the assets held by the business (valued at replacement cost for identical items) are:

	£
Van	12,000
Motor car (owned outright and used for both business and private purposes)	14,000
Sports training equipment	1,000

The van and equipment items will be sold over the next few months. Charlie will keep the car for his own personal use.

You are required to outline for VAT purposes how Charlie and Bella must proceed following their decision to retire. (5 marks)

6   In December 2010 Simply Bags Ltd made the following transactions of which the new chief accountant requires advice as to their VAT treatment.

(1) Sale of 600 ladies handbags to Cordes SARL – a company based in France.
(2) Purchase of fine leather from a supplier in Brazil.
(3) Purchase of 1,000 metal hinges for bags from a supplier in Italy.

You are required to discuss the VAT implications of the above three transactions. (5 marks)

7   Hermione opened a clothes shop on 1 July 2009. Since then her sales have been consistent at £5,000 per month, apart from each December when, due to Christmas demand, turnover is £24,000. Hermione does not sell children's clothes.

Hermione didn't register for VAT until 29 March 2011.

You are required to discuss the penalty HMRC will charge for the late registration. (5 marks)

8 Olivia runs a village post office and general store. In the quarter to 31 March 2010, she had the following:

	£
Standard rated supplies (excluding VAT)	53,000
Zero-rated supplies	7,000
Exempt supplies	12,500
Attributable to taxable supplies	6,800
Input tax:	
Attributable to exempt supplies	1,500
Residual	1,000

Taxable supplies include £4,000 (excluding VAT) for the sale of a computer, printer and scanner, which Hermione had previously used in her business.

You are required to calculate the VAT payable by/repayable to Olivia in her return for the quarter to 31 March 2010, based on the above information. (5 marks)

9 The structure for the Marlowe Group is as below.

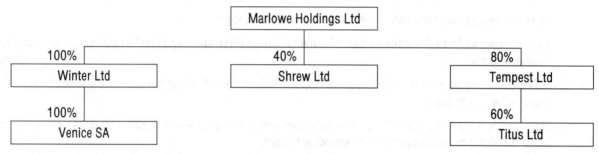

All companies except Venice SA have a place of business in the UK.

Titus Ltd runs children's day nurseries and makes wholly exempt supplies. All other companies make taxable supplies.

Which companies can be included in a VAT group registration and what are the effects of a group VAT registration? (5 marks)

10 Tempest Ltd ordered a consignment of widgets from Caliban Ltd on 12 December 2009 paying a £2,000 deposit.

The widgets are dispatched from Caliban Ltd's factory on 15 January 2010.

An invoice is issued on 20 January 2010. Tempest Ltd paid the balance of £18,000 on 29 January 2010.

Briefly explain the VAT tax points for the deposit and for the balance. (5 marks)

11 Gower Ltd submits its VAT returns and pays its VAT as follows:

Quarter ended	VAT due £	Date return submitted	Date VAT paid
30 June 2009	22,000	25 August 2009	25 August 2009
30 September 2009	28,000	25 October 2009	25 October 2009
31 December 2009	30,000	14 February 2010	14 February 2010
31 March 2010	(5,000)	31 May 2010	-
30 June 2010	7,000	29 July 2010	5 August 2010

You are required to outline how the default surcharge rules will apply to Gower Ltd. (5 marks)

12 Harry granted a 45-year lease on a commercial property to Richard on 12 June 2010. The premium was £95,000 and the net present value of the rent is £180,000. Annual rents under the lease are £1,100 per month.

What is the Stamp Duty Land Tax payable on the grant of the lease and what is the due date for payment?

(5 marks)

Module B

1. Paul gifts £275,000 to an interest in possession trust on 3 April 2010. The beneficiaries of the trust are his three teenage children.

    His only other lifetime gifts have been a gross chargeable transfer of £115,500 on 14 June 2006 and gifts of £100 to each of his four nieces and nephew at Christmas every year since 2001.

    Paul always pays any Inheritance Tax due in connection with his lifetime gifts.

    You are required to calculate how much Inheritance Tax Paul must pay. You should also state Paul's gross chargeable transfer in respect of the April 2010 gift. (5 marks)

2. Anne is a very wealthy 62 year old looking for Inheritance Tax advice.

    She is UK domiciled and intends to leave all her assets to her husband, Gus, aged 47.

    Gus was born in New Zealand. He moved to England when he married Anne, eleven years ago, and has told Anne that he intends to return to New Zealand if Anne dies before him.

    Anne has no other relations and has made no other substantial gifts.

    You are required to advise Anne on her Inheritance Tax position and any potential planning opportunities available to her. (5 marks)

3. In May 2004 Lisa sold her family home for £650,000. She gave £400,000 to her son, David, who bought a property for Lisa to live in.

    The property is currently worth £475,000 and has an annual rental value of £18,525. Lisa does not pay rent to David. No elections have been made in respect of the gift.

    Lisa is a higher rate taxpayer.

    You are required to calculate and explain Lisa's tax liability for 2009/10 in respect of the property and to advise her how she can avoid any tax charge. (5 marks)

4. Kari dies on 8 October 2009.

    In her estate were the following assets:

    (1) *15,000 Smoky plc shares*

    At the date of her death the shares were quoted at 230.25 – 235, with bargains at 231, 233.25 and 234.

    The shares had gone ex-dividend on 28 September 2009 and the dividend of 19p per share was paid on 12 October 2009.

    (2) *Holiday home in France*

    Kari had purchased the property for €127,500 when the buying exchange rate was €1.39 and the selling rate was €1.20. At the date of her death the villa is worth €622,000. The buying exchange rate is €1.51 and the selling rate is €1.32.

    (3) *1,000 shares in Fire Ltd*

    Fire Ltd is an unquoted trading company valued at £725,000. Kari had owned the shares for ten years. The company does not hold any investments.

    The costs of dealing with the overseas property came to €5,852.

    Funeral expenses were £1,200.

    Kari had made no gross chargeable lifetime transfers and left her entire estate to her son, Nick.

    You are required to calculate the Inheritance Tax liability on Kari's estate. (5 marks)

5. The trustees of the Conn Family Discretionary Trust pass a property worth £725,000 out of the trust to one of the beneficiaries on 1 June 2009. The trust had been set up by Janet Conn on 12 April 2003 with cash of £450,000.

    Janet's only other lifetime gift had been a gift of £50,000 to her daughter on her wedding day on 25 April 2002.

    You are required to calculate the exit charge when the property leaves the trust, assuming the beneficiary pays any Inheritance Tax due. (5 marks)

6   The trustees of the Slocombe Discretionary Trust have a tax pool brought forward at the beginning of the tax year of £625.

   They receive dividend income of £19,800 and have no trust management expenses.

   They make an income payment of £9,000 to a beneficiary.

   You are required to calculate the trustees' Income Tax liability for 2009/10 and state the balance on the tax pool at the end of the year. (5 marks)

7   Alan sets up a discretionary trust on 15 May 2009 for his two children, Samantha (age 12) and Jake (age 9).

   The trust property consists of 50,000 shares in Loaded plc, a quoted trading company, and an investment property that is currently rented out. The annual trust income is expected to be in the region of £25,000 and expenses are expected to be approximately £1,500.

   The plan is for the trustees to pay the children's school fees from trust income.

   You are required to explain to Alan how the trust income will be taxed. You should ignore both Capital Gains Tax and Inheritance Tax. (5 marks)

8   Henry acquired some shares in York Ltd (an unlisted trading company) in June 2008. In March 2010 he settled them on to a trust for his children and grandchildren.

   Briefly explain the circumstances in which Business Property Relief will be available to reduce the transfer of value made by Henry to the trust. (5 marks)

9   **Give five instances where a donor can give away an asset, be able to benefit from the use of the asset after the gift and not be caught by the rules regarding Gifts With Reservation of Benefit.** (5 marks)

10   William is a company director earning £100,000 per annum. In June 2006, William created a discretionary trust for the benefit of his three minor children by settling an investment property (then worth £400,000). The chargeable gain of £120,000 on settlement was held over under s.260 TCGA 1992.

   In March 2010 the trustees sold the property for £600,000. This was their only disposal in 2009/10.

   You are required to calculate the Capital Gains Tax position in respect of the above. (5 marks)

11   Mrs Hathaway died on 5 April 2009 leaving her estate to her daughter Anne. The estate consisted of the family home, an investment property and a bank deposit.

   The Executors completed the administration of the estate on 31 January 2010. The income and expenses during the administration period were as follows;

	£
Rental income	24,000
Bank deposit interest (net)	4,800
Letting expenses	(4,000)
Estate management expenses	(400)
Interest on short term loan to pay the IHT	(2,500)

   You are required to show the entries required for form R185 (Estate Income) to be given to the residuary beneficiary. (5 marks)

12   (1)   Small-holding of arable pasture in northern France. Farmed by a tenant under a long lease since 1997.

   (2)   Cattle farm in North Yorkshire farmed by the taxpayer and his wife in partnership.

   (3)   Farmhouse (situated on the farmland) in which they live.

   (4)   Cattle herd.

   (5)   Tenanted land used by a sheep farmer in North Wales. 30 year lease signed in 1993 (due for renegotiation in 2013).

   Briefly explain whether the above assets will qualify for agricultural property relief and (if so) at what rate. You should assume all assets have been held for many years. (5 marks)

Module C

1. Harrap Ltd recently acquired 100% of the shares in Overseas Inc, a company incorporated in a country which is not in the European Union. Following the acquisition, a number of directors of Harrap Ltd will join the board of directors of Overseas Inc.

   Overseas Inc's main trading operations are outside of the UK but it operates a small manufacturing unit in the UK.

   You are required to advise Harrap Ltd on how the UK residency position of Overseas Inc will be determined and the Corporation Tax implications of Overseas Inc being UK or non-UK resident. (5 marks)

2. Gardener Ltd prepares accounts to 31 October. During the year to 31 October 2009 the following transactions took place:

		Cost/proceeds £
1 May 2009	Car acquired; CO_2 emissions 134g/km	11,000
1 June 2009	Van acquired	13,000
1 June 2009	Mercedes car sold	15,000
1 July 2009	Machine sold (original cost £35,000)	40,000

   The car acquired on 1 May 2009 was for the use of the sales manager and 25% of his annual mileage was for private purposes.

   The balances on the capital allowance pools as at 1 November 2008 were:

	£
Main pool	45,000
Mercedes car	24,000
Short life asset (acquired 1 May 2004)	4,000

   You are required to calculate the capital allowances available to Gardener Ltd for the year ended 31 October 2009. (5 marks)

3. Marine Ltd manufactures speedboats and prepares accounts to 31 March. In the year to 31 March 2010 the following transactions took place:

   (1) On 1 April 2009 the company issued £200,000 10% debentures. The funds were used to purchase an investment property which was rented out from 1 June 2009 at an annual rent of £25,000, payable quarterly in advance. The company incurred professional fees of £1,800 in connection with the issues of the debentures.

   (2) On 1 June 2009 the company took out a bank loan to fund the purchase of plant and machinery. Interest of £2,000 was paid during the year. Interest payable of £800 was accrued as at 31 March 2010.

   You are required to explain how the above income and expenditure will be treated in the Corporation Tax computation of Marine Ltd for the year to 31 March 2010. (5 marks)

4. Mammoth Ltd, an electrical engineering company, has always prepared accounts to 30 June. In 2009 it decided to change its accounting date and prepared accounts for the six months to 31 December 2009.

   The company's trading profit for the six months to 31 December 2009 was £200,000. This figure is adjusted for tax purposes, with the exception of the following items:

   (1) An amortisation charge of £20,000 in relation to the goodwill of a business acquired in May 2007 has not yet been charged in the profit and loss account.

   (2) Capital allowances for the year have not yet been computed. The balance on the capital allowance main pool as at 1 July 2009 was £50,000.

   On 1 August 2009 the company acquired plant and machinery for £15,000.

   Mammoth Ltd has no other income in the period.

   You are required to calculate Mammoth Ltd's Corporation Tax liability for the six months to 31 December 2009. (5 marks)

5   Circle Ltd owns 100% of the share capital of Oblong Ltd and 80% of Square Ltd. Square Ltd owns 80% of the share capital of Triangle Ltd.

All companies are UK resident.

The results of Circle Ltd and Oblong Ltd for the year ended 31 December 2009 are as follows:

Year ended:	Circle Ltd £	Oblong Ltd £
Trading profit/(loss)	50,000	(220,000)
Chargeable gain/(loss)	15,000	Nil
Bank interest	10,000	5,000
Charges on income – Gift Aid	2,000	6,000

You are required to:

(1) **State, giving reasons, whether Square Ltd and Triangle Ltd are in a group for group loss relief purposes with Circle Ltd and Oblong Ltd.** (2 marks)

(2) **Calculate the amount of losses of Oblong Ltd which are available for group relief and the maximum amount of loss that Circle Ltd could claim from Oblong Ltd.** (3 marks)

Total (5 marks)

6   Hotspur Ltd was incorporated on 1 January 2009. Its shares are wholly owned by Mr Percy.

Hotspur Ltd opened a bank account and began trading on 1 April 2009. The first accounts were drawn to 31 May 2010 and showed the following results;

	£
Adjusted trading profits before capital allowances	448,000
Bank interest receivable	7,000
Rental income (see below)	120,000

Plant and equipment was bought on 1 April 2009 for £53,000. Some equipment was sold in April 2010 for £1,000.

An investment property was acquired on 1 December 2009 and was immediately leased out at an annual rent of £120,000 payable in advance.

Compute the profits chargeable to Corporation Tax in respect of the period to 31 May 2010 and show the due date(s) for the submissions of forms CT 600. (5 marks)

7   Verona Ltd (a large company) has traditionally drawn up accounts to 30 April. It joined the Swan plc group on 1 May 2009 and, to coincide with that of its new parent company, duly changed its accounting reference date to 31 December.

Verona Ltd estimated that its chargeable profits for the eight months to 31 December 2009 would be £5 million. At their board meeting on 6 April 2010, the directors signed off the accounts and provisional tax computations showing chargeable profits of £6 million.

You are required to calculate the Corporation Tax payment required to be made on 14 April 2010. (5 marks)

8   **Give four ways in which a deficit on a non-trading loan relationship may be relieved.** (5 marks)

9   Orsino Ltd incorporated a new wholly owned subsidiary (Viola Ltd) on 1 January 2009. Viola Ltd opened a bank account and started to trade on 1 February 2009. First accounts are drawn to 30 September 2009. Orsino Ltd has one other subsidiary.

The accounts of Viola Ltd for its first accounting period show the following:

	£
Tax adjusted profit	125,000
Bank interest receivable	8,000
Dividend received on quoted investment	1,000

Viola Ltd's only capital acquisition was a car (CO_2 emissions 187g/km) costing £19,000 on 1 May 2009.

You are required to calculate the Corporation Tax payable by Viola Ltd for the period ended 30 September 2009. (5 marks)

10 **Briefly outline the circumstances in which the carry forward of trading losses could be denied on a change of ownership of a company.** (5 marks)

11 Lysander Ltd is a property investment company, wholly owned by Theseus Ltd. Theseus Ltd had incorporated Lysander Ltd in 2001 when it subscribed for 100,000 £1 ordinary shares at par.

In 2010, Quince Ltd paid £10m for all of the share capital of Lysander Ltd.

The main asset of Lysander Ltd is an office block that it rents out to various third party tenants.

The office block was originally owned by Puck Ltd, another 100% subsidiary of Theseus Ltd. Puck Ltd had constructed the office block for £1 million in 2000. It was transferred to Lysander Ltd in 2007 for £3 million, when its market value was £6 million.

You are required to calculate the chargeable gains arising as a result of the above transactions, stating clearly which company will be chargeable. You should ignore indexation allowance. (5 marks)

12 Cressida Ltd is a small company which manufactures paint. In its year ended 31 December 2009, it had the following income and expenditure:

	£	£
Income		
Paint sales		312,000
Patent royalty received from Mr Paris (UK trader)		8,000
		320,000
Expenses		
General manufacturing costs	120,000	
Research expenditure into new paint making methods	40,000	
Acquisition cost of business goodwill (Note)	100,000	
		(260,000)
Profit		60,000

Note

On 1 July 2009, Cressida Ltd paid £100,000 for the goodwill of a tin-making company. It will write the goodwill off over 5 years.

Calculate the Corporation Tax payable by Cressida Ltd for the year ended 31 December 2009. (5 marks)

Module D

1. A new client, Reginald, has advised you that he purchased an investment property and started receiving rental income of £10,000 per month from 1 January 2010. He notified HMRC of this new source of income on 15 September 2010 and was issued with a 2009/10 tax return on 10 November 2010. He filed this return online on 13 February 2011.

   You are required to advise Reginald on the following matters, providing reasons for your conclusions:
   (1) Whether he notified HMRC of his new source of income on time
   (2) Whether he filed his 2009/10 tax return on time
   (3) The deadline for Reginald to make amendments to his tax return
   (4) The deadline for HMRC to open an enquiry into Reginald's 2009/10 tax return
   (5) Any penalties which Reginald may have incurred in respect of the above matters.

   Assume FA 2009 penalty provisions apply. (5 marks)

2. Mr Falstaff is 76. In 2009/10 he received the following income:

	£
State pension	5,200
Employers pension (PAYE deducted £2,400)	16,000
Rental profits	4,800
Bank interest	750

   On 15 November 2009 he married Celia (63). Celia has self-employed trading profits of £30,000.

   On 1 January 2010 Mr Falstaff made a donation to charity of £500 under Gift Aid.

   You are required to calculate the Income Tax payable by Mr Falstaff for 2009/10. (5 marks)

3. Antony joined Cleo plc as a HR manager on 1 July 2009 on a salary of £60,000. His benefits package included the following:

   (1) Company car, list price £20,000, CO_2 emissions 168 g/km, all petrol costs reimbursed by the company.

   (2) Use of an unfurnished company-owned flat until such time as he found suitable family accommodation in the area. The flat cost £250,000 in 2006 and has an annual rental value £1,000. Antony paid a notional rent of £200 per month for the use of the flat. He bought a family house on 31 January 2010 and duly moved out of the flat.

   You should assume HM Revenue & Customs' official interest rate is 4.75%.

   You are required to calculate the taxable benefits arising in 2009/10. Assume Cleo plc has paid other relocation costs for Antony in excess of £8,000. (5 marks)

4. Eleanora was born in Australia, but moved to the UK 19 years ago to work for a UK company and has lived here ever since. She plans to return to Australia on her retirement in around five years' time.

   During 2009/10, Eleanora had the following income:

	£
UK employment income	70,000
Rent from letting out her house in Sydney (credited to her Australian bank account)	12,000
Dividend income from an overseas company (of which £11,000 was transferred to her UK account)	20,000

   You are required to discuss Eleanora's current residence and domicile status for UK tax purposes and explain the UK tax treatment of her various sources of income in 2009/10. You may assume that no overseas tax is payable on any of Eleanora's income and that she makes any beneficial claims. (5 marks)

5   On 15 March 2007, Jemima was granted share options to acquire 5,000 shares in her employer company, Puddle plc, at a price equal to the March 2007 market value of £6.80 per share. The options were granted under the company's Enterprise Management Incentive scheme.

   Jemima exercised her options in November 2009, by which time the shares were valued at £14.50 each. She sold the shares one month later for £14.70 per share.

   Jemima's shareholding represents less than 1% of the company's shares.

   You are required to explain (with supporting calculations where appropriate) Jemima's Income Tax, National Insurance Contributions and Capital Gains Tax position on grant and exercise of the options and on sale of the shares, assuming that she is a higher rate taxpayer and that she made no other chargeable gains during 2009/10. (5 marks)

6   Roderigo sold some quoted shares in 2007 making a substantial capital gain. In 2008 he subscribed for shares in a qualifying EIS company and elected to defer the gain arising.

   You are required to list five events which will result in the deferred gain becoming chargeable. (5 marks)

7   Jamie lets out a furnished flat in the UK and receives the following rent:

	£
18 December 2008: Annual rental to 31 December 2009	15,000
22 December 2009: Annual rental to 31 December 2010	15,600

   He also incurred the following expenditure on the property:

   (1)   Insurance premiums paid in advance for the next 12 months: £3,600 on 1 August 2008 and £4,200 on 1 August 2009.

   (2)   Council tax of £1,100 for the year to 31 March 2010.

   (3)   Replacement of a chimney in November 2009 at a cost of £800, following damage in a storm.

   (4)   Interest at 3% per annum on the outstanding loan of £200,000 which Jamie took out a few years ago in order to finance the purchase of the property.

   You are required to calculate Jamie's taxable property income for the 2009/10 tax year. (5 marks)

8   Emily is a director of Arcite Ltd with a salary of £50,000 per annum. During 2009/10 she also received the following remuneration:

   (1)   Bonus of £36,000 for year ended 31 March 2009 paid on 20 July 2009.

   (2)   Private medical insurance costing the company £480.

   (3)   Free accommodation in a flat which has a market value of £180,000 and is rented by the company at a rate of £10,800 per annum.

   (4)   Reimbursement of personal telephone bills totalling £650.

   You are required to calculate the 2009/10 National Insurance Contributions payable by Emily and the company in respect of her remuneration, assuming that Emily is not contracted out of S2P. (5 marks)

Question 9 has been amended for changes to capital gains tax legislation.

9   Maria made a number of disposals in February 2010, realising the following gains.

Date of purchase	Type of asset	Gain £
6 May 1971	Painting	Note
14 August 2007	Shares in West Ltd (20% shareholding)	45,000
2 November 2004	Shares in Coach plc (1% shareholding)	24,000

Note. The painting was acquired for £3,000. It was sold for £6,860, net of 2% auctioneers' fees. It was valued for insurance purposes at £4,000 in March 1982.

Both West Ltd and Coach plc are trading companies. Maria has been employed by West Ltd since 2004. Maria had capital losses brought forward at 6 April 2009 of £5,000.

You are required to calculate Maria's CGT payable for 2009/10. (5 marks)

10 Henry Percy sold his house in Scotland on 30 September 2009 realising a gain (after selling expenses) of £272,000.

He had bought the house in October 1978. On 1 April 1997 he bought a flat in Newcastle and elected for this property to be his main residence. He worked in Newcastle but continued to use the house in Scotland on occasional weekends. He sold the Newcastle flat in September 2008 and returned permanently to the house in Scotland.

In 2009/10, Henry had self-employed trading profits of £37,500 and made no other gains.

You are required to calculate Henry's Capital Gains Tax payable for 2009/10. (5 marks)

11 Oswald gave the following assets to his family members in 2009/10:

(1) In January 2010 he sold his shares in Shrew Ltd (an unlisted trading company) to his son Edmund for £40,000. He had bought the shares in February 2008 for £12,000 and they were worth £95,000 at the date of transfer. Oswald has never worked for Shrew Ltd.

(2) On 3 February 2010 he sold a painting to his daughter Cordelia for £10,000. He had inherited it in 2006 when it has a probate value of £25,000. It was worth £20,000 at the date of the transfer.

(3) In March 2010 he gave some shares in Southern Stone plc to his nephew Edgar. The shares had cost him £20,000 in May 2001 and were worth £8,000 at the date of the gift.

You are required to calculate the net gains arising and state the base cost of the assets for the recipients. Assume all appropriate claims are made. (5 marks)

12 Miranda bought 10,000 shares in Tempest plc in June 2006 for £80,000. On 1 July 2008, Tempest plc was taken over by Prospero plc. For each of their Tempest plc shares, the shareholders received the following:

Two new Prospero plc ordinary shares worth £4.75 each
£10 of non-convertible loan stock (valued at par)
£5.50 cash

In December 2009, Miranda redeemed her loan stock and received £85,000.

Miranda's shareholdings in Tempest plc and Prospero plc represented less than 1% of the companies' shares.

Miranda has never worked for Tempest plc.

You are required to calculate the gain / loss on redemption of the stock. (5 marks)

Module E

1. Albert is in business running a café. His accounts for the year to 30 June 2009 show a trading profit of £35,000, after deducting the following:

    (1) Legal fees of £500 in respect of renewing the ten year lease on the cafe.

    (2) Repair costs of £200 in respect of a second-hand refrigeration unit which was acquired during the year. The repairs were required prior to using the unit in order to comply with health and safety regulations.

    (3) Cost of acquiring a delivery van on 1 June 2009 for £6,000. The van is used 20% of the time by Albert for private purposes.

    (4) Parking fine of £50 incurred by Albert whilst making a delivery of sandwiches to a local business.

    You are required to calculate Albert's taxable trading profit for the year to 30 June 2009 giving an explanation for your treatment of the repair costs. (5 marks)

2. Maggie commenced business as a self-employed beautician on 1 February 2009. Her results for her first set of accounts for the fifteen month period to 30 April 2010 are as follows:

	£	£
Gross operating profit		120,000
Less : Wages (Note 1)	80,000	
Rent and rates (Note 2)	10,000	
Depreciation	2,000	
Telephone and utilities	2,500	
Sundry expenses (all allowable)	800	
		(95,300)
Net profit		24,700

    Notes

    (1) Wages includes £45,000 in respect of Maggie and £10,000 in respect of Maggie's daughter who works full time in the business.

    (2) Rent and rates relate to the whole of the building. The beauty salon occupies three of its rooms; Maggie's son lives in the fourth room.

    (3) During the period Maggie used goods which had cost £500 for her own personal use. The usual retail price of these goods was £850. No adjustments have been made in the accounts for the goods removed.

    You are required to calculate Maggie's taxable trading profit for the fifteen month period to 30 April 2010 and to state the basis period for the trading income assessment in 2009/10. (5 marks)

3. Karen operates a dress-making business as an unincorporated trader. The following capital transactions took place in the year to 31 August 2010:

		Cost £
Acquisitions		
1 October 2009	Jaguar car (40% private use; CO_2 emissions 178g/km)	25,000
1 December 2009	Ford car (20% private use; CO_2 emissions 154g/km)	10,000
1 April 2010	Delivery van	15,000

		Proceeds £
Disposals		
15 September 2009	Expensive car (Volvo) (40% private use)	12,000

    The Jaguar car acquired and the Volvo car disposed of during the year were used by Karen. The Ford car was used by the sales manager.

    The original cost of the Volvo car was £22,000.

The value of the capital allowance pools as at 1 September 2009 were:

	£
Main pool	25,000
Expensive car (Volvo)	16,000

You are required to calculate the capital allowances available to Karen for the year to 31 August 2010. Assume tax rates and allowances for 2009/10 continue into the future. (5 marks)

4 Gerald has traded as a self-employed carpenter for a number of years. On 31 December 2009 he ceased to trade.

Gerald's taxable trading profits had been as follows:

	£
Year to 30 June 2008	38,000
Year to 30 June 2009	34,000

His final accounts for the six months to 31 December 2009 show a tax adjusted trading profit before capital allowances of £15,000.

The only assets used in the business were a van, which he retained for his personal use, and items of plant and machinery which he sold for £6,500. Gerald had only ever used the van for business purposes.

The van had cost £15,000 in April 2003 and had a market value of £8,500 at 31 December 2009. None of the individual items of plant and machinery were sold for more than their original cost.

The tax written down value of the main capital allowances pool as at 1 July 2009 was £4,000.

Gerald had overlap profits in respect of his opening years' assessments of £8,000.

You are required to calculate Gerald's trading income assessment for 2009/10. (5 marks)

5 Brooke has been trading as a self-employed hairdresser for a number of years.

Her recent tax adjusted trading results have been as follows:

	£
Year to 31 May 2007	45,000
Year to 31 May 2008	26,000
Year to 31 May 2009	(10,000) loss

Brooke expects to have a tax adjusted trading profit of £500 for the year to 31 May 2010.

In addition to her trading income Brooke has other taxable income of £5,000 each year.

You are required to set out the options available to Brooke to utilise the loss arising in the year to 31 May 2009 and to explain the implications of each of the options. You do NOT need to quantify the amount of tax saved under each option. (5 marks)

6 Richard sold a freehold building for £850,000 on 1 August 2009. The building had always been used for business purposes. Richard had acquired the building on 1 July 2001 for £400,000.

On 1 September 2009 he acquired a new freehold building, for use in his business, for £750,000.

You are required to:

(1) **Calculate the chargeable gain arising on the sale of the building assuming that Richard will not claim to rollover the gain into the cost of the building acquired on 1 September 2009.** (2 marks)

(2) **Calculate the revised base cost of the building acquired on 1 September 2009 assuming that Richard claims to rollover the gain arising on the old building into the cost of the new building.** (3 marks)

Total (5 marks)

7   Antonio and Bassanio are in partnership sharing profits equally. Their only asset is the business goodwill, which they purchased in April 1991 for £200,000.

On 1 January 2010, Portia was admitted to the partnership and profits were thereafter split 50:30:20 between Antonio, Bassanio and Portia. No adjustment was made to the partnership accounts, although Portia made a direct payment of £80,000 to Bassanio for his share of the goodwill.

You are required to explain (with calculations) the capital gains consequences of Portia joining the partnership and show the base cost of her 20% share. (5 marks)

8   Horatio and Claudius have been in partnership for many years drawing up accounts annually to 30 November. Profits are split 3:2 after a salary of £15,000 to Claudius.

Horatio retired on 31 December 2009, so Claudius took the opportunity to move the accounts date to 31 December and thereafter continue as a sole trader. Profits for the period 1 December 2008 to 31 December 2009 were £260,000.

Both Horatio and Claudius had overlap profits carried forward of £15,000.

You are required to calculate the taxable trading profit for 2009/10 for Horatio and Claudius. (5 marks)

9   Toby started trading on 1 May 2008. His results have been as follows:

	Profit/(loss)
	£
1 May 2008 to 31 January 2009	60,000
1 February 2009 to 30 April 2009	(30,000)
1 May 2009 to 30 April 2010	90,000

You are required to calculate the National Insurance Contributions payable by Toby for 2009/10. (5 marks)

10 Florence owned a gift shop. She retired on 31 March 2010 and sold the business to an unconnected buyer, Oliver. Oliver paid Florence £400,000 for the business and the two parties agreed that this be broken down as follows.

	£
Business premises	220,000
Goodwill	100,000
Stock	60,000
Plant and machinery	20,000
	400,000

The stock cost £10,000 and had an estimated market value of £25,000. Florence has trading losses brought forward to offset any trade profits arising.

You are required to show the adjustment, if any, which should be made to Florence's final trading profits in respect of her stock. (5 marks)

11 Warwick started trading as a wedding singer on 1 January 2009. His tax adjusted profits have been as follows:

	£
Year ended 31 December 2009	12,000
Period ended 30 April 2011	30,000

His only asset is his electric keyboard and amplifier bought in December 2008 for £6,000.

You are required to calculate the taxable trading profits for 2010/11 and show any overlap profits to be carried forward. (5 marks)

12 Morgan started trading on 1 May 2008. He notified his chargeability to Income Tax in July 2009 and was duly sent a 2008/09 tax return, which he filed on 29 January 2010. The Income Tax and Class 4 National Insurance Contributions due for 2008/09 totalled £16,000.

Within the return, Morgan made a claim to reduce his payments on account for 2009/10 to £5,500 each.

Morgan submitted his 2009/10 return on 27 February 2011 showing tax and National Insurance Contributions due for the year of £13,000. No claim was made to reduce his payments on account for 2010/11.

The following tax payments have been made:

	£
29 January 2010	21,500
30 September 2010	5,500
31 March 2011	8,500

Assume HM Revenue & Customs' official interest rate is 2.5%.

You are required to calculate the interest and penalties for which Morgan is liable. (5 marks)

Assume FA 2009 penalty provisions apply.

Mock Exam 1: Answers

Module A

1 Alpha Developments

(1) Recovery on computer:

In year to 31 March 2008 (interval 1 – initial recovery): (70% × £24,500) = £17,150
In year to 31 March 2009 (interval 2 – annual adjustment): 1/5 × £24,500 × (85% – 70%) = £735

In both cases, the input tax can be reclaimed.

(2) The sale of the computer is a taxable supply and the VAT on the remaining adjustment periods will be made on the basis that the computer was wholly used for taxable purposes (Regulations 115(3)).

In the year to 31 March 2010 the adjustment percentage is 75% (ie. taxable use of computer in period prior to sale).

Adjustment (credit) is (75 – 70)% × £24,500 × 1/5 = £245

For the years to 31 March 2011 and 2012 the adjustment is (100 – 70)% × 24,500 × 2/5 = £2,940

As the VAT charged on the sale of the computer is £6,130, the whole of the sale credit of £2,940 can be reclaimed (Regulation 115(3)).

Total adjustment (credit to business) = £3,185

2 Categorise

(1) Standard rated supply of the freehold of a 'new' (less than 3 years old) commercial building. As this supply is already standard rated the option to tax is not applicable.

(2) Exempt supply of land, however, Farmer Giles may opt to tax the land prior to the sale to standard rate the supply.

(3) Exempt supply. The option to tax cannot be exercised in respect of buildings which will be used as a dwelling.

(4) Exempt supply of lease. Zero rating does not apply since 'major interest' has not been supplied by constructor. Option to tax cannot be exercised in respect of buildings which will be used as a dwelling.

(5) Exempt supply of a commercial lease. Stats Construction may opt to tax the supply to standard rate the sale.

3 Horricks Ltd

(1) The sale of the business is a transfer of a going concern and is therefore outside the scope of VAT, assuming certain conditions are met, eg JL Industries Ltd uses the assets acquired from Horricks Ltd for the same kind of business, there is no significant break in trade, etc. However, unless JL Industries complies with additional obligations, TOGC treatment will not apply to the warehouse since it is 'new' (less than three years old) and if sold in isolation would be a standard rated supply.

(2) VAT due

Warehouse £250,000 × 17.5% = £43,750

Goodwill and plant/machinery are outside the scope of VAT on this transfer.

However, if JL Industries Ltd complies with certain additional obligations, the sale of the warehouse will fall within the TOGC and will therefore will not be subject to VAT. In order for this to be the case, JL Industries must:

- Opt to tax the warehouse
- Notify HMRC of this option to tax, and
- Notify Horricks that this option to tax will not be disapplied under special anti-avoidance rules

JL Industries must do all of this by the 'relevant date' (usually the date of completion).

If JL Industries Ltd does opt to tax, it will have to charge VAT on any supplies it makes in the future with respect to the warehouse (eg if it leases the building to another party).

4 Lancashire Candles Ltd

Scents Ltd

The debt is over six months old. VAT due is 3/23 × £2,000 = £261. This can be claimed as bad debt relief on next return to 30 June 2010 if debt is written off in Company's accounts.

Hope Ltd

The VAT relating to the debt would have been £1,304 (£10,000 × 3/23). The date on which the debt can be written off for BDR purposes is 10 December 2009 so the debt is over six months old. As for Scents above, bad debt relief is available if the debt is written off in the company's accounts.

Dot Ltd

£5,000 was due and £1,500 is repaid (by way of dividend) so £3,500 is outstanding. The debt is six months old (the date on which the debt can be written off for BDR purposes is 30 December 2009) so, as above, bad debt relief is due for £457 (£3,500 × 3/23) if the debt is written off in the company's books.

Jingle Ltd

The debt is not yet six months old (the date on which the debt can be written off for BDR purposes is 25 April 2010) so bad debt relief is not available on either the quarter ended June 2010 return or the quarter ended September 2010 return. The company must wait until the quarter ended 31 December 2010 return to claim £446 (£3,000 × 7/47 – the VAT rate reverts to 17.5% from 1 January 2010).

5 Charlie and Bella Royle

The business must notify HMRC of a need to deregister by 30 May 2010 as it ceased to trade on 30 April 2010.

The following assets had input tax reclaimed on them and were in the business on the last day of registration.

	£
Van	12,000
Sports equipment	1,000
	13,000

Note: VAT was not recovered on the purchase of the car so it is ignored in the above calculation.

VAT must be accounted for on the above assets. As the VAT on the deemed supply is not below the de minimis of £1,000, the partnership must declare the VAT due on the final VAT return of the business.

When the van and equipment are later sold VAT is not charged as the business is no longer VAT registered.

6 Simply Bags Ltd

The VAT implications of the transactions are as follows:

(1) This is a dispatch to an EU customer in France. If Simply Bags Ltd has the French VAT registration number of Cordes SARL it may zero rate the sale of bags. If not it must charge VAT at the standard rate. It must also obtain and retain commercial evidence to show that the goods were despatched to another member state.

(2) This is an import. The goods will be held at the port of entry until Simply Bags Ltd pays the standard rate VAT (and other taxes) due to release the goods. This VAT is input tax and can be recovered in the normal way on the VAT return covering the date of importation.

(3) This is an acquisition from an EU supplier. If Simply Bags Ltd gave the supplier its UK VAT registration number the goods will arrive at the premises of the company VAT free. Simply Bags Ltd must charge itself standard rate VAT on these goods. This will be in the form of acquisition tax which must be declared on the VAT return covering the date of acquisition. Subject to the usual rules, Simply Bags may deduct this as input tax on the same VAT return.

7 Hermione

2009	£
July	5,000
August	5,000
September	5,000
October	5,000
November	5,000
December	24,000
2010	
January	5,000
February	5,000
March	5,000
April	5,000
Total	69,000

Hermione should have notified her liability to register for VAT by 30 May 2010 and should have charged VAT on sales from 1 June 2010. She is therefore 10 months late.

The penalty will be a percentage of the potential lost revenue ie the amount of VAT due from 1 June 2010 to the date HMRC received notification (29 March 2011). The percentage will be based on the behaviour causing the failure. The maximum percentage is 100% (if the failure is deliberate and concealed). The penalty will be reduced if there is disclosure. As the failure in this case was rectified within 12 months, if the failure was not deliberate and there was unprompted disclosure, the penalty may be reduced to nil.

8 Olivia

$$\frac{\text{Taxable supplies}}{\text{Total supplies}} = \frac{60,000 - 4,000}{60,000 - 4,000 + 12,500} = 81.75\% \text{ (round to 82\%)}$$

Note: exclude supplies of capital items in partial exemption fraction.

Input tax recoverable:	£
Taxable supplies	6,800
Non-attributable (£1,000 × 82%)	820
Recoverable input tax	7,620

Exempt input tax is:	
Exempt	1,500
Non attributable £(1,000 – 820)	180
De minimis (< £625 per month and less than 50% of the total input VAT for the period) thus recoverable in this period)	1,680

VAT due:	
Output tax	£
£53,000 × 17.5%	9,275
Input tax recoverable £(7,620 + 1,680)	(9,300)
VAT repayable	(25)

9 Marlowe Group

The following companies CANNOT be within the VAT group:

- Shrew Ltd (not under common control – ie < 50% owned)
- Venice SA (no UK place of business / fixed establishment in the UK)

The other companies can form a VAT Group (including the exempt company, Titus Ltd).

The main effects of group VAT registration are:

(a) The group is treated as one single taxable person.

(b) One company (the 'representative member') is responsible for all VAT accounting including the completion and submission of VAT returns.

(c) All the companies within the group registration are jointly and severally liable for any VAT due.

(d) Any supplies made between members of the VAT group are ignored (ie such supplies are outside the scope of VAT).

10 Tempest Ltd

Deposit

The basic tax point is the date the goods are dispatched – ie 15 January 2010.

However, a deposit is paid before this date, so the earlier date becomes the tax point but only to the extent of the deposit paid.

The tax point for the deposit is therefore 12 December 2009.

Balance

The basic tax point is the date the goods are dispatched – ie 15 January 2010.

An invoice is issued within 14 days of the basic tax point, so the invoice date becomes the tax point.

The tax point for the balance is therefore 20 January 2010.

The date of payment of the balance has no impact here.

11 Gower Ltd

30.6.09	Late return and VAT. SLN issued covering period from 1.7.09 to 30.6.10. No penalty charged.
30.9.09	Return & VAT on time.
31.12.09	Late return and VAT. 2% penalty applies. 2% × £30,000 = £600. Surcharge period extended to 31.12.10.
31.3.10	Return late. Repayment return so no penalty charged but surcharge period extended to 31.3.11.
30.6.10	Late payment of VAT. 5% penalty applies. 5% × £7,000 = £350. This is less than £400 so it will not be collected. Surcharge period extended to 30.6.11

12 Harry

The SDLT on the lease is:

	£
Duty on premium: £95,000 × 1% (note)	950
Duty on rent: £(180,000 – 150,000) × 1%	300
Total duty	1,250

Note

The zero rate charge does not apply because the annual rental exceeds £1,000 and the land is non-residential property.

The SDLT is payable by Richard no later than 12 July 2010 (30 days from completion).

Module B

1 Paul

Any gift to a trust during a person's lifetime (except to a bare trust or trust for a disabled person) is a chargeable lifetime transfer as the trust is a relevant property trust. This trust cannot be a bereaved minor trust or age 18-25 trust as it is being set up during Paul's lifetime.

The tax due is:

	£	£
Transfer of value		275,000
Less: AE 2009/10 (Note)		(3,000)
AE 2008/09 b/f		(3,000)
CLT		269,000
Less: nil rate band	325,000	
Less: GCTs	(115,500)	
		(209,500)
Chargeable		59,500
Tax @ 20/80 or 25%		14,875

Note: The full annual exempt amount for both 2009/10 and 2008/09 are available as the Christmas gifts to Paul's nieces and nephews come within the small gifts exemption as they are below £250.

The GCT is the total amount that leaves Paul's estate as a result of the gift (ie the chargeable gift PLUS the tax):

£269,000 + £14,875 = £283,875

2 Anne

Gifts between spouses are usually exempt from IHT. However, Gus has arguably retained his New Zealand domicile of origin because he intends to return to New Zealand if Anne dies before him, which is likely considering the age difference. He has no intention to make England his permanent home.

Since only the first £55,000 of transfers from a UK domiciled spouse to a non-UK domiciled spouse are exempt, only gifts up to this amount from Anne to Gus will be exempt.

Anne should consider making gifts up to this amount now. She will be able to use her annual exempt amount of £3,000 for the year of the gift and the exemption from the previous year as this has not already been used. The annual exempt amount is not available for transfers on death.

If she gifts more than the £55,000 limit, the excess will be a potentially exempt transfer (PET) for IHT purposes. A PET is exempt during the donor's lifetime and only becomes chargeable if they die within seven years of making the gift. So, if Anne survives more than seven years from making the gift, it will be completely exempt.

A final planning consideration could be for Anne to make regular gifts out of income. These are fully exempt from IHT so long as she can show a regular pattern of giving and that the gifts do not affect her standard of living.

3 Lisa

As Lisa provided the funds for the purchase of the property that she now lives in the property is caught by the Pre-Owned Asset Tax (POAT) rules.

There is an income tax charge equivalent to the annual value of the land less any amount paid by the individual for their use of it.

The charge in respect of Lisa's occupation of the property is:

£18,525 @ 40% = £7,410.

Lisa can avoid an income tax charge by paying David a market rent for her occupation of the property.

4 Kari

	£
Death estate	
Quoted shares (W1)	37,566
Holiday home (W2)	411,921
Unquoted shares (W3)	NIL
Total	449,487
Less: administration costs	
$5,852 ÷ 1.51	(3,875)
	445,612
Less: reasonable funeral expenses	(1,200)
Death estate	444,412
Less: nil rate band	(325,000)
	119,412

Tax @ 40% = £47,765

Workings

(1) Quoted shares

Quoted shares are valued at the lower of the quarter-up and mid bargain values. As the shares had gone ex-div at the date of death, the value of the next dividend must be included in the value.

15,000 shares @ lower of:

(i) $\frac{1}{4}$-up:

$(235 - 230.25) \div 4 + 230.25 = 231.4375$

(ii) Mid bargain:

$\frac{231 + 234}{2} = 232.50$

	£
ie £2.314375 × 15,000 =	34,716
Add: dividend 15,000 × 19p	2,850
Probate value	37,566

(2) Foreign property

Valued at the buying (ie the lower) exchange rate: €622,000 ÷ €1.51 = £411,921

(3) Unquoted shares

BPR is available for the shares as they are unquoted trading company shares that Kari has owned for more than two years.

	£
Shares	725,000
Less: BPR @ 100%	(725,000)
	NIL

5 Conn Family Discretionary Trust

Exit charge

	£
Transfer to trust	450,000
Less: nil rate band (Note)	(325,000)
	125,000

Tax @ 20% = £25,000

Effective rate:

$$\frac{25,000}{450,000} \times 100 = 5.55555\%$$

Actual rate:

$5.55555\% \times 30\% \times {}^{24}/_{40} = 0.99999\%$

Exit charge:

$0.99999\% \times £725,000 = £7,250$

Note. The PET to her daughter on her wedding day does not use up any of the nil rate band as it is exempt during lifetime.

6 Slocombe Discretionary Trust

Income payments to discretionary trust beneficiaries come with a 40% tax credit. The trustees must have paid sufficient tax to cover this tax credit. They keep a tally of all the tax paid to HMRC in the 'tax pool'.

If there is insufficient tax paid to HMRC in the tax pool, the trustees have an additional liability that must be paid over with any other income tax liability. If there is sufficient tax, the balance is carried forward to cover payments in future years.

	£
Dividend income × $^{100}/_{90}$	22,000
Taxable income	22,000
Basic rate band:	
£1,000 @ 10%	100
£21,000 @ 32.5%	6,825
Income tax liability	6,925
Less: 10% tax credit: £22,000 × 10%	(2,200)
Income tax due (and entering the tax pool)	4,725

The balance on the tax pool is:

	£
Tax pool b/f	625
Add: tax paid in current year	4,725
Available tax credits	5,350
Less: tax required to cover beneficiary's payment:	
£9,000 × $^{40}/_{60}$	(6,000)
Additional tax liability	650
Total tax liability: £650 + £4,725	5,375
Tax pool c/f	NIL

7 Alan

The first £1,000 of non-savings income will be taxed at the basic rate.

In addition any income used to pay trust expenses is also taxed at the basic rate depending on the type of income used to pay them (dividend income first).

The balance of non-savings income will be taxed at 40% and the dividends at 32.5%.

When the beneficiaries either receive income from the trust or funds are used for their benefit (eg when the trustees pays their school fees) that income is usually taxable on them. Such payments come with a 40% tax credit.

However, as Alan's unmarried minor children can benefit from the trust it is a settlor interested trust. This means that any income paid to or used for the benefit of the children will be taxed on Alan unless it is below the annual de minimis limit of £100 (gross).

It is unlikely that the school fees will be below this limit so the income used to pay the fees will not be taxed on the children but instead on Alan.

8 Henry

Where relevant business property has not been owned for 2 years, BPR will still be given if:

(a) 'Old' business property has been sold in the prior 3 years and replaced with the York Ltd shares. BPR will be given on the York Ltd shares if the aggregated ownership periods total at least two of the five years immediately preceding the transfer, or

(b) If Henry had acquired the York Ltd shares on the death of his spouse and the joint ownership period was at least 2 years, or

(c) Henry has acquired the shares on the death of a person within the last 2 years and that death transfer had qualified for BPR.

[see s.107 – 109 IHTA 1984]

9 Gifts with Reservation of Benefit

- Where the donor pays full consideration for the use of the asset
- Where the donor gives away half of a house then shares that house with the donee (provided that the donor pays a reasonable share of all outgoings) (see IRPR 15.5.87)
- Where the donor gives away a house and stays with the donee for less than one month a year in total (or less than 2 weeks if the donee is not present)
- Where the donor gives a house to a donee then stays with the donor for a short-term purpose (eg while convalescing after medical treatment)
- Where the donor gives away land then uses that land to walk dogs etc, as long as this does not restrict the donee's use.

(+ marks for other examples in HMRC Tax Bulletin November 1993).

10 William

Capital gain arising

	£	£
Proceeds		600,000
Cost	400,000	
Less: held over gain	(120,000)	
		(280,000)
Trustees gain		320,000
Less: AE		(5,050)
Taxable gain		314,950

CGT @ 18% = £56,691

11 Mrs Hathaway

	Non savings £	Interest £
2009/10		
Rental profit	20,000	
Interest (× 100/80)		6,000
Less: deductible payment (loan interest)	(2,500)	
Taxable income	17,500	6,000
Less: tax suffered at 20%	(3,500)	(1,200)
Net income	14,000	4,800
Less: estate expenses		(400)
Net distributable income	14,000	4,400

R185 (Estate income)	Gross £	Tax £	Net £
Non savings	17,500	3,500	14,000
Interest	5,500	1,100	4,400

12 Agricultural property relief

- Yes – APR available on land situated in EEA.
- Yes – relief given at 100% × agricultural value. BPR may be available on residual value.
- Yes – assuming that the farmhouse is 'of a character appropriate to the property'.
- No – livestock may instead qualify for BPR.
- Yes – relief given at 50% × agricultural value as lease signed pre 1.9.95 and has more than 2 years left to run.

Module C

1 Overseas Inc

Overseas Inc is incorporated outside of the UK. It will therefore only be resident in the UK if its central management and control is exercised in the UK. If the central management and control is exercised by the board of directors, the place where the board meetings are held will be an important factor in determining the residence of the company.

If Overseas Inc is deemed to be UK resident it will be subject to UK corporation tax on its worldwide profits. The profits arising from both the UK and overseas operations will therefore be taxed in the UK.

A non-UK resident company is only taxed in the UK on profits arising from a trade carried on through a permanent establishment in the UK, eg the manufacturing unit. If Overseas Inc is non-UK resident it will only be taxed in the UK on the profits arising from the UK manufacturing operations.

Double tax relief may be available for income which is taxed both in the UK and overseas.

2 Gardener Ltd

Capital allowances computation for the year to 31 October 2009

	AIA £	Main Pool £	Expensive Car £	Short life asset (SLA) £	Allowances £
TWDV at 1.11.08		45,000	24,000	4,000	
SLA transfer (held > 5 APs)		4,000		(4,000)	
Acquisitions					
1.5.09 Car (<160g/km)		11,000			
1.6.09 Van	13,000				
AIA	(13,000)				13,000
Disposals:					
1.7.08 Machine (limited to cost)		(35,000)			
1.6.08 Expensive car			(15,000)		
		25,000	9,000		
Balancing allowance			(9,000)		9,000
WDA @ 20%		(5,000)			5,000
TWDV cfwd		20,000	–	–	
Total allowances					27,000

3 Marine Ltd

(1) The debentures were issued to raise funds for non-trade related purposes and are therefore a non-trading loan relationship. The interest payable, on an accrued basis, of £20,000 will be a debit on a non-trading loan relationship. The associated professional fees will be treated in the same way.

The accrued rent for the 10 months to 31 March 2010 of £20,833 (£25,000 × 10/12) will be taxed as property income.

(2) The bank loan was used for trading purposes and is therefore a trade related loan relationship. Interest payable is an allowable deduction from trading income. The interest is deductible on accrued basis and £2,800 will therefore be an allowable deduction from trading profits.

4 Mammoth Ltd

Corporation tax liability for the six months ended 31 December 2009

	£
Trading income:	
Trading profit per accounts	200,000
Amortisation charge	(20,000)
Capital allowances:	
Pool WDA £50,000 × 20% × 6/12	(5,000)
Plant AIA £15,000 × 100%	(15,000)
Profits chargeable to corporation tax	160,000
Corporation tax liability (W):	
£160,000 × 28%	44,800
Less marginal relief:	
7/400 × (£750,000 − £160,000)	(10,325)
	34,475

Working

Rate of corporation tax

The accounting period is 6 months long. The limits used to determine the rate of corporation tax are therefore multiplied by 6/12:

Upper limit: £1,500,000 × 6/12	£750,000
Lower limit £300,000 × 6/12	£150,000

The company is therefore a small companies' marginal relief company for the period.

5 Circle Ltd

(1) Loss relief group

Circle Ltd owns at least 75% of Square Ltd. They therefore form a loss relief group.

Triangle Ltd is not in a loss relief group with Circle Ltd as Circle Ltd's indirect holding in Triangle Ltd is less than 75% ie 64% (80% × 80%).

Square Ltd and Triangle Ltd can form a separate loss relief group.

(2) Group relief − Year ended 31 December 2009

Oblong Ltd can surrender its current year trading loss of £220,000 and its excess charges on income of £1,000 (£6,000 − £5,000).

Circle Ltd can claim losses of £73,000 from Oblong Ltd, ie the amount of its profits chargeable to corporation tax (ie total profits (including gains) less charges on income).

6 Hotspur Ltd

	12 m/e 31.3.10 £	2 m/e 31.5.10 £
Adjusted profit before CAs (12:2)	384,000	64,000
CAs: AIA £50,000 (max)	(50,000)	
Balance £3,000 × 40%	(1,200)	
£(3,000 − 1,200 − 1,000) × 20% × 2/12		(27)
Trading Income	332,800	63,973
Profit on non-trading loan relationship (12:2)	6,000	1,000
Property income (4/12 : 2/12)	40,000	20,000
PCTCT	378,800	84,973
Due dates for CT 600	31.5.11	31.5.11

7 Verona Ltd

8 month CAP, therefore 3 payments on account required.

Initial payments based on profit estimate of £5m.

Instalment	Due	Working	£
1	14.11.09	£5m × 28% × 3/8	525,000
2	14.2.10	£5m × 28% × 3/8	525,000
			1,050,000
3	14.4.10	Balance required (N)	630,000
Total tax payable			1,680,000

Note. Revised tax due = £6m × 28% = £1,680,000.

8 Non-trading loan relationship

(1) Against profits of the same accounting period before charges and s.393A loss relief.
(2) Surrendered as group relief.
(3) Carried back 12 months against credits on non-trading loan relationships.
(4) Against non-trading profits of the next accounting period.

9 Orsino Ltd

The chargeable accounting period is 1.2.09 to 30.9.09 (ie 8 months)

	£	£
Tax adjusted profit	125,000	
Less: capital allowances		
£19,000 × 10% × 8/12	(1,267)	
Trading profit		123,733
Profit on non-trading loan relationship		8,000
PCTCT		131,733
FII (£1,000 × 100/90)		1,111
Notional profits		132,844

There are 3 associated companies:

	£
Upper limit (£1.5 m × 1/3 × 8/12)	333,333
Lower limit (£300,000 × 1/3 × 8/12)	66,667

Marginal relief applies.

	£
CT due:	
£131,733 × 28%	36,885
7/400 × £(333,333 – 132,844) × $\frac{131,733}{132,844}$ ×	(3,479)
Corporation tax payable	33,406

10 Trading losses

The carry forward of trading losses is denied where within a three year period there is BOTH

(1) a change of ownership of a company, AND
(2) a 'major change in the nature or conduct of the trade' carried on by the company.

A change will be 'major' if there is a change in any of the following:

- The type of property dealt in
- The type of services provided
- The facilities provided
- Customers
- Outlets
- Markets.

The carry forward of trading losses is also denied where:

(1) The company's activities had become small or negligible, and
(2) There is a change of ownership of the company, and
(3) Following the change of ownership there is a considerable revival in the scale of activities.

11 Lysander Ltd

The sale of the shares in Lysander Ltd will result in a gain chargeable on Theseus Ltd.

	£
Proceeds	10,000,000
Less: cost 2001	(100,000)
Gain chargeable	9,900,000

The substantial shareholding exemption does not apply as Lysander Ltd is not a trading company.

There will also be a de-grouping charge as the office block had been transferred to Lysander Ltd in a no gain/ no loss transfer within 6 years of Lysander leaving the group:

	£
Market value at transfer in 2007	6,000,000
Less: Cost to group in 2000	(1,000,000)
Gain chargeable	5,000,000

This gain will be chargeable on Lysander Ltd.

12 Cressida Ltd

	£	£
Trading income:		
Paint sales		312,000
Patent royalty ($\times$ 100/80)		10,000
		322,000
Expenses:		
General manufacturing costs	120,000	
R&D expenditure (£40,000 $\times$ 175%)	70,000	
Amortisation of goodwill:		
£100,000 $\times$ 1/5 $\times$ 6/12	10,000	
		(200,000)
PCTCT		122,000

Small company.

Tax:	£
£122,000 $\times$ 21%	25,620
Less: income tax suffered on patent royalty income	(2,000)
	23,620

Module D

1 Reginald

Reginald has notified chargeability on time. The deadline is 5 October 2010 for 2009/10.

As HMRC issued the tax return after 31 October, the deadline for filing online was 3 months after the tax return was issued, ie by 10 February 2011. Therefore, Reginald filed his return late.

Reginald can amend his return within 12 months of the filing deadline – ie up until 10 February 2012.

If a return is filed late, HMRC has until the quarter day following the first anniversary of the actual filing date to open an enquiry, ie 30 April 2012.

As Reginald filed his return three days late, he will incur a penalty of £100.

2 Mr Falstaff

	Non savings £	Savings £
State pension	5,200	
Employer's pension	16,000	
Rental profits	4,800	
Bank interest ($\times ^{100}/_{80}$)		937
Net income	26,000	937
Less: PAA (W1)	(7,934)	
Taxable income	18,066	937

Tax		£
18,066 @ 20%		3,613
937 @ 20%		187
Tax liability		3,800
Less: PAYE		(2,400)
Tax on interest		(187)
Tax payable		1,213

Working

	£
Income	26,937
Less: gift aid (£500 × $^{100}/_{80}$)	(625)
Income for PAA purposes	26,312

	£
PAA (>75)	9,640
Less $^{1}/_{2}$ × (26,312 − 22,900)	(1,706)
	7,934

Note. As marriage takes place after 5 December 2005, the married couples allowances goes to the one with the highest income (in this case this is Celia).

3 Antony

	£	£
Car: £20,000 × 21% × 9/12 $\frac{(165-135)}{5} + 15 = 21\%$		3,150
Fuel: £16,900 × 21% × 9/12		2,662
Accommodation:		
Annual value	1,000	
Additional yearly rent		
£(250,000 − 75,000) × 4.75%	8,312	
	9,312	
× 7/12	5,432	
Less: rent paid (£200 × 7)	(1,400)	
		4,032
Total taxable benefits		9,844

4 Eleanora

Eleanora is currently resident and ordinarily resident, but non-domiciled in the UK. Even though she has lived here for many years, she retains her non-domicile status because she has a clear intention to return to live in Australia.

Her UK employment income will be taxable in full in the UK on an arising basis.

As a non-domiciled individual, she may claim for her overseas income to be taxable in the UK only to the extent that it is remitted to the UK, which would mean that the rental income of £12,000 is not taxable in the UK.

The overseas dividend income would only be taxable to the extent that it was remitted to the UK (ie £11,000). This amount would be taxed as non-savings income at a rate of 40%.

However, as Eleanora has been resident in the UK for at least 7 out of the preceding 9 tax years she would be subject to the £30,000 remittance basis charge if she claims to be taxed on the remittance basis. This is in addition to the tax charged on her remitted income. It would not therefore be beneficial for Eleanora to claim the remittance basis in respect of 2009/10 and she will be taxed on all her foreign income on an arising basis.

5 Jemima

Grant

There is no tax or NIC on the grant of options under the EMI scheme.

Exercise

There is no tax or NIC on the exercise of the EMI options, because the exercise price was not less than the market value of the shares at the date of grant.

Sale of shares

The gain on the sale of shares is subject to CGT, as follows:

	£
Proceeds (£14.70 × 5,000)	73,500
Cost (£6.80 × 5,000)	(34,000)
	39,500
Annual exempt amount	(10,100)
	29,400

CGT @ 18% = £5,292

6 Roderigo

The deferred gain will crystallise if:

(1) Roderigo disposes of the shares (other than by way of a gift to his spouse/civil partner)

(2) After transferring the shares to his spouse/civil partner, the spouse/civil partner then disposes of the shares

(3) Roderigo becomes neither resident nor ordinarily resident within 3 years from the issue of the shares

(4) After giving the shares to the spouse/civil partner, the spouse/civil partner becomes neither resident nor ordinarily resident within 3 years from the issue of the shares

(5) The EIS shares cease to be eligible for relief.

7 Jamie

		£	£
Rent	($^9/_{12}$ × £15,000)	11,250	
	($^3/_{12}$ × £15,600)	3,900	
			15,150
Less allowable expenses:			
Insurance	($^4/_{12}$ × £3,600)		(1,200)
	($^8/_{12}$ × £4,200)		(2,800)
Council tax			(1,100)
Chimney replacement (Note)			(800)
Interest	(3% × £200,000)		(6,000)
Wear and tear allowance	(10% × £(15,150 – 1,100))		(1,405)
Property income (2009/10)			1,845

Note. Replacement of a subsidiary part of an asset (eg chimney) is treated as revenue expenditure and therefore allowable.

8 Emily

Class 1 primary – payable by Emily

	£
Earnings	
Salary	50,000
Bonus	36,000
Telephone bills	650
	86,650
Class 1 primary: £(43,875 – 5,715) × 11%	4,198
£(86,650 – 43,875) × 1%	428
	4,626

Class 1 secondary – payable by Arcite Ltd

£(86,650 – 5,715) × 12.8% = £10,360

Class 1A – payable by Arcite Ltd

	£
Accommodation (note)	10,800
Medical insurance	480
	11,280

£11,280 × 12.8% = £1,444

Note. No additional benefit in respect of the accommodation as the property is not owned by the employer.

9 Maria

Capital gains tax computation 2009/10

		£	£
1	*Painting*		
	Proceeds	6,860	
	31.3.82 MV	(4,000)	
	Gain	2,860	
	Restricted to:		
	$5/3 \times £(7,000 - 6,000)$ (gross proceeds used)		1,667
2	*West Ltd*		
	Gain before reliefs	45,000	
	Less Entrepreneurs' relief		
	£45,000 × 4/9	(20,000)	
	Gain		25,000
3	*Coach plc*		24,000
	Total gains		50,667
	Less losses brought forward		(5,000)
			45,667
	Less annual exempt amount		(10,100)
	Taxable gain		35,567

CGT at 18% = £6,402

10 Henry Percy

	£
Gain	272,000
Less: PPR relief $18/27.5 \times £272,000$ (W1)	(178,036)
Gain	93,964
Less: AE	(10,100)
Taxable gain	83,864

CGT: £83,864 @ 18% = £15,096

WORKING

	Occupied years	*Absent years*
1.4.82 – 31.3.97	15	
1.4.97 – 30.9.06		9.5
1.10.06 – 30.9.09	3	
(last 3 years)		
Total	18	9.5

11 Oswald

	£	£
Shares to son:		
MV	95,000	
Less: cost	(12,000)	
Gain	83,000	
Less: s.165 gift relief	(55,000)	
Chargeable gain £(40,000 – 12,000)	28,000	
		28,000

Base cost for son: £95,000 – 55,000 = £40,000

Painting to daughter:		
MV	20,000	
Less: cost	(25,000)	
Loss	(5,000)	
'Connected persons' loss so no relief against other gains		NIL

Base cost for daughter: £20,000

Shares to nephew:		
MV	8,000	
Less: cost	(20,000)	
Loss	(12,000)	
Nephew not a 'connected person' so general loss relief allowed		(12,000)

Base cost for nephew: £8,000

Net gains 2009/10		16,000

12 Miranda

Apportionment of consideration on takeover

	Value £	%
20,000 ordinary shares in Prospero plc	95,000	38
£100,000 of loan stock in Prospero plc	100,000	40
Cash	55,000	22
Total	250,000	100

Gain on receipt of loan stock in 2008/09 will be frozen until loan stock is sold/redeemed:

	£
Value of loan stock at takeover	100,000
Less: base cost	
£80,000 × 40%	(32,000)
Frozen gain	68,000

This gain crystallises in 2009/10 when the loan stock is redeemed.

The loss on redemption is not allowable as the loan stock is exempt from CGT.

Module E

1 Albert

Tax adjusted trading profit for the year ended 30 June 2009

	£
Profit per accounts	35,000
Add: Legal fees	–
Repair costs (Note)	200
Delivery van – cost	6,000
Parking fine	50
	41,250
Capital allowances (AIA) on van £6,000 × 100% × 80%	(4,800)
Tax adjusted trading profit	36,450

Note. The repair costs were initial repairs to a recently acquired asset and were necessary in order for the asset to be used in the business. The costs are therefore disallowed as capital.

2 Maggie

Tax adjusted trading profit for the fifteen months to 30 April 2010

	£
Net profit per accounts	24,700
Plus: Maggie's wages (appropriation of profit)	45,000
Rent and rates (private use £10,000 × 1/4)	2,500
Depreciation	2,000
Goods own use	850
Tax adjusted trading profit	75,050

2009/10 Trading income assessment

2009/10 is Maggie's second tax year of trade. The basis period for the 2009/10 trading income assessment is 6 April 2009 to 5 April 2010 (the actual basis as no accounting period ends in 2009/10).

3 Karen

Capital allowances computation for the year to 31 August 2010

	AIA £	Main pool £	Expensive Car 1 (PU 40%) £	Expensive Car 2 (PU 40%) £	Allow-ances £
TWDV at 1.9.09		25,000	16,000		
Additions not qualifying for AIA:					
Jaguar car (>160g/km)				25,000	
Ford car (<160g/km)		10,000			
Addition qualifying for AIA:					
Van	15,000				
Disposal			(12,000)		
	15,000	35,000	4,000	25,000	
Balancing allowance			(4,000) × 60%		2,400
AIA	(15,000)				15,000
WDA @ 20%		(7,000)			7,000
WDA @ 10%				(2,500) × 60%	1,500
TWDV c/fwd		28,000	–	22,500	
Total allowances					25,900

4 Gerald

2009/10 Trading income assessment

Basis of assessment: 18 month period to 31 December 2009

	£	£
Year ended 30 June 2009 – taxable profit		34,000
6 months to 31 December 2009 – Adjusted trading profit	15,000	
Plus: Balancing charge (W)	11,000	
		26,000
Less: Overlap profits		(8,000)
Trading income assessment		52,000

WORKING

Capital allowances for the 6 months to 31 December 2009

	Main pool £	Allowances £
TWDV bfwd	4,000	
Disposals:		
Van (MV)	(8,500)	
Plant and machinery	(6,500)	
	(11,000)	
Balancing charge	11,000	11,000

5 Brooke

The loss arises in the tax year 2009/10.

Options available

(1) Carry forward against the first available future trading profits of the same trade.

Under this option £500 of the loss would be offset in 2010/11 (year ended 31 May 2010). The balance of £9,500 would be carried forward to future years. The benefit of the loss will therefore be delayed into the future.

(2) Offset against general income

The loss can be offset against general income of the current tax year (2009/10) and/or the previous tax year (2008/09).

In 2009/10 Brooke's other income is £5,000 which would be covered by the personal allowance. Offsetting the loss in this year would waste most of the personal allowance and is not therefore advisable.

In 2008/09 Brooke has trading income of £26,000 (year ended 31 May 2008) and other income of £5,000. The loss would be fully utilised, save tax at the basic rate and result in a repayment of tax.

(As the loss occurred in 2009/10 the temporary extension to carry back relief applies. However, a current or prior year claim must be made first, so the additional relief is not applicable here as the loss is utilised in full when the carry back claim is made.)

6   **Richard**

   (a) *Disposal of building – August 2009*

	£
Proceeds	850,000
Less: cost (July 2001)	(400,000)
Chargeable gain	450,000

   Note: Entrepreneurs' relief is not available for the disposal of a single business asset.

   (b) *Base cost of new building - assuming rollover relief claimed*

	£
Rollover relief – restricted as proceeds are not fully reinvested.	
Proceeds not reinvested (£850,000 – £750,000)	100,000
Gain eligible to be rolled over (£450,000 – £100,000)	350,000
Cost of new building	750,000
Less: gain rolled over	(350,000)
Revised base cost	400,000

7   **Antonio, Bassanio and Portia**

Portia is acquiring a 20% interest in the partnership goodwill on 1 January 2010.

Bassanio is disposing of a 20% interest in the partnership goodwill on 1 January 2010.

No adjustment is made via the partnership accounts, so the transaction takes place at no gain, no loss under SP D12 para 4.

As Portia makes a payment to Bassanio outside the accounts, this payment is treated as additional consideration.

Bassanio's CGT computation is therefore as follows:

Gain on 1.1.10:	*Bassanio*
	£
'Deemed proceeds' (20% share)	40,000
Less: cost (£200,000 × 20%)	(40,000)
Gain	NIL
Actual consideration paid	80,000
Gain	80,000

Bassanio is therefore deemed to have sold his 20% interest to Portia for £(40,000 + 80,000) = £120,000. This is Portia's CGT base cost for her 20% share.

8   **Horatio and Claudius**

	Total	Horatio	Claudius
	£	£	£
P/e 31.12.09 (13 m)	260,000		
Salary (× ¹³/₁₂)	16,250		16,250
Balance (3:2)	243,750	146,250	97,500
	260,000	146,250	113,750
2009/10:			
P/e 31.12.09		146,250	113,750
Less: overlap relief (W)		(15,000)	(3,750)
Taxable profits		131,250	110,000

Working

Claudius's overlap profits	£
B/f (relates to 4 months as November year end)	15,000
Used on change of accounts date:	
£15,000 × ¼	3,750
c/f	11,250

9 Toby

		£
2008/09:		
1.5.08 – 5.4.09		
£60,000 + £(30,000) × $^2/_3$		40,000
2009/10:		
1.5.08 – 30.4.09		
1.5.08 – 31.1.09		60,000
1.2.09 – 30.4.09: £(30,000) less £(20,000) allocated to 2008/09		(10,000)
		50,000
NIC 2009/10:		
Class 2 (£2.40 × 52)		125
Class 4 £(43,875 – 5,715) × 8%		3,053
£(50,000 – 43,875) × 1%		61
Total NIC		3,239

10 Florence

As stock is transferred along with other assets, under s.176 ITTOIA 2005, the value placed on stock has to be 'just & reasonable' to prevent manipulation of consideration to obtain a tax advantage.

HMRC will therefore expect the value to be placed on the stock at cessation to be its market value of £25,000.

As £60,000 has been accounted for in respect of the stock, £35,000 will therefore need to be deducted from the final trading profit.

The cost of the stock for Oliver will now be £25,000 (not £60,000 as agreed).

11 Warwick

			£
Capital allowances:			
Year ended 31 December 2009	£6,000 × 100% (AIA)		6,000
Period ended 30 April 2011			NIL
Trading profits:			
Year ended 31 December 2009	£(12,000 – 6,000)		6,000
Period ended 30 April 2011			30,000

Assessable profits and overlap

		£	£
2008/09	1.1.09 – 5.4.09		
2009/10	1.1.09 – 31.12.09		
Overlap	1.1.09 – 5.4.09		
	$^3/_{12}$ × £6,000	1,500	
2010/11 (year of change)	1.5.09 – 30.4.10		
	$^8/_{12}$ × £6,000		4,000
	+ $^4/_{16}$ × £30,000		7,500
			11,500
Overlap	1.5.09 – 31.12.09		
	$^8/_{12}$ × £6,000	4,000	
2011/12	1.5.10 – 30.4.11		
Overlap c/f	From opening years		1,500
	Created on change of accounts date		4,000
			5,500

12 Morgan

Interest charges:

	£
2nd POA for 2009/10 (due 31.7.10) £5,500 × 2/12 × 2.5%	23
Balancing payment for 2009/10 (due 31.1.11) £2,000 × 2/12 × 2.5%	8
Over-reduction of POAs for 2009/10 (by £1,000 each) £1,000 × 12/12 × 2.5%	25
£1,000 × 6/12 × 2.5%	12
1st POA for 2010/11 (due 31.1.11) £6,500 × 2/12 × 2.5%	27
Total interest charges	95
Late payment penalty as 2009/10 balancing payment > 30 days (but < 6 months) late: £2,000 × 5%	100
Late return penalty for 2009/10 (not more than 3 months late)	100
Grand total	295

Mock Exam 2: Questions

CTA Awareness Paper

Mock Examination 2 (May 2009)

Question Paper	
Time allowed	*3 hours*

Attempt all questions

DO NOT OPEN THIS PAPER UNTIL YOU ARE READY TO START UNDER EXAMINATION CONDITIONS

CTA Awareness Paper

Mock Examination 2
(May 2009)

Attempt all questions

DO NOT OPEN THIS PAPER UNTIL YOU ARE READY TO START UNDER EXAMINATION CONDITIONS

Module A

1. A transaction is only within the scope of UK VAT if a number of conditions are met.

   You are required to explain what those conditions are.

2. **You are required to explain when a tax point is created, and what, if any, differences there are between the tax point for a supply of goods, and the tax point for a supply of services.**

   (You should ignore any special rules applicable to continuous supplies, self supplies, and reverse chargeable supplies, and any special tax point rules for specific trades, professions, or industries).

3. The case of *Card Protection Plan Ltd* produced case law from both the European Court of Justice, and the House of Lords, which established some basic principles to assist in determining whether a multi-element transaction should be treated as multiple supplies with the appropriate VAT liability for each element, or as one single supply with just one VAT liability.

   You are required to indicate what those principles are.

4. **You are required to list the eligibility criteria for VAT grouping in the UK.**

5. You have a new client who has recently been made redundant from his previous employment. He has decided to invest his redundancy payment in buying a small engineering business from its current owner, a sole proprietor who is retiring. The business your client is buying only has one customer, with whom there is a long-term contract which generates £6,000 a month.

   Your client has no plans to expand the business he is buying and he feels that it would be better for him if he could delay having to register for VAT until the latest possible time

   You are required to explain what the rules are for determining when a new business undertaking must register for VAT, and based on the information available to you, when you think your client will have to register.

6. Your client, Acme General Services Ltd, made the following supplies in the VAT quarter ended 31 March 2010.

	£ (VAT exclusive)
Standard rate supplies	47,000
Reduced rate supplies	8,000
Zero rated supplies	9,000
Exempt supplies	17,500

The input tax incurred in the same period is as follows	£
Attributable to standard rate supplies	4,000
Attributable to reduced rate supplies	1,500
Attributable to zero rate supplies	500
Attributable to exempt supplies	1,500
VAT on overheads not attributable to specific supplies	2,500

   Acme General Services Ltd does not operate any special VAT accounting schemes or methodologies.

   You are required to calculate the output tax payable and input tax recoverable by your client, for that period.

7. VAT registered businesses which implement, or are party to, two broadly defined categories of "avoidance schemes", must disclose their use to HM Revenue & Customs.

   You are required to explain, briefly, what the two categories of schemes are.

   (You are NOT required to give examples of either category).

8. UK VAT is chargeable on taxable supplies of goods and services made in the UK.

   You are required to briefly explain what is meant by the UK for VAT purposes and to state why UK VAT may be charged on supplies not directly made in the UK.

9   A taxable person may sell a business, or part of a business as a Transfer of a Going Concern ("TOGC"), and thereby legitimately sell that business without having to charge VAT which would otherwise be chargeable.

   You are required to list any five of the conditions which have to be met for a VAT-free TOGC.

   (You should ignore the special conditions which apply to property, when property is part of a TOGC).

10 **You are required to list the particulars which a VAT invoice to a UK customer must contain.**

11 Stamp Duty Land Tax is chargeable on the acquisition of a "chargeable interest".

   You are required to briefly define "a chargeable interest" and to state three examples of chargeable interests.

12 When Stamp Duty Land Tax is payable by a tenant, the default position is that it is due on the net present value of rent payable for the duration of the tenancy. Even if the value of the rent is not known at the start of the tenancy, Stamp Duty Land Tax is still payable.

   You are required to explain how a tenant should calculate and account for Stamp Duty Land Tax in such circumstances.

Module B

1 Margaret died on 18 May 2008. She left cash of £62,400 to her brother and the residue of her estate which comprised residential property and was valued at £450,000, to her husband George. George died on 20 October 2009, when his total death estate, which comprised residential property and cash, was worth £825,000. He left this to his children.

Neither Margaret nor George had made any lifetime transfers and both were domiciled within the UK for Inheritance Tax purposes

State, and calculate where necessary, the Inheritance Tax consequences of each death, assuming any beneficial claims are made.

2 Jean-Paul had lived in the UK for two years before he died on 10 April 2010. He had always retained his French domicile. At the date of death, he owned the following assets:

(1) Birmingham penthouse.

(2) Paris home.

(3) Shares in Gates Bank plc, quoted on the London Stock Exchange.

(4) Loan to his daughter, who lives in France. This was made to help her clear her student debts and is repayable on demand.

On 10 April 2010, the title deeds of both houses, and the share certificates in Gates Bank plc were held by Jean-Paul's solicitor in Paris.

Briefly explain, whether each of the assets listed above should be included in, or excluded from, Jean-Paul's death estate for the purpose of UK Inheritance Tax.

3 The Robinson Trust was created for the benefit of John and his brother in equal portions. At 6 April 2009, the trust assets consisted of a portfolio of quoted investments and neither of the beneficiaries had an interest in possession.

On 1 July 2009, John became absolutely entitled to his portion of the trust assets. If the whole of the trust assets had been sold on this date, a gain of £32,000 would have arisen.

On 1 December 2009, John's portion of the trust assets was sold, by which time a further gain of £12,000 had accrued on this portion.

Calculate the Capital Gains Tax consequences of the transactions in the year 2009/10, assuming that no other capital disposals were made in the year.

4 On 15 July 2009, Sam turned 30 years old. He then gave up his job, sold his house in Manchester and moved to Australia where he bought a vineyard to start his own wine business. He had been born in the UK and has lived here all his life, as have his parents and grandparents, but he has told his family that he does not plan to live in the UK again.

Explain Sam's domicile status for the purposes of UK Inheritance Tax, before and after the move to Australia

5 Jayne gifted £500,000 into a discretionary trust on 10 September 1999. She had made one previous gross chargeable transfer of £57,000 on 19 October 1998.

On 10 July 2004, the trustees made a gross capital distribution of £100,000 to one beneficiary.
The value of the trust property at 10 September 2009 was £625,000.

Calculate the principal charge arising on 10 September 2009.

6   On 2 January 2009, Mills Forest Ltd, a marketing company began to trade. Elizabeth Mills became the managing director, and the shares were held as follows:

   20% by a trust in which Elizabeth had the sole interest in possession
   40% by Elizabeth
   40% by Alfie, the finance director

   There were no changes to the officers or shareholdings until 14 March 2010, when the shares held by the trust were sold to a third party investor.

   Explain why this disposal qualifies for entrepreneurs' relief.

7   Shares in TJ Ltd, a TV production company, were owned from 1 January 2005 to 31 December 2009 as follows:

Tariq Jay	500
Sheena, Tariq's wife	300
Jamie, Tariq's son	200
Total	1,000

   On 1 January 2010, Tariq gifted 200 of his shares into a discretionary trust at which time the values of shareholdings of various sizes were as follows:

Less than 50%	£50 per share
50% to 74%	£120 per share
More than 74%	£150 per share

   The balance sheet of TJ Ltd at the time was as follows:

	£
Leasehold improvements	40,000
Plant and equipment	25,000
Investments in quoted shares	10,000
Other net assets	20,000
	95,000

   The market value of the investments was £30,000; otherwise the balance sheet values shown represent market value

   You are required to calculate:

   (1)   The transfer of value for Inheritance Tax purposes when the shares are gifted into the trust, and

   (2)   The business property relief available on this transfer Brian's chargeable estate showing how any reliefs will be given.

8   In the year 2009/10, the Rachel Jones Discretionary Trust received rental income of £8,800, and net dividends of £2,818.

   There were no trustee expenses and no distributions were made to beneficiaries.

   Calculate the Income Tax payable by the trustees for 2009/10

9   Mary gifted her house to her son on 18 August 2007 when it was worth £450,000. She continued to live in the house but made no financial contribution. On 20 July 2009, Mary died when the house was worth £550,000. She had made no other lifetime gifts.

   You are required to explain the Inheritance Tax relating to the house, which arises on Mary's death. Calculations are not required.

10 On 1 July 2005, Sarah gave her friend Vicky cash of £350,000. She had made no previous lifetime transfers. On 1 July 2006, Sarah died. Vicky died on 1 October 2009 leaving a chargeable estate of £1 million.

   Calculate the quick succession relief available on Vicky's death. Ignore annual exemptions.

11 On 15 October 2009, Richard transferred cash of £400,000 and a property valued at £350,000 into a discretionary trust. The property has been used by Richard and his business partners as premises for their accountancy business for many years.

The trustees paid the Inheritance Tax due on the gift into trust.

Richard had made no previous lifetime gifts.

Calculate the initial value of the assets in the trust.

12 Sally runs a successful clothing design business, employing two staff members. She carried out the following transactions in the year 2009/10.

(1) She sold her holiday home for £210,000. The asking price had been £235,000 but Sally accepted a lower offer as she wanted the money quickly for use in the business.

(2) She paid £500 a month for nursing assistance for her elderly father who lives with her.

(3) She gave each of her employees a watch worth £650 for Christmas.

State, with brief explanations, whether each of the transactions constitutes a transfer of value for Inheritance Tax purposes

Module C

1. On 1 June 2009 Petott Ltd purchased 20% of the ordinary share capital of Jescan Ltd. Both Petott Ltd and Jescan Ltd are trading companies. Petott Ltd has recently received an offer from an unconnected company to purchase the entire 20% shareholding in Jescan Ltd. However, due to difficulties in raising the necessary finance, the board have been asked to consider a sale in stages over a number of years.

   Outline the chargeable gains position of the proposed sale, indicating any relevant relief available and any effect that the proposed staggered sale may have on such relief. Your answer should clearly state the conditions for the identified relief.

2. MP plc is a UK resident trading company, preparing accounts to 30 June annually. It has always paid Corporation Tax at the small company rate. The accountant acting for the company died on 31 March 2010, having not yet prepared or filed the company's accounts to 30 June 2009, although all previous returns have been filed on time.

   Advise MP plc of the deadlines in relation to payment of the Corporation Tax liability and filing of the Corporation Tax return, stating any implications of being late. Assume that the FA 2009 penalty provisions apply and that there is no deliberate withholding of information from HMRC.

3. RI Ltd purchased the business of IB Ltd on 1 May 2010 as a going concern. The purchase price of the business included goodwill and a freehold office building used in the trade of IB Ltd. IB Ltd was an unrelated company. RI Ltd have been advised that they may be able to claim some allowances for the cost of purchase against their profits.

   Outline the manner in which each element of the purchase price will be treated for Corporation Tax purposes, clearly stating any allowances available.

4. It is necessary to establish a company's residence position in order to establish the liability to UK Corporation Tax.

   Explain how a company's residence status affects its liability to UK corporation tax and state when a company is resident in the UK.

   Tutorial note: This question replaces the original question set, which is no longer relevant.

5. Alpha plc owns 80% of the ordinary share capital of Beta plc and 90% of the ordinary share capital of Ceta plc. All companies prepare accounts annually to 31 March. None of the companies paid or received any dividends. The results for the year ended 31 March 2010 are as follows:

	Alpha plc £	Beta plc £	Ceta plc £
UK Trading profit/(loss)	600,000	(100,000)	130,000
Property business profits	50,000	20,000	-
Interest receivable	-	40,000	10,000
Gift aid donations	-	-	(5,000)

   Assuming the group wishes to claim losses in the best manner to minimise the total Corporation Tax liability for the year ended 31 March 2010, calculate profits chargeable to Corporation Tax for each of the companies for the year ended 31 March 2010.

6. Pumpkin Ltd has brought forward trading losses at 1 January 2010 of £200,000. Ghost Ltd intends to purchase the shares of Pumpkin Ltd within the next couple of months. The accountants for Pumpkin Ltd have included in their valuation of the business the potential Corporation Tax saving available from use of the unrelieved losses. Both Ghost Ltd and Pumpkin Ltd make up their accounts to 31 December each year.

   Advise Ghost Ltd as to whether the brought forward trading losses of Pumpkin Ltd may be used against the profits of Pumpkin Ltd or Ghost Ltd for the year to 31 December 2010.

7   For many years X Ltd has owned 100% of the ordinary share capital of each of Y Ltd and Z Ltd. On 1 June 2010, X Ltd will sell the shares in Z Ltd to another unconnected company.

Z Ltd owns the following assets, which were previously transferred to it from group members:

- A factory transferred from X Ltd on 1 December 2008
- Fixed machinery transferred from Y Ltd on 1 June 2003

Outline any capital gains implications arising as a result of Z Ltd leaving the group.

8   To raise finance on the formation of the company, BB Ltd borrowed £100,000 from individuals and £50,000 from another company. Both loans have been used for trading purposes, and are subject to interest at a rate of 7% per annum.

Calculate the sums to be paid to each lender and indicate the extent of any tax relief available to BB Ltd on the borrowings.

9   Sally was made redundant on 31 March 2009 and formed a company, SAL Ltd, through which she has contracted to provide services to her former employer.

Sally accepts that the contract with her former employer falls within the provisions of the IR35 Personal Service Companies legislation and has provided you with the following information for the year ended 5 April 2010:

	£
Total invoiced for services	155,000
Salary paid in the year (including employers' NIC)	10,000
Travel expenses (including £2,000 for home to work travel)	5,000
Employer pension contribution for Sally paid by SAL Ltd	8,000
Dividends paid (net of tax credit)	40,000

Prepare the deemed employment income calculation for 2009/10.

10   The premises of Loopy Ltd were refurbished during the company's nine month accounting period to 31 December 2009. The following assets were acquired:

		£
1 May 2009	Ventilation system for building	50,000
1 Sept 2009	Computer equipment	30,000

The tax written down value of the main pool at 1 April 2009 was £120,000.

Calculate the maximum capital allowances available to Loopy Ltd for the nine months to 31 December 2009.

11   Sugar Ltd, a small trading company, and Tea Ltd, a large trading company, incurred research and development costs in the year to 31 March 2010, as follows:

	Sugar Ltd	Tea Ltd
	£	£
Staff costs	20,000	40,000
Consumables	40,000	20,000
Apportionment of general overheads	10,000	–
Software	–	40,000

Both companies made losses in the year to 31 March 2010 of £200,000.

Calculate the amount of relief available to each company for the research and development expenditure incurred.

12   The entire share capital of D Ltd is owned by Mr and Mrs Jenkins, and D Ltd has no associated companies. The income and expenditure of the company for the year to 31 March 2010 was as follows:

	£
Dividends received on quoted UK investments (net of tax credit)	90,000
Bank/building society interest receivable	55,000
Loan stock interest receivable	80,000
Management expenses paid	30,000
Gift aid donations paid	5,000

Calculate the Corporation Tax payable for the year to 31 March 2010.

Module D

1. Jerome has been self-employed for many years. His total Income Tax liability for 2008/09 was £26,568. Some of this was paid by deduction at source as follows:

	£
Tax deducted on savings income	3,150
Dividend tax credit	1,200
Tax deducted on REIT income	424

   In respect of 2008/09, Jerome also paid Capital Gains Tax of £258

   Jerome made his first payment on account for 2009/10 on 31 January 2010 and paid an amount of £9,800, based on estimated computations.

   In 2009/10, Jerome made a gain on a gift to his brother, of shares in an unquoted investment company resulting in a Capital Gains Tax liability for 2009/10 of £10,120. Jerome's brother intends to keep the shares as a long-term investment.

   You are required to:

   (1) Calculate the amount of any further payment to be made to HM Revenue & Customs by 31 July 2010.

   (2) Identify an option that is available to Jerome to reduce the amount of Capital Gains Tax payable by 31 January 2011.

   You are NOT required to consider interest on late paid tax.

2. Miguel is a director of Blake Ltd. The employment package provided to him during 2009/10 includes the following:

Salary		£43,000
Car		
-	original list price	£45,000
-	accessories added later	£2,000

   The car has carbon dioxide emissions of 194g/km. Blake Ltd does not pay for any petrol for private use.

   In addition Miguel borrowed £25,000 interest free from the company in August 2006 to help fund the purchase of a holiday home. He repaid £6,000 of the loan on 5 July 2009.

   You are required to calculate Miguel's assessable employment income for 2009/10.

3. Sanish has been UK resident for the last 15 years, but is Indian domiciled. He has received overseas dividends of £120,000 (gross), and has remitted £25,000 of this to the UK during 2009/10. He has made a remittance basis election for 2009/10. Sanish also has UK income of approximately £100,000 each year.

   You are required to:

   (1) Calculate Sanish's UK Income Tax liability due to the overseas income. Ignore double tax relief.

   (2) Identify two situations where an individual who is UK resident but not UK domiciled can apply the remittance basis without having to make an election.

4. Angelina is the managing director of Ballet Ltd. She is considering ways of creating incentives for key members of staff. She has heard about Enterprise Management Incentives (EMIs), but knows very little about them. Ballet Ltd is owned by a number of individuals and has no subsidiaries.

   You are required to:

   (1) State the main conditions that the company must fulfil to qualify under an EMI scheme.

   (2) Briefly explain the Income Tax treatment, for the key employees, of the options under an EMI scheme.

5   Evie, aged 50, has the following income and payments for 2009/10:

	£
Salary from Shaming Ltd	46,190
Dividends (net of tax credit)	486
Gift aid payment (net)	1,880
Interest paid	4,200

The interest paid of £4,200 is made up of £4,000 on the loan to purchase Evie's house, and £200 to purchase shares in Shaming Ltd, an employee controlled company.

Calculate Evie's Income Tax liability for 2009/10.

6   The employees of Dane plc have the choice between contributing into the company's occupational pension scheme or contributing into their own personal pension schemes.

The company will also contribute into whichever scheme an employee chooses.

The employees earn between £12,000 and £250,000 per annum.

Explain the Income Tax implications of both the employer and employee contributions, and explain how relief will be given to the individual. You should ignore the pension anti-forestalling provisions.

7   Imogen has two investment properties that she let out during 2009/10.

2 Watson Street

This property was first let on 6 October 2009. The tenant paid a premium of £10,000 for the five year lease.

6 Dooher Gardens

This property qualifies as a furnished holiday letting.

You are required to:

(1)   **Calculate the amount of the lease premium subject to Income Tax.**
(2)   **State three tax advantages of a property being treated as a furnished holiday letting in 2009/10.**

8   Flea Ltd has approximately 20 employees on the payroll, including the following:

(1)   Abdul

He has a salary of £40,000 per annum and is paid 45p per business mile for using his own car.

(2)   Shonay

Shonay is 68 years old, and in addition to her £15,000 salary, she is provided with private medical insurance paid for by the company.

The company also pays for an annual dinner costing £180 per person for all employees. There is a PAYE settlement agreement in place relating to this cost.

For each element of remuneration mentioned above, briefly explain which classes of National Insurance Contributions apply, identifying whether it is payable by the employee or Flea Ltd.

You are NOT required to perform any calculations.

9 David and Doreen own the entire share capital of Willis Ltd, They each subscribed for 500 ordinary shares of £1 each in January 1983.

David has always worked as a full-time director of the company, whilst Doreen has had no involvement other than owning the shares. David and Doreen also personally own the freehold building from which Willis Ltd operates. They let the building rent free to the company. David and Doreen purchased the building in February 1983.

David now wishes to retire, and the couple intend to buy a second home. To fund this purchase, David and Doreen sold their shares in March 2010, each realising a gain on disposal before reliefs of £449,500. In the same month, they also sold the freehold building each realising a gain before reliefs of £650,000. David and Doreen made no other disposals during 2009/10, and David has capital losses brought forward at 6 April 2009 of £20,000.

You are required to calculate the Capital Gains Tax payable by David and Doreen for 2009/10, assuming all relevant claims and elections are made.

10 Pardeep purchased 5,000 ordinary shares of £1 each in Puck plc for £20,000 on 20 January 1999. On 25 May 2009, Puck plc was taken over by Creed plc. The shareholders received the following for each £1 ordinary share in Puck plc:

	Market Value at 25 May 2009
Two ordinary shares in Creed plc	£7.16 per share
£3 Qualifying Corporate Bonds (QCBs) in Creed plc	£0.96 per £1 of QCBs

On 26 March 2010 Pardeep sold all 10,000 of the ordinary Creed plc shares for £43,000, and £10,000 of QCBs in Creed plc for £21,000. Pardeep has never worked for either company and his shareholdings have always been less than 1% of the issued share capital.

Calculate Pardeep's chargeable gains arising on the disposals in 2009/10.

11 Gordon has recently left university and is planning to purchase his first house. He is still unsure about what to do next with regard to work and/or travelling the world.

Gordon assumes that the gain on the eventual sale of the house will be exempt from Capital Gains Tax whatever life choices he makes.

Identify five periods during which Gordon may not be living in the house, but in respect of which part of the eventual gain on sale may still be exempt from Capital Gains Tax.

12 Theo disposed of two assets during 2009/10 as follows:

(1) Land

Theo inherited 25 acres of land in July 2000 when the probate value was £400,000. On 5 August 2009 he sold 15 acres to a developer for £986,800, from which solicitor's fees totalling £6,800 are to be deducted. The remaining 10 acres were valued at £600,000 on that date.

(2) Lease

Theo acquired a 15 year lease on 10 January 2004 for £20,000. On 10 January 2010 he sold the lease for £13,425.

Calculate Theo's Capital Gains Tax payable for 2009/10.

Module E

1. Ivor and Joseph have been in partnership for several years. They prepare accounts annually to 30 April. Profits have always been shared equally.

   Kieran joined the partnership on 1 July 2009. He was entitled to a prior share of £18,000 per annum and the profit sharing ratio for the balance of profits changed to 2:2:1 (Ivor:Joseph:Kieran) from that date.

   The partnership had an adjusted trading profit for the year ended 30 April 2010 of £90,000.

   Calculate the taxable trading profit for all partners for the year ended 30 April 2010 and state the amount to be assessed on Kieran in 2009/10.

2. Nigel is a self-employed wine merchant. His latest accounts were prepared for the year ended 30 November 2009. The trading profit for the year was £67,000 including the following:

   (1) Lease costs of £6,400 have been deducted in arriving at trading profit in respect of a lease entered into in 2007. These relate to an Audi car that is used by Nigel. The car had a retail price when new of £20,000 and CO_2 emissions of 171g/km. Nigel uses the car 20% for private purposes.

   (2) A charge of £2,000 for the legal fees to arrange the lease of new business premises.

   (3) An amount of £3,600 described as subscriptions has been deducted in arriving at the profit figure. This includes £900 for the wine merchants' trade journal and £2,700 membership fee for the local golf club where Nigel only entertains clients.

   Calculate the adjusted trading profit for Nigel for the year ended 30 November 2009 after taking account of items 1) to 3) above. Briefly explain your treatment of each item.

3. Olivia has completed a university course in engineering and is currently unemployed. In the past she collected old pieces of furniture and restored them as a hobby. In January 2010 she bought an old table and chairs at auction and restored them. In March 2010 she sold the table and chairs at auction and used the proceeds to fund the purchase of three further pieces of furniture that she is currently restoring. She is still looking for employment and knows that she will have less time for her hobby once she is employed.

   Briefly state and explain the factors that HM Revenue & Customs will take into account when determining whether the profit Olivia made on the sale of the furniture will be assessed to tax as a trading profit.

4. Alastair is a self-employed car retailer. He purchased a showroom in 1995 at a cost of £64,000. He decided to relocate his business premises and sold the original showroom in August 2009 for £320,000. The new premises were purchased in June 2009 at a cost of £290,000. They are however bigger than Alastair needs and he rents out one fifth of the new premises to XJ Ltd who sell electrical goods.

   Explain whether Alastair will be able to claim rollover relief for the gain of £256,000 on the sale of his original showroom. Calculations are not required.

5. Faisal, who is self-employed, has seen trading conditions deteriorate and decided to cease trading on 31 January 2010. His adjusted trading profits/(loss) over recent periods have been as follows:

	£
Year ended 31 October 2006	23,000
Year ended 31 October 2007	20,000
Year ended 31 October 2008	8,000
Year ended 31 October 2009	2,000
Period ended 31 January 2010	(14,000)

   Faisal had unrelieved overlap profits of £3,800.

   Faisal has other taxable income of £6,000 each year from various investments.

   Assuming that Faisal makes only a terminal loss relief claim, calculate Faisal's terminal loss and show, with a brief explanation, how it can be relieved.

6   Caroline has been a self-employed florist for several years and prepares accounts to 31 August annually. She has found that the summer is a very busy time for her business and decided to change her accounting date to 31 January. The adjusted trading profits for her business have been as follows:

	£
Year ended 31 August 2008	30,000
Period ended 31 January 2010	45,000

Caroline had seven months of unrelieved overlap profits with a value of £9,800.

(1) **Calculate the trading profits to be assessed for 2009/10 and state the value of any overlap profits to be carried forward.**

(2) **Advise Caroline of two conditions she must meet for the change of accounting date to be valid.**

7   Albert and Ian are market traders and are each self-employed individuals.

Albert was born on 10 May 1941. He had an adjusted trading profit for 2009/10 of £17,000.

Ian was born on 16 July 1975. He had an adjusted trading profit for 2009/10 of £28,000. Ian made a trading loss of £5,000 in 2008/09. He made a claim to relieve the trading loss against general income in 2008/09.

Calculate, with brief explanations, the Class 4 National Insurance Contributions payable by Albert and Ian for 2009/10.

8   Sabrina paid Income Tax by self-assessment of £26,000 for 2009/10. She made the required payments on account for 2010/11 on their due dates. The Income Tax due by self-assessment for 2010/11 totalled £40,000. Sabrina paid the balancing payment for 2010/11 on 30 September 2012.

Briefly explain and calculate the amount of any interest and penalties for late payment that Sabrina will have to pay on the amounts due in respect of 2010/11.

Assume the rate of interest on overdue tax is 2.5% per annum and that the FA 2009 penalty provisions apply.

9   Abdul, a sole trader, made an adjusted trading loss for the year ended 31 March 2010.

The adjusted trading profits/(loss) of his business are as follows:

	£
Year ended 31 March 2009	17,000
Year ended 31 March 2010	(11,000)
Year ended 31 March 2011 (estimated)	3,000

Abdul also has rental income of £6,000 per year from an investment property he owns.

Abdul has never made any chargeable disposals for Capital Gains Tax.

Explain the options available to Abdul to relieve the trading loss of the year ended 31 March 2010, and advise him as to which option he should choose. You are not required to calculate Abdul's tax saving from the use of the loss.

10   Simon prepared accounts for the year ended 31 March 2010. He had the following tax written down values brought forward at 1 April 2009:

	£
Main pool	5,700
Expensive Car – used by Simon 80% for business purposes	13,000

During the year ended 31 March 2010, Simon had the following transactions:

	£
Purchased a new computer	16,000
Disposed of machinery that had originally cost £7,000	2,500
Installed a ventilation system and external solar shading	40,000

Calculate the maximum capital allowances that Simon may claim for the year ended 31 March 2010.

11 Michael decided to incorporate his long established sole trader business on 1 January 2010. All of the business assets except cash were transferred to a newly formed company, M Ltd. The market value of the net assets, at incorporation was £250,000. The only chargeable assets were a property and goodwill as follows:

	Cost	Market Value at 1 January 2010
	£	£
Property (purchased March 1994)	45,000	130,000
Goodwill	-	80,000

On incorporation, Michael received consideration of 10,000 ordinary shares of £1 each in M Ltd together with £40,000 cash.

Michael made other chargeable disposals in 2009/10 sufficient to use the annual exempt amount. He has not invested in any other assets or shares.

Assuming Michael wants to utilise all possible reliefs, calculate the chargeable gain on incorporation.

12 Julie and Anna have been in partnership for many years sharing capital and trading profits and losses equally. They have built up the goodwill of their business from nothing. In May 2009 they decided to admit Emma into the partnership. Prior to this, on 30 April 2009, they revalued the goodwill in the accounts at a value of £120,000. After Emma joined the partnership the capital and trading profits and losses were shared 2:2:1 (Julie:Anna:Emma).

Explain the Capital Gains Tax issues arising from Emma joining the partnership and from the revaluation of the goodwill.

Mock Exam 2: Answers

Module A

1   The transaction is a supply of goods or services.

   "Supply" includes all forms of supply, but not anything done otherwise than for a consideration.

   The transaction takes place in the UK.

   The transaction is undertaken by a taxable person (who is someone who is registered, or is required to be registered, for VAT).

   The transaction is undertaken in the course or furtherance of a business carried on by a taxable person.

   Note: An additional mark up to the maximum available may be awarded to candidates who mention that supply is not defined in the VAT legislation but is widely interpreted according to the principles laid down in VAT case law.

2   The basic tax point for supplies of goods is when the goods are delivered to/collected by the customer, or are made available to the customer.

   The basic tax point for supplies of services is when the services are performed.

   An actual tax point is created if before the basic tax point, the supplier issues a VAT invoice or receives payment, in which case the applicable tax point will be the time the invoice is issued or the payment received, whichever occurs first.

   If an invoice is raised by the supplier, within 14 days after the basic tax point, then the tax point will become the date of that invoice.

3   (1)   Can one or more elements be regarded as a principal supply, or are they merely ancillary to the principal supply?

   (2)   An element is ancillary to the principal supply if that element is not an aim in itself but is simply a means of better enjoying the principal supply.

   (3)   The fact that there is a single price is not determinative.

   (4)   Where there is a bundle of elements, and/or features, and/or acts, it is necessary to have regard to all the circumstances in which the transaction takes place.

   (5)   From an economic perspective, elements must not be artificially split, or artificially aggregated.

4   Members of VAT groups must be bodies corporate.

   Members must meet the control test, which is that one body corporate, one person, or two or more persons in partnership, controls all the bodies in the VAT group.

   Members must also meet the residency test, which is that all members must be established, or have a fixed establishment in the UK.

   Note: An extra mark may be awarded to candidates who state that achieving VAT grouping is not something which happens by default and, to form a VAT group, a written application must be made to HMRC.

5   (1)   A business must register when the taxable turnover reaches the currently extant VAT registration limit (currently £68,000 per annum). This is determined by either:

   - The backward look (or 'historic') test which means that the obligation to register is triggered if at the end of any month, the taxable turnover in the past year has exceeded the turnover limit, or

   - The forward look (or 'future') test which means that at any point there are reasonable grounds for believing that the value of the taxable supplies in the next 30 days will exceed the turnover limit.

   (2)   Prima face the new client will only be obliged to register in 12 months time when the turnover exceeds £68,000 per annum.

   (3)   However, the sale of the business by the vendor would appear to fall to be treated as a TOGC and so the client will be obliged to register immediately.

6   (1) Output tax due: £47,000 × 17.5% = £8,225

   £ 8,000 × 5% = £400

   Total £8,625

(2) Input tax recoverable: £4,000 + £1,500 + £500 plus percentage of £2,500 as follows.

No special method, therefore standard method based on percentage of taxable supplies over total supplies:

$$\frac{47,000 + 8,000 + 9,000}{47,000 + 8,000 + 9,000 + 17,500} = 78.52\% \text{ rounded up to } 79\%$$

79% of £2,500 = £1,975

Recoverable therefore £6,000 + £1,975 = £7,975

Exempt input tax = £1,500 plus £525 = £2,025 which exceeds de minimis limit of <£625 per month and <50% of total – therefore NOT recoverable in this case.

7   Listed schemes are named and defined schemes, the details and workings of which are specifically described in the legislation.

Hallmark schemes are not specifically named or described schemes, but are transactions which:

(a) Will or may be expected to enable a person to obtain a tax advantage;

(b) That advantage is the main or one of the main benefits of the scheme; and

(c) Incorporate certain features – "hallmarks" – which are stated in the legislation.

8   The UK consists of

(1) England, Scotland, Wales and Northern Ireland.

(2) The territorial sea of the UK which are the waters within the 12 mile limit.

(3) The Isle of Man is treated as part of the UK for VAT purposes.

(4) UK VAT is payable by the importer of goods into the UK.

(5) UK VAT is payable by the recipient of certain services received from abroad if received for a business purpose under the reverse charge provisions.

9   (1) The assets are to be used by the purchaser in carrying on the same kind of business.

(2) The purchaser must either already be registered for VAT, or become liable to register as a result of the transaction.

(3) If only part of an existing business is transferred, that part must be capable of separate operation.

(4) The effect of the transfer is to put the new owner in possession of a business which can be operated as such.

(5) The business (or part) being transferred must be a going concern at the time of transfer.

(6) There must not be a series of immediately successive transfers, ie the purchaser must not immediately sell on the assets to a third party.

(7) There should be no significant break in the normal trading pattern before or immediately after the transfer.

10 (1) The name, address and VAT registration number of the supplier

(2) The name and address of the customer

(3) The date of issue, the tax point and invoice number

(4) A description sufficient to identify the goods or services supplied

(5) For each description, the quantity supplied, unit price, the rate of VAT applicable and the amount payable excluding VAT

(6) The gross amount payable (excluding VAT)

(7) The rate of any cash discount offered

(8) The total amount of VAT payable

(9) The unit price.

11 A chargeable interest is an estate, interest, right or power in or over land in the UK, or the benefit of an obligation, restriction or condition affecting the value of any such estate, interest, right or power (s.48(1) FA 2003).

Examples of chargeable interests are:

- A freehold estate (the nearest equivalent to absolute ownership, sometimes referred to as an 'estate in fee simple')
- A leasehold estate (sometimes referred to as a 'term of years')
- An undivided share in land
- A right in or over land such as an easement or profit a prendre
- A rent charge
- In Northern Ireland, a ground rent or fee farm rent
- The right to receive rent
- The benefit of a restrictive covenant
- The benefit of a positive covenant
- An equitable interest in land such as a life interest or an interest in reversion or in remainder.
- An executor's or trustee's power of appointment.

12 (1) When rent is unknown at the start of a lease, the value is calculated based on an estimate of the rent.

(2) A "land transaction return" (LTR) is submitted to HMRC along with payment.

(3) Once any unknown rent amounts are determined, it is necessary to calculate whether any further SDLT is payable.

(4) If so, a further LTR should be submitted together with the additional tax, plus interest.

Module B

1. *Margaret's death* – transfer to spouse exempt from IHT

   Transfer to brother covered by nil rate band of £312,000, so no IHT

   (Note. Mark awarded if this is shown numerically but has to be shown/stated somehow)

   Percentage of Margaret's NRB used = 62,400/312,000 = 20%

   George's NRB is increased by 80% × £325,000 = £260,000

   George's death

	£
Value of estate	825,000
Less: Enhanced nil rate band £(325,000 + 260,000)	(585,000)
	240,000

   IHT = 40% × £240,000 = £96,000

2. Only assets situated in the UK are included as Jean-Paul was French domiciled

   Birmingham penthouse – include, as physically situated in the UK

   Paris home – exclude, as physically situated in France

   Shares in Gates Bank plc – include, as registered on UK Stock Exchange

   Loan to daughter – exclude, as situated in France (where debtor resides)

   Note. Any wording of explanation that demonstrates knowledge of the rules will score, but some explanation required, eg "exclude as daughter lives in France" sufficient for last point.

3.
	£
Deemed disposal by trust when John becomes entitled to assets	
Gain is ½ of £32,000	16,000
Less annual exempt amount (2009/10)	(5,050)
	10,950
CGT @ 18%	1,971
Disposal by individual (note)	
Gain	12,000
Less annual exempt amount (2009/10)	(10,100)
	1,900
CGT @ 18%	342

   Note. When a beneficiary becomes absolutely entitled to trust assets, the trustees hold those assets on bare trust for them until they are transferred to the beneficiary or sold, as in this case. When assets are held on bare trust any actions by the trustees are treated as those of the beneficiary, which is why the gain is taxed on John.

4. Prior to the move, Sam had a domicile of origin within the UK which he obtained from his father.

   (Note. "Domicile of origin" or reference to that of father would get this mark)

   It appears that he may have lost his domicile within the UK because he intends to live permanently outside the UK (as evidenced by the sale of his house/giving up job/owning business in Australia).

   It appears that he may have gained a domicile of choice in Australia.

   However, in order to gain a domicile of choice in Australia he would need to intend to remain permanently in Australia. We are not told that this is the case and if he does not so intend he will neither gain a domicile of choice in Australia nor lose his domicile within the UK

   Sam will still be deemed domiciled in the UK for IHT purposes for the next 3 years.

5

		£	£
Gift' (ie value of trust property at 10 September 2009)			625,000
Less: nil rate band		325,000	
Less: chargeable transfers in prior 7 years		(57,000)	
capital distributions		(100,000)	
			(168,000)
			457,000
IHT:			
20% × £457,000			£91,400
91,400/625,000 × 100			14.624%
14.624% × £625,000 × 30%			£27,420

Alternative: IHT payable = £457,000 × 20% × 30% = £27,420

6   Elizabeth had an interest in possession in the shares and so was a 'qualifying beneficiary'

For a period of more than one year (ending within the three years) up to date of disposal:

- The company was a trading company
- Elizabeth was a director/officer of the company
- The company was Elizabeth's personal company/Elizabeth owned more than 5% of the share capital

7   Related property valuation

	£
Value of Tariq's shareholding before transfer	
500 × £150 (80% shareholding of him and wife)	75,000
Value of Tariq's shareholding after transfer	
300 × £120 (60% shareholding of him and wife)	(36,000)
	39,000
Normal valuation	
Value of Tariq's shareholding before transfer	
500 × £120 (50% shareholding)	60,000
Value of Tariq's shareholding after transfer	
300 × £50 (<50% shareholding)	(15,000)
	45,000

Transfer of value ignoring related property comes to £45,000 which is higher, therefore would use that.

Therefore, part of transfer which is eligible for relief:

$$\frac{95,000 - 10,000}{95,000 + 20,000} \times £45,000 \times 100\% = £33,261$$

8

	£
Rental income	8,800
Dividend income £2,818 × 100/90	3,131
Tax:	
Rental income	
£1,000 @ 20%	200
£7,800 @ 40%	3,120
Dividends: £3,131 @ 32.5%	1,018
Less: Tax credit on dividend	(313)
	4,025

9   This was a PET (gift to an individual) which was also a gift with reservation of benefit, as Mary continued to live in the house rent-free

Inheritance Tax due on the house at the date of Mary's death is the higher of:

- That if the PET is charged (and the probate value (ie value at date of death) excluded from the death estate)
- That if the PET is ignored, and the house is instead included in the death estate at the value on death

As the value of the house has increased significantly, then the IHT is higher if the PET is ignored, and the house value is included in the death estate.

10 As a result of Sarah's death, PET becomes chargeable:

	£
PET	350,000
Less NRB	(285,000)
	65,000
IHT payable on PET by Vicky on Sarah's death = £65,000 × 40%	26,000
Vicky's estate increased by £350,000 − £26,000	324,000

Period between gift and 2nd death: 1.7.05 − 1.10.09 = 4 − 5 years: 20%

Therefore, QSR = 20% × $\frac{324,000}{350,000}$ × £26,000 = £4,814

11

	£
Cash	400,000
Property	350,000
BPR @ 50% × £350,000	(175,000)
AE (2009/10)	(3,000)
AE (2008/09)	(3,000)
Transfer of value	569,000
NRB	(325,000)
	244,000
IHT @ 20%	48,800
Initial value =	400,000
	350,000
	(48,800)
	701,200

12 (1) Holiday home – no transfer because no gratuitous benefit intended/arm's length

(2) Nursing assistance – no transfer because payment for care/maintenance of dependent relative

(Note. Mark also available if normal payment out of income (s.11 IHTA 1984) given as a reason. Although strictly this is still a transfer of value, it would be exempt so the examiner would accept this as an alternative).

(3) Staff Christmas presents – no transfer because allowable as a deduction from profits of business

Module C

1. Provided the sale takes place after 31 May 2010 the disposal qualifies for the substantial shareholding exemption. The conditions are that Petott Ltd:

   - Has owned at least 10% of the ordinary share capital, giving entitlement to ≥ 10% of profits available for distribution and assets on a winding up, (a substantial shareholding), and
   - Has held the substantial shareholding for at least 12 months in last 2 years.

   The implications of a staggered sale are:

   - Conditions must be met for any 12 month period in 2 years before sale, and
   - Tranches will qualify for exemption provided can meet conditions in any 12 month period.

2. Corporation tax is payable by 9 months and 1 day after the end of the accounting period, ie by 1 April 2010 for the year ended 30 June 2009. Interest will be charged at the statutory rate from 1 April 2010 up to the date of payment.

   The corporation tax return is due for filing by 30 June 2010.

   If it is filed late, the penalties are:

   - An initial fixed penalty due of £100
   - Once 3 months late, ie on 30 September 2010, daily penalties of £10 per day can be imposed for a maximum of 90 days.
   - If it is filed more than 6 months late, an additional penalty of 5% of the tax due will be charged.
   - If it is filed more than 12 months late, a further penalty of 5% of the tax due will be charged.

3. Property – No allowance available against profits. Cost will be carried forward and deducted in arriving at any chargeable gain/allowable loss on the eventual sale

   Goodwill – If amortised in line with GAAP, allowable deduction from profits
   Otherwise, company can elect for a 4% pa write down
   Election must be made within 2 years of end of accounting period in which the asset was acquired.

4. UK resident companies are liable to UK Corporation Tax on their worldwide income.

   Non resident companies are not liable to UK Corporation Tax unless they are carrying on a trade in the UK via a permanent establishment.

   A company will be resident in the UK if it is incorporated in the UK.

   If not incorporated in the UK, a company will still be resident in the UK if it is centrally managed and controlled in the UK.

5. 3 associated companies

   UL £1,500,000 ÷ 3 = £500,000, LL £300,000 ÷ 3 = £100,000

	Alpha plc £	Beta plc £	Ceta plc £
Trading profits	600,000	-	130,000
Property business profits	50,000	20,000	-
Interest receivable	-	40,000	10,000
Gift aid	-	-	(5,000)
	650,000	60,000	135,000
Marginal rate of tax	28%	21%	29.75%
Group relief	(65,000)	-	(35,000)
PCTCT	585,000	60,000	100,000

6   *Ghost Ltd*

The losses were made in a period before acquisition by Ghost and therefore group relief will not be available.

Pumpkin Ltd

Anti avoidance provisions exist to restrict the use of trading losses where within any period of three years there is both:

- A change in ownership of the company, and
- A major change in the nature or conduct of trade.

Here, Pumpkin Ltd undergoes a change of ownership but we need to consider whether there is any major change in the nature of trade within 3 years. If there is there will be no relief for the pre change losses against profits arising after the change in ownership.

7   Transfers between members of a gains group are at a value giving no gain/ no loss at the time of the transfer.

De-grouping provisions apply where the transferee company leaves the group within 6 years of the transfer and still owns the asset.

The de-grouping charge is calculated as if the asset had been sold at market value on the date of the original transfer.

Fixed machinery transferred from Y Ltd 1 June 2003 is more than 6 years before leaving the group so no de-grouping charge applies.

Premises transferred from X Ltd 1 December 2008 is less than 6 years before leaving the group so de-grouping provisions apply.

The gain is chargeable on Z Ltd on the first day of the accounting period in which it leaves the group.

8   *Loan from individuals £100,000*

Interest at 7% = £7,000 fully deductible from profits on an accruals basis.

Income tax needs to be deducted at 20% = £1,400 before actual payment.

Net interest paid to individuals = £5,600.

Loan from company £50,000

Interest at 7% = £3,500 fully deductible from profits on an accruals basis.

No income tax deduction necessary as company to company.

9

	£
Total invoiced	155,000
Less 5% statutory deduction	(7,750)
	147,250
Less Allowable expenditure	
Salary including NIC	10,000
Travel excluding home to work	3,000
Pension contribution	8,000
	(21,000)
Deemed payment (inc employers' NIC)	126,250
Employers' NIC = 12.8 / 112.8	(14,326)
Deemed employment income	£111,924

10

		Main Pool £	Integral Features £	Allowances £
Tax written down value b/fwd		120,000		
1 May 2009	50,000			
Less Annual Investment Allowance*	(37,500)			37,500
	12,500			
Transfer to pool	(12,500)		12,500	
1 September 2009	30,000			
FYA @ 40%	(12,000)			12,000
	18,000			
WDA – 20% × 9/12		(18,000)		18,000
WDA – 10% × 9/12		-	(938)	938
Transfer to pool	(18,000)	18,000		
Tax written down value c/fwd		£120,000	£11,562	
Total allowances				£ 68,438

* Maximum AIA = 9/12 × £50,000 = £37,500

11 Sugar Ltd (small company)

175% × qualifying expenditure

175% × £60,000 (exclude overheads) = £105,000.

As it is a loss making company, the £105,000 (as less than the available loss) can be surrendered in exchange for a repayable tax credit equal to £14,700 (14% × £105,000). This is not allowed to exceed the total PAYE/NIC payable by the company for the year.

Tea Ltd (large company)

130% × qualifying expenditure

130% × £100,000 = £130,000

12

	£
Interest receivable	55,000
Loan stock interest receivable	80,000
	135,000
Less: management expenses	(30,000)
	105,000
Less: Gift aid donations	(5,000)
Profits Chargeable to Corporation Tax	100,000
Corporation tax @ 28%	£28,000
(close investment holding company)	

Module D

1. (1) Payment due 31 July 2010 - 2009/10 Payment on account

    2008/09 self assessment liability

	£
Total liability	26,568
Less: tax credits	
on savings income	(3,150)
on dividends	(1,200)
on REIT income	(424)
	21,794

    Payments on account due 31 January and 31 July 2010 are £10,897 (50% × £21,794). However only £9,800 was paid in January 2010.

    Payment due by 31 July 2010 is £10,897. The under payment of £1,097 on the 31 January instalment should be paid as soon as possible.

    (2) Option open to Jerome

    As the disposal of shares does not qualify for gift relief then the Capital Gains Tax can be paid in 10 equal annual instalments where an election is made in writing.

    Hence only £1,012 would be due by 31 January 2011.

2. Miguel

    Employment income 2009/10

	£
Salary	43,000
Car benefit 26% (W1) × £47,000	12,220
Beneficial loan interest (W2)	974
	56,194

    Workings

    (1) Car benefit

    $\dfrac{190-135}{5} = 11\%$ Therefore car benefit percentage = 26% (15 + 11)

    (2) Beneficial loan (employee would select the lower figure)

    Averaging method

    $\dfrac{25,000 + 19,000}{2} \times 4.75\% =$ £1,045

    Strict method

3/12 × £25,000 × 4.75% =	297
9/12 × £19,000 × 4.75% =	677
	£974

3 (1) Sanish

UK income tax

Remittance Basis User

	£
Overseas dividends remitted	25,000
Taxed at 40% (treated as if non-savings)	10,000
Additional remittance basis charge	30,000
TOTAL	40,000

(2) A UK resident but non-domiciled individual automatically applies the remittance basis (without election) if:

- The individual has unremitted gains and income in the year below £2,000

or

- The individual has no UK income or gains in the tax year, or only has UK taxed investment income of £100 or less, and
- Does not remit any foreign income or gains in the tax year, and
- Either has been resident for no more than 6 out of the last 9 years or is under 18 at the end of the tax year.

4 **Angelina**

(1) The main conditions to be fulfilled by Ballet Ltd are:

- It must be a trading company not carrying on excluded activities
- Gross assets must not exceed £30 million
- The company must have less than 250 full time equivalent employees
- It must not be under the control of another company.

(2) Income tax treatment for employees:

- No income tax on grant of the options
- No income tax on exercise of the options unless the exercise price is less than the market value at grant
- If it is less, income tax is charged on the difference between exercise price and market value at grant.

5 **Evie**

Income tax computation 2009/10

		£
Salary		46,190
Dividends £486 × 100/90		540
		46,730
Less Interest on share loan (Note)		(200)
		46,530
Less Personal allowance		(6,475)
		40,055

		£
£39,515	× 20% (non-savings)	7,903
£235	× 10% (dividends)	24
£39,750	(W)	
£305	× 32 ½ %	99
£40,055		
		£8,026

	£
Working	
Basic rate band	37,400
Gift aid £1,880 × 100/80	2,350
	39,750

Note: There is no relief for the interest on Evie's home loan.

6 Dane plc

Individuals receive income tax relief on contributions up to the higher of:

- £3,600, and
- 100% × relevant earnings (up to a maximum of £245,000 in 2009/10)

Contributions made by Dane plc are a tax free benefit, regardless of whether they are paid into a personal or occupational pension.

Occupational pension schemes

Individual's contributions are deducted gross from their earnings before operating PAYE. Hence relief at all rates is given at source.

Personal pension schemes

Individual's contributions are paid net of basic rate tax. Higher rate relief is given by increasing the basic rate band by the gross amount of the contribution.

7 Imogen

(1) Lease premium subject to income tax

$$\frac{50-4}{50} \times £10,000 = £9,200$$

(2) Furnished holiday lettings advantages

- Losses can be relieved as if they are trading losses (ie against general income).
- Capital allowances are available in full (ie including on furniture) to replace wear and tear allowance.
- Profits are treated as relevant earnings for pension purposes.
- Capital gains tax reliefs such as gift relief, rollover relief and entrepreneurs' relief are available.

8 Flea Ltd

Abdul

Salary	Class 1 primary payable by Abdul
	Class 1 secondary payable by Flea Ltd
Mileage allowance	
Excess over 40p pm	Class 1 primary & secondary (as above)

Shonay

Salary	Class 1 secondary payable by Flea Ltd
	(over 60 years old – no primary contributions)
Private medical insurance	Class 1A payable by Flea Ltd
Annual dinner	Class 1B payable by Flea Ltd on the cost grossed up for income tax

9 David & Doreen

Capital Gains Tax payable

	David £	Doreen £
Gain on shares	449,500	449,500
Gain on freehold building (associated disposal)	650,000	650,000
Total gains	1,099,500	1,099,500
Less: entrepreneurs' relief		
4/9 × £1,000,000 (maximum)	(444,444)	
	655,056	1,099,500
Less losses brought forward	(20,000)	
	635,056	1,099,500
Less annual exempt amount	(10,100)	(10,100)
	624,956	1,089,400
CGT @ 18%	£112,492	£196,092

Note. As Doreen has never worked for Willis Ltd, there is no entrepreneurs' relief on the gain relating to her share disposal. Therefore the disposal of her share of the building is not an associated disposal and there can be no entrepreneurs' relief on the gain.

10 Pardeep

Chargeable gains

Creed plc ordinary shares

	£
Sale proceeds	43,000
Cost (W)	(16,651)
Gain	26,349

Creed plc Loan stock

Gain on loan stock is exempt. However, the gain that arose on takeover would have been frozen at that date and becomes chargeable now.

	£
Sale proceeds (MV May 2009) £0.96 × 10,000	9,600
Cost (10,000/15,000 × £3,349)) (W)	(2,233)
Gain	7,367

Working

Creed plc shares at takeover

	Market Value 25 May 2009 £	Cost £
10,000 ordinary shares	71,600	16,651
£15,000 loan stock	14,400	3,349
	86,000	20,000

11   Gordon

PPR

The gain on the house will be exempt in the following circumstances:

For periods of deemed occupation which are both preceded and (usually) followed by actual occupation. Deemed occupation is one of:

- Any period(s) of non occupation up to 3 years for any reason
- Any period where the owner had to live abroad due to his employment
- Any period(s) up to 4 years where the owner was away from home due to work

Also

- The last 36 months is exempt even if it is not occupied, provided it has been the owner's PPR at some time
- A gain of up to £40,000 may be exempt if it relates to a period where the PPR was let.
- Living in Job Related accommodation s.222(8)
- Up to 12m for alterations / redecorations (ESC D49)

12   Theo

Capital gains tax 2009/10

(1) Land - part disposal

	£
Sale proceeds	986,800
Less selling costs	(6,800)
	980,000
Less cost	
$\dfrac{986,800}{986,800 + 600,000} \times £400,000$	(248,752)
	731,248

(2) Lease - wasting asset

	£
Sale proceeds	13,425
Less cost	
$\dfrac{43.154 \text{ (9 yrs)}}{61.617 \text{ (15 yrs)}} \times £20,000$	(14,007)
Allowable loss	(582)

	£
Net gains (£731,248 − £582)	730,666
Less annual exempt amount	(10,100)
Taxable gains	720,566
CGT @ 18%	129,702

Module E

1 Ivor, Joseph and Kieran

	Total £	Ivor £	Joseph £	Kieran £
Year ended 30 April 2010				
1.5.09 to 30.6.09				
2/12 × £90,000	15,000			
Balance (1:1)	(15,000)	7,500	7,500	
	–			
1.7.09 to 30.4.10				
10/12 × £90,000	75,000			
Salary 10/12 × £18,000	(15,000)			15,000
Balance (2:2:1)	(60,000)	24,000	24,000	12,000
	–			
		31,500	31,500	27,000

Assessment

	£
2009/10	
1.7.09 to 5.4.10	
9/10 × £27,000	24,300

2 Nigel

	£	
Trading profit	67,000	
Lease costs	6,400	
Allowable proportion of lease costs 12,000 + 20,000/(2 × 20,000) × £6,400 = £5,120 × 80%	(4,096)	Only a proportion of the lease charge is allowed as the car is expensive. It is restricted to the proportion the car is used in the business by Nigel.
Legal fees for new premises	2,000	Capital expenditure
Golf club membership	2,700	Entertaining expenditure is not deductible - ITTOIA 2005 s.45
Adjusted trading profit	74,004	

Note: The new rules in respect of leased cars do not apply as the lease was entered into before 6.4.09.

3 Olivia

Factor

Subject matter of the transaction	Antiques often held as investment so may indicate that not trading.
Frequency of transactions	If Olivia continues to resell items quickly and purchase further ones this may be seen as trading.
Length of ownership	Olivia only held furniture for short period of time which is not typical for antiques held as an investment.
Supplementary work	The act of restoring the items in order to resell may indicate trading.
Profit motive	If there is a profit motive then this would imply trading.
The way in which the asset sold was acquired and held	The fact Olivia is purchasing the items herself might indicate trading.
Method of funding	Olivia has not taken out any short term finance for the purchases.

The indication that Olivia will stop doing the restoration should she find employment might indicate that it is not a trade.

4 Alastair

Rollover relief is available because:

- The new and old assets are buildings
- Both are used in the trade
- The new premises were acquired in the period 1 year before to 3 years after the sale of the old premises.
- Relief will be restricted for those proceeds not reinvested.
- Relief will be restricted as the new premises are only used 80% for the trade.

5 Faisal

The assessment for 2009/10 is:

	£	£
Year ended 31 October 2009	2,000	
Period ended 31 January 2010	(14,000)	
2009/10 result		(12,000)
Overlap		(3,800)
		(15,800)

Calculation of the terminal loss (loss of the last 12 months of trading)

	£	£
Period 6 April 2009 – 31 January 2010		
6.4.09 to 31.10.09 7/12 × £2,000	1,167	
1.11.09 to 31.1.10	(12,000)	
Loss		10,833
Add overlap relief		3,800
		14,633
Period 1 February 2009 – 5 April 2009		
Profit so treated as nil		–
Total terminal loss		14,633

The terminal loss can be relieved against trading income of the year of cessation and the three years of assessment prior to that of cessation on a LIFO basis:

Therefore it will be set off as follows:

	£
2009/10	Nil
2008/09	8,000
2007/08	6,633
	14,633

6 Caroline

Assessment is calculated as follows:

		£	£
2009/10			
17 months ended 31 January 2010		45,000	
Less 5 months of overlap	5/7 × £9,800	(7,000)	
			£38,000
Unrelieved overlap profits:			
7 months brought forward			9,800
5 months used in 2009/10			(7,000)
2 months carried forward			2,800

Conditions (ITTOIA 2005 s.217 – 218):

The accounting period which effects the change of accounting date must not exceed 18 months.

Caroline must not have changed her accounting date within the last five years unless she agrees with HMRC that the change is for a valid commercial reason.

Caroline must elect for the change of accounting date by 31 January following the tax year of the change (ie 31 January 2011).

7 Albert and Ian

£

Albert

Albert is 67 at the start of the tax year. As he is over 65 he is not liable for Class 4 NIC on his trading profits.

—

Ian

The loss in 2008/09 will be carried forward to offset the trading profit in 2009/10 for NIC purposes, irrespective of the treatment of the loss for Income Tax purposes.

	£
Trading profit	28,000
Less trading losses	(5,000)
Assessable to NIC	23,000

(£23,000 − £5,715) @ 8% 1,383

8 Sabrina

Interest on late payment of tax

The balancing payment of £14,000 was due on 31 January 2012 and was paid on 30 September 2012, thus there is interest of:

2.5% × £14,000 × 8/12   233

Penalty for late payment of tax

The tax was unpaid 30 days after the due date therefore a penalty will be charged of 5% of the tax due.

5% × £14,000   700

The tax was still not paid 5 months after the first penalty date therefore a further 5% penalty will be charged.

5% × £14,000   700

9 Abdul

Abdul will have a trading loss for 2009/10 of £11,000.

Options for loss:

ITA 2007 s.83

Carry forward the loss against first future trading profits of the same trade.

This will take at least two years as the expected trading profit for 2010/11 is only £3,000 leaving £8,000 to carry forward to 2011/12.

ITA 2007 s.64

The loss can be used against general income of the year of loss and/or the previous year.

General income in 2009/10 is £6,000 which will be fully covered by the personal allowance.

General income in 2008/09 is (£6,000 + £17,000) £23,000 which would fully utilise the loss and not waste the personal allowance. This would save tax at the basic rate. This is the option Abdul should choose unless he expects 2011/12 results to be such that he will be a higher rate taxpayer.

ITA 2007 s.71

Abdul has no chargeable gains so there is no possibility of a claim under s.71.

Note: Although the temporary extension to loss relief provisions apply to losses in 2009/10, the relief has no impact here as the loss is less than the trading profit in 2008/09 and therefore utilised in full in this year against trading profits, leaving no losses to carry further back.

10 Simon

	AIA £	Main pool £	Car with private use (80% bus) £	Total allowances £
TWDV b/f		5,700	13,000	
Additions qualifying for AIA				
Ventilation (special rate asset)	40,000			
AIA	(40,000)			40,000
Computer	16,000			
AIA (Balance of £50,000)	(10,000)			10,000
	6,000			
FYA @ 40%	(2,400)			2,400
	3,600			
Disposal		(2,500)		
		3,200		
WDA @ 20%		(640)		640
WDA @ 20%			(2,600)	2,080
Transfer to pool	(3,600)	3,600		
TWDV c/f	–	6,160	10,400	
				55,120

11 Michael

	£	£
Property		
Proceeds	130,000	
Cost	(45,000)	
Gain	85,000	85,000
Goodwill		
Proceeds	80,000	
Cost	(0)	
Gain	80,000	80,000
		165,000
Incorporation relief		
(£250,000 – £40,000)/£250,000 × £165,000		(138,600)
		26,400
Entrepreneurs' relief (4/9 × £26,400)		(11,733)
Chargeable gain		14,667

12 Julie, Anna and Emma

When Emma joins the partnership this is a disposal for Julie and Anna. Before Emma joins they received 50% of the capital profits. Once Emma joins this reduces to 40% and therefore they are each treated as disposing of a 10% share and Emma receives a 20% share.

As the goodwill had been revalued prior to admitting Emma the disposal is treated as taking place at balance sheet value. Julie and Anna have proceeds of (10% × £120,000) £12,000. There is no cost and so they have a chargeable gain at this time of £12,000. Their cost carried forward on the remainder of their share of the goodwill is nil but Emma has a cost carried forward of £24,000.

Mock Exam 3: Questions

CTA Awareness Paper

Mock Examination 3 (November 2009)

Question Paper	
Time allowed	**3 hours**

Attempt all questions

DO NOT OPEN THIS PAPER UNTIL YOU ARE READY TO START UNDER EXAMINATION CONDITIONS

CTA Awareness Paper

Mock Examination 3
(November 2009)

Attempt all questions.

DO NOT OPEN THIS PAPER UNTIL YOU ARE READY TO START UNDER EXAMINATION CONDITIONS

Module A

1. You are required to list five situations where the period covered by a VAT return may not be for a three month period.

2. Acme General Services Ltd incurred the following capital expenditure during the last 10 years:

    (1) Financial year ended 31 October 2003: Extension to its existing single storey warehouse which increased the floorspace by 25%, for which it paid £255,000 (inclusive of VAT)

    (2) Financial year ended 31 October 2004: A new mini mainframe computer to run Acme's SAP based stock control and accounts system, for which it paid £115,000 (inclusive of VAT).

    (3) Financial year ended 31 October 2009: The freehold of a new office block for its own use which it paid £295,000 (inclusive of VAT).

    Acme recovered all of the VAT it incurred on the above capital expenditure, as its intention and expectation was that it would only make taxable supplies. In the financial year ended 31 October 2010, Acme started making some VAT exempt supplies for the first time.

    You are required to explain whether Acme must repay some of the VAT it recovered on its capital expenditure.

    You are not required to calculate any VAT repayable.

3. Rents charged by the landlord of commercial and industrial properties will sometimes be liable to VAT, and sometimes not. You are required to explain why this can be the case.

    You should ignore the VAT rules for rents charged on domestic/residential property.

4. **You are required to give five examples of the specific records that HM Revenue & Customs require all VAT registered businesses to keep and maintain.**

5. Sometimes, a person will sell goods, or perform services, and charge others for doing so, but that person's activities will not be regarded as business activities. Only business activities are within the scope of VAT, and hence there is a 'business test' to be applied to determine whether a person is undertaking a business activity. This test is based on principles laid down in case law.

    You are required to explain the five basic principles of this 'business test'.

6. HM Revenue & Customs have powers to raise a VAT assessment in certain circumstances.

    You are required to give five examples of the circumstances where HM Revenue & Customs have the power to raise an assessment for VAT.

    You are not required to consider any time limits which may apply.

7. The terms 'imports' and 'acquisitions' are often both used in relation to goods and services coming into the UK, from countries outside the territorial borders of the UK. Similarly, the terms 'exports' and 'dispatches' are often both used in relation to goods and services leaving the UK, going to countries outside the territorial borders of the UK. When used correctly, the terms have different applications, and are not interchangeable.

    You are required to explain what the correct meaning of each term is, and what the practical difference is between an import and an acquisition.

8. **You are required to state five conditions to be met by a business seeking to claim relief for the VAT element of an unpaid debt.**

9. **You are required to explain what is, and what is not, 'business entertainment', giving three examples of what HM Revenue & Customs regard as being included within 'business entertainment'.**

10. If the exact amounts of output VAT due or input VAT recoverable are not known a business may submit an estimated VAT return, without triggering any liability for any penalty, subject to certain conditions.

    You are required to state those conditions.

11. **You are required to state what interests in land are exempt from Stamp Duty Land Tax.**

12. Stamp Duty Land Tax is charged as a percentage of the 'chargeable consideration' for a land transaction.

    You are required to explain what is meant by the 'chargeable consideration'.

Module B

1. Valerie has made the following gifts during her lifetime:

		£
January 2010	Cash to her grandson as a wedding present	20,000
March 2010	£200 into separate discretionary trusts for each of her other 10 grandchildren	2,000

    In addition, for each of the last 10 years she has given £4,000 to each of her four children as birthday presents. She is able to do this out of her excess income.

    Briefly explain whether any exemptions are available to reduce the value of Valerie's gifts for Inheritance Tax purposes.

2. In July 2007 Kadan gave shares in an unquoted investment company to his sister. However they agreed that Kadan would still receive the dividend income from the shares. Kadan died in March 2010.

    Explain the two possible Inheritance Tax treatments of Kadan's gift to his sister, and identify which treatment will be used. You are not required to make any calculations.

3. Erin died in May 2008 leaving an estate that included a house worth £300,000. In April 2009 her executors sold the house for gross proceeds of £270,000, before deducting selling costs of £8,500. In July 2009 they purchased an apartment for £120,000. Erin made lifetime gifts that utilised all of her nil rate band at death.

    Calculate the final Inheritance Tax payable by Erin's executors in relation to the house. Assume all beneficial claims are made.

4. **Briefly explain whether Business Property Relief (BPR) is available on the following transfers made in March 2010. If it is available, state the rate of BPR which will apply.**

    (1) Peter Smith died leaving shares in an unquoted trading company to his brother John. Peter had acquired the shares in February 2009 on the death of his wife, who had purchased the shares in January 2007.

    (2) Mr Jones gave his share in the family partnership, a greengrocer's business, to his daughter. At the same time he gave the shop premises, which he owned personally, to his son. Mr Jones bought the shop in October 1984, at the same time that the partnership commenced.

5. Xavier made the following gifts during 2009/10:

May 2009	£250,000 cash to an interest in possession trust for the benefit of his grandchildren
August 2009	£180,000 cash to a discretionary trust for the benefit of his son

    His only other lifetime gift was a gross chargeable transfer of £133,000 in July 2007. The trustees agreed to pay any lifetime tax due on the August 2009 transfer.

    Calculate the Inheritance Tax payable on Xavier's gifts. Ignore annual exemptions.

6. Cobey, who is not UK domiciled, moved to the UK ten years ago. He currently owns a large number of assets which include the following:

    (1) A holiday home in Florida
    (2) Bank deposits at the London branch of a French bank
    (3) A debt of £100,000 owed by a business associate who is resident in Spain.

    Identify which of these assets would be included in his estate at death if he were to die today. Briefly explain whether this will change if he remains in the UK.

7. Malcolm, a single man, died on 2 April 2010 leaving an estate worth £480,000 to his brother. His only previous gifts had been two payments into a discretionary trust for the benefit of his nephews and nieces as follows:

February 2003	Gross chargeable transfer £220,000. No lifetime tax was payable at that time.
January 2005	Gross chargeable transfer £150,000. Lifetime tax of £21,400 was paid by the trustees.

    Calculate the Inheritance Tax payable as a result of Malcolm's death.

8   On 31 March 2010, Mohammed owned the following assets:

    5,000 shares in Mirror plc quoted at 308 – 316, with recorded bargains of 310, 312 and 318

    2,000 of the 6,000 shares in Catcher Ltd. Mohammed's wife owns 3,000 shares and his daughter owns the remaining 1,000 shares in the company.

    At 31 March 2010 the shares in Catcher Ltd were valued as follows:

Size of holding	£ per share
<25%	10
25 – 49%	15
50 – 74%	20
75 – 90%	30
91-100%	50

    He gave these assets to his sister on 31 March 2010.

    Calculate the value, before any reliefs, of the gifts made by Mohammed on 31 March 2010.

9   On 10 August 2009 the trustees of the Clear Family Discretionary Trust distributed assets worth £120,000 out of the trust to one of the beneficiaries.

    The trust had been created by Amy Clear on 10 March 2004 with cash of £500,000. She paid any lifetime tax due.

    Amy had previously made a gross chargeable transfer of £198,000 in December 1999.

    Calculate the Inheritance Tax payable when the assets leave the trust, assuming that the beneficiary pays any tax due.

10 The Baird Family Discretionary trust received the following income during 2009/10:

	£
Rental income	12,000
Dividend income (net)	890

    The trustees incurred administration expenses of £460 during the year.

    Calculate the Income Tax payable by the trustees for 2009/10.

11 On 15 September 2005 Grainne set up her only trust, making her sister Orla life tenant, and her nephew Sean the remainderman. She immediately put the following assets into the trust:

    •   A painting worth £123,000.

    •   Ordinary shares in Metro Ltd worth £210,000. Orla has worked for Metro Ltd and also personally owned 8% of the ordinary share capital in the company for many years.

    During 2009/10 the trustees made the following disposals to unconnected parties:

    •   The painting was sold for £105,000
    •   The shares in Metro Ltd were sold for £324,750

    Calculate the Capital Gains Tax payable by the trustees for 2009/10, assuming all beneficial claims are made.

12 Abdul died on 1 September 2009, leaving his estate to his wife Louisa. The executors expect to complete the administration of the estate in December 2010.

    The income and expenses of the estate during 2009/10 were:

	£
Rental income	6,200
Dividends (net)	7,695
Estate management expenses	720

    The executors made an interim payment of £6,400 to Louisa on 5 April 2010.

    Show the entries required on form R185 (Estate Income) for 2009/10, and identify the remaining gross income to be taxed on completion of the administration in 2010/11.

Module C

1. Jonathans Ltd is an office cleaning company. During the year ended 31 March 2010, the following transactions took place:

    (1) The company took out a loan to finance the purchase of equipment. The loan interest paid during the year totalled £1,000. A further £200 was owed as at 31 March 2010.

    (2) The company paid interest of £125 to HM Revenue & Customs in respect of Corporation Tax paid late.

    (3) The company arranged a mortgage to purchase new office premises. The interest payable on this mortgage in the period to 31 March 2010 was £3,500, all of which was paid during the period.

    Explain how the above interest expenditure should be treated in the Corporation Tax computation of Jonathans Ltd for the year ended 31 March 2010.

2. Andrews Lorries Ltd, a haulage company, sold a warehouse on 30 April 2009 for £780,000. The company incurred legal fees on the sale of £7,000. The warehouse had been purchased on 31 March 1996 for £390,000.

    On 31 July 2009, the company purchased land to be used to park lorries overnight. The cost of the land was £700,500. The land was immediately brought into use.

    Calculate the chargeable gain on the sale of the warehouse, assuming all available reliefs were claimed.

3. Jane and Peter Lane are directors and shareholders of Meat Pies Ltd, a UK company. They wish to expand into an overseas market, and plan to set up a new company which will own plant and premises in an overseas country for the production of pies, which will then be sold in that country.

    The shares in the new company will be owned by Jane and Peter, who will be the only directors. A local manager will be appointed to operate the plant, appoint suppliers and recruit staff, but Jane and Peter will make decisions involving investment, financing and sales strategy, in the UK.

    You are required to:

    (1) **Explain whether the new company will be considered resident in the UK for Corporation Tax purposes.**

    (2) **If the new company is considered UK resident, state the deadline for informing HM Revenue & Customs that the company is within the charge to Corporation Tax.**

4. Ant Ltd owns 80% of the ordinary share capital of Buttercup Ltd. Buttercup Ltd owns 80% of the ordinary share capital of Caterpillar Ltd. Ant Ltd also owns 65% of the ordinary share capital of Daisy Ltd.

    You are required to:

    (1) **Explain whether each of the companies is associated with Ant Ltd.**
    (2) **Explain whether each of the companies is a member of Ant Ltd's chargeable gains group.**

5. Balcony Ltd, a company with no subsidiaries or associates, had the following results for the first three years of trade, ended 31 March 2010, shown before any loss relief.

	Year ended 31 March		
	2008	2009	2010
Trading profits/(losses)	13,000	(45,000)	28,000
Profit on non-trading loan relationship	2,000	3,000	4,000
Chargeable gains	500	2,000	1,000
Gift aid donations paid	(500)	(700)	(600)

    Assuming that Balcony Ltd claims relief for trading losses as early as possible, calculate the profits chargeable to Corporation Tax for each of the three years, ending 31 March 2010.

6. Pitt Enterprises Ltd was incorporated on 18 January 2008, and on 10 March 2008 opened an interest-bearing bank account with an initial deposit of £10,000. On 18 June 2008, the company began to trade. It prepared its first set of accounts to 31 July 2009. The company ceased to trade on 18 March 2010 and the company's bank account was closed on 30 April 2010 when the remaining cash was paid out to shareholders.

    State, with brief explanations, the dates of all of the chargeable accounting periods for Pitt Enterprises Ltd which fall in the period from 18 January 2008 to 30 April 2010.

7   Bricks Ltd is a property investment company which has owned 100% of the ordinary share capital of Luxury Offices Ltd, a property development company for many years. Both companies prepare their accounts to 31 December each year.

   On 18 April 2009, Bricks Ltd transferred an office building to Luxury Offices Ltd for £500,000 which was the market value of the building at that time. The building had cost £600,000 in October 2007.

   Luxury Offices Ltd used its established sales and marketing channels to advertise and sell the property to a third party for £450,000, completing the transaction on 20 March 2010.

   Explain the Corporation Tax implications of these transactions. You should ignore indexation.

8   Arkwright Industrials Ltd owns industrial units which it rents out to third parties on a commercial basis. It is wholly owned by Al Holdings Ltd. In the year ended 31 March 2010, Arkwright Industrials Ltd made a property income loss of £10,000 and a chargeable gain of £5,000. In the same period, Al Holdings Ltd had property income of £4,000 and gains of £150,000.

   Explain the different ways in which the property income loss of Arkwright Industrials Ltd could be relieved.

9   Annabel Ltd has traded for many years, and its profits chargeable to Corporation Tax have exceeded £1,500,000 in each accounting period. It has no associated companies.

   The company's Corporation Tax liability for the seven months ended 31 January 2010 was £966,000.

   State the due dates for payment of Corporation Tax in respect of the liability for the period ended 31 January 2010, quantifying the amounts due on each date.

10 City Ltd has held 100% of the ordinary share capital of Village Ltd, and 70% of the ordinary share capital of Town Ltd for several years. On 1 April 2009, City Ltd acquired 100% of the ordinary share capital of County Ltd.

   During the year ended 31 December 2009, City Ltd made a trading loss of £65,000, property income of £1,800. For the same period, the trading profits of the other companies were as follows. These companies had no other income or gains.

   Village Ltd £10,000
   Town Ltd   £15,000
   County Ltd   £20,000

   Calculate and explain the maximum amount of group relief which can be surrendered by City Ltd in respect of the year ended 31 December 2009, to each of Village Ltd, Town Ltd and County Ltd.

11 Stars & Moon Ltd, a company which organises corporate events, has no associated companies.

   The company's trading profit for the year ended 30 September 2009 was £400,000. This was before any adjustment for capital allowances.

   The tax written down value of the main pool at 1 October 2008 was £19,000. The company acquired plant costing £65,000 on 1 August 2009. It also acquired the following two vehicles during the year:

		£
(1)	Volvo XC70 for the Finance Director – CO_2 emissions of 159 g/km; 75% private use	30,250
(2)	Toyota Prius for the HR Manager – CO_2 emissions of 89 g/km; 40% private use	19,090

   The company had no other income or gains in the year ended 30 September 2009.

   Calculate the Corporation Tax liability for the year ended 30 September 2009.

   Tutorial Note: This question originally examined the CT rate change between FY 2007 and FY 2008 and the hybrid rate for CAs. The question has therefore been updated to examine an area that is topical for FY 2009.

12 Roman & Fox Ltd, a catering company, was incorporated on 1 January 2009, and prepared its first set of accounts to 31 December 2009. The company had draft trading profits for the period of £158,000, before deduction of the following expenses.

		£
(1)	Legal fees regarding the issue of share capital	2,000
(2)	Arrangement fee for a bank loan to buy a van	500
(3)	Fees for registering the company's logo as a trade mark	1,500
(4)	Fine for breach of Health and Safety rules	2,500
(5)	Legal advice regarding non-payment by a customer	80

Calculate the revised trading profits for Roman & Fox Ltd for the year ended 31 December 2009, briefly explaining your treatment of each of the expenses.

Module D

1. Harlan received a salary of £48,000 from Crescent Ltd in 2009/10. In addition Crescent Ltd provided him with the following benefits:

    - A diesel car with CO_2 emissions of 192g/km. The car had a list price when new of £37,000. Harlan had contributed £6,000 to its capital cost at the time of purchase, in May 2007. Crescent Ltd provided all the fuel for both business and private mileage.

    - Childcare vouchers at a value of £75 per week to help fund the childcare costs for Harlan's daughter. She attends a day nursery which is an approved childcare provider.

    (1) **Calculate the value of Harlan's taxable benefits subject to Income Tax for 2009/10.**

    (2) **Identify on which elements of the above remuneration package Harlan is personally subject to National Insurance Contributions. You are not required to calculate the value of the contributions payable.**

2. David had an Income Tax liability for 2008/09 of £15,265 and for 2009/10 of £6,120. On 10 May 2009 David invested £70,000 in qualifying EIS shares. This was his first investment in EIS shares.

    (1) **Explain, with the aid of calculations, how David can obtain the maximum tax relief on his investment in the qualifying EIS shares.**

    (2) **State the condition that David will need to meet in order for his investment to be a qualifying EIS investment.**

    Tutorial Note: This question originally tested the EIS carry back rules which were more complex prior to FA 2009. The element in respect of the investor condition has been added to ensure the question remains worth 5 marks.

3. On 1 October 2008 Joshi paid a premium of £35,000 to take out a 25 year lease on premises.

    On 1 October 2009 Joshi granted a five year sub-lease on the premises to Elisabeth who will use them in her business. Elisabeth paid a premium of £8,000 to Joshi on the grant of the sub lease.

    Elisabeth has for many years prepared accounts annually to 31 December.

    Calculate the effect on the amounts subject to Income Tax for 2009/10 for both Joshi and Elisabeth.

4. On 1 August 2009 Hassan was granted options to acquire 10,000 shares in his employer Deuce Ltd. The market value of the shares on 1 August 2009 was £2.90 per share.

    You are required to:

    (1) **Outline the conditions that must be fulfilled in order that the share options meet the criteria of an approved company share option plan.**

    (2) **State Hassan's liability to tax at the future date of exercise assuming the scheme meets the criteria.**

5. Jamie was born on 18 November 1936. He is married to Amy who was born on 7 May 1928. They have been married for twenty years. Jamie had pension income of £25,800 in 2009/10. He also received £6,210 in dividends from shares in quoted companies and interest from a cash ISA of £760. Jamie pays a donation of £20 per month under Gift Aid to his local church.

    Amy had net income of £11,000 from her pension and investments in 2009/10.

    Calculate Jamie's entitlement to allowances for 2009/10.

6. In the input period ending in 2009/10 Andreas paid £15,000 per month into his pension scheme. His employer made a further contribution of £65,000 to the scheme in the same period. This is the same pattern of contributions as in earlier years. Andreas has earned in excess of £300,000 per annum for the last few years.

    Andreas' father, Jose, retired on 1 September 2009 and vested his pension benefits at that date. The value of Jose's fund at that date was £1,900,000. He took the maximum amount possible as a lump sum.

You are required to:

(1) Calculate the value of any Income Tax charge Andreas will have for 2009/10 in respect of the contributions paid into his pension fund.

(2) Calculate the post tax cash amount of the lump sum Jose received from his pension fund.

7   Norma worked for Sporin Ltd for 16 years up to 30 November 2009 when she was made redundant. Norma was entitled to a statutory redundancy payment of £4,800. In addition she received £69,000 as an ex gratia payment from Sporin Ltd. Norma was also allowed to retain her company car. It had a market value on 30 November 2009 of £11,300.

Sporin Ltd also made a payment to Norma of £22,000 to prevent her from working for a similar company within a 50 mile radius of their head office for a period of a year.

All amounts were received by Norma on 30 November 2009.

Calculate, with brief explanations, the taxable income arising from Norma's redundancy.

8   Grace purchased 1,200 shares in Zed Ltd in July 2002 for £30,000. Zed Ltd had 10,000 shares in issue. In June 2009 Zed Ltd was taken over by Exe plc. Exe plc gave Zed Ltd shareholders three ordinary shares in Exe plc and £50 cash for each share they owned in Zed Ltd. The Exe plc shares were worth £6.70 each at the date of the takeover. After the takeover Exe plc had one million shares in issue.

Grace sold 1,000 of her Exe plc shares in February 2010 for £6 per share. Grace made no other chargeable disposals in 2009/10. Grace has worked for Zed Ltd since March 2001.

Calculate Grace's chargeable gains after all reliefs (but before the annual exempt amount) for 2009/10.

9   Mite Ltd has four shareholders who each own 25% of the ordinary shares in the company. These are the only shares in issue and carry equal voting rights. On 6 April 2006 Mite Ltd made an interest free loan of £80,000 to one of the shareholders who does not work for the company. The shareholder did not repay any of the loan and Mite Ltd wrote off the loan on 6 October 2009.

Explain the Income Tax consequences of the loan to the shareholder for 2009/10.

10   Anoop had an Income Tax liability of £22,000 in 2008/09 of which Income Tax payable by self assessment was £400. He has an Income Tax liability of £29,000 for 2009/10 of which £6,100 is payable by self assessment. Prior to 2008/09 Anoop's Income Tax liability had been settled in full via PAYE.

State, together with brief explanations, the due dates and amounts of Income Tax payable by Anoop during 2010/11.

11   Desmond made the following disposals during 2009/10:

- A 20% share in a racehorse which had been purchased in May 2002 for £17,400. It was sold in July 2009 for £29,500.

- A painting that he had bought at auction in March 1996 for £1,150. The artist has since become very collectable and Desmond sold the painting at auction in August 2009 for £11,600 net of commission of £350.

- An antique sideboard for £4,800 on 25 November 2009. He had inherited the sideboard from his godmother in March 2007 when it was worth £8,350.

Calculate Desmond's chargeable gain/allowable loss arising on each of the disposals in 2009/10.

12   Steven earned a salary of £7,200 in 2009/10. In addition he was provided with accommodation by his employer. The accommodation was a flat which had been purchased by his employer in May 2000 and was first made available to Steven in November 2007. The flat had cost £85,000 and was worth £97,000 by November 2007. It has an annual value of £1,600.

Steven's employer furnished the flat at a cost of £8,400 in November 2007. The cleaning and heating and lighting bills totalled £1,350 for 2009/10 and were paid in full by Steven's employer.

Calculate the amount that would be assessable as a benefit on Steven in respect of the accommodation for 2009/10, assuming he is not in job related accommodation.

Module E

1. Peter decided to close the business he had run for many years. His recent tax-adjusted trading profits were as follows:

	£
Year to 30 June 2009	50,000
Period to cessation	32,000
Overlap profits brought forward	8,000

   Peter had no other sources of income in 2009/10 or 2010/11.

   You are required to:

   (1) **Calculate the trading profits to be assessed in 2009/10 and 2010/11 assuming:**

   (a) **Peter ceased to trade on 31 March 2010.**
   (b) **Peter ceased to trade on 30 April 2010.**

   In both cases assume the tax-adjusted trading profits for the final period remain the same.

   (2) **State two advantages to Peter's tax position if he had delayed cessation until 30 April 2010.**

2. Matthew and Robert began trading in partnership on 1 October 2008 and decided to prepare the first accounts for the period ended 31 March 2010. Their partnership agreement stated that they share profits equally. The business had a profit of £145,000 for the period ended 31 March 2010, after adjustment for all items except for capital allowances on their vehicles.

   They each drive a car (CO_2 emissions 167g/km) purchased for £18,000 by the business in October 2008. Matthew estimates his private use at 15% and Robert estimates his private use at 20%.

   Calculate the assessable profits for each partner for 2009/10.

3. Val, Derek and Michael have been trading in partnership for several years. Val is aged 55, Derek is aged 70 and Michael is aged 30. The adjusted trading profit for the year ended 31 March 2010 was £94,000, which they shared in the ratio 50:10:40 (Val:Derek:Michael).

   Calculate the total National Insurance payable by each partner, in respect of their trading profits from the partnership, for 2009/10.

4. After many years of trading successfully, Ben decided to incorporate his business on 1 April 2010, by transferring the trade and assets to Ben Ltd.

   Explain the Capital Gains and Income Tax implications for Ben of transferring the business to Ben Ltd.

5. Kim started a florist business on 1 November 2009. She has not yet registered the business in any way with any tax authorities and doesn't understand how she will pay tax on her income.

   Explain the requirements under self assessment in relation to starting to trade and declaring the trading income annually thereafter.

6. Mark worked as a mechanic for a local garage for many years until he was made redundant in April 2010. He had previously changed his personal car regularly, often selling the cars for significantly more than he purchased them for.

   Whilst seeking new employment, Mark began buying cars at auction, restoring them and selling them on, until finally finding a new job which he will start on 1 December 2010.

   Briefly state and explain the factors HM Revenue & Customs will consider when determining whether Mark was trading in used cars between April 2010 and December 2010.

7 Sally prepared accounts for her marketing business for the year ended 31 August 2010, including the following items of expenditure:

		£
(1)	Advertising	1,300
(2)	Staff canteen/refreshments	800
(3)	Client entertaining	400
(4)	Software upgrades	2,150
(5)	Donations to charity	500

Explain whether each of the items (1) to (5) are allowable in computing the adjusted trading profit of the business for the year ended 31 August 2010. In each case state what, if any, adjustment would be needed to calculate the adjusted trading profit for the year.

8 James decided to gift his engineering business to his son Sam on 30 September 2009. The business as a whole was valued at £1,500,000 on that date, which was analysed as follows:

	£	
Goodwill	600,000	
Freehold premises	650,000	(Originally cost £150,000 in December 2002)
Stock	25,000	
Plant and machinery	65,000	
Net current assets	160,000	
Total value	£1,500,000	

You are required to:

(1) Calculate the chargeable gains arising on James during 2009/10.
(2) Identify and explain two possible forms of relief available to James to reduce these gains.

9 Debbie has run her market stall based business for several years and has historically realised tax-adjusted trading profits of at least £15,000 per annum. She has no other sources of income.

Due to the credit crunch, her accounts for the year ended 31 December 2009 are expected to show a tax adjusted loss of £50,000. Debbie is currently unsure whether to continue with the business or cease trading on 31 December 2009.

You are required to:

(1) Explain how Debbie could relieve the trading loss arising in 2009/10.

(2) Explain how terminal loss relief would be available if she were to cease trading on 31 December 2009.

10 Terry and Sue run a local general store. During the year ended 31 March 2010 they made the following additions and disposals:

		£
1 May 2009	New heating/air-conditioning system	60,000
1 December 2009	New car for Sue (no private use): CO_2 emissions 176g/km	14,000
	Old car originally cost £8,000: Sale proceeds	2,000
1 February 2010	Sold a spare coffee-vending machine	
	Original cost £5,000: Sale proceeds	2,500
1 March 2010	Replacement computers	5,000
	Old computers scrapped	

The tax written down values brought forward on 1 April 2009 were:

	£
General pool	45,000
Terry's car 25% private use	16,000

Calculate the maximum capital allowances the business may claim for the year ended 31 March 2010.

11 Jack runs a small sole trader business with minimal help from his wife, Jill, who occasionally types his invoices or makes appointments for him.

In February 2010, Jill was made redundant from her employment with the local council.

Jack is considering whether they can ensure they use Jill's full personal allowance and basic rate tax band by deducting a salary payable to her by his business.

Explain whether such a deduction would be allowable against Jack's profits and how this income would be treated for Jill.

12 Shane sold the freehold office building used by his sole trade business on 1 November 2009 for £300,000, incurring selling and legal fees of £5,000.

Shane had originally purchased the offices in May 2005 for £200,000 on the sale of a freehold factory used by the business. The factory had been purchased in January 2000 for £90,000 and sold for £400,000.

Shane made no other chargeable disposals in 2009/10 and his sole trade business continued after the sale of the office in November 2009.

Calculate the Capital Gains Tax payable by Shane on the sale of the office block, assuming rollover relief was claimed on the earlier gain arising in May 2005.

Mock Exam 3: Answers

Module A

1. Any 5 of the following:
   - Annual returns.
   - Monthly returns
   - The first return period.
   - Bespoke VAT periods as approved and authorised by HMRC (for example to comply with a businesses' own accounting period if they are not based on calendar months).
   - When a trustee in bankruptcy, administrative receiver, liquidator or similar person tales control of the assets of a registered person.
   - The final VAT return on deregistration.

2.
   (1) The extension is not a VAT Capital Items Scheme asset as although the floor space was increased by more than 10%, the VAT exclusive value was less than £250,000.

   (2) Neither is the VAT recovered on the extension subject to adjustment under partial exemption regulations as the VAT was incurred more than 6 years prior to the generation of VAT exempt income.

   (3) The mini-mainframe is a VAT Capital Items Scheme asset as it cost more than £50,000, but it is now outside the time period for adjustment, being more than 5 years since purchase.

   (4) The new freehold office block is a VAT Capital Items Scheme asset, as the VAT exclusive value was greater than £250,000, and an adjustment is therefore required under the terms of the Capital Items Scheme.

3.
   (1) The default position is that the letting and leasing of non-residential properties is a supply of an interest in or right over land, which is VAT exempt.

   (2) But a landlord has the ability to choose to charge VAT on these supplies.

   (3) This is referred to as the "option to tax".

   (4) If a Landlord opts to tax, his supplies change from VAT exempt, to liable to VAT at the standard rate.

   (5) But sometimes, having made an option to tax, that option can be disapplied, and the supply reverts to being VAT-exempt.

4.
   - The general business and accounting records which include order & delivery books sales and purchase books, cash books, till rolls, bank statements and paying in slips, annual accounts and trading and profit and loss accounts
   - VAT account
   - Copies of all VAT invoices issued
   - All VAT invoices received
   - All credit notes and debit notes received and/or issued
   - A copy of any self billing agreement entered into
   - Details of the name, address and VAT number of any supplier with whom the business has a self billing arrangement
   - Documentation relating to imports and exports by the business
   - Documentation relating to acquisitions and despatches by the business.

5   (1)   Is the activity a serious undertaking, or a serious occupation, earnestly pursued?

    (2)   Is the activity actively pursued with reasonable or recognisable continuity?

    (3)   Does the activity have a measure of substance when measured by the quarterly or annual value of supplies made?

    (4)   Is the activity conducted in a regular manner and on sound and recognised business principles?

    (5)   Is the activity predominantly concerned with the making of taxable supplies, to consumers, for a consideration?

    Credit would also be given for:

    (6)   Are the taxable supplies that are being made of a kind which, subject to differences of detail, are commonly made by those who seek to profit from them?

6   (1)   When a business has not submitted one or more periodic VAT returns due

    (2)   The business has not retained documents and hence HMRC are unable to verify the returns submitted

    (3)   It is HMRC's view that the returns submitted are incomplete or incorrect

    (4)   Where in any VAT period, an amount of VAT has been paid to, or credited to, a person by HMRC and that amount should not have been so paid or credited

    (5)   A business has acquired goods in the course or furtherance of its business activities and cannot prove that those goods have been on supplied or exported or are in stock and available to be on supplied

    (6)   A business has acquired goods in the course or furtherance of its business activities and those goods are not on hand/in stock and the business cannot prove that they have been lost or destroyed

    (7)   A fiscal warehouse keeper has failed to pay VAT on missing or deficient gods, or goods otherwise removed from a warehouse without payment of VAT

    (8)   VAT has been lost as a result of fraudulent or dishonest conduct.

7
- Imports refers to goods/services brought into the UK from outside the EU
- Acquisitions refers to goods/ services brought into the UK from another EU member state
- Export refers to goods/services sent to a destination outside the EU
- Dispatches refers to goods/ services sent to another EU member state
- It is not necessary to make an import declaration on acquisitions of goods from another EU country, or to pay VAT at the frontier/border whereas it is for imports.

8
- The business had made a supply of goods or services and has accounted for and paid the VAT due on that supply to HMRC
- Six months or more must have elapsed since the date the customer was due to have made the payment
- The transaction must have been written off as a bad debt in the business accounts
- The value of the supply must not exceed open market value
- The debt must not have been sold, assigned or factored
- The business must have retained a copy of the invoice, or if there was no obligation to issue an invoice, have retained a document showing details of the supply and when it was made
- Claim must be made within the period of 4 years (3 years pre 1.4.09) and 6 months following the later of:
    - The date on which the consideration which has been written off becomes due and payable, and
    - The date of the supply.

9   Business entertainment means any hospitality of any kind provided by a business, in the course or furtherance of that business

EXCEPT entertainment provided to employees, & Directors of the company

Examples: any three of the following:
- Provision of food and drink
- Provision of accommodation
- Provision of theatre and concert tickets
- Tickets to sporting events
- Entry to clubs, nightclubs, casinos etc
- Use of capital goods such as yachts, aircraft, etc for the purpose of entertainment.

10
- Permission to submit an estimated VAT return must be obtained from HMRC, in advance
- The estimated VAT return is submitted by the due date
- The estimated vat due (is any) is paid by the due date
- The estimate must be adjusted and exactly accounted for in the next VAT return
- If HMRC are satisfied that the exact amount is still not known when the next VAT return is due, the estimate can be adjusted in the next return after that.

11
- A security interest including any interest or right (other than a rent charge) held for the purpose of securing the payment of money or the performance of any other obligation (eg a mortgage)
- A licence to use or occupy land
- any personal right which in land law does not constitute an estate, interest or right over land
- A tenancy at will
- An advowson
- A franchise
- A manor interest.

12
- The chargeable consideration is any consideration in money or money's worth
- The expression money or money's worth is not defined for SDLT, although it must be something that is capable of being sold
- It includes consideration given or received in respect of a non-land transaction where that transaction is 'involved in connection with' a land transaction
- It includes consideration given directly or indirectly by the purchaser or a person connected with him
- It also includes the carrying out of building works or the provision of services as consideration
- The carrying out of certain specified building works is however specifically excluded from constituting chargeable consideration.

Module B

1 The following exemptions are available:

		£
Jan 2010	Wedding present to grandson	
	Gift in contemplation of marriage by a remoter ancestor	2,500
	Annual exemptions for 2009/10 and 2008/09 (2 × £3,000)	6,000
Mar 2010	No exemptions	-
	Small gifts exemption only applies to outright gifts	
Annual gifts	Normal expenditure out of income as	16,000
	Part of normal expenditure	
	Out of income	
	Sufficient income to maintain her normal lifestyle	

2 Kadan has made a gift with reservation of benefit. The two possible treatments are

(a) The gift is treated as a PET in July 2007 valued at market value.
It may be eligible for annual exemptions.
As Kadan died within 7 years, the PET becomes chargeable subject to the nil rate band.

(b) The shares are included in Kadan's death estate at probate value.

HMRC will choose whichever of treatment (a) or (b) that gives the higher total tax.

3

	£
Probate value	300,000
Less: gross sale proceeds	(270,000)
Loss	30,000

As the loss is more than £1,000, the loss is taken into account in reducing the value subject to IHT on death.

Allowable loss

		30,000
Less: restriction (for purchase)		
$\frac{120,000}{270,000}$	× £30,000	(13,333)
		16,667

IHT on house = 40% × £(300,000 – 16,667) = **£113,333**

4 *Peter Smith*

Property inherited on death of a spouse is deemed acquired on the date the deceased spouse acquired it, ie it is treated as held for more than 2 years.

100% BPR will therefore be available.

Mr Jones

Interest in a partnership held for more than 2 years – 100% BPR will be available

Building owned personally and used by the partnership - 50% BPR will be available.

5

	£	
May 2009		
IIP trust	250,000	
Remaining nil rate band £(325,000 – 133,000)	(192,000)	
	£58,000	
Tax on gift (20/80)		£14,500
August 2009		
Discretionary trust	180,000	
No remaining NRB		
Tax (at 20%)		£36,000

6   As Cobey is not UK domiciled only his UK assets would be included in his death estate. The following treatment applies:

Holiday home — not in estate
Deposit with London branch — in estate
Spanish debtor — not in estate

If Cobey remains in the UK he will acquire a UK deemed domiciled once he has been resident for 17 out of the last 20 years.

All UK and overseas assets will then be included in his estate.

7

	£
Feb 2003	
No tax payable as the gift was more than 7 years before death.	
Jan 2005	
CLT	150,000
Remaining NRB £(325,000 – 220,000)	(105,000)
	45,000
Tax at death @ 40%	18,000
Less taper relief (5 – 6 years) @ 60%	(10,800)
	7,200
Less tax already paid	(21,400)
Further tax payable	Nil
April 2010	
Death estate	480,000
Remaining NRB £(325,000 – 150,000)	(175,000)
	305,000
Tax @40%	122,000

8

		£
Mirror plc		
Lower of:		
Quarter up	308 + ¼ (316 – 308) = 310	
Mid bargain	½ × (310 + 318) = 314	
	£3.10 × 5,000	15,500
Catcher Ltd		
Related property		
Pre transfer	2,000 × £30 (83.3% related)	60,000
Post transfer	Nil × £20 (50% related)	(0)
		60,000

(Ignoring related property gives clearly lower result (2,000 × £15) (33% holding))

9

	£	£
Initial value		500,000
NRB on 10 August 2009	325,000	
Transfers in 7 years before March 2004	(198,000)	
Remaining NRB		(127,000)
		373,000
Notional tax @ 20%		74,600
Effective rate $\frac{74,600}{500,000}$ × 100%	14.92%	
Complete quarters since creation (5 yrs 5 mths)	21	
Actual tax rate 14.92% × 30% × 21/40	2.3499%	
Tax payable by beneficiary 2.3499% × £120,000		£2,820

10

	£
Rental income	12,000
Dividend income (£890 × 100/90)	989
	12,989

Tax on:
Rental income
- First £1,000 @ 20% — 200
- Balance (12,000 – 1,000) @ 40% — 4,400

Dividend income
- For trustees expenses
  (£460 × 100/90 = £511) @ 10% — 51
- Balance £(989 – 511) @ 32.5% — 155

	4,806
Less Tax credit on dividend	(99)
Tax payable by trustees	4,707

11

	£	£
Painting		
Sale proceeds	105,000	
Cost	(123,000)	
Allowable loss		(18,000)
Shares in Metro Ltd		
Sale proceeds	324,750	
Cost	(210,000)	
	114,750	
Less Entrepreneurs' relief		
(Orla's personal company for at least one year)		
4/9 × £114,750	(51,000)	
		63,750
Gains		45,750
Less annual exemption		(5,050)
		40,700
CGT @ 18%		7,326

12

	Non savings £	Divs £
Rental income	6,200	
Dividends (× 100/90)		8,550
Less: tax @ 20%/10%	(1,240)	(855)
Net income	4,960	7,695
Expenses (paid from dividend income first)		(720)
Net distributable income	4,960	6,975
Less distributed (matched with non savings income first)	(4,960)	(1,440)
Remaining net income to be taxed in 2009/10	Nil	5,535
Gross income (× 100/90)		6,150

R185

	Total	Non savings	Divs
Net	6,400	4,960	1,440
Tax	1,400	1,240	160
Gross	7,800	6,200	1,600

Module C

1 The loan is for a trading purpose and so interest is allowable as a deduction from trading income on an accruals basis, ie £1,200 is deductible

   Interest on Corporation Tax paid late is allowable as a non-trading loan relationship deduction

   The mortgage interest is an allowable trading income deduction.

2 Sale of warehouse

	£
Proceeds	780,000
Less legal fees	(7,000)
Net proceeds	773,000
Less cost	(390,000)
	383,000
IA	
April 2009 = 210.8	
March 1996 = 151.5	
0.391 × £390,000	(152,490)
	230,510
Rollover relief (balance)	(158,010)
Chargeable gain	
Proceeds not reinvested = £773,000 - £700,500 =	£72,500

3 (1) If the new company is incorporated in the UK, it will be UK resident.

   Even if the company is incorporated overseas, if the central management and control of the company is in the UK, it will be UK resident.

   The central management and control of a company is exercised where the highest level of control is exercised/major not operational decisions.

   Therefore, as Jane and Peter will make all the strategic decisions in the UK, the new company will be UK resident.

   (2) Notification within three months of coming within the charge to Corporation Tax.

4 (1) Buttercup Ltd, Caterpillar Ltd and Daisy Ltd are associated with Ant Ltd because they are all under the control of Ant Ltd.

   (2) Buttercup Ltd and Caterpillar Ltd are in a gains group with Ant Ltd

   Direct holdings are at least 75%

   Ant Ltd has an effective holding of more than 50% in Caterpillar Ltd

   Daisy Ltd is not in a gains group as direct holding is less than 75%

5

	Year ended 31 March		
	2008	2009	2010
Trading profits	13,000		28,000
Carry forward against trading profits			(24,500)
Profit on non-trading loan relationship	2,000	3,000	4,000
Chargeable gains	500	2,000	1,000
Current year claim against profits		(5,000)	
Carry back loss against profits	(15,500)		
Gift aid donations paid	–	–	(600)
PCTCT	NIL	NIL	7,900

Loss memo

Loss for year ended 31 March 2009	45,000
Used against current year profits	(5,000)
Used against prior year profits	(15,500)
	24,500
Carried forward against trading profits, 2010	(24,500)
Carried forward	NIL

6 *10 March 2008 – 17 June 2008*

Company first comes into the charge to corporation tax when acquires a source of taxable income, here, bank interest

Next period starts when company commences trade

18 June 2008 – 17 June 2009

12 month period expires before next accounting date, so accounting period end

18 June 2009 – 31 July 2009

Accounting period ends with the accounting date of the company

1 August 2009 – 18 March 2010

Cessation of trade

19 March 2010 – 30 April 2010

Within the charge to corporation tax until cash taken off deposit

7 Bricks Ltd and Luxury Offices Ltd are in a group for chargeable gains purposes so the transfer between companies is at no gain/ no loss, ie the transfer is at cost of £600,000.

Luxury Offices Ltd is deemed to have immediately appropriated the building into stock at market value £500,000.

A capital loss of £100,000 therefore arises in Luxury Offices Ltd in the year ended 31 December 2009.

The sale in March 2010 creates a trading loss of £50,000 in Luxury Offices Ltd (£450,000 – £500,000) in the year ended 31 December 2010.

8 The loss must first be set against gains of the current year

The remaining £5,000 can be carried forward, to be used against future total profits, (provided the same property income business is carried on in subsequent periods)

Alternatively, the £5,000 can be group relieved to AI Holdings for use against that company's profits chargeable to Corporation Tax

Note: Only *excess* property income losses can be group relieved.

9 Corporation Tax for seven months ended 31 January 2010:

14 January 2010 = 3/7 × £966,000 = £414,000
14 April 2010 = 3/7 × £966,000 = £414,000
14 May 2010 = £966,000 – £414,000 × 2 = £138,000

10 Available loss of City Ltd = £65,000

City Ltd does not need to make a current year loss claim first

Village Ltd
Lower of £10,000 and £65,000. Therefore, £10,000

Town Ltd
No group relief possible as shareholding less than 75% so not in a group for loss relief.

County Ltd
Lower of £20,000 × 9/12 = £15,000 and £65,000 × 9/12 = £48,750. Therefore, £15,000.

11

	£
Trading profit	400,000
Less capital allowances (W)	(84,940)
Adjusted trading profit	315,060
FY 2009	
CT @ 28%	88,217
less 7/400 × (1,500,000 − 315,060)	(20,736)
	67,480

Working: Capital allowances

	AIA/FYA £	Main pool £	Allowances £
TWDV b/f		19,000	
Additions			
Low emission car	19,090		
FYA @ 100%	(19,090)		19,090
Plant	65,000		
AIA (max £50,000)	(50,000)		50,000
	15,000		
Less: FYA @ 40%	(6,000)		6,000
	9,000		
FD's car (<160g/km)		30,250	
		49,250	
WDA @ 20% =		(9,850)	9,850
Transfer to main pool	(9,000)	9,000	
TWDV c/f		48,400	
Total allowances			84,940

12

	£
Draft trading income	158,000
Less:	
Legal fees regarding the issue of share capital	
Disallowed, as capital in nature (relating to shares)	nil
Arrangement fee for a bank loan to buy a van	
Specifically allowable by legislation	(500)
Fees for registering the company's logo as a trade mark	
Specifically allowable by legislation	(1,500)
Fine for breach of Health & Safety rules	
Disallowed, as not wholly and exclusively for the purpose of trade	nil
Legal advice regarding non-payment by a customer	
Allowable, as relates to the trade	(80)
Revised trading income	155,920

Module D

1

	£
Car	
(190 − 135)/5 = 11 + 15 + 3 (diesel) = 29%	
29% × (£37,000 − £5,000 (max))	9,280
Fuel	
29% × £16,900	4,901
Childcare vouchers	
(£75 − £55) × 52	1,040
	15,221

National Insurance

Class 1 primary payable by Harlan on cash earnings of £48,000 plus the childcare vouchers of £1,040.

Note. The remainder of the benefits are subject to Class 1A National Insurance payable by Crescent Ltd.

2 (1) Income tax relief of 20% of the value invested is available as a reduction against the Income Tax liability. The maximum relief available to David is therefore £70,000 × 20% = £14,000. It is however restricted to the amount of the tax liability.

A claim can be made to treat all or part of the amount invested as made in the previous tax year.

Therefore:

	2008/09 £	2009/10 £
Income Tax liability	15,265	6,120
Carry back claim	(7,880)	
Current year claim		
Restricted to amount of liability		(6,120)
Revised Income Tax liability	7,385	-

(2) David must not be connected with the company. This means that he must not be an employee of the company and cannot control, together with his associates, more than 30% of the company.

3

Joshi

	£	£
Grant of sub lease to Elisabeth		
Premium	8,000	
Less: 2% × (5 − 1) × £8,000	(640)	
Assessable as property income for Joshi (or £8,000 × $\frac{50-4}{50}$)	7,360	7,360

Deduction for premium assessed on the head lease for the period covered by the sub lease

Premium	35,000	
Less: 2% × (25 − 1) × £35,000	(16,800)	
	18,200	
£18,200 × 5/25 (or £35,000 × $\frac{50-24}{50}$ × 5/25)		(3,640)
Amount assessable as property income in 2009/10		3,720

Elisabeth

A proportion of the premium is deductible as a business expense. This is based on the amount of the premium assessable on Joshi as rental income.

Allowable deduction in year ended 31 December 2009 (deductible in 2009/10)
£7,360 ÷ 5 × 3/12   368

4 *Sch 4 ITEPA 2003*

(1) The maximum value of the shares, measured at the time the options are granted, cannot exceed £30,000.

The 10,000 options granted to Hassan are worth £29,000 and meet this criteria.

The options must not be exercisable less than three years from the date of grant (ie 1 August 2012) or more than 10 years from the date of grant (ie 1 August 2019).

The price at which the options are acquired cannot be manifestly less than the market value at the date the option is granted. Therefore Hassan must have to pay at least £2.90 per share at exercise.

Hassan must be a full time director or qualifying employee of Deuce Ltd.

Hassan must not have a material interest in Deuce Ltd (25%).

(2) If the conditions are met there will be no tax consequences at the date of exercise.

5

	£	£
Pension		25,800
Interest – Exempt as from an ISA		-
Dividends – £6,210 × 100/90		6,900
Net income		32,700
Personal allowance		
Age 73	9,490	
Abatement		
½ ((£32,700 − £300) − £22,900) = £4,750	(3,015)	
(Net income adjusted for gross gift aid payment, ie £20 × 12 × 100/80)		(6,475)
MCA (Amy born before 6 April 1935)		6,965
Remaining abatement £4,750 - £3,015		(1,735)
MCA		5,230

6

(1)

	£
Andreas' contributions	
12 × £15,000 × 100/80	225,000
Employer contributions	65,000
	290,000
Less: annual allowance 2009/10	(245,000)
	45,000
Additional charge	
40% × £45,000	18,000

(2) Lump sum

25% of the value of the fund, up to the lifetime allowance, can be taken as a tax free lump sum, ie (25% × £1,750,000) = £437,500

The value of the fund is in excess of the lifetime allowance of £1,750,000 by £150,000.

The excess can be taken as a lump sum but there is a tax charge of 55% = £150,000 × 55% = £82,500

	£
Maximum tax free lump sum	437,500
Additional lump sum (£150,000 − £82,500)	67,500
	505,000

7

	£	£
Statutory redundancy – exempt	4,800	
Ex gratia payment	69,000	
Exempt	(30,000)	
		43,800
Car – assessed at market value (no exemption remains to cover this)		11,300
		55,100
Restrictive covenant payment - taxable		22,000
Total taxable amount		77,100

8

	MV at takeover £	Cost £
Ordinary shares in Exe plc (1,200 × 3 × £6.70)	24,120	8,602
Cash (1,200 × £50)	60,000	21,398
	84,120	30,000

Disposal of shares for cash

	£
Proceeds	60,000
Cost	(21,398)
Gain before reliefs	38,602
Entrepreneurs' relief	
4/9 × £38,602	(17,156)
	21,446

Disposal of Exe plc shares

	£
Proceeds (1,000 × £6)	6,000
Cost (1,000/3,600 × £8,602)	(2,389)
	3,611
Chargeable gains	25,057

9

The shareholder is assessed on the amount that would have been assessed as a beneficial loan benefit, if they were an employee. This amount is assessed as a distribution.

The benefit for 2009/10 is (£80,000 × 4.75% × 6/12) = £1,900

The gross taxable distribution is (£1,900 × 100/90) = £2,111

Waiver of the loan

The amount waived is treated as a distribution.

The gross dividend is (£80,000 × 100/90) = £88,889

10

	£
31 July 2010	
Interim payments	
As tax payable by self assessment for 2008/09 was less than £1,000 (and less than 20% of the Income Tax liability) no interim payments are due for 2009/10.	-
31 January 2011	
Balancing payment for 2009/10	6,100
Interim payment due for 2010/11 as tax due by self assessment of £6,100 is greater than 20% of the Income Tax liability of £29,000 (£5,800).	
50% × £6,100	3,050
Total	9,150

11

	£	£
Racehorse		
Exempt disposal as it is a wasting chattel	-	-
Painting		
Gross proceeds	11,950	
Commission	(350)	
Proceeds (net)	11,600	
Cost	(1,150)	
Gain	10,450	
Restricted to a maximum of:		
5/3 (£11,950 – £6,000)	9,917	
Lower gain taken		9,917
Sideboard		
Proceeds (deemed)	6,000	
Cost	(8,350)	
Loss	(2,350)	(2,350)

12

	Not job related
	£
Annual value	1,600
Additional charge (based on MV as > 6 yrs before Steven moves in)	
(£97,000 - £75,000) × 4.75%	1,045
Furnishing (chargeable as once benefit is taken into account have earnings in excess of £8,500)	
20% × £8,400	1,680
Expenses paid for by employer	1,350
Taxable benefit	5,675

Module E

1 *Cease 31 March 2010*

2009/10	Year to 30 June 2009	50,000
	Period to 31 March 2010	32,000
	Less overlap relief	(8,000)
	Assessable profit	£74,000

Cease 30 April 2010

2009/10	Year to 30 June 2009	£50,000
2010/11	Period to 30 April 2010	32,000
	Less overlap relief	(8,000)
	Assessable profit	£24,000

Delaying cessation will mean (any two from):

– Unused personal allowance of 2010/11 can be used against profits
– More profits can be assessed at basic rate of tax
– Delay payment of tax on £24,000 income by 1 year

2

	£
Period ended 31 March 2010	145,000
Less: Capital allowances (W1)	(7,425)
Adjusted profit for period	£137,575
50% share each	£68,788

2009/10 assessment
2nd year of trading – 12 months to acc date (31/3/10)
12/18 × £68,788   £45,859

(W1) Capital allowance computation

	Expensive car 1 85% bu	Expensive car 2 80% bu	Allowance
Qualifying expenditure	18,000	18,000	
Writing down allowance			
Restrict to £3,000 pa × 18/12	(4,500)	(4,500)	9,000
Private use adjustment	675	900	(1,575)
Total allowances			£7,425

3

	Val 50%		Derek 10%		Michael 40%	
Share of profit	£47,000		£9,400		£37,600	
Class 2	52 × £2.40 =	125	Over 65 so none payable		52 × £2.40 =	125
Class 4	£5,715 – £43,875 @ 8%	3,053			£5,715 – £37,600 @ 8%	2,551
	£43,875 – £47,000 @ 1%	31				
Total NIC		£3,209				£2,676

4 • Gain arises on sale of chargeable assets

  – Based on market value at date of transfer of business
  – May be relieved by gift relief / incorporation relief / entrepreneurs' relief

  • Election can be made for assets to be transferred at tax WDV

  • Final year of assessment = 2009/10

  – Will be able to claim overlap relief against profits

  • Future income tax will be based on income drawn from company (salary and/or dividends).

5
- Needs to notify trade immediately for Class 2 NIC purposes.
- Needs to notify chargeability for income tax and Class 4 NIC purposes by 5 October 2010.
- Self Assessment tax return will be required to show assessable profits
    - If filed on paper, deadline is 31 October following the end of the tax year
    - If filed online, deadline is 31 January following the end of the tax year.
- Started to trade 1 November 2009 so first return due is for 2009/10.
- 1st payment of tax will be 31 January 2011.

6 "Badges of trade"

Motive	Needed cash to replace salary so may be seen to be a profit motive which may be considered as a trade
Frequency	Unusual to change personal car regularly so may be a trade
Item	Cars can be personal assets so may not be a trade
Length of ownership	If owned for very short periods (whilst being worked on) would suggest trade
Supplementary work	His expertise can clearly be used to make money out of the cars.

7

Advertising	£1,300	Allowable	No adjustment
Staff canteen	£800	Allowable	No adjustment
Client entertaining	£400	Not allowable	Add back to profits
Software upgrades	£2,150	Allowable	No adjustment
Donations	£500	Not allowable unless to a local charity	Add back to profits
		Will instead extend basic rate tax band if it is made under gift aid.	

8 (1) Calculation of gains

	Goodwill £	Freehold £
Market Value	600,000	650,000
Original cost		(150,000)
Potential gain	£600,000	£500,000

Stock, plant and machinery and net current assets not chargeable assets for capital gains tax purposes.

(2) Gift relief is available — Must be agreed by both James and his son
Form of relief = deferral, so son takes assets on at lower value

Entrepreneurs' relief — Available on first £1million of gains
Form of relief = exemption

9 (1) Without cessation, options are:

Current year — No other income so no loss can be offset

Prior year — Set against total income. Profits £15,000. Leaving £35,000 loss to carry forward.

An extended carry back claim can be made to offset the loss against the trade profits of the previous 3 years on a LIFO basis. This would utilise £45,000 of the loss and leave £5,000 to carry forward.

(2) Terminal loss relief — Loss arising in last 12 months can be carried back 3 tax years, on a LIFO basis.

As Debbie has profits of at least £15,000 per annum then at least £45,000 of the loss will be relieved. Any unrelieved amounts would be lost.

10

	General pool £	Special rate Pool £	Expensive car – Terry £	Allowances £
Tax WDV b/f	45,000		16,000	
AIA additions				
Air conditioning unit		60,000		
Computers	5,000			
FYA @ 40%	(2,000)			2,000
	3,000			
AIA		(50,000)		50,000
Disposals				
Sue's car	(2,000)			
Coffee machine	(2,500)			
	40,500	10,000	16,000	
Non AIA addition				
Sue's car (>160g/km)		14,000		
WDA @				
20%/10%	(8,100)	(2,400)		10,500
Max £3,000			(3,000) ×75%	2,250
Transfer to pool	(3,000)	3,000		
Tax wdv c/f	£35,400	£21,600	£13,000	
Total allowances				£64,750

11 Jack can pay a commercial rate for any work Jill does

Any more than this will not be allowable for deduction from his trading profits

Jill must be paid as an employee

Subject to employer's NIC, payable by Jack (deductible)

Subject to PAYE/employee's NIC before paid to Jill

Wages must be physically paid to be allowable.

12

			£
November 2009		Proceeds	300,000
		Legal/selling fees	(5,000)
		Net sale proceeds	295,000
May 2005		Original cost W1	(90,000)
			205,000
Less annual exempt amount			(10,100)
Taxable gain			194,900
Capital Gains Tax @ 18%			35,082

(W1) £

Sale of factory May 05	Proceeds	400,000
	Less: cost	(90,000)
	Gain	310,000
Rollover relief		
	Proceeds	400,000
	Reinvested	(200,000)
	Not reinvested	200,000
	Rollover relief claimed £(310,000 – 200,000)	(110,000)
Chargeable May 2005		200,000
Base cost of new offices May 2005		
Purchase price		200,000
Held over gain		(110,000)
Revised base cost		90,000

Tax Tables

CTA EXAMINATIONS
MAY AND NOVEMBER 2010
TAX TABLES

THE CHARTERED INSTITUTE OF TAXATION

INCOME TAX	2009-10	2008-09
Rates	%	%
Starting rate for savings income [1] [2]	10	10
Basic rate [3]	20	20
Higher rate [3]	40	40
Trust rate	40	40
	£	£
Savings income starting rate band [1] [2]	1 – 2,440	1 – 2,320
Basic rate band	1 – 37,400	1 - 34,800
Standard rate band for trusts	1,000	1,000

Notes
(1) Savings income is taxed at 10%, 20% or 40%.
(2) If an individual's taxable non-savings income exceeds £2,440, the 10% starting rate for savings will not apply.
(3) Dividend income is taxed at 10% up to the basic rate limit and at 32.5% thereafter.

Income Tax reliefs	2009-10	2008-09
	£	£
Personal allowance	6,475	6,035
– age 65–74	9,490	9,030
– age 75 or over	9,640	9,180
Married couple's allowance [1] [2]		
– age under 75	NA	6,535
– age 75 or over	6,965	6,625
– Maximum income before abatement of relief - £1 for £2	22,900	21,800
– Minimum allowance	2,670	2,540
Blind person's allowance	1,890	1,800
'Rent-a-room' limit	4,250	4,250
Enterprise investment scheme relief limit [3]	500,000	500,000
Venture capital trust relief limit [4]	200,000	200,000
Employer supported childcare	£55 per week	£55 per week

Notes
(1) Relief restricted to 10%.
(2) Only available where at least one partner was born before 6 April 1935.
(3) Relief at 20%.
(4) Relief at 30%.

Pension contributions

	Annual allowance	Lifetime allowance
	£	£
2006-07	215,000	1,500,000
2007-08	225,000	1,600,000
2008-09	235,000	1,650,000
2009-10	245,000	1,750,000
2010-11 to 2015-16	255,000	1,800,000

Basic amount qualifying for tax relief   £3,600

Company cars and fuel

Car benefit   15% of list price for cars emitting 135g/km, increased by 1% per 5g/km over the limit
Capped at 35% of list price
10% of list price for cars emitting 120g/km or less
3% supplement on diesel cars
Fuel benefit - £16,900 multiplied by the percentage used in calculating the car benefit (ie based on CO_2 emission rating)

Van benefit   £3,000
Fuel benefit - £500

ITEPA Mileage Rates

2009-10 and 2008-09

Car or van[1]	First 10,000 business miles	40p
	Additional business miles	25p
Motorcycles		24p
Bicycles		20p
Passenger payments		5p

Note (1) For NIC purposes, a rate of 40p applies irrespective of mileage.

Official rate of interest	2009-10	2008-09
	4.75%	6.10%

VALUE ADDED TAX

	From 1.1.10	1.12.08 to 31.12.09	To 30.11.08
Standard rate	17½%	15%	17½%
VAT fraction	7/47	3/23	7/47

Limits	From 1.5.09	1.4.08 to 30.4.09
Annual registration limit	£68,000	£67,000
De-registration limit	£66,000	£65,000

Thresholds	Cash accounting	Annual accounting
Turnover threshold to join scheme	£1,350,000	£1,350,000
Turnover threshold to leave scheme	£1,600,000	£1,600,000

CAPITAL ALLOWANCES

	6.4.09 – 5.4.10[1]	6.4.08 – 5.4.09[1]
Annual investment allowance (AIA)[2]	100%	100%
First year allowance (FYA)[3]	40%	N/A
WDA on plant and machinery in main pool[4]	20%	20%
WDA on plant and machinery in special rate pool[5]	10%	10%
Writing down allowance on patent rights and know-how	25%	25%

Notes
(1) Dates for companies are 1 April - 31 March.
(2) 100% on the first £50,000 of investment in plant and machinery (except cars).
(3) A FYA is available for expenditure in the main pool. FYA is given after the AIA.
(4) A rate of 20% applies to cars with CO_2 emissions greater than 110g/km but not more than 160 g/km acquired on or after 6 April 2009 (1 April for companies).
(5) A rate of 10% applies to cars with CO_2 emissions greater than 160 g/km acquired on or after 6 April 2009 (1 April for companies).
(6) Cars acquired prior to 6 April 2009 (1 April for companies) continue to be written down based on cost rather than emissions.

100% First year allowances available to all businesses

1) New energy saving plant and machinery, and water efficient plant and machinery.
2) New cars registered between 16 April 2002 and 31 March 2013 if the car either emits not more than 110 g/km (120g/km prior to 1 April 2008) of CO_2 or it is electrically propelled.
3) Renovation or conversion of vacant business premises, in a designated Enterprise Area, for the purpose of bringing those premises back into business use.
4) Converting or renovating an empty or under-used space above a commercial property into qualifying residential accommodation.
5) Capital expenditure incurred by a person on research and development.

CORPORATION TAX

Financial year	2009	2008
Full rate	28%	28%
Small companies' rate	21%	21%
Profit limit for small companies' rate	£300,000	£300,000
Profit limit for small companies' marginal relief	£1,500,000	£1,500,000
Marginal relief fraction for profits between £300,000 and £1,500,000	7/400	7/400

Research and development expenditure

	SMEs	
	From 1.8.08	From 1.1.05
Employees - less than	500	250
Turnover - not more than	€100m	€50m
Balance sheet assets - not more than	€86m	€43m

SMEs must meet the employees criteria and *either* the turnover *or* the balance sheet assets criteria.

NATIONAL INSURANCE CONTRIBUTIONS

	2009-10			2008-09		
Class 1 contributions	Annual	Monthly	Weekly	Annual	Monthly	Weekly
Lower earnings limit	£4,940	£412	£95	£4,680	£390	£90
Earnings threshold	£5,715	£476	£110	£5,435	£453	£105
Upper accruals point	£40,040	£3,337	£770	N/A	NA	N/A
Upper earnings limit	£43,875	£3,656	£844	£40,040	£3,337	£770

Employee's contributions in 2009-10 (2008-09)

Not contracted out:	11% (11%) on earnings between £110 (£105) and £844 (£770)
	1% (1%) above £844 (£770) per week
Contracted out:	9.4% (9.4%) on earnings between £110 (£105) and £770 (NA)
	11% (NA) on earnings between £770 (NA) and £844 (NA)
	1% (1%) on earnings above £844 (£770) per week
	1.6% rebate on earnings between £95 (£90) and £110 (£105)

Employer's contributions in 2009-10 (2008-09)

Not contracted out:	12.8% (12.8%) on earnings in excess of £110 (£105)
Contracted out:	
Salary related:	9.1% (9.1%) on earnings between £110 (£105) and £770 (£770)
	12.8% (12.8%) on earnings in excess of £770 (£770)
	3.7% (3.7%) rebate on earnings between £95 (£90) and £110 (£105)
Money purchase:	11.4% (11.4%) on earnings between £110 (£105) and £770 (£770)
	12.8% (12.8%) on earnings in excess of £770 (£770)
	1.4% (1.4%) rebate on earnings between £95 (£90) and £110 (£105)

	2009-10	2008-09
Class 1A contributions	12.8%	12.8%
Class 1B contributions	12.8%	12.8%
Class 2 contributions		
Normal rate	£2.40 pw	£2.30 pw
Small earnings exception	£5,075 pa	£4,825 pa
Class 3 contributions	£12.05 pw	£8.10 pw
Class 4 contributions		
Annual lower earnings limit (LEL)	£5,715	£5,435
Annual upper earnings limit (UEL)	£43,875	£40,040
Percentage rate between LEL and UEL	8%	8%
Percentage rate above upper earnings limit	1%	1%

CAPITAL GAINS TAX	2009-10	2008-09
Annual exempt amount	£10,100	£9,600
CGT rate for individuals and trusts	18%	18%

Entrepreneurs' relief: Disposals in 2009-10 (and 2008-09)

Relevant gains (lifetime maximum)	£1,000,000
Reducing fraction	4/9

Lease percentage table

Years	Percentage	Years	Percentage	Years	Percentage
50 or more	100.000	33	90.280	16	64.116
49	99.657	32	89.354	15	61.617
48	99.289	31	88.371	14	58.971
47	98.902	30	87.330	13	56.167
46	98.490	29	86.226	12	53.191
45	98.059	28	85.053	11	50.038
44	97.595	27	83.816	10	46.695
43	97.107	26	82.496	9	43.154
42	96.593	25	81.100	8	39.399
41	96.041	24	79.622	7	35.414
40	95.457	23	78.055	6	31.195
39	94.842	22	76.399	5	26.722
38	94.189	21	74.635	4	21.983
37	93.497	20	72.770	3	16.959
36	92.761	19	70.791	2	11.629
35	91.981	18	68.697	1	5.983
34	91.156	17	66.470	0	0.000

Retail Prices Index

Where Retail Price Indices are required, it should be assumed that they are as follows.

	Jan	Feb	Mar	Apr	May	Jun	Jul	Aug	Sep	Oct	Nov	Dec
1982	–	–	79.44	81.04	81.62	81.85	81.88	81.90	81.85	82.26	82.66	82.51
1983	82.61	82.97	83.12	84.28	84.64	84.84	85.30	85.68	86.06	86.36	86.67	86.89
1984	86.84	87.20	87.48	88.64	88.97	89.20	89.10	89.94	90.11	90.67	90.95	90.87
1985	91.20	91.94	92.80	94.78	95.21	95.41	95.23	95.49	95.44	95.59	95.92	96.05
1986	96.25	96.60	96.73	97.67	97.85	97.79	97.52	97.82	98.30	98.45	99.29	99.62
1987	100.0	100.4	100.6	101.8	101.9	101.9	101.8	102.1	102.4	102.9	103.4	103.3
1988	103.3	103.7	104.1	105.8	106.2	106.6	106.7	107.9	108.4	109.5	110.0	110.3
1989	111.0	111.8	112.3	114.3	115.0	115.4	115.5	115.8	116.6	117.5	118.5	118.8
1990	119.5	120.2	121.4	125.1	126.2	126.7	126.8	128.1	129.3	130.3	130.0	129.9
1991	130.2	130.9	131.4	133.1	133.5	134.1	133.8	134.1	134.6	135.1	135.6	135.7
1992	135.6	136.3	136.7	138.8	139.3	139.3	138.8	138.9	139.4	139.9	139.7	139.2
1993	137.9	138.8	139.3	140.6	141.1	141.0	140.7	141.3	141.9	141.8	141.6	141.9
1994	141.3	142.1	142.5	144.2	144.7	144.7	144.0	144.7	145.0	145.2	145.3	146.0
1995	146.0	146.9	147.5	149.0	149.6	149.8	149.1	149.9	150.6	149.8	149.8	150.7
1996	150.2	150.9	151.5	152.6	152.9	153.0	152.4	153.1	153.8	153.8	153.9	154.4
1997	154.4	155.0	155.4	156.3	156.9	157.5	157.5	158.5	159.3	159.5	159.6	160.0
1998	159.5	160.3	160.8	162.6	163.5	163.4	163.0	163.7	164.4	164.5	164.4	164.4
1999	163.4	163.7	164.1	165.2	165.6	165.6	165.1	165.5	166.2	166.5	166.7	167.3
2000	166.6	167.5	168.4	170.1	170.7	171.1	170.5	170.5	171.7	171.6	172.1	172.2
2001	171.1	172.0	172.2	173.1	174.2	174.4	173.3	174.0	174.6	174.3	173.6	173.4
2002	173.3	173.8	174.5	175.7	176.2	176.2	175.9	176.4	177.6	177.9	178.2	178.5
2003	178.4	179.3	179.9	181.2	181.5	181.3	181.3	181.6	182.5	182.6	182.7	183.5
2004	183.1	183.8	184.6	185.7	186.5	186.8	186.8	187.4	188.1	188.6	189.0	189.9
2005	188.9	189.6	190.5	191.6	192.0	192.2	192.2	192.6	193.1	193.3	193.6	194.1
2006	193.4	194.2	195.0	196.5	197.7	198.5	198.5	199.2	200.1	200.4	201.1	202.7
2007	201.6	203.1	204.4	205.4	206.2	207.3	206.1	207.3	208.0	208.9	209.7	210.9
2008	209.8	211.4	212.1	214.0	215.1	216.8	216.5	217.2	218.4	217.7	216.0	212.9
2009	210.1	211.4	211.3	210.8*	210.3*	209.8*	209.3*	208.8*	208.3*	207.9*	207.5*	207.2*
2010*	206.8	206.5	206.2	205.9	205.7	205.5	205.4	205.4	205.5	205.6	205.7	205.9

* = assumed

STAMP DUTY / STAMP DUTY RESERVE TAX

Shares   0.5%

Stamp duty land tax

Rate (%)	Residential	Non-residential
Zero	Up to £125,000[1][2]	Up to £150,000[3]
1	Over £125,000[1][2] - 250,000	Over £150,000 - 250,000
3	Over £250,000 - 500,000	Over £250,000 - 500,000
4	Over £500,000	Over £500,000

Note   (1)   A higher threshold of £150,000 applies to transactions in residential land in disadvantaged areas.

(2)   From 3.9.08 to 31.12.09 a higher threshold of £175,000 applies.

(3)   For non-residential property, where the land is a grant of a lease, the zero rate band is not available if annual rent exceeds £1,000.

New leases - Stamp duty land tax on rent

Rate (%)	Net present value of rent	
	Residential	Non-residential
Zero	Up to £125,000[1]	Up to £150,000
1%	Excess over £125,000[1]	Excess over £150,000

Notes   (1)   The higher threshold of £175,000 applies between 3.9.08 and 31.12.09. For the period from 3.9.08 to 21.4.09, the higher threshold did not apply to leases which were granted for a term of less than 21 years or assigned with a term of less than 21 years to run. In addition, SDLT was payable on the excess of chargeable consideration above £125,000. From 22.4.09 to 31.12.09, the higher threshold applies to all leases of residential accommodation and SDLT is payable on the excess of chargeable consideration above £175,000.

INHERITANCE TAX

	Nil rate band		Nil rate band
6 April 1996 – 5 April 1997	up to £200,000	6 April 2003 – 5 April 2004	up to £255,000
6 April 1997 – 5 April 1998	up to £215,000	6 April 2004 – 5 April 2005	up to £263,000
6 April 1998 – 5 April 1999	up to £223,000	6 April 2005 – 5 April 2006	up to £275,000
6 April 1999 – 5 April 2000	up to £231,000	6 April 2006 – 5 April 2007	up to £285,000
6 April 2000 – 5 April 2001	up to £234,000	6 April 2007 – 5 April 2008	up to £300,000
6 April 2001 – 5 April 2002	up to £242,000	6 April 2008 – 5 April 2009	up to £312,000
6 April 2002 – 5 April 2003	up to £250,000	From 6 April 2009	up to £325,000

Death rate	40%	Wedding gifts - Child	£5,000
Lifetime rate	20%	- Grandchild or remoter issue	£2,500
Annual exemption	£3,000	- Other party to marriage	£2,500
Small gifts	£250	- Other	£1,000

Taper relief		Quick succession relief	
Death within 3 years of gift	Nil%	Period between transfers less than one year	100%
Between 3 and 4 years	20%	Between 1 and 2 years	80%
Between 4 and 5 years	40%	Between 2 and 3 years	60%
Between 5 and 6 years	60%	Between 3 and 4 years	40%
Between 6 and 7 years	80%	Between 4 and 5 years	20%

OTHER INDIRECT TAXES

		2009-10	2008-09
Insurance Premium Tax[1]	Standard rate	5%	5%
	Higher rate	17.5%	17.5%
Landfill Tax[2]	Per tonne	£40	£32
	Qualifying material	£2.50 per tonne	£2.50 per tonne
Landfill Communities Fund (LCF)	Relief for 90% of qualifying contributions	6.0% × landfill tax liability	6.0% × landfill tax liability
Aggregates Levy[2]	Per tonne	£2.00	£1.95
Climate Change Levy[3]	Electricity	0.470p per kwh	0.456p per kwh
	Gas	0.164p per kwh	0.159p per kwh
	Liquid hydrocarbons	1.050p per kg	1.018p per kg
	Any other taxable commodity	1.281p per kg	1.242p per kg

Notes   (1)   Premium is tax inclusive – IPT is 1/21 or 7/47 of the premium.

(2)   Pro rated for part tonnes.

(3)   Where the reduced rate applies it is 20% of the rate shown in the table.

Notes page

Notes page

Notes page

Notes page